Becoming a teacher

Second edition

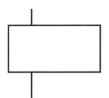

Becoming a teacher

Issues in secondary teaching

Second edition

Edited by
Justin Dillon and Meg Maguire

Open University Press
Buckingham · Philadelphia

Open University Press
Celtic Court
22 Ballmoor
Buckingham
MK18 1XW

email: enquiries@openup.co.uk
world wide web: www.openup.co.uk

and
325 Chestnut Street
Philadelphia, PA 19106, USA

First Published 2001

A catalogue record of this book is available from the British Library

ISBN   0 335 20861 4 (pb)

Library of Congress Cataloging-in-Publication Data
Becoming a teacher: issues in secondary teaching / [edited by] Justin Dillon and
Meg Maguire.—2nd ed.
    p. cm.
  Includes bibliographical references and index.
  ISBN 0–335–20861–4 (pbk.)
  1. High school teaching–Great Britain.   2. High school teaching–Social
aspects–Great Britain.   3. Classroom management–Great Britain.
4. Curriculum planning–Great Britain.   I. Dillon, Justin.   II. Maguire,
Meg. 1949–
LB1737.G7B43   2001
373.1102′0973–dc21   00–068825

Typeset by Graphicraft Limited, Hong Kong
Printed in Great Britain by Biddles Limited, Guildford and King's Lynn

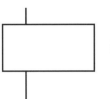

Contents

Notes on contributors   ix

Introduction   xv
Justin Dillon and Meg Maguire

Part 1   First thoughts   1

   1 Developing as a student teacher   3
      Meg Maguire and Justin Dillon

   2 Better read: theorizing the teacher!   10
      Stephen J. Ball

Part 2   Policy, society and schooling   23

   3 Ideology, evidence and the raising of standards   25
      Paul Black

   4 Values and schooling   37
      Alan Cribb and Sharon Gewirtz

   5 School and teacher quality: problem-solving and critical
      perspectives   50
      Martin Thrupp

   6 Reforming teachers and their work   63
      Meg Maguire, Justin Dillon and Gill Close

   7 Inspection   74
      Alison Millett, Justin Dillon and Jenny Adey

  8 Social justice in schools   87
     Brenda Gay

  9 Parents and schooling   98
     Diane Reay

 10 Excellence in cities   109
     Meg Maguire and Justin Dillon

 11 Teachers and the law   120
     Dylan Wiliam

Part 3   Teaching and learning   133

 12 Adolescence   135
     John Head

 13 Learning in the classroom   142
     Martin Monk

 14 Managing effective classrooms   150
     Sheila Macrae and Mike Quintrell

 15 Differentiation in theory and practice   162
     Christine Harrison

 16 Setting, streaming and mixed ability teaching   173
     Jo Boaler and Dylan Wiliam

 17 Assessing pupils   182
     Bob Fairbrother and Christine Harrison

 18 Special educational needs – becoming more inclusive   192
     Chris Abbott

 19 English as an additional language: challenges of language
     and identity in the multilingual and multiethnic classroom   203
     Roxy Harris and Constant Leung

Part 4   Across the curriculum   217

 20 Literacy   219
     Bethan Marshall

 21 Citizenship: what does it mean to be a good citizen?   229
     Ann-Marie Brandom

 22 Spiritual education   239
     Ann-Marie Brandom, Mike Poole and Andrew Wright

 23 Healthy schools: health education and health promotion
     for the twenty-first century   250
     Faith Hill and Margaret Sills

24 Information and communications technology: policy and
    practice   262
    Deryn Watson

25 14–19 education: broadening the curriculum   273
    Peter Gill and Sally Johnson

26 Beyond the subject curriculum: the form tutor's role   284
    Jane Jones

    Index   295

Notes on contributors

Chris Abbott taught in primary, secondary and special schools for 16 years. He joined King's in 1994 and has taught on the English and ICT PGCE as well as developing Masters modules on information and communication technology (ICT), literacy and the Internet. He has been an ICT consultant for the DfEE and for governments in other countries, most recently South Africa and Uzbekistan. He is the author of *ICT: Changing Education* (2000) and *Symbols Now* (2000). His research interests include young people and the Internet, special schools and online education, and the processes by which ICT is changing schooling.

Jenny Adey was the headteacher of a mixed London comprehensive school for 10 years. Previously she had taught in schools in London and in the Caribbean and was involved in a primary teacher training project in Indonesia. Now, as well as Ofsted inspections, she carries out consultancy work in schools, contributes to the King's MA programme and works for a management company specializing in equal opportunities. She recently qualified as a DfEE external assessor and performance management consultant.

Stephen J. Ball left King's in 2001, after 15 years, to become Karl Mannheim Professor of the Sociology of Education at the University of London Institute of Education. He is editor of the *Journal of Education Policy* and a fellow of the Academy of Social Sciences. He is author of *The Micropolitics of the School* (1987), *Politics and Policy-making in Education* (1990), *Education Reform* (Open University Press 1994), *Markets, Choice and Equity in Education* (with Sharon Gewirtz and Richard Bowe, Open University Press 1995) and *Choice, Pathways and Transitions Post-16* (with Meg Maguire and Sheila Macrae, 2000). He is the editor of *Sociology of Education: Major Themes* (4 Volumes) (2000).

Paul Black is Professor Emeritus of Science Education at King's. He was Chair of the Government's Task Group on Assessment and Testing in

1987–88 and Deputy Chairman of the National Curriculum Council from 1989 to 1991. He is currently engaged in a research collaboration with science and mathematics teachers in six schools to develop classroom practices in formative assessment.

Jo Boaler is an associate professor at Stanford University, specializing in mathematics education. She is a former secondary school teacher of mathematics and researcher at King's. She taught in diverse, inner London comprehensive schools, across the 11–18 age range and is the author of two books, including *Experiencing School Mathematics: Teaching Styles, Sex and Setting* (Open University Press 1997) that won the Outstanding Book of the Year award for education in Britain.

Ann-Marie Brandom taught religious education (RE) in central London for 10 years before joining King's in 1998 where she is now responsible for the PGCE in RE and the RE INSET programme. Her research interests include the cognitive abilities of pupils in relation to religious and theological understanding. She co-edited *Learning to Teach Religious Education in the Secondary School* (2000).

Gill Close was the head of mathematics in a London comprehensive school before joining Chelsea College in 1983, prior to it merging with King's. From 1989–94 she directed the team writing the first Key Stage 3 Mathematics tests. She has worked on and directed a number of assessment projects and has research interests in both assessment and initial teacher education. She is currently the PGCE Director.

Alan Cribb joined King's in 1990 having previously worked for the Centre for Social Ethics and Policy and the Department of Epidemiology and Social Oncology, University of Manchester. His research interests include moral and political philosophy and applied ethics. He is the editor of *Health Care Analysis, An International Journal of Health Philosophy and Policy.*

Justin Dillon taught in London schools for nine years. Since joining King's in 1989, he was the deputy course director for the PGCE for several years and the course organizer of the part-time PGCE. He is now the director of the International Education Unit. He is a primary school governor and co-edited *Learning to Teach Science* (1995) with Martin Monk. He is the assistant editor of *Science Education* and his research interests include teacher development and environmental education.

Bob Fairbrother has taught science in a number of schools, has been an examiner and awarder for the GCSE and A level, and was a member of the SEAC/SCAA Science Subject Committee. He has done research into problems of assessment, has many publications in this area of work and has lectured widely at home and abroad. He is currently a visiting senior lecturer at King's.

Brenda Gay has taught in both the independent and maintained sectors, was headmistress of a girls' independent school and has worked in teacher education and educational research. She joined King's in 1996 and coordinates the PGCE in classics education. She is the programme director for the MA in classics education and has published in a wide range of areas, including religion in the independent school, accountability and the management of conflict in the classroom. Brenda's current research interests are focused on teacher induction, classics teaching and learning as part of global communication and the religious dimension of independent schools.

Sharon Gewirtz is a professor of education at King's. Her books include *Markets, Choice and Equity in Education* (with Stephen Ball and Richard Bowe, Open University Press 1995), *New Managerialism, New Welfare?* (with John Clarke and Eugene McLaughlin, 2000) and *The Managerial School: Post-welfarism and Social Justice in Education* (2001).

Peter Gill taught physics and mathematics at secondary and tertiary level for 18 years including four as head of science in a large comprehensive school. After joining King's, originally to run INSET courses on National Curriculum assessment, he took over responsibility for the mathematics PGCE for three years. His main research interest is the learning of mathematics within the context of science. He has recently become involved in a number of projects associated with widening access to higher education.

Roxy Harris is a lecturer in the Department of Education at King's. He has worked extensively with teachers on questions of language and education. He has a particular interest in the relationships between language, power, ethnicity and culture and has researched and published on these issues, including *My Personal Language History* (1988) and *Language and Power* (1990).

Christine Harrison taught for 13 years in secondary schools in and around London, before moving on to a curriculum development project and consultancy work in science education. She has research interests in assessment, science education and in-service training and is responsible for the biology PGCE at King's.

John Head is a former secondary schoolteacher who has worked in the UK and the USA. His current research interests, as a visiting senior lecturer at King's, encompass psychology applied to issues of adolescence such as identity development and gender differences.

Faith Hill has taught health education in secondary schools and has run national projects for the Health Education Authority. She has trained teachers throughout the UK and has published widely in the area of health promotion, particularly for young people aged 16–19. For many years she ran a Masters programme in health education and health promotion at King's. She was the joint academic director of the Learning and Teaching Support Network (LTSN) 'Health Sciences and Practice' until 2001 when she took up a post at the University of Southampton.

Sally Johnson taught biology and environmental science for 13 years in London and has extensive experience of post-16 education. She was the senior tutor for A level students in a college of further education and was also interested in the provision of vocational courses. Sally joined King's in 1991 and is involved in initial teacher education as well as large in-service programmes in Nigeria and South Africa. Her research interests include the implementation of General National Vocational Qualification

(GNVQ) in the UK and educational capacity building in developing countries.

Jane Jones taught for many years in primary and secondary schools in London and Kent and her last school post was as senior teacher responsible for profiling and assessment in a large comprehensive school in Wandsworth. Her research interests include school leadership and governance, counselling in schools and all aspects of language learning. She is responsible for modern foreign languages in initial teacher education at King's and directs the UK aspects of several EU-funded projects.

Constant Leung taught in schools and worked as advisory teacher and manager in local education authorities for 15 years. His research interests include curriculum development and language policy. He joined King's in 1999 and is active in promoting continuous professional development for teachers working with linguistically diverse students. He was the founding chair of the National Association for Language Development in the Curriculum (NALDIC). He has written and published widely on additional/second language education issues both nationally and internationally. His publications include *English as a Second Language in the Mainstream: Teaching, Learning and Identity* (with Bernard Mohan and Chris Davison, 2001).

Sheila Macrae taught in secondary schools over a period of 17 years in Scotland and England and in a pupil referral unit in Inner London. Since 1992, she has worked as a research fellow at King's where her main interests are in the psychological and social development of adolescents.

Meg Maguire taught for many years in London including a spell as a headteacher. She is the course leader of the modular MA at King's and has published widely on teacher education and issues of equity.

Bethan Marshall taught English in West London comprehensives for nine years before taking up her current post at King's, a job she combined for five years with that of advisory teacher in English, media and drama. She has written widely on the subject of English teaching and is author of *English Teachers – The Unofficial Guide* (2000).

Alison Millett has considerable experience in primary teaching and management in Inner London and has also managed and taught on an early years course in further education. Since moving to King's she has held the post of research fellow on the Evaluation of the implementation of National Curriculum mathematics; completed a PhD on innovation and change in primary mathematics; and been project director of the ESRC funded OFSTED and Primary Maths study. She is currently working on 'Whole School Action on Numeracy', part of a large programme of research funded by the Leverhulme Trust.

Martin Monk has worked as a science teacher and teacher trainer for 30 years. He contributed to and was the joint editor of *Learning to Teach Science* (1995) and *Good Practice in Science Teaching* (Open University Press 2000). He has published research on teacher development, science education and classroom practice. His work has taken him to Belize, the former Czechoslovakia, Egypt, India, Indonesia, Lesotho, Nigeria, South Africa and Uzbekistan.

Michael Poole taught physics and religious education during a period of 14 years at Forest Hill School in London. He then spent three years preparing and broadcasting radio programmes on science and religion before taking up a post as Lecturer in Science Education at King's. His research interests are in the interplay between science and religion, with special reference to its educational context, and his research includes a study of sixth formers' views on these issues. In 1998 he was presented with an international award from the Templeton Foundation for quality and excellence in teaching science and religion. He has written a number of books as well as some sixty papers and articles on issues of science and religion, their relevance for science teachers, religious education specialists and for general readership.

Michael Quintrell was a comprehensive school teacher for 17 years (including 13 as head of an English faculty) before working for an LEA inspectorate in the development and evaluation of INSET. During his time at King's he was responsible for the English PGCE before becoming PGCE Director. His research interests include the promotion of speaking and listening and their assessment, class management, pastoral care and pupil grouping. He has now returned to teaching English.

Diane Reay taught in inner London schools for 20 years. For much of that time she was responsible for home-school liaison. Her doctoral work, published as *Class Work* (1998) was an ethnographic study of parental involvement in primary schools. Since joining King's she has continued to research and publish widely in the area of home and school relationships across both primary and secondary sectors. Currently she is co-organizer of an ESRC seminar series, 'Parents and Schools: Diversity, Participation and Democracy'.

Margaret Sills taught physical education and human biology in London before studying for her Masters degree in health education. She was awarded her PhD from King's in 1990 having completed her thesis on perceptions of influences on health and change. She has undertaken health promotion consultancy work for health and education authorities, universities and the Health Development Agency. She recently spent two years as the health promotion and health systems officer in the human resources development division of the Commonwealth Secretariat. She has been a visiting teacher at King's for 10 years and is now sharing the role of academic director for the Learning and Teaching Support Network (LTSN) Centre for Health Sciences and Practice with Faith Hill. She is also currently a National Healthy Schools Standard assessor for the Health Development Agency.

Martin Thrupp joined King's in 2000 after moving to the UK from New Zealand. Previously he was a secondary school teacher for six years, and lectured at the University of Waikato where he edited the *New Zealand Journal of Educational Studies*. His research interests include educational reform, social class and education, and critical approaches to school effectiveness, school improvement and educational management. He edited *A Decade of Reform in New Zealand Education: Where to Now* (1999) and is the author of *Schools Making a Difference: Let's Be Realistic!* (Open University Press 1999) which won the 1999 Standing Conference on Studies in Education (SCSE) Education Book Prize.

Deryn Watson taught geography in inner London secondary schools for seven years before becoming actively involved in the research and development of computer assisted learning materials in the humanities, with concerns for both models of software development and the potential for interactive learning. She was a member of the ImpacT project and her current research interests include influences on the take-up and use of IT in schools, institutional policies and practices for IT, ICT in teacher education, and teachers' responses to innovation and change through IT. She is the programme director for the professional doctorate in education at King's and editor of the international journal, *Education and Information Technologies*.

Dylan Wiliam taught in inner London for seven years before joining the Graded Assessment in Mathematics project in 1984, developing innovative assessment materials in mathematics. He ran the mathematics PGCE at King's from 1986 to 1989 after which he coordinated the work of the Consortium for Assessment and Testing in Schools developing assessment tasks for the National Curriculum. It was during this period that he developed his interest in education law. He divides his research time between educational assessment and mathematics education, where his main interest is the effects of ability grouping. He is currently Professor of Educational Assessment and Assistant Principal at King's.

Andy Wright is a lecturer in religious and theological education at King's. Before entering higher education he was head of religious education in three contrasting secondary schools. He has been responsible for PGCE religious education courses at the London Institute of Education, Roehampton Institute and King's. He is currently director of King's MA Religious Education programme and coordinator of religious education research students. He is the author of *Spiritual Pedagogy* (1998), *Spirituality and Education* (2000) and co-editor, with Ann-Marie Brandom, of *Learning to Teach Religious Education in the Secondary School* (2000). His research interests currently focus on the development of religious literacy.

Introduction

Justin Dillon and
Meg Maguire

If you are learning how to be a teacher, then this book has been written for you. It has been written by a group of people who have two things in common. The first is that they have devoted most of their lives to education – teaching, researching or a combination of the two. The second thing that they have in common is that they have all worked in the Department of Education at King's College London. Those two powerful bonds have resulted in what you hold in your hands – thoughts, ideas, words, questions, answers, wit and wisdom.

Some time ago, a visit from Her Majesty's Inspectorate encouraged us to look at the amount of reading that our own PGCE students did. For many reasons, including accessibility of libraries, the cost of books and funding, the amount of reading that students did was much less than we thought appropriate. Looking around we could not find an appropriate textbook that addressed the issues that we knew concerned our students. So we wrote one ourselves – for internal consumption. It proved to be popular so, with the help of Open University Press, we produced, in 1997, a more polished version. The first edition proved to be popular and had to be reprinted. However, education changes rapidly and books date – even if many ideas remain valid over decades. We decided that a second edition could and should be written.

This edition contains three more chapters than the first edition. There are new chapters on inspection, parents, citizenship and school and teacher quality. There are some new contributors and many new ideas and issues. However, the overall philosophy of the book remains unchanged. This is not a tips for teachers book – although some chapters do focus on technical issues. Each chapter is designed to give you some background in terms of, say, historical context and to illuminate the key issues that you will be faced with every day. Some of the chapters should enable you to make sense of what goes on in school and should help you to gain an overview of a particular topic. The authors have tried to give you evidence to support points of view – there is too much unsubstantiated opinion in education that has affected teachers and children detrimentally for too many years. This book will give you some evidence from the literature to back up, or maybe to challenge, your own opinions and experience.

Much of teaching relies on confidence. You need to be confident in your knowledge of your subject. Your students need to be confident in you as a teacher. You need to appear confident when you work with a class. Confidence can develop through experience and through feedback from other people. This book is designed to help you to become more confident in your understanding of what learning to teach involves. There will be much in this book that you have not thought of before – things that you disagree with or things that you feel are obvious. It is designed to be dipped into rather than read sequentially and, we hope, will point you in the direction of further reading.

How to use the book

Each chapter is designed to be read on its own although you will find recurrent themes. If you are doing an essay on a topic such as learning or special educational needs or you feel that there are areas of education about which you know very little, then you can use the chapters here as starting points. Some of the chapters are linked in terms of content, so if you're interested in learning, you will find that the chapters on adolescence, differentiation and assessment are interrelated. Indeed, the complexity of education is what makes it such an interesting area to work in.

The book is divided into four major sections. We have called Part 1, First thoughts, because it sets the scene – addressing some fundamental areas of concern for a new teacher.

Part 2, Policy, society and schooling, provides a grounding in the broader context in which education sits. As well as looking at the historical roots of the problems facing teachers and learners, particularly in the inner city, the part provides a vision of alternative and possible futures.

In the classroom, most of your concerns will be more immediate than those outlined above and Part 3, Teaching and learning, is a collection of interrelated articles addressing issues such as classroom management, adolescence and assessment. In each chapter you will find practical advice based on sound theoretical understandings as well as some key issues to consider.

Part 4, Across the curriculum, appears daunting. The responsibilities of teachers beyond that of subject specialist has grown steadily over the years. The authors of the chapters in this part provide information about roles and responsibilities in areas including health education, information technology, literacy and citizenship. A key role that almost all new teachers now find themselves in is that of form tutor – the final chapter in the part looks at some of the roles and responsibilities involved.

And finally

In putting together this book we have tried to emphasize the three Rs: reading, reflection and research. Good teachers are able to learn from their experiences, reflecting on both positive and negative feedback. The best teachers are often those who not only learn from their experience but also learn from the experiences of others. Reading offers access to the wisdom of others as well as providing tools to interpret your own experiences. We have encouraged the authors contributing to this book to provide evidence from research to justify the points that they make. We encourage you to reflect on that evidence and on the related issues during the process of becoming a teacher. Over to you.

Part 1 | First thoughts

1 Developing as a student teacher

Meg Maguire and Justin Dillon

Anticipating teaching

If you are engaged in a course of teacher training you face what may be the most challenging period of your life. But take heart – the stimulation and the enjoyment of working with learners can be immense. Looks on faces, words of thanks, the physical excitement that young people are able to generate come frequently enough to justify the effort.

Most of your own experience of education will probably have been spent sitting down, facing the front being directed by an older person. Your teacher training will involve a series of rapid dislocations; some of the time you will be the teacher and some of the time you will be a learner. It is not a dichotomous situation though – you will be learning and teaching simultaneously.

What sort of teacher are you going to be? At the moment your model may be based on teachers that you have had or, possibly, based on the teachers you wished that you had had. This is common in new teachers and you will find yourself saying and doing things that your teachers said and did to you. Your first concern may well be with the behaviour of your students and there will be times, usually just before a lesson, when you look back at your decision to become a teacher and think, 'Why did I do that?' As you become more confident and more competent at teaching your concern will shift from behaviour to learning. The two are intrinsically linked. It is difficult for students to learn if they are not working in a well-managed environment and if they feel they are learning something worthwhile they are more likely to re-spond to being managed (see Chapter 14 for a full discussion of classroom management).

Learning to teach involves a range of practical skills 'and a subtle appre-ciation of when and how to apply them' (Claxton 1990: 16).

Whether you like it or not, how you teach and how you learn to teach are bound up with your own personality, philosophy and values. Somewhere inside there is a set of personal standards – whether tacit or articulated, ill-informed or carefully thought out – that determine what shocks you, interests you or angers you about schools, and that serve as the benchmarks which you will use to guide and evaluate your progress as a teacher.

(Claxton 1990: 18)

Training to become a teacher can therefore be a challenging as well as a frustrating business. A lot of ground is covered in a short time and this can result in feelings of stress and anxiety (Troman 2000). Your under-graduate learning experience may have focused on a formalized acquisi-tion of content. In seminars you may well have looked at prepared papers or had content-driven academic debates. While these forms of learning feature in current teacher training, and while there is a necessary emphasis on classroom techniques and skills, learning to teach is fundamentally a personal challenge where practical, personal and emotional attributes are just as salient as intellectual capacities. The PGCE provides a vocational training built around a demanding and challenging induction into the teaching profession. 'The PGCE is a complex and unique part of becoming a teacher' (Head *et al.* 1996: 83).

Many secondary trainee teachers (but not all) come into teaching as mature students, with a rich and broad experience of working in a variety of settings. Many are parents and have first-hand experience of their own children's schooling. Sometimes in the light of these experiences, teach-ing can seem to be a common-sense affair – all about conveying some useful and hopefully interesting aspects in a lively manner which motivates young people to succeed. For people who think this way, becoming a teacher can sometimes explode any 'simple' model of teaching and learning. Teaching children who are less motivated than ourselves or who do not seem like the children we know, can present practical and personal diffi-culties where we may 'blame' the children instead of our own inexperience. However, it can also make for a stimulating and rewarding work setting.

Teacher qualities

At the heart of this book is a concern with becoming a teacher. Teachers are in an extremely privileged position; educating other people's children is a critical and influential task in any society. But this job is made more complex in times of acute social, economic and political change. One way in which to approach becoming a contemporary teacher is from the trainee perspective – hinted at above. Another way might be to ask what is involved in teaching and what might we, as a society, want to prioritize at particular moments in time? Do we want compliant pupils who can apply what they have learned? Do we want problem-solvers and flexible learn-ers? Do we want specialists or generalists? Are there any common strands that are recognizable as key components of a good teacher? In what follows we will consider four main themes through which we hope to raise questions about the central qualities involved in being and becoming a teacher: classroom management, the wider role of the teacher, professional and personal qualities.

Classroom management

There are some well-known key aspects that are fundamental to good teaching. Good classroom management and organization, the capability of teaching effectively in a mixed 'ability' classroom (and are not all classrooms mixed ability, however they are arranged?), good knowledge of subject and subject application, assessment, record-keeping and all the other criteria listed by the government are important. But what is important to recognize is that all of these variables depend on the degree to which a teacher can maintain a positive and open climate in the classroom. The research into classroom life demonstrates that teachers and school students are in constant negotiation over boundaries, relationships, curriculum content sequencing and pacing (Beynon 1985; Delamont 1990). This means that there are not simple codes or regimes which have a totality of application. This does not mean that new teachers cannot be helped with these issues either, but these are not just aspects of performance that are incrementally added to the teaching repertoire. They require a different type of learning and a different type of understanding.

We all know that the very best teaching depends on sensitive communication. We all know very well qualified people who really understand their subject but cannot help others into it in a user-friendly manner. It is not only important to be able to help our school students understand by clear and effective communication modes, it is important that teachers listen, observe and become sensitive to the children and 'where they are at' in relation to their understanding. Teachers need to be able to listen to and 'read' their students. This too takes time and practice to refine, and even for the most experienced of teachers, it sometimes goes wrong. Dealing with adolescent people is not always straightforward or predictable. Sometimes it is the unrecognized forms of communication – non-verbal expressions or aspects of body language that need consideration (Neill 1991; Wooton 1993). At other times there is the basic issue of respect for persons, sometimes ignored when dealing with youngsters. Thus, 'every job that requires significant interaction with other people (such as teaching) is an emotional practice' (Hargreaves 1999: 8).

Trainee teachers frequently worry about 'control' and eagerly seek out strategies to help them in their school experience settings. Experienced teachers know only too well that controlling – or creating a climate to allow learning to happen – is intimately bound up with a knowledge of the children. Trainee teachers are placed in a novel situation of attempting to manipulate the atmosphere in large grouped settings. This is an unusual skill to develop and is not the same as managing adults in a workplace setting. It takes time and personal investment in good relationships with school students and it would be unrealistic for new teachers to achieve this overnight. All this suggests that 'control' is more related to relationships than external strategies or mechanistic skills.

The wider role of the secondary school teacher

Teaching in contemporary schools involves building relationships with many different students with a variety of backgrounds, needs, expectations, motivations and aspirations. It is not possible to help children learn effectively unless you have some knowledge and insight into their concerns. The pastoral role of a teacher is related to the widest aims of teaching (see Chapter 26 for a discussion of a teacher's pastoral role). The National Curriculum places a statutory responsibility upon schools to promote 'the spiritual, moral, cultural, mental and physical development' of the school students. This means being interested in the children, getting to know them, feeling comfortable about discussing issues related to their learning and perhaps advising them in certain ways. The revised National Curriculum, launched in 2000, introduced the theme of citizenship in order to address important matters which had perhaps become marginal to the work of schools (see Chapter 21 on citizenship). At particular times issues related to health, sexuality, substance abuse, and so on, become salient in the classroom, and society expects schools to address and educate round these concerns. Teachers need to know what they can do, as well as what they cannot, in this context (see Chapter 23 on 'Healthy schools').

From this pastoral role comes an obvious extension – working with parents. In the current policy setting, this aspect of the role of the teacher has significance for the maintenance of a healthy developing school (Munn 1993; Gewirtz *et al.* 1995). Communicating clearly and professionally with parents is a core attribute for effective teaching; it is recognized that parents and schools working together provides a continuity and coherence for the school student and is critical for achievement (Vincent 1996; see also Chapter 9 on parents and schooling).

Professional qualities

New teachers do need to be oriented to the fact that becoming a teacher means entering into membership of a particular community. They are members of a school staff, they are involved in a profession that needs to hold debates within itself and they have to participate in these debates. They need to keep up with their subject(s) and should be encouraged to join a relevant subject association or phase-specific group. Essentially teachers need a feeling of responsibility and control over their work. They need to participate in decision-making and indeed hopefully will develop over time to take a lead in this process. The General Teaching Council (established in 2000) will have a role to play in this development. Other professional qualities which we believe are required are related to the structural elements of the job. Teachers need to be on the inside of professional concerns and issues related to their salary, pay structure and conditions of service as well as issues of professionalism (see Furlong *et al.* 2000).

Another important dimension to all this is the capacity to relate with colleagues and to work collaboratively. Teachers need the confidence to challenge assumptions about their work and the way in which it proceeds.

They need to be in a position where not only can they work with colleagues but they are able collectively as a staff as well as individuals to ask fundamental questions about what they are doing. Is it worthwhile? It is this capacity that is characteristic of a professional teacher as opposed to a 'deliverer' of a curriculum devised elsewhere.

Personal qualities

Typically, new teachers experienced their school days as well-behaved and well-motivated students. Their role model of what it is to be a teacher may well have been constructed from this experience. For intending teachers who may have experienced selective schooling and may have been in top sets, the challenges of working with different types of students may be initially daunting. Children who have come to a recognition that school has little to offer them, that school only confirms in them a sense of failure and of 'being stupid' are going to be harder to reach and harder to teach (Hargreaves 1982). In some of our schools, beginning teachers may well meet many different types of children from the sort of children that they were – restless, unable to concentrate, demotivated or perhaps with some particular learning difficulty. They will also meet students who are assertive, who demand respect and who will not be passive recipients of teachers' knowledge. Students will challenge what they perceive to be unfair or unjust in a way that might sometimes be constructed as provocative.

Beginning teachers will discover that they need lots of different responses – different ways of being with children in the school setting. They will need to experiment with different strategies. They will need to develop a flexible and adaptive repertoire of teaching. They will need to see themselves as learners throughout their lives and see this as a challenge and an opportunity, not a threat. At the heart of these personal qualities for teachers and student teachers must be the capacity to see their professional life as one of continual growth and development. For new teachers what is required is a state of adaptability, an experimental attitude, a capacity to recognize that they are going through a period of 'transitional incompetence', perhaps learning to tolerate their own fallibility and accepting that they can make mistakes as part of this process of becoming a teacher.

Concluding comments

The teacher is the ultimate key to educational change and school improvement. The restructuring of schools, the composition of national and provincial curricula, the development of benchmark assessments – all these things are of little value if they do not take the teacher into account. Teachers do not merely deliver the curriculum. They develop, define it and reinterpret it too. It is what teachers think, what teachers believe and what teachers do at the level of the classroom that ultimately shapes the kind of learning that young people experience.

For some reformers, improving teaching is mainly a matter of developing better teaching methods or of improving instruction. For them, training teachers in new classroom management skills, in active learning, cooperative learning, one-to-one counselling and the like are the main priorities. These things are important, but we are also increasingly coming to understand that developing teachers and improving their teaching involves more than giving them new tricks. Teachers need to be creative and imaginative in their work, they need to be able to use 'intuitive, rational and reflective thinking' as well as having the 'confidence to take risks in learning and a sense of cognitive self-efficacy in a range of learning contexts' (Eraut 2000: 267).

Teachers teach in the way they do not just because of the skills they have or have not learned. The ways they teach are also grounded in their backgrounds, their biographies, in the kind of teachers they have become. Their careers – their hopes and dreams, their opportunities and aspirations, or the frustration of these things – are also important for teachers' commitment, enthusiasm and morale. So too are relationships with their colleagues, either in supportive communities, or as individuals working in isolation, with the insecurities that this sometimes brings.

> As we are coming to understand these wider aspects of teaching and teacher development we are also beginning to understand that much more than pedagogy, instruction or teaching method is at stake. Teacher development, teachers' careers, teachers' relations with their colleagues, the conditions of status, reward and leadership under which they work – all these affect the quality of what they do in the classroom.
>
> (Hargreaves and Fullan 1992: ix)

For those of you who are reading this and who are in the process of becoming a teacher there is one more fundamental issue which has to be addressed. There is a distinction between being a good teacher and someone who helps school students become good learners: those whom Claxton (1990) calls mentors. Claxton has set up a simple model to illustrate his point. He talks about the traditional 'good teacher' as someone who tells things clearly, points out the key features, and maximizes the training procedures through which pupils 'perform smoothly and successfully in situations – like most exams – that ask them to apply familiar operations to familiar content' (Claxton 1990: 154). One consequence can be the development of an unimaginative and inflexible learner.

> Good pupils often perform well and look good but at the expense of precisely those qualities that distinguish good learners: resourcefulness, persistence and creativity. And it is just this kind of quality that mentors care about. Their main concern is to equip their pupils with the ability to be intelligent in the face of change.
>
> (Claxton 1990: 154)

Becoming a teacher is not just a matter of training in basic skills and classroom procedures, essential as these all are as a starting place. It is also a matter of choice and of various personal and professional decisions, judgement and even intuitions (Atkinson and Claxton 2000). That is why teaching is such a tantalizing, challenging and rewarding occupation.

References

Atkinson, T. and Claxton, G. (eds) (2000) *The Intuitive Practitioner. On the Value of Not Always Knowing What One is Doing.* Buckingham: Open University Press.

Beynon, J. (1985) *Initial Encounters in the Secondary School: Sussing, Typing and Coping.* London: Falmer Press.

Claxton, G. (1990) *Teaching to Learn. A Direction for Education.* London: Cassell.

Delamont, S. (1990) *Interaction in the Classroom.* London: Routledge.

Eraut, M. (2000) The intuitive practitioner: a critical overview, in T. Atkinson and G. Claxton (eds) *The Intuitive Practitioner. On the Value of Not Always Knowing What One is Doing.* Buckingham: Open University Press.

Furlong, J., Barton, L., Miles, S. *et al.* (2000) *Teacher Education in Transition. Reforming Professionalism?* Buckingham: Open University Press.

Gewirtz, S., Ball, S.J. and Bowe, R. (1995) *Markets, Choice and Equity in Education.* Buckingham: Open University Press.

Hargreaves, A. (1999) Classrooms, colleagues, communities and change: the sociology of teaching at the turn of the century. Keynote address given at 50th Anniversary of the Japanese Society of Sociology of Education, Tokyo, August.

Hargreaves, A. and Fullan, M.G. (eds) (1992) *Understanding Teacher Development.* London: Cassell.

Hargreaves, D.H. (1982) *The Challenge for the Comprehensive School: Culture, Curriculum and Community.* London: Routledge and Kegan Paul.

Head, J., Hill, F. and Maguire, M. (1996) Stress and the postgraduate secondary trainee teacher: a British case study, *Journal of Education for Teaching,* 22(1): 71–84.

Munn, P. (ed.) (1993) *Parents and Schools: Customers, Managers or Partners.* London: Routledge.

Neill, S. (1991) *Classroom Nonverbal Communication.* London: Routledge.

Troman, G. (2000) Teacher stress in the low-trust society. Conference paper, Annual Meeting of the American Education Research Association, New Orleans, April.

Vincent, C. (1996) *Parents and Teachers: Power and Participation.* London: Falmer Press.

Wootton, M.J. (1993) *Not Using Your Voice: Non-Verbal Communication Skills in Teaching.* Upminster: Nightingale Teaching Consultancy.

Further reading

Borich, G.D. (1995) *Becoming a Teacher: An Inquiring Dialogue for the Beginning Teacher.* London: Falmer Press.

Hargreaves, A. (1999) The psychic rewards (and annoyances) of classroom teaching, in M. Hammersley (ed.) *Researching School Experience: Ethnographic Studies of Teaching and Learning.* London: Falmer Press.

Kohl, H.R. (1986) *On Becoming a Teacher.* London: Methuen.

Better read: theorizing the teacher!

Stephen J. Ball

Introduction

In this chapter I intend to reflect upon the role and purpose and thus the education and continuing professional development of the teacher. I have two related starting points for my discussion. First, I want to assert a key role for the teacher as a 'public intellectual' (Aronowitz and Giroux 1991) in late modern society. I shall argue that teachers are important, but not as important as all that. Second, I intend to deplore the use of the teacher as political folk devil and criticize the ongoing attempts by governments in the UK and elsewhere to reduce the role of the teacher to that of classroom technician. From these starting points and in a roundabout way I will examine recent developments in educational 'research', or more precisely *educational science*, and education policy which contribute very forcefully to the reworking of the teacher as technician.

The politics of education since the early 1980s can be interpreted as centring upon a primary concern – the taming of teachers. The major thrust of much of the eruption of education policy during that period has been to control and discipline teachers. The work of teaching has become increasingly overdetermined and overregulated. Policy has been constructed in fear and loathing of the teacher. Four main forms of control are being used in the UK in an attempt to capture, specify and delineate 'the teacher' and to reconstruct and redefine the meaning and purpose of teaching, both as vocational practice and mental labour; they are: the curriculum, the market and management, and most recently, and somewhat paradoxically, educational science.

Here I am drawing on Brian Fay's (1975) distinction, also used by Gerald Grace, between policy science and policy scholarship. As Grace (1995: 3) explains

Policy scholarship resists the tendency of policy science to abstract problems from their relational settings by insisting that the problem can only be understood in the complexity of those relations. In particular, it represents a view that a social-historical approach to research can illuminate the cultural and ideological struggles in which schooling is located.

Fay (1975: 14) defines policy science as:

> that set of procedures which enables one to determine the technically best course of action to adopt in order to implement a decision or achieve a goal. Here the policy scientist doesn't merely clarify the possible outcomes of certain courses of action, he actually chooses the most efficient course of action in terms of the available scientific information.

Policy science, Fay suggests, is a type of 'policy engineering': the 'policy engineer . . . is one who seeks the most technically correct answer to political problems in terms of available social scientific knowledge'. Here policy is both depoliticized and thoroughly technicized; the purview of the policy scientist is limited to and by the agenda of social and political problems defined elsewhere and by solutions already embedded in scientific practice, which is what Fay (1975: 27) calls 'the sublimation of politics'. It also produces, I suggest, another effect, that is – by a combination of financial restructuring and Faustian deal-making – 'the taming of the academy'. As a result, research perspectives and research funding are increasingly tightly tied to the policy agendas of government; the already weak autonomy of higher education having been redefined as part of the cause of Britain's economic problems. Further, this problem-solving technicism rests upon an uncritical acceptance of moral and political consensus and operates within the hegemony of instrumental rationalism or as Fay (1975: 27) puts it 'man [sic] must plan, and the function of the social sciences is to provide the theoretical foundation that makes this planning possible'. In this scientific and technical project for research the debates and conflicts that link policies to values and morals is displaced by bland rationalist empiricism, and the best we can aspire to is to be 'integrated critics' (Eco 1994). I take school effectiveness research as a case in point of policy engineering.

The curriculum and the classroom

Put in simple terms, here I refer to the imposition of a national curriculum and national testing and direct and indirect interventions into pedagogical decision-making. The three basic message systems of schooling – curriculum, assessment and pedagogy (Bernstein 1971) – are thus subject to change, and changes in any one system interrelate with and affect the others. In general terms there is an increase in the technical elements of teachers' work and a reduction in the professional. Significant parts of teachers' practice are now codified in terms of attainment targets, programmes of study, teaching requirements (1999) and measured in terms of national tests. The spaces for professional autonomy and judgement are (further) reduced (cf. Dale 1989). A standardization and normalization of classroom practice is being attempted. The curriculum provides for standardization and testing for normalization – the establishment of measurements, hierarchy and regulation around the idea of a distributionary statistical norm within a given population. This begins with the testing of students, but raises the possibility of monitoring the performance of teachers and schools and making comparisons between them. There is also the capacity to link these comparisons to appraisal and to performance related pay awards (Richardson 1999).

Furthermore, significant changes in teachers' classroom practice can now be achieved by decisions taken at a distance about assessment regimes or curriculum organization. Thus the reduction of coursework elements in GCSE assessment has profound implications for classroom work. And the introduction of separate programmes of study in national curriculum subjects (most recently English) can dictate the form of student grouping in the school (Reay 1998). The possibility of the publication and comparison of examination and test scores may also play a part in teachers' decision-making about how much time to devote to whole class and individual work, or their distribution of attention between different students in the classroom, particularly in Years 10 and 11 when, in some schools, students on the GCSE C/D boundary are targeted for special attention. In all this there is an increasing concern about the quality, character and content of teachers' labour and increasingly direct attempts made by the state to shape the character and content of classroom practice (Gewirtz 1997).

Another form of intervention into pedagogy is the campaign among conservative cultural restorationists and some educational researchers to re-establish streaming and class teaching. Concomitantly, methods associated with progressivism have been under attack for some time (Alexander *et al.* 1992; *Panorama*, BBC TV,10 June 1996). What is important here is not so much what is being asserted in the debate over methods as the effect of these assertions in decentring the teacher. What is achieved is a redistribution of significant voices. As always it is not just a matter of what is said but who is entitled to speak. The teacher is increasingly an absent presence in the discourses of education policy, an object rather than a subject of discourse.

> We're into a situation now where I think we are definitely not in control, I don't feel in control. I may feel consulted, but the consultations are more or less about what has been discussed and decided . . . even the style of heads of departments is becoming like that too, they're finding their room for manoeuvre is not that great either. So I'm not blaming them so much, they're being told to implement things, therefore they're coming over as being quite, not perhaps dictatorial, that's too harsh a phrase, but perhaps as being determinedly persuasive, 'that's what's going to happen'. And no doubt they're looking over their shoulder, because they're being told, 'look, you are the one that's accountable, so get these things done'. And that's it, the directive is taking shape.
>
> (experienced teacher, Flightpath Comprehensive, quoted in Ball 1994: 94)

One of the worst things about the changes here is that we are not allowed to discuss them properly at staff meetings. If we raise an intelligent question, we are accused of being negative. Critical thinking, logical reasoning, all outlawed. You have to decode everything these days. When they say, 'we had a productive meeting', they mean no real discussion took place. Everyone nodded approval. Another success for the mindless public relations world we are creating.

> (Mr Osborne, Brian Boru School,
> quoted in Mac an Ghaill 1991: 307)

The market

The second element in the changing matrix of power within which schools are set also has far-reaching implications for the redefinition of teachers' work. The introduction of market forces into the relations between schools means that teachers are now working within a new value context in which image and impression management (the deliberate manipulation of messages and symbols to represent the schools as they would want to be known) are becoming as important as the educational process. The market is a disciplinary system and within it education is reconstructed as a consumption good. Children and their performances are traded and exchanged as commodities. In relations between schools, the key element of the market is competition. 'The competitive process provides incentives and so evokes effort . . . The essence of the whole process is choice by the consumer; emulation, rivalry and substitution by the producer' (Reekie 1984: 37). Teachers' work is thus increasingly viewed and evaluated solely in terms of output measures (test scores and examination performance) set against cost (subject time, class size, resource requirements). Ofsted (Office for Standards in Education) intends to pursue the calculability of the teacher further by grading them during school inspections from 'excellent' to 'failing' (see Chapter 7 in this volume).

The processes of competition in education are driven by price and by supply and demand, much the same as other markets, except, in contrast to most commodity markets, prices are fixed in relation to LEA budgets and a DfEE approved formula. Nonetheless, the onus is upon schools to attract clients and maximize income. Marketing and income-generation are presently major priorities in the planning and decision-making activities of senior managers in many schools (Foskett 1998). In some schools the discourses of financial planning and economic rationalism now operate in an antagonistic relation to the discourses of teaching and learning and pupil welfare (Mahony and Hextall 2000). The relationship of schools to 'consumers', the priorities of school organization and the ethics of impression management are all affected by the market context. Impression management and responsiveness to the consumer reorientate the values of the institution and subvert and reorder the priorities and purposes through which it presents itself. In crude terms, the important thing is to reflect back to parents their prejudices, setting aside experience and judgement. Traditionalism and academicism are accented, expertise in special needs provision is underplayed, for fear of giving the wrong impression.

Management

The scenario outlined above already begins to point up the intimate relationship between the control exercised over teachers by the National Curriculum, parental choice and competition and the role of management. Management and the market are clearly closely intertwined in UK government thinking. As the Department for Education and Science explained:

> Local management is concerned with far more than budgeting and accounting procedures. Effective schemes of local management will enable governing bodies and headteachers to plan their use of resources – including their most valuable resource, their staff – to maximum effect in accordance with their own need and priorities, and to make schools more responsive to their clients – parents, pupils, the local community and employers.
>
> (DES 1988: 3)

The crucial point about both management and the market is that they are 'no hands' forms of control as far as the relationship between education and the state is concerned. They provide, in Kickert's (1991: 21) terms, 'steering at a distance' – a new paradigm of public governance. Steering at a distance is an alternative to coercive/prescriptive control. Constraints are replaced by incentives. Prescription is replaced by ex post accountability based upon quality or outcome assessments – the strategies of performativity (Ball 1998). Coercion is replaced by self-steering – the appearance of autonomy. Opposition or resistance are side-stepped, displaced. From this perspective acquiring a market awareness and the skills of a self-monitoring and individual accountability within the context of 'normal' school activities, would, at least in theory, consolidate the basic principles of self-management within teachers' individual consciousness – decreasing the need for overt control. The individualization of consciousness oriented towards performativity constitutes a more subtle, yet more totalizing form of control of teachers than is available in the top-down prescriptive steering of bureaucratic state planning. 'Resistance' in this context threatens the survival of the institution. It sets the dissenters against the interests of colleagues rather than against policies. Values and interests are thoroughly conflated. The use of discretionary payments, loyalty and commitment become criteria for preferment alongside other aspects of 'performance'.

In all this some decisive shifts are achieved – from public debate to private choice, from collective planning to individual decision-making. Together, management and the market remove education from the public arena of civil society, from collective responsibility, and effectively privatize it. The scope and availability of provision are no longer matters of national or local political debate or decision-making. They rest, on the one hand, with consumer choice and competitive individualism and, on the other, with the responsive, entrepreneurial decision-making of senior managers in schools. We have the closure and atomization of civil society. In general terms, at the heart of this reforming thrust, what is being attempted is a breakdown of the distinction between public and private goods and the public and private sectors.

Educational science

Management theories as modes of objectification place human beings as subjects – to be managed. This is a 'discourse of right' which legitimates the exercise of authority. Its primary instrument is a hierarchy of continuous and functional surveillance. School effectiveness research can be seen to have played a crucial role in laying the groundwork for the reconceptualization of the school within which management discourses operate and has played its part in providing a technology of organizational measurement and surveillance (Thrupp 1999). First, effectiveness studies and school difference studies recentred the school as the focus of causation in explanations of student performance and variations in levels of achievement, displacing or rendering silent other explanations related to the embeddedness of education in social and economic contexts. Further, in so far as the gaze of 'effectiveness' provides a scientific basis for the possibility of blaming the school, it fits perfectly into the 'discourses of derision' (Ball 1990a) which target schools as causes of general social and economic problems within society at large. In addition, the focus on measurable outcomes also articulates directly with the political process of the commodification of education involved in the creation of an education market. Second, this research provides a scientific concomitant to the political re-emphasis on excellence, diversity and selection and the attempt to develop methods of appraisal that can be used to identify (and punish) 'weak' and 'inadequate' teachers. Third, the effectiveness studies develop a technology of control which enables the monitoring and steering of schools by applying 'neutral' indicators. In its ambition as policy engineering, effectiveness research continually attempts to tap and measure more of that which is schooling, including 'the "deep structure" of pupil attitudes and perceptions' (Reynolds 1990: 21). Thus significant discursive and disciplinary work is done by effectiveness research. We can see the play and effects of power and domination at work in the direct relationships and immediate structures of school organization.

In effect, through such schemes, teachers are entrapped into taking responsibility for their own 'disciplining'. Indeed teachers are urged to believe that their commitment to such processes will make them more 'professional' (Clarke and Newman 1997). Moreover, effectiveness is a technology of normalization. Such research both constructs a normative model of the effective school and abnormalizes the ineffective or 'sick' school. In relation to the concepts of 'review', 'development' and 'self-evaluation' it then draws upon the 'confessional technique' (an admission of transgressions and a ritual of atonement) as a means of submission and transformation. The secular confession is founded on the notion of normal as against abnormal transposed from the religious opposition of sin and piety. Such a transposition is most clearly evident in the methods of 'appraisal'.

The normalizing effects of 'effectiveness' are noted by Laurie Angus. In a review of school effectiveness literature, he comments that 'predictability and efficiency are valued to the extent that schools would surely become dramatically more boring places than they are already' (1993: 343). He goes on to suggest that:

> not only is there a lack of engagement with sociological (or other theory), but also effectiveness work is largely trapped in a logic of common sense which allows it, by and large, to be appropriated into the Right's hegemonic project . . . it advocates an isolationist, apolitical approach to education in which it is assumed that educational problems can be fixed by technical means and inequality can be managed within the walls of schools and classrooms provided that teachers and pupils follow 'correct' effective school procedures.
>
> (Angus 1993: 343)

By such means 'normalizing judgements' are turned upon the whole school and each school is set in a field of comparison – which again articulates with other current aspects of educational policy. An 'artificial' order is laid down, 'an order defined by natural and observable processes' (Foucault 1979a: 179). The definitions of behaviour and performance embedded in the order and the norm are arrived at 'on the basis of two opposed values of good and evil' (Foucault 1979a: 180). The good school and the bad school, effective and ineffective practice, excellent and failing teachers. Through 'value-giving' measures the constraint of a conformity that must be achieved is introduced.

If self-examination fails, the expert, the consultant, the moral disciplinarian is at hand to intervene with their models of 'effective practice'. In this role the scientific and the moral are tightly intertwined. In effect, given the logic of management, ineffectiveness is seen as a disorder of reason and as such susceptible to cure by the use of appropriate techniques of organization.

It is in this way that epistemological development within the human sciences, like education, functions politically and is intimately imbricated in the practical management of social and political problems. The scientific vocabulary may distance the researcher (and the manager) from the subjects of their action but, at the same time, it also constructs a gaze that renders the 'landscape of the social' ever more visible. Through methodical observation the 'objects of concern' identified in this landscape are inserted into a network of ameliorative or therapeutic practices. The point is that the idea that human sciences, like educational studies, stand outside or above the political agenda of the management of the population or somehow have a neutral status embodied in a free-floating progressive rationalism are dangerous and debilitating conceits.

Theory, intellect and the postmodern teacher

As I have intimated at several points thus far all of the developments outlined above have been set against, and in part made possible by, the continuing 'discourse of derision' aimed at the teacher. This discourse, focused in particular on the practices of comprehensive education and educational 'progressivism', in effect blames teachers for various aspects of the UK's social and economic problems. The UK's position in international comparisons of test performance serves as a recurring source of panic and recrimination aimed at teachers in general, their education and training, and particular practices – like group work or mixed ability teaching. An example comes from *The Daily Mail*; under the headline: 'College crackdown as study highlights Britain's slide – Trainee teachers go back to basics', it was reported:

> Teacher training will undergo a revolution in a desperate attempt to improve school leavers' skills. Stung by alarming new evidence that Britain is lagging dangerously behind its competitors in literacy and numeracy, the Cabinet has ordered drastic reforms. All trainees will have rigorous instruction in the skills of teaching children the three Rs under a new 'national curriculum' for colleges . . . Government insiders say that the crisis in standards reveals the effect of decades of trendy and politically correct training at colleges.
>
> (*Daily Mail*, 12 June 1996: 2)

There are three particularly significant things to note about such discursive activity. First, there is the issue of what does and does not get 'blamed' in such attacks. That is to say, teachers and their 'training' are the objects of derision, the policies that frame and orient their work rarely are. This displacement also serves to exclude other possibilities for blame – like working conditions, levels of funding, social problems or changes within society generally. It is always and obviously the teacher.

Second, these 'attacks' typically rest upon simple but powerful polarities – in this case 'basic skills' as against 'trendy and politically correct training'. The 'effectiveness' of such polarities is related both to the divisions they generate and the unities they conjure up. Thus, basic skills are the one straightforward solution to the problem identified: all teachers are trained in 'trendy and politically correct' methods (whatever they might be) which are taught in all 'colleges' and these are the cause of all 'the problems'. The problems are 'elsewhere', and can be fixed by a direct intervention that has the effect of even closer specification of teacher preparation and teachers' work (which brings me to the issue of teacher education more generally; see below).

Third, within this rhetorical structure holdouts against change, defenders of 'the trendy and politically correct', can be picked off as both subversive, damaging to the interests of children and the nation, and reactionary, irrationally persisting with the old, disreputable ways. In terms of education policy and practice the sayable and unsayable, doable and undoable, are carefully demarcated. A classic division between madness and reason is enacted. Teachers and teacher educators are effectively silenced in all this. Their contributions to 'debate', such as it is, are tainted by their positioning within the discourse of derision as 'the problem'. Any response, and counter-arguments are, a priori, self-interested or politically motivated – 'They would say that wouldn't they?'. Of course, this tactic, which has been used repeatedly since the early 1980s, is self-defeating in educational terms but politically expedient. It is self-defeating in that it both undermines the morale and commitments of teachers and steadily weakens parents' and students' respect for and commitment to education and the teacher.

The question begged by the rather sad and depressing account presented here is what kind of teacher do we want or need, or indeed, deserve as we start the twenty-first century? Therefore how should we educate our teachers? In terms of current policies in play the answer is fairly obvious. Teachers are cast as state technicians whose work is doubly, and contradictorily, determined by government prescriptions on the one hand and the requirements of the education marketplace on the other. Alongside this goes the notion that teachers and teaching are nothing special. That many people could be teachers, as so defined. That teaching involves transmission of a variety of 'basic skills' by the application of simple classroom technologies and management tactics. These can be acquired primarily through an on-the-job apprenticeship. These ideas lay behind older attempts to open up new routes into teaching – licensed and articled teachers and the 'Mums' army' – and the ongoing redefinition and reorientation of teacher education – as teacher training, as specified by the Teacher Training Agency, as school-based, as basic skills (see the *Daily Mail* extract above). Again all this is set within a powerful binary. The conception of teaching as constituted, practised and 'taught' as a set of specified skills and competencies is set over and against the role of theory in the education of teachers. One of the intentions embedded in UK government policies for 'teacher training' since the mid-1980s has been to expunge 'theory'. Theory is seen as both irrelevant and dangerous. (I shall return to the issue of theory below). Thus, writing in *The Times* in 1992, Sheila Lawlor (education director of the New Right Centre for Policy Studies) accepted the usefulness of government reforms which intended to put 'more emphasis on subject teaching and classroom work' but believed that they did not go far enough.

> Those reforms may have led to some changes in the broad division of courses and the allocation of time but the heart of the problem remained. Training was in the hands of those whose livelihood rested on the propagation of some educational theory or other.
>
> (*The Times*, 6 January 1992)

There is a second response to the question of the future of 'the teacher'. That is the one which sees teachers as increasingly irrelevant as new technologies take over more and more of the role of schools in 'educating' society. This may be so, who knows; there is some evidence of such developments, but not so much in the UK. It would seem that we will be relying on the older, solid, fixed technologies of classrooms and teachers for some time to come.

So I turn to a third conception of 'the teacher' and thus teacher education – the teacher as public intellectual or what we might call 'the postmodern teacher'. Aronowitz and Giroux (1991: 109) assert that

We believe that teachers need to view themselves as public intellectuals who combine conception and implementation, thinking and
practice, with a political project grounded in the struggle for a culture
of liberation and justice.

They go on to suggest that 'Teachers need to provide models of leadership that offer the promise of reforming schools as part of a wider revitalization of public life'. Clearly, the emphasis on technical–rational goals,
prescribed knowledge and teaching competencies has sidelined (to the
extent that they were ever present) issues such as the need for critical
reflection, the need to focus on learning rather than teaching, issues of
social justice, and praxis as opposed to poiesis (Carr 1987). All of this
attributes significant responsibilities to the teacher *for* and *in* society; not
simply in teaching subjects or functional skills in traditional classroom
contexts and relationships but in developing intellect and citizenship (see
Chapter 21 for a discussion of citizenship). As educational leaders, such
teachers would 'create programs that allow them and their students to
undertake the language of social criticism, to display moral courage'
(Aronowitz and Giroux 1991: 109). Here education and the teacher are
privileged in the sense that they play a central role, but certainly not an
exclusive one, in the revitalization of political culture, civic virtue and
intellectual intelligence. Theory is central to this conception of teaching
and would have a central place in the initial and continuing education
and professional development of the postmodern teacher, and in their
practice.

Why is theory regarded with such suspicion? Why go to such lengths
to exclude it from the preparation of teachers? The point is that theory
can separate us from 'the contingency that has made us what we are, the
possibilities of no longer seeing, doing or thinking what we are, do or
think' (Mahon 1992: 122). Theory is a vehicle for 'thinking otherwise'; it
is a platform for 'outrageous hypotheses' and for 'unleashing criticism'.
Theory is destructive, disruptive and violent. It offers a language for challenge, and modes of thought, other than those articulated for us by
dominant others. It provides a language of rigour and irony rather than
contingency. The purpose of theory is to defamiliarize present practices
and categories, to make them seem less self-evident and necessary, and to
open up spaces for the invention of new forms of experience.

The point about theory is not that it is simply critical. In order to go
beyond the accidents and contingencies that enfold us, it is necessary to
start from another position and begin from what is normally excluded.
Theory provides this possibility, the possibility of disidentification – the
effect of working 'on and against' prevailing practices. The point of theory
and of intellectual endeavour in the social sciences should be, in Foucault's
words, 'to sap power', to engage in struggle to reveal and undermine what
is most invisible and insidious in prevailing practices. Theories offer
another language, a language of distance, of irony, of imagination. Part of
this, as Sheridan (1980: 223) puts it, is 'a love of hypothesis, of invention'
which is also unashamedly 'a love of the beautiful' – as against the bland,
technical and desolate languages of policy science and policy entrepren-
eurship. However, in taking such a stance public intellectuals (in schools,

universities and elsewhere) cannot simply seek to reinhabit the old re-
demptive assumptions based upon an unproblematic role for themselves
in a perpetual process of progressive, orderly growth or development
achieved through scientific and technological 'mastery' or control over
events or by the assertive recycling of old dogmas and tired utopias. The
process of disidentification also involves a transformation of intellectuals
and their relationship to the 'business of truth'. What I am groping towards
here is a model of the teacher as a cultural critic offering perspective
rather than truth, engaged in what Eco (1994) calls 'semiotic guerrilla warfare', or to put it another way:

> Criticism is a matter of flushing out that thought (which animates
> everyday behaviour) and trying to change it: to show that things are
> not as self-evident as one believed, to see that what is accepted as self-
> evident will no longer be accepted as such . . . As soon as one can no
> longer think things as one formerly thought them, transformation
> becomes both very urgent, very difficult and quite possible.
>
> (Foucault 1988: 154)

For Foucault, freedom lies in our ability to transform our relationship to
the past, to tradition and much less in being able to control the form and
direction that the future will take. In the mad scramble of late modernist
life we seem to need to latch on to elusive images of who we are and what
our existence means. But in the place of such rigid and anterior norms
and discourses, we must, as Richard Rorty suggests, locate a playing field
on which ideas are toyed with and radical ironies explored. In Rorty's
post-epistemological view, edifying conversations, rather than truth-
generating epistemological efforts must be the staple of a poststructural
social science (Rorty 1979) and by extension, the staple of teacher development and classroom interaction.

References

Alexander, R.J., Rose, A.J. and Woodhead, C. (1992) *Curriculum Organisation and
  Classroom Practice in Primary Schools: A Discussion Paper.* London: Department of
  Education and Science.
Angus, L. (1993) The sociology of school effectiveness, *British Journal of Sociology of
  Education*, 14(3): 333–45.
Aronowitz, S. and Giroux, H. (1991) *Postmodern Education: Politics, Culture and Social
  Criticism.* Oxford, MN: University of Minnesota Press.
Ball, S.J. (1990a) *Politics and Policymaking in Education.* London: Routledge.
Ball, S.J. (1994) *Education Reform: A Critical and Post-Structural Approach.* Bucking-
  ham: Open University Press.
Ball, S.J. (1998) Educational reform and the struggle for the soul of the teacher.
  Lecture given at the Chinese University of Hong Kong, 27 November.
Bernstein, B. (1971) On the classification and framing of educational knowledge, in
  M.F.D. Young (ed.) *Knowledge and Control.* London: Collier-Macmillan.
Carr, W. (1987) *For Education: Towards Critical Educational Inquiry.* Milton Keynes:
  Open University Press.
Clarke, J. and Newman, J. (1997) *The Managerial State.* London: Sage Publications.
Dale, R. (1989) *The State and Education Policy.* Milton Keynes: Open University Press.

Department of Education and Science (DES) (1988) *The Local Management of Schools*, Circular 7/88. London: DES.

Eco, U. (1994) *Apocalypse Postponed*. London: BFI Publishing.

Fay, B. (1975) *Social Theory and Political Practice*. London: Allen & Unwin.

Foskett, N.H. (1998) Schools and marketization, *Educational Management and Administration*, 26(2): 197–210.

Foucault, M. (1979a) *Discipline and Punish*. Harmondsworth: Peregrine.

Foucault, M. (1988) Truth, power, self: an interview with Michel Foucault, in L.H. Martin, H. Gutman and P. Hutton (eds) *Technologies of the Self*. Amherst, MA: The University of Massachusetts Press.

Gewirtz, S. (1997) Post-welfarism and the reconstruction of teachers' work in the UK, *Journal of Education Policy*, 12(4): 217–31.

Grace, G. (1995) *School Leadership: Beyond Education Management: An Essay in Policy Scholarship*. London: Falmer Press.

Kikert, W. (1991) *Steering at a Distance; a New Paradigm of Public Governance in Dutch Higher Education*. European Consortium for Political Research: University of Essex.

Mac an Ghaill, M. (1991) State school policy: contradictions, confusions and contestation, *Journal of Education Policy*, 6(3): 299–314.

Mahon, M. (1992) *Foucault's Nietzscean Genealogy: Truth, Power and the Subject*. Albany, NY: State University of New York.

Mahony, P. and Hextall, I. (2000) *Reconstructing Teaching: Standards, Performance and Accountability*. London: Routledge.

Reay, D. (1998) Setting the agenda: the growing impact of market forces on pupil grouping in British secondary schools, *Journal of Curriculum Studies*, 30(3): 545–58.

Reekie, W.D. (1984) *Markets, Entrepreneurs and Liberty*. Brighton: Wheatsheaf.

Reynolds, D. (1990) Research on school/organizational effectiveness: the end of the beginning, in R. Saran and V. Trafford (eds) *Management and Policy: Retrospect and Prospect*. London: Falmer Press.

Richardson, R. (1999) *Performance Related Pay in Schools. An Assessment of the Green Paper*, a report prepared for the National Union of Teachers. London: London School of Economics.

Rorty, R. (1979) *Philosophy and the Mirror of Nature*. New York: Routledge.

Sheridan, A. (1980) *Michel Foucault: The Will to Truth*. London: Tavistock.

Thrupp, M. (1999) *Schools Making a Difference: Let's Be Realistic! School Mix, School Effectiveness and the Social Limits of Reform*. Buckingham: Open University Press.

Part 2 | Policy, society and schooling

Ideology, evidence and the raising of standards

Paul Black

Introduction

A teacher's classroom work is strongly constrained by a framework of rules and beliefs about curriculum and assessment. In England and Wales that framework underwent a revolution when a national curriculum and assessment system was put in place, for the first time, by the Education Reform Act of 1988 (the ERA). This chapter is about that revolution. The first section discusses the background – the ideas and beliefs that helped drive the development of the new policies. Subsequent sections will discuss the developments, first of the National Curriculum, and then of the assessment system. These accounts will concentrate on the period between 1988 and 1997 under Conservative governments, with brief mentions only of subsequent developments. The purpose here is both to help us understand our present systems in the light of their origin, and to help us reflect on obstacles to helpful reform in the future. A final section addresses these purposes by returning to the themes of the first, looking more deeply at beliefs and assumptions that have to be changed if public policy is to be more coherent and effective in improving education. This chapter should be read in conjunction with Chapter 17 which deals with the more technical aspects of assessment.

Nostalgia, fear and myth

The world of politics is driven by a mixture of rationality, myth and political expediency. In education, three powerful myths have driven political thinking and public opinion. This section examines those myths in turn.

The first is that standards have fallen. This myth, which has been a feature of public debate for well over a century, is not confirmed by any thorough review of evidence. For example, the independent National Commission on Education (NCE 1993) concluded that we do not have an effective system for monitoring changes, so claims that standards have fallen cannot be based on firm evidence (Foxman *et al.* 1993). Policy has been driven by selective evidence and hearsay.

Between 1970–71 and 1991–92, the percentage of pupils obtaining no graded examination results as school leavers fell from 44 per cent to 6.2 per cent (due in part to the raising of the school leaving age from 15 to 16 so that all pupils were in school to take the age 16 examinations). The percentage of those leaving school before the age of 17 who gained five or more higher grades at GCSE (or the earlier equivalents) rose from 7.1 per cent to 13.2 per cent (DfE 1994). Subsequent changes have continued this trend, which points to the enormous success of teachers in our comprehensive schools.

A second myth is that this 'fall in standards' has been due to the adoption of 'progressive' methods of teaching. Again this flies in the face of the evidence of Eric Bolton, former head of the national inspectorate, based on his experience of thousands of hours of observation by his staff:

> The evidence of inspection is that poor standards of learning are more commonly associated with over-direction by teachers, rather than with teachers opting out and allowing pupils to set the pace and style of learning.
>
> Far from having an education service full of trendy teachers led, willy-nilly, this way and that by experts and gurus (the 'Educational Mafia'), we have a teaching profession that is essentially cautious and conservative: a profession that is highly suspicious of claims from within or without its ranks that there is a particularly fool-proof way of doing things. Teachers are too close to the actual, day-to-day complexity of classrooms, and to the variability of people and pupils, to be anything else but pragmatic and commonsensical in their thinking and actions.
>
> (Bolton 1992: 16–19)

The third myth is that learning would be improved by a return to traditional methods. Here again the evidence contradicts the myth. Numerous research studies have shown the debilitating consequences of rule-bound traditional learning (for example, Benezet 1936). The study of Nuthall and Alton-Lee (1995) on the methods pupils use to answer tests showed that long-term retention depends on the capacity to understand and so reconstruct procedures, and the work of Boaler (1997) shows that more open methods produce better attitudes and performance in mathematics than traditional methods (see also Chapter 16). The results of such studies are entirely consistent with contemporary research on the ways that children learn (Pellegrino *et al.* 1999). Consider the following from a review of such work:

> Even comprehension of simple texts requires a process of inferring and thinking about what the text means. Children who are drilled in number facts, algorithms, decoding skills or vocabulary lists without developing a basic conceptual model or seeing the meaning of what

they are doing have a very difficult time retaining information (because all the bits are disconnected) and are unable to apply what they have memorised (because it makes no sense).

(Shepard 1992: 303)

This dominance of mythology is linked to neglect of research. The report of the NCE (1995) deplored the rapid decline in government spending on research in education and the absence of any significant research into the effects of its own reforms. The following quotations help to explain this neglect (the first is about a former Conservative Minister – Sir Keith Joseph):

Here Joseph shared a view common to all conservative educationists: that education had seen an unholy alliance of socialists, bureaucrats, planners and Directors of Education acting against the true interests and wishes of the nation's children and parents by their imposition on the schools of an ideology (equality of condition) based on utopian dreams of universal co-operation and brotherhood.

(Knight 1990: 155)

Tories really do seem to believe in the existence of left-wing, 'education establishment' conspiracies.

(Lawton 1994: 145)

Thus one can understand why research evidence is untrustworthy – those responsible for this evidence are part of the conspiracy.

One possible origin for this conspiracy theory is suggested by Lawton:

The dominant feature of the Tory Mind that has emerged from this study is, unsurprisingly, an exaggerated concern for tradition and past models of education and society. But what did surprise me when reading so many speeches and autobiographies was the Tory *fear* of the future and of the non-traditional. I was even more surprised by the kind of fear which took the form of an almost paranoid belief in conspiracies among the 'educational establishment'.

(Lawton 1994: 144)

Another relevant policy initiative has been the application of the ideology of the marketplace to education – more eagerly taken up because it promised to weaken local education authorities and the comprehensive system. The application of a market model to education has been criticized by many, notably in the reports of the NCE (1995), in the analysis offered by Stephen Ball (Ball 1994: Chapter 7), and in a review of the effect of over a decade of parental choice of schools in Scotland:

Parental choice has led to an inefficient use of resources, widening disparities between schools, increased social segregation and threats to equality of educational opportunity.

(Adler 1993: 183)

A market implies consumer choice between expensive products of high quality and cheaper products of poorer quality, while demand is linked to willingness and ability to pay, not to need. The right-wing Hillgate

Group has commented that 'Consumer sovereignty does not necessarily guarantee that values will be preserved' (McKenzie 1993). Keith Joseph believed in the 'blind, unplanned, uncoordinated wisdom of the market', but it is clear that markets favour those who have the knowledge and the power to choose effectively – the children of the less well informed will suffer (Ball 1994).

Thus it seems that the revolution in our education policy was based on a combination of nostalgia and fear of change, with an inappropriate market model for education. This basis is supported by myths that are protected by a neglect of evidence, so that we shall not learn from experience. Moreover, many of the features with origins in these beliefs, notably about the inevitability of a decline in standards ('if more students succeed in GCSE that *must* be because the standards have fallen') and about the value of the market model for education, have hardly been affected by the change in the governing party in 1997.

The curriculum – pragmatic, traditional, unprincipled

The Education Reform Act devoted about three lines to the principles on which the curriculum should be based – it was to promote the spiritual, moral, cultural, mental and physical development of pupils. It then moved to list the 10 subjects, which were thereby established as if they were self-evident 'goods'. Then, as the separate formulations for these subjects were developed, and have since been revised, there has been no attempt to check that they serve these principles either separately or in a mutually coherent way. Furthermore, these subjects, with the notable exception of design and technology, were the subjects which constituted my own grammar school education in the 1940s and 1950s. It is easy to expose the intellectual poverty of this way of specifying a national curriculum and its consequences (White 1990), but the specification survived the 1997 change in government and is enshrined without debate.

Some other countries have policies in education that contrast sharply with the UK's and do not share these weaknesses. In Finland, for example, a policy document on the framework for the curriculum (National Board 1994) discusses changes in social needs and values, and goes on to emphasize that our new understanding of learning shows the need to emphasize 'the active role of the student as the organiser of his [*sic*] own structure of knowledge' and the need for 'organising teaching into inter-curricular issues and subjects'.

The Norwegian Ministry document on the Core Curriculum (Royal Ministry 1994) was in chapters with titles as follows:

- The spiritual human being
- The creative human being
- The working human being
- The liberally educated human being
- The social human being
- The environmentally aware human being
- The integrated human being.

Here we have governments who, in sharp contrast to our own approach since 1988, present to their country a deeply argued rationale for the aims of their curriculum.

Education policy has to confront concerns about the changing world of the child and the adolescent (see also Chapter 12 for a discussion of the pressures of adolescence). Changes in family stability and in the stability of employment, and the increasing power of the media, have meant that young people face an environment that is rich in information and vicarious experience, poor in first-hand experience, weaker than it ever was in emotional security and support, and overshadowed by the threat of unemployment (Beck 1992). Where the world of the child has been impoverished, the task of the school is both more complex and more vital. Yet it has to be carried out in a society where the authority of teachers, as with other professionals, is no longer taken for granted.

A nostalgia-driven return to traditional policies ignores such problems, and cannot provide for the contemporary needs of young people and of society. In 1995 a group of European industrialists stressed the importance of literacy, numeracy and of science and technology, but added to these critical thinking, decision-making, the need to be able to learn new skills, the ability to work in groups, a willingness to take risks and exercise initiative, curiosity, and a sense of service to the community (ERT 1995). British employers see the same needs (Ball 1990: 103). More recent debates in the UK that have expressed similar concerns, some to do with basic literacy and numeracy skills, some with such broader issues as citizenship, and spiritual and moral education, are all evidence of the inadequacy of the 1988 formulations which subsequent revisions have failed to redress.

National assessment – the rise and fall of the TGAT

In 1987 the Cabinet Minister then responsible for education, Kenneth Baker, invited me to chair the Task Group on Assessment and Testing (TGAT) to advise on assessment policy for the new national curriculum. I accepted because my experience made me optimistic that valid, and therefore helpful, external national tests could be set up. I was also optimistic because government statements seemed to recognize the importance of teachers' own assessments in any national scheme (DES 1987: para. 29; 1988a: Appendix B). The task group members represented a wide range of interests and relevant experience. Five had been members of public examination boards – one as chairman, two had directed different subject areas of the government's Assessment of Performance Unit, one was director of the National Foundation for Educational Research, another the director of one of the leading agencies for post-16 vocational examinations, while two others were distinguished researchers in examining. The group also included the Chief Education Officer of one of the largest local authorities, a senior Her Majesty's Inspector (HMI) (the national inspectorate) and two headteachers, one secondary, one primary.

The TGAT proposals (DES 1988a, 1988b) emphasized the centrality of teachers' own assessments in promoting the day-to-day learning of pupils.

They went on to recommend that national assessments should be based upon a combination of teachers' own assessments and the results of external tests, on the grounds that external tests helped establish common standards and criteria, but were of limited reliability and limited in the range of learning aims that they could validly test.

These proposals were at first accepted as government policy, and then abandoned one by one in the next few years (Black 1993, 1996). It was clear at an early stage that Baker's acceptance of the TGAT report might not have wholehearted support from his Prime Minister:

> The fact that it was then welcomed by the Labour Party, the National Union of Teachers and the *Times Educational Supplement* was enough to confirm for me that its approach was suspect. It proposed an elaborate and complex system of assessment – teacher dominated and uncosted. It adopted the 'diagnostic' view of tests, placed the emphasis on teachers doing their own assessment and was written in an impenetrable educationalist jargon.
>
> (Thatcher 1993: 594–5)

A more explicit rejection was delivered later by Thatcher's new Education Minister, Kenneth Clarke:

> The British pedagogue's hostility to written examinations of any kind can be taken to ludicrous extremes . . . This remarkable national obsession lies behind the more vehement opposition to the recent introduction of 7 year old testing. They were made a little too complicated and we have said we will simplify them . . . The complications themselves were largely designed in the first place in an attempt to pacify opponents who feared above all else 'paper and pencil' tests.
>
> (Clarke 1991)

The background to such views may be understood from the following quotation from a pamphlet with the exciting title *The Empire Strikes Back*:

> This wretched tale shows how the National Curriculum was subverted and undermined by the very Education Empire whose ideas it was meant to eradicate. Ministers were duped . . .
>
> Their aim was to sabotage the government policies of 'back to basics' in schools . . . Their strategy was simple: infiltration, then subversion.
>
> (Marsland and Seaton 1993: 2, 27)

The TGAT argument that priority should be given to supporting assessment by teachers was accepted by Kenneth Baker. However, the agencies responsible for developing the national assessment policy devoted hardly any of their time or resources to it – they concentrated on external testing (Daugherty 1995; Black 1997). This should not have been a surprise in view of earlier reversals. Consider for example Baker's statement in 1989:

> The balance – characteristic of most GCSE courses – between coursework and an externally set and marked terminal examination has worked well. I accept the Council's judgement that assessment by means of coursework is one of the examination's strengths.
>
> (quoted in Daugherty 1995: 131)

In 1991 the Prime Minister, John Major, reversed this conclusion:

> It is clear that there is now far too much coursework, project work and teacher assessment in GCSE. The remedy surely lies in getting GCSE back to being an externally assessed exam which is predominantly written. I am attracted to the idea that for most subjects a maximum of 20 per cent of the marks should be obtainable from coursework.
>
> (quoted in Daugherty 1995: 137)

This speech led to government directives to reduce the coursework component of GCSE. This change was not preceded either by public consultation or by any review of evidence.

Underlying this flux of debate is a basic question – how can policy and practice in testing and assessment raise the standards of pupil work in schools? Many politicians have a simple answer to this question – set tests and make schools accountable for them and improvements will follow automatically. There is hardly any evidence to support this belief. Indeed, such policies lead to a system where short, written, external tests dominate the curriculum, tests which cannot reflect some of the important aims of education. Yet the pressure on schools to do well in them means that they will distort and damage learning (Fairbrother *et al.* 1995b; Gipps *et al.* 1995); there is also alarming evidence that while above average pupils have improved on tests, the absolute standards of those well below the average have fallen (Bell 1995). Furthermore, as schools concentrate on drilling pupils to do well in sets of short test items, they can improve their scores on these particular tests, but do so by giving less attention to developing in pupils the skills needed to apply their learning to complex and realistic tasks.

To make matters worse, it is also clear that the results of short external tests are bound to be of limited reliability. The evidence available (Black 1963, 1990; Wiliam 1995) indicates that *if* we had sound data for the short national tests, or for GCSE, or for A-levels, these would all turn out to involve rather large margins of error. However, while these tests are the basis on which teachers are to be judged and pupils' life chances determined, such data are not available. Other countries have accepted this view. In Sweden, national tests calibrate schools but the results for individual pupils are left to teachers to determine (Eckstein and Noah 1993). In the Australian state of Queensland external testing for pupils' certification was abandoned in 1982 and to date there is no sign that they will ever be reintroduced (Butler 1995; Maxwell 2000).

Research evidence clearly indicates a quite different answer to the basic question. Dramatic improvement in pupils' achievement can be made by changes in the way that teachers use assessment to give feedback to guide pupils' learning, the key to raising standards lies in supporting the work of teachers in the classroom, not in attempting to control and harass them from the outside (Black and Wiliam 1998a, 1998b).

Other countries have realized this. In France, national testing has been deployed, not to blame teachers at the end of a teaching year, but to help them by providing diagnostic information about their new classes of pupils at the start of a school year (Black and Atkin 1996). The National Board of Education in Finland has written (1994: 29) that:

The task of evaluation is to encourage the student – in a positive way – to set his [sic] own aims, to plan his work and to make independent choices. For this to take place, the student gradually needs to learn to analyze his own studies and those of others through the use of self-evaluation and group evaluation . . . The ability to do that in the future means the ability to survive in a situation where there is more and more uncertainty and where the individual is subjected to all kinds of choices and sudden changes.

Work with schools in England (Fairbrother *et al.* 1995a) reinforces this argument, showing that science teachers anxious to improve learning and assessment soon see the need to develop pupils' self-assessment. There are signs that such arguments are at last being taken seriously in this country; government initiatives to develop and support assessment for learning are now being developed.

Can we find new directions?

My aim here is to discuss six issues which need to be confronted in any attempt to formulate a coherent policy for the improvement of education.

The first is concerned with the process of change. An OECD review of 23 case studies, spread over 13 countries, which examined the progress of different educational innovations, revealed striking differences between the models of change that were adopted (Black and Atkin 1996). At one extreme there were top-down models in which central authority tells everyone what to do. Where this was done, either very little happened at classroom level, or teachers, being disoriented, delivered an impoverished interpretation of the intentions.

The opposite approach, which was to leave as much as possible in the hands of schools and of teachers, also had difficulties, for the process was slow and such delegation implied that only a very general framework could be prescribed. However, there are powerful arguments, of principle and from empirical evidence, that this is the most effective and acceptable strategy (Fullan 1991; Posch 1994). Where matters are interlinked in complex ways and where one has to be sensitive to the local context in which this complex is situated, then only those who have freedom of manoeuvre can turn a good idea into a really effective innovation. This approach has been adopted in business and industry (Peters and Waterman 1982), where the response has been to move from long hierarchical chains to so-called 'flat' management structures. If new aims for education are to be achieved, we have to give teachers freedom to work out the best ways for their school:

While the existence of central national institutions is necessary to guarantee social equity in education and to supply guidelines and expertise, it is essential that educational institutions at every level should have autonomy to implement the changes they see as necessary.
(ERT 1995: 18)

This need is stronger if schools are to form those links with local communities and with local employers, which they need if they are to help pupils to make successful transition from schools to working life.

The OECD study also concluded that worthwhile educational reform cannot happen quickly – it takes several years for the majority of teachers to grasp new curriculum ideas and to put them into practice through changes in their classroom work. This time scale is long compared with the interval between elections. More alarmingly, it may be too long in relation to the pace at which our society is changing and – therefore – at which its needs in education are changing.

Teachers are the focus of my second issue. Where teachers have low status, they become targets for blame, and are treated with remarkable insensitivity:

> We are struck by the extent to which German and French education systems place responsibility on the shoulders of professional teachers. It contrasts sharply with the mood of distrust of professionals which has grown in this country in recent years, not without government encouragement. This mood has been carried too far and must be reversed.
>
> (NCE 1993a: 340)

Such treatment is not only unjust, it is also counter-productive, for in any but the most narrow mechanical view of teaching, it must be recognized that teachers are the sole and essential means to educational improvement. If they do not share the aims, and do not want to do what needs to be done, it cannot happen effectively.

Furthermore, to define teachers as mere providers of the market goods that the parent customers require is to misconstrue their fundamental role. A former Chair of the Headmasters' Conference, Father Dominic Milroy, wrote:

> They [parents] know that, for the child, the encounter with *the teacher* is the first major step into outside society, the beginning of a long journey towards adulthood, in which the role of the teacher is going to be decisive . . . all education is an exercise in collaborative parenting, in which the profession of teaching is seen as a complement to the vocation of parenthood . . . Teachers are, therefore, not in the first instance agents either of the National Curriculum Council (or whatever follows it) or of the state. They are bridges between individual children and the culture to which they belong . . . This culture consists partly of a heritage, which links them to the past, and partly of a range of skills and opportunities, which links them to the future. The role of the teachers is, in this respect, irreplaceable.
>
> (Milroy 1992: 57–9, original emphasis)

This perspective rejects the notion of teachers as paid agents, and replaces it with a concept of partnership in which teachers, by virtue of their role, must take authority for developing young adults. Indeed, parents give this authority to the school and the teachers because they want their children to learn the myriad of ideas and behaviours that they cannot themselves give them, and society reinforces this when it sets up a curriculum within which parents are not free to pick and choose if their children go to schools funded by their taxes. Thus the teacher is the pivotal agent of change, sharing authority with parents for the development of children, and representing society as the agent to put into effect any nationally agreed plans for education.

A third issue is the need to clarify what society wants teachers to achieve, which is to say that we need a fresh consensus about the educational aims that society wants schools to pursue. This is lacking because of rapid social change, because our society is divided about its fundamental beliefs and values and because society has weakened in many ways the support given to the developing child outside school.

A national curriculum which stresses details of subjects, flimsily related to a few very broad aims, leaves schools in a very difficult position. It might make sense to give schools no direction at all. It might be better to set out for them the broad framework of aims that society wants them to achieve and leave them to find the detailed ways to achieve such aims. It surely makes no sense at all to specify the detailed ways but to leave them to decide the overall aims.

My fourth issue has already been discussed above. We need a new policy for assessment, one which will support the assessment aspect of teachers' work, which will have helpful rather than damaging effects on good teaching by assessing those aspects of learning that young people need to be effective in a changing society, and which will give information, to individuals and to the public, that is both relevant and trustworthy.

The fifth issue is that we need to have a proper respect for evidence, which means that we have to be willing to review existing evidence, to monitor the progress of our educational changes and to research in depth some of the most important problems that they raise. This implies that the level of investment in research in education should be very sharply increased above the derisory level to which it has sunk in recent years.

If we are to be able to work effectively at these five issues, I believe we shall need to take up a sixth, which is that we need to build up a much better public understanding of the complexities of teaching and learning. The public ought to be, and needs to be, far better informed about educational issues than at present. Myths about our schools are too powerful and policy thinking about our education is too weak. There ought to be a sustained effort to help the public, and especially politicians and their policy advisers, to achieve a more realistic, and therefore more complex, understanding of the realities of schools, of classrooms, of testing and of educational change.

References

Adler, M. (1993) An alternative approach to parental choice, in National Commission on Education, *Briefings*. London: Heinemann.

Ball, S.J. (1990) *Politics and Policy Making in Education*. London: Routledge.

Ball, S.J. (1994) *Education Reform: A Critical and Post-structural Approach*. Buckingham: Open University Press.

Beck, U. (1992) *Risk Society: Towards a New Modernity*. Newbury Park, CA: Sage.

Bell, C. (1995) In a different league? *British Journal of Curriculum and Assessment*, 5(3): 32–3.

Benezet, L.P. (1936) The teaching of arithmetic III: the story of an experiment, *Journal of the National Education Association*, January.

Black, P.J. (1963) Examinations and the teaching of science, *Bulletin of the Institute of Physics and the Physical Society*, August: 202–8.

Black, P.J. (1990) APU science: the past and the future, *School Science Review*, 72(258): 13–28.

Black, P.J. (1993) The shifting scenery of the National Curriculum, in P. O'Hear and J. White (eds) *Assessing the National Curriculum*. London: Paul Chapman.

Black, P.J. (1997) Whatever Happened to TGAT? in C. Cullingford (ed.) *Assessment vs. Evaluation*. London: Cassell.

Black, P.J. and Atkin, J.M. (eds) (1996) *Changing the Subject*. Routledge: London.

Black, P. and Wiliam, D (1998a) Assessment and classroom learning, *Assessment in Education*, 5(1): 7–71.

Black, P.J. and Wiliam, D. (1998b) *Inside the Black Box: Raising Standards Through Classroom Assessment*. London: School of Education, King's College London.

Boaler, J. (1997) *Experiencing School Mathematics: Teaching Styles, Sex and Setting*. Buckingham: Open University Press.

Bolton, E. (1992) The quality of teaching, in Various Authors, *Education – Putting the Record Straight*. Stafford: Network Press.

Butler, J. (1995) Teachers judging standards in senior science subjects: fifteen years of the Queensland experiment, *Studies in Science Education*, 26: 135–57.

Clarke, K. (1991) Education in a classless society, 'The Westminster Lecture'. Given to the Tory Reform Group, June.

Daugherty, R. (1995) *National Curriculum Assessment. A Review of Policy 1987–1994*. London: Falmer.

Department of Education and Science (DES) (1987) *The National Curriculum 5–16: A Consultation Document*. London: Department of Education and Science and the Welsh Office.

Department of Education and Science (DES) (1988a) *Task Group on Assessment and Testing: A Report*. London: Department of Education and Science and the Welsh Office.

Department of Education and Science (DES) (1988b) *Task Group on Assessment and Testing: Three Supplementary Reports*. London: Department of Education and Science and the Welsh Office.

Department for Education (DfE) (1994) *Educational Statistics for the United Kingdom*, Statistical Bulletin 1/94. London: DfE.

Eckstein, M.A. and Noah, H.J. (1993) *Secondary School Examinations: International Perspectives on Policy and Practice*. New Haven, CT: Yale University Press.

European Round Table of Industrialists (ERT) (1995) *Education for Europeans: Towards the Learning Society*. Brussels: ERT.

Fairbrother, R.W., Black, P.J. and Gill, P. (eds) (1995a) *Teachers Assessing Pupils: Lessons from Science Classrooms*. Hatfield: Association for Science Education.

Fairbrother, R.W., Dillon, J. and Gill, P. (1995b) Assessment at Key Stage 3: teachers' attitudes and practices, *British Journal of Curriculum and Assessment*, 5(3): 25–31, 46.

Foxman, D., Gorman, T. and Brooks, G. (1993) Standards in literacy and numeracy, in *Briefings*. National Commission on Education, London: Heinemann.

Fullan, M.G. with Stiegelbauer, S. (1991) *The New Meaning of Educational Change*. London: Cassell.

Gipps, C., Brown, M., McCallum, B. and McAlister, S. (1995) *Intuition or Evidence? Teachers and National Assessment of 7-year-olds*. Buckingham: Open University Press.

Knight, C. (1990) *The Making of Tory Education Policy in Post-War Britain 1950–1986*. London: Falmer.

Lawton, D. (1994) *The Tory Mind on Education 1979–94*. London: Falmer.

Marsland, D. and Seaton, N. (1993) *The Empire Strikes Back: The Creative Subversion of the National Curriculum*. York: Campaign for Real Education.

McKenzie, J. (1993) *Education as a Political Issue*. Aldershot: Avebury.

Maxwell, G. (2000) Private communication (University of Queensland).

Milroy, D. (1992) Teaching and learning: what a child expects from a good teacher, in Various Authors, *Education – Putting the Record Straight*. Stafford: Network Press.

National Board of Education (1994) *Framework for the Comprehensive School 1994*. Helsinki: Painatuskeskus (in English).

National Commission on Education (NCE) (1993a) *Learning to Succeed: Report of the National Commission on Education*. London: Heinemann.

National Commission on Education (NCE) (1995) *Learning to Succeed: The Way Forward*. London: NCE.

Nuthall, G. and Alton-Lee, A. (1995) Assessing classroom learning: how students use their knowledge and experience to answer classroom achievement test questions in science and social studies, *American Educational Research Journal*, 32(1): 185–223.

Pellegrino, J.W., Baxter, G.P. and Glaser, R. (1999) Addressing the 'two disciplines' problem: linking theories of cognition with assessment and instructional practice, *Review of Research in Education*, 24: 307–53.

Peters, T. and Waterman, R. (1982) *In Search of Excellence*. New York: Harper and Row.

Posch, P. (1994) Strategies for the implementation of technology education, in D. Layton (ed.) *Innovations in Science and Technology Education Vol. V*. Paris: UNESCO.

Royal Ministry of Church, Education and Research (1994) *Core Curriculum for Primary, Secondary and Adult Education in Norway*. Oslo: Akademika a/s (in English).

Shepard, L.A. (1992) Commentary: what policy makers who mandate tests should know about the new psychology of intellectual ability and learning, in B.R. Gifford and M.C. O'Connor (eds) *Changing Assessments: Alternative Views of Aptitude, Achievement and Instruction*. Boston, MA: Kluwer.

Thatcher, M. (1993) *The Downing Street Years*. London: Harper Collins.

White, J. (1990) *Education and the Good Life: Beyond the National Curriculum*. London: Kogan Page.

Wiliam, D. (1995) It'll all end in tiers, *British Journal of Curriculum and Assessment*, 5(3): 21–4.

4 | Values and schooling

Alan Cribb and
Sharon Gewirtz

Introduction

In this chapter we explore some of the ways in which fundamental questions about values and schooling are currently 'asked' and 'answered'. We will argue that in many respects these questions are marginalized, or even buried, and that there is a widespread and understandable scepticism about them. We will also argue, however, that this scepticism is an important feature of what might be called 'the prevailing values climate' – a climate that has a neutral and common-sense face but that is by no means neutral. Most of the chapter will be given over to sketching out some of the features of this value climate. The first part of this sketch covers features of the general philosophical and ethical context, particularly the role of value scepticism and value neutrality. The second part of the sketch focuses in on aspects of the current social and political context of English schooling, and the value shifts inherent in the reforms of the 1980s and 1990s.[1] Such broad coverage makes it impossible to cover issues in much depth or to trace through all the themes, or possible links between the features discussed. However, we hope that there are also advantages in working on a broad canvas. In particular we hope to draw attention to a powerful compound of factors which serve to undermine the critical function of value debate.

What are schools for?

Virtually all questions about schooling are value questions – but some of these are fundamental in the sense that the answers we give to them determine our answers to the others. 'What are schools for?' is an example of one of the most fundamental value questions that needs to be asked. The issues raised by this question are the most far-reaching and arguably the most practical matters facing a prospective teacher. The way in which schools are organized, priority setting and the allocation of resources, the attitudes towards (and attention given to) different sorts of tasks, the general modes of behaviour, and the nature and quality of relationships will all be shaped by beliefs about the purpose of schooling. Mike Bottery makes this point nicely in his book, *The Ethics of Educational Management* (1992). He identifies a number of different philosophical perspectives on the ultimate purposes of education and argues that these produce very different relationships and approaches to management within schools. For example, the 'cultural transmission' perspective:

> values knowledge which is perceived as part of a country's cultural heritage. It sees the child as essentially a passive imbiber . . . Teachers, therefore, are seen as guardians, transmitters of appropriate values, and as headteachers will be transmitters, and supervisors of those below them who are also transmitting, the situation will be an essentially hierarchical one.
>
> (Bottery 1992: 12)

The 'child-centred' perspective, on the other hand:

> sees the curriculum as based on each individual child's experiences and interests, each of them being active, involved, unique constructors of their own reality . . . The teacher, in this situation, becomes a facilitator, a constructor of beneficial situations for the child, but in no way a transmitter . . . Hierarchy makes little sense, and one moves increasingly towards a model of democracy.
>
> (Bottery 1992: 13–14)

These are just examples. Others include the 'social reconstruction' perspective, which 'sees schools as essentially concerned with pressing social issues which need to be resolved', and the 'gross national product' perspective, which 'values knowledge which is conducive to the furtherance of national economic well-being' (Bottery 1992: 12). Such approaches are not necessarily all mutually exclusive and can be interpreted and combined in various ways. This is exemplified in the Australian sociologist, R.W. Connell's seminal 1985 ethnographic study, *Teachers' Work*. Connell's teachers hold a range of views on the fundamental purposes of education, which is reflected in their different approaches to teaching.

Our purpose here has not been to answer the question 'what are schools for?' but merely to underline its fundamental nature for anyone pursuing a career in teaching. Although there is no doubt some wisdom, as well as a legal and moral obligation, in taking a lead from the policies and ethos generated by one's employing institution and one's colleagues, anyone who wants to make a contribution to the policy-making process operates, implicitly or explicitly, with a view of schooling. Even if a teacher were to retreat to a position of mere employee, virtually every practical decision they made, every conversation they had in the classroom or the corridor, would betray a personal conception of what schools are for.

Thus the challenge could be issued to everyone embarking on a career as a teacher – 'How will you affect the balance of the debate? What are your conceptions of the aims of education, and of schooling? What do you see as the role of schools in society?' Perhaps it would be foolish to start a career with a set of confident and dogmatic answers, yet not to have any answers might be deemed professionally negligent.

It is not as simple as this, however. There is a whole array of factors that militate against individuals forming such a personal vision of the role of education. In fact when it comes to answering questions about values and schooling there is a loosely related range of 'licensed avoidance tactics'. In answer to the question 'What are schools for?' you could say, in short, 'There are no right answers'; and/or 'There are different answers – and you have to be neutral between them' and/or 'You need to use a neutral mechanism to determine what people want from schools'. These avoidance tactics will be explored further in the sections that follow, but they all have the effect of marginalizing both value debate and teachers' own personal value positions.

Scepticism

It is easy to stress the practical importance of questions about values and schooling, but it is much more difficult to answer them. What is an individual teacher to do? What is the appropriate stance towards ethical and political issues? This is where scepticism enters the picture.

At base, scepticism is the view that knowledge of something is impossible – in this case ethical or political matters – that there is no procedure for arriving at, or demonstrating, the truth or falsity, rightness or wrongness, of value claims. This is not the place to discuss the nature of scepticism in any depth, but perhaps it is worth mentioning that it is very difficult to argue convincingly against scepticism in any area of knowledge. However, for a number of reasons scepticism about value judgements is peculiarly pervasive in everyday culture. Indeed, the phrase 'It's a value judgement' is often treated as synonymous with expressions like 'It's just a personal opinion' or 'Who can say?'

The growth of value scepticism has been a long and complex process (MacIntyre 1985), but to a large extent it is the product of the modern fixation with certain models of knowledge, in particular models of rationality, observability and testability associated with the natural sciences which seek to separate out the 'hard' public realm from the 'soft' realm of personal beliefs and feelings, the 'objective' from the 'subjective', facts from values. In the twentieth century a number of philosophical theories were advanced to the effect that ethical judgements are nothing more than expressions of emotions, attitudes, or preferences. At one extreme these would entail that no ethical position is better grounded, or more warranted, than any other. Something very like this has also become a major current in common-sense thinking. If this was treated as the whole story, however, the implications would be drastic. There would be no basis on which to criticize any ethical or political position. A teacher would be on an equally strong footing whether they pulled their value judgements out of a hat or whether they deliberated carefully about them.

Asking about the aims of schooling would be asking a question for which there were no right answers.

Although value scepticism is prevalent in theoretical and popular discourse, it is only part of the picture. Other aspects of everyday culture tell a different story. First, there are of course people who are comfortable maintaining that they do have good grounds, and justified beliefs, regarding their moral and political judgements, the most clear-cut, and most visible, being religious fundamentalists of one kind or another. Second, even people who dismiss the idea that they operate with defensible moral convictions tend to change their minds in practice if certain lines are crossed (for example, if their flat-mate turns out to be a cannibal). Third, very many people take overt moral and political stances, and show conviction and commitment in the pursuit of these stances, and may simply leave the question of the epistemological status of these stances on one side (although, once again, in practice they will typically offer reasons and arguments in the defence of these stances). The powerful convictions surrounding conflicts around racism or animal welfare testify to the limits of scepticism in practice.

These two facts about current values talk – the widespread currency of scepticism and the vigorousness of moral challenge and argument – appear to be contradictory. However, they are probably better seen as two complementary facets of a new orthodoxy.

Neutrality

Whether or not ethical systems are rationally defensible, ethics does not require a rational foundation. All that is required is a shared tradition and framework of beliefs, feelings and habits. Within such a tradition there can be scope for rational debate and disagreement about principles and ideals, and how they should be interpreted and applied. The difficulty is to know what to do if the reality, or even the idea, of a shared tradition breaks down and is replaced by a situation of moral or value pluralism. In many respects value scepticism is a response to value pluralism. Ours is a society that is suspicious of the controlling use of ethical traditions and systems, one that contains people with different worldviews, that encompasses different cultures and traditions, and in which there is increasingly less consensus about the right starting point for debate.

In the context of pluralism, the combination of scepticism and conviction mentioned above appears more coherent, although this combination is perhaps better understood as a consequence of the 'privatization of morality' and as a weak version of moral relativism, which allows scope for value divergence between individuals and groups within society but which draws the line at stronger versions of relativism. (Stronger versions would accord equal status to outlooks which sought to destroy this equilibrium.) This combination is characteristic of what might be called a 'liberal ethic', which is arguably the dominant outlook in the contemporary values climate and the orthodoxy of value pluralism! A liberal ethic allows for alternative beliefs about 'what is good' to operate at the private level, or within relatively self-contained groups, while preserving a thin framework of public morality. The latter is necessary to protect the private sphere and to ensure that people rub along together satisfactorily (Mulhall and Swift 1993). The primary value in a liberal ethic is autonomy, and respect for autonomy. According to liberal political philosophy the role of the state is to be, as far as possible, neutral between competing conceptions of the good. Individual conceptions of the good are to be autonomously determined and pursued. We can have our personal value convictions providing we do not use the public realm to impose them on anyone else.

From this standpoint, developing and promoting the autonomy of young people becomes the central aim of education. The role of schools as public institutions is to introduce young people to the different perspectives that make up the pluralist culture and to support them in finding their own path through it and arriving at their own convictions. This approach is largely incompatible with the advocacy of any particular value position, and some might feel it should entail playing down the overt ethical and political dimensions of education.

The problem for this sort of liberalism is that, not only do public institutions tend not to be neutral in practice, but it is far from clear that neutrality is a possibility even in principle. This is particularly evident in the case of schools. In practice, a liberal ethos is overlaid with some favoured value system. The role of Christianity or particular attitudes towards sexuality will serve as examples. But how could a school be organized in such a way as not to favour certain world views? This may be a useful ideal for some purposes (up to a point it would serve to support a tolerant, respectful and inclusive ethos) but is surely not a realizable one. One reason it is unrealizable is that a liberal ethos can conflict with some of the standpoints it might seek to embrace – for example, how could a school be neutral between sexual equality on the one hand and anti-homosexual beliefs on the other?

Scepticism and neutrality provide avoidance tactics for teachers who are asked to make value judgements about the purpose, content and organization of schooling. Indeed, there are good reasons for teachers to be cautious. It would seem arrogant to set oneself up as an authoritative arbiter of political and ethical matters. Surely it is necessary to recognize that there are very different beliefs about these matters, and there is a need to recognize this diversity, and to treat different views with respect? Perhaps those people who determine the organization and ethos of schools should try to steer a middle course, and to avoid extremes? Up to a point this attitude is plausible but it is also highly prone to exploitation. Forms of scepticism and neutrality serve as very fertile conditions for the spread of dominant norms and ideologies. Teachers who retreat behind them – as a way of avoiding engagement with challenging value questions – may be in an unwitting conspiracy with some strongly 'non-neutral' stances.

Effectiveness and efficiency

In the practical contexts of politics and policy-making there is not very much talk about 'neutrality'; the idea is rarely advocated explicitly, but it is an important implicit dimension of real world politics. Some very sophisticated mechanisms exist to present value laden positions as if they were value neutral. In fact, one aspect of the politics of policy-making is to 'neutralize', and thereby help to legitimize, certain value judgements – to render ideology into common sense. A good example of this manoeuvre in recent UK politics has been the championing of the goals of effectiveness and efficiency in the reformed public sector.

It would be perverse not to be in favour of effective schools, or to favour wasteful schools. Here is a language that everyone can share, which – at least on the face of things – is outside of ethical and political ideology. However, in reality the use of these ideas within education policy has been part and parcel of the deliberate imposition of a specific ideological framework on schooling and the reinforcement and creation of specific value environments for schools. We will look at some features of this process in more detail below, but first we will briefly review the two main 'neutralizing mechanisms' of efficiency: utilitarianism and markets.

Utilitarianism

Faced with the task of evaluating social institutions, and given the diversity and contestability of possible criteria, there is a tendency to identify, or stipulate, some lowest common denominator to serve as the arbiter of success or effectiveness, and as the means of comparing performance over time or between institutions. These measures of output or performance indicators will need to be publicly observable and easily measurable. An efficient institution will be one that achieves the highest score of success at lowest cost. Of course this has the effect of replacing all of the complexity and value debate (about, for example, what schools are for) with whatever measure happens to be identified or stipulated. There will always be pressure to introduce more sophisticated and multidimensional criteria of success but equally inevitably there will always be countervailing pressures to simplify complex measures in order to provide definitive and decisive scores and comparisons.[2]

Markets

Resorting to 'markets' of one kind or another represents the other main mechanism for smoothing out value diversity and conflict. The market can be represented as a neutral mechanism for efficiently aggregating and responding to the variety of 'consumer' preferences – for providing what it is people actually want. The market, it is claimed, merely reflects preferences rather than imposing some external standard on institutions, which would also mean deliberately imposing a contestable value position on people who do not share it. It does not follow from the fact, however, that a market mechanism may be an effective way of circumventing open-ended value debate, that its effects are more defensible or acceptable, or that its consequences because they are 'unplanned' amount any less to an imposition. War is another mechanism that serves to circumvent debate but it is common to resist the accompanying idea that 'might is right'.

Although they are only two threads of a complicated picture, utilitarian and market thinking are undoubtedly important currents in recent public and education policy. In some varieties they are in strong tension with one another, because utilitarianism tends towards simple specified yardsticks, whereas market ideology emphasizes process and diversity. They can be combined in various ways, however, and they are linked by a preoccupation with efficiency and the attempt to cut through the contestability of values. It is this combination that makes them – along with the language of 'standards' and 'effectiveness' – suitable vehicles to import a specific value climate under the guise of neutrality.

Reform in England since 1988

We now want to turn to more concrete matters and in particular to sketch the specific form in which utilitarian and market principles have been combined in the restructuring of the English education system since 1988. We will then look at some of the particular ways in which this restructuring has begun to generate a shift in the values climate of the English school system. In doing so, our aim is to use the concrete example of school reform in England to illustrate the general point that utilitarianism and markets represent key policy mechanisms for imposing, under the guise of neutrality, a particular set of values on schooling. We should say at once that the following account is only one interpretation of this specific values shift; our main intention is to draw attention to the process that is taking place. This is an important task, because in order for practising teachers to be reflexive about their own values they need to be aware of the ways in which these values, and the opportunities to act on them, are shaped and constrained by the values embedded within the structures of the school and the education system as a whole.

Those currently working within schools do not only suffer from living within a general philosophical climate that marginalizes value debate. They are also being bombarded with a particular genre of 'new managerialist' literature designed to help them 'improve' and be more 'efficient' and 'effective' (Angus 1994). Most of this literature tends to neglect the social and value context of schooling, except in so far as it relates to the 'image' of the school in the education 'marketplace'. Some of it goes further and seeks positively to discourage school managers and teachers from concerning themselves with such things that are deemed to be beyond their control and an unnecessary distraction from the core tasks of being efficient and effective. However the New Labour government elected in 1997, unlike its Conservative predecessor, has at least explicitly addressed the fundamental issue of what values it wishes to promote in education. These are set out in the *Revised National Curriculum* for England (QCA/ DfEE 1999) as follows:

Foremost is a belief in education, at home and at school, as a route to the spiritual, moral, social, cultural, physical and mental development, and thus the well-being, of the individual. Education is also a route to equality of opportunity for all, a healthy and just democracy, a productive economy, and sustainable development. Education should reflect the enduring values that contribute to these ends. These include valuing ourselves, our families and other relationships, the wider groups to which we belong, the diversity in our society and the environment in which we live. Education should also reaffirm our commitment to the virtues of truth, justice, honesty, trust and a sense of duty.

(QCA/DfEE 1999)

Thus for New Labour, education has a range of purposes, reflecting what Bottery (1992) has called the 'gross national product' perspective, alongside an environmentalist perspective and concerns more traditionally associated with liberal humanism, including equality of opportunity, democracy and valuing diversity. This liberal humanist perspective is also reflected in the decision to include citizenship as part of the statutory curriculum from 2002. The importance of collaboration between schools and of the inclusion of families deemed to be 'socially excluded' are other values emphasized in New Labour policies – for example, the Sure Start, Education Action Zones and Excellence in Cities initiatives.

New Labour education policies can, therefore, be differentiated in specific respects from the policies of the preceding Conservative governments. There are also some important continuities, however. There has, for example, been no increased level of public debate about what schools are for under New Labour, and the list of 'value outputs' in the revised National Curriculum has not been accompanied by any discussion of value issues relating to the processes or contexts of schooling. Moreover New Labour has inherited, and in some respects reinforced, the four key mechanisms that the Conservatives had introduced to create a market in schooling. These mechanisms – choice, diversity, per capita funding and devolved management – were first introduced by the 1988 Education Reform Act (ERA).

In the rhetoric justifying the 1988 legislation, choice and freedom were presented both as good things in themselves and as mechanisms for raising standards. Standards would improve, it was suggested, because within the market 'good/strong' schools would thrive, while 'poor/weak' ones would go to the wall or have to improve. In this survival-of-the-fittest approach to educational provision, good schools and colleges are defined as those that are popular with consumers (parents and/or students), and poor schools as those that are unpopular.[3]

The market introduced by the Conservatives and retained by New Labour cannot be characterized as a free market, nor as a neutral mechanism of resource allocation, but is more accurately described as a form of what Hayek (1980) has termed 'ordered competition'. This is because in addition to the market mechanisms of choice, per capita funding and devolved management, mentioned above, the Conservatives also introduced – under the 1988 Act – a set of specific performance indicators based on a centrally prescribed National Curriculum and a system of national testing at four key stages. These components incorporate utilitarian aspects into the reforms.

The system of information established by the 1988 Act is constituted by published league tables of national test results based on the National

Curriculum, as well as Ofsted inspection reports. This information is meant to enable consumers to compare the performance of schools and assist them in making their choices. The 1988 legislation was therefore designed to encourage schools to respond to consumer wishes, but at the same time the government was trying to send very clear messages about what consumers should be looking for in a school. Under New Labour, these messages have arguably been articulated even more forcibly and extensively. For example, the government has set up a website for parents which both promotes and provides information on school choice and includes links to the schools results tables and Ofsted reports. In addition to an intensification of consumerist rhetoric, there has arguably also been an intensification of utilitarian currents through an increased emphasis on target setting and performance monitoring – and utilitarian discourses of efficiency and effectiveness are threatening to further penetrate teachers' professional identities with the introduction of performance-related pay (Waine 2000).

The ostensibly neutral formal arrangements identified in the preceding paragraphs – markets, national testing, the publication of test results and Ofsted inspection reports, and performance management – inevitably carry a set of beliefs about what schools are for and about how those involved in managing them should behave. For example, although on the surface the market reforms value freedom of choice, that value is compromised by an alternative set of values embedded within legislation. First, the introduction of markets means that the concept of neighbourhood schooling is devalued through the effective abolition of catchment areas. Neighbourhood schooling is based on the idea that children should go to their local school with other local children. Within the marketized system however it is assumed that consumers (or responsible ones at any rate) will only choose the local school if it performs well in the league tables. If sufficient parents in a neighbourhood choose not to send their children to a local school, then there is, in effect, no longer a neighbourhood school for other parents in that area to choose. This means that freedom of choice espoused by supporters of marketization does not necessarily include the choice of a neighbourhood school.

Second and relatedly, the emphasis within both the 1988 legislation and New Labour's reforms established a decade later by the 1998 School Standards and Framework Act appear to us to be mainly focused upon the instrumental goals of education. More specifically, legislation is geared towards the improvement of 'standards' that are narrowly defined in terms of output: for example, test results, attendance levels and school leaver destinations. The implication is that 'good' schools are those that perform well in league tables – either on the basis of their raw scores or their rates of improvement. The information required to be published is limited, and despite more recent adjustments to make the measures more representative of schools' 'added value', some important characteristics are ignored.

For example, there is no requirement for schools to publish information on: the expressive, cooperative and community aspects of schooling, on levels of enjoyment, happiness, stimulation and challenge for teachers and students, on degrees of innovation and creativity in school approaches to teaching and learning, on the quality of special needs provision, on the pastoral, social and extracurricular dimensions of schooling, nor on collaborative relationships within and between schools. Good attendance might be a reflection of these things, but then again it may well be a reflection of other factors, such as the kind of students who attend the institution.

Values drift

It can be argued that the overall effect of these arrangements for the control and management of schools is a process of values drift. This argument (set out in much greater length as part of research reported in Ball 1994, Gewirtz et al. 1995 and Gewirtz 2001) suggests that in practice the market constitutes an incentive structure that rewards schools for particular kinds of behaviour and values and penalizes them for others. The argued drift consists of a diminishing concern with need, equity, community and cooperation and an increasing concern with image, discipline, output measures, academic differentiation and competition. (Talk of 'a drift' is a simplification, and reflects a general tendency – the effects of which are partial and patchy – not a universal before-and-after switch!)

It is argued that values drift occurs in large measure because school managers perceive that their schools will be judged on the basis of their exam league table performance. This leads them to implement policies that they feel will make their schools more attractive to children with a high measured 'ability'. Such students are likely to enhance the schools' league table performances at lowest cost. At the same time, many schools seem to be concerned not to attract too many students with learning, emotional or behavioural difficulties. Such students demand a high level of investment while producing little return in terms of exam league table performance (Housden 1993).

According to this interpretation, it appears that prospective students are effectively being divided into two categories by schools – those students whom they desire to attract and those whom they do not. The former category consists of children of a high measured 'ability', those who are perceived to be committed to education and those with supportive parents. A particularly desirable category of children are girls, who are perceived as behaviourally more amenable than boys and academically more highly achieving. Some groups of South Asian students are also treated as valuable commodities in the marketplace. The second category of consumers, the undesirables, consists of the less 'able', children who have emotional problems or who are behaviourally disruptive, working-class children whose parents are viewed as not valuing education, who 'just' send their children to the school because it is local, and children with learning difficulties and other special needs (although there are some exceptions) who are expensive to educate and who threaten 'balanced' intakes. Schools with strong special needs departments need to be concerned about the image conveyed by strength in this area as well as by the financial consequences of having large numbers of children with learning difficulties. There is no conclusive evidence that schools are identifying particular ethnic groups within the 'undesirables' category, but national statistics on exclusions do suggest that African-Caribbean boys are at least covertly being assigned to this group (Bourne *et al.* 1994; Gillborn and Gipps 1996).

Within some schools resources appear to have shifted from students with special needs to students defined as being more able. Special needs departments have contracted and in some schools, under New Labour, special needs teachers are effectively being replaced by classroom assistants who need no formal qualifications. At the same time a number of schools have established and drawn attention to programmes for 'gifted children'. Most recently, through the Excellence in Cities Programme, New Labour has introduced additional funding specifically targeted at students deemed to be 'gifted and talented'. These shifts in the balance of targeting affect all children and not just those deemed to be 'special' for one reason or another. Increasingly schools have invested energy and resources on students judged to be at the threshold of achieving more than five A–Cs or at least one A–G at GCSE (the key indicators used to compile the exam league tables) (Gillborn and Youdell 1999).

Developments noted by other researchers lend support to the argument that values drift is a reality in English schools. For example, Woods (1993) in his study of 11 secondary schools in three LEAs pointed to 'indications . . . of senior staff in the case study schools giving emphasis to middle-class parental perspectives, by making changes which it is assumed will be attractive to them'. Among the changes the author noted were more attention to discipline, uniform, homework and examination policies. Two of his case study schools systematically identify the primary schools whose pupils go on to achieve the best GCSE results in order to target their promotional activity. Fitz *et al.* (1993) noted what they refer to as a 'reinvigorated traditionalism' in a number of the grant maintained schools they studied:

> several had strengthened their dress codes and reinforced school uniform codes; others were giving increased emphasis to customary standards of pupil behaviour, including ways of approaching and addressing teachers; while at least one had banned the use of 'biros' in favour of fountain pens.
>
> (Fitz *et al.* 1993: 73)

Once again it is plausible that the 'reinvigorated traditionalism' that Fitz *et al.* describe represents efforts to make schools more attractive to middle-class students with good GCSE potential who will help to raise the league table position of the schools.

At the heart of the 'values drift' thesis is a concern that the fundamental value axis of English schooling is changing; that there is a gradual erosion of the principle 'that the education of all students is intrinsically of equal value' (Daunt 1975) which underpinned much educational thinking (if not always practice) in the pre-1988 'comprehensive era'. In opposition to this principle, it is argued, forms of marketization and utilitarianism work to promote the values of competitive individualism within the English school system.

It is important to note that the evidence upon which the values drift thesis was originally based was assembled before New Labour's coming to power in 1997. It remains to be seen what the overall effects of New Labour's more complex policy mix will be, with its concurrent emphasis on markets and utilitarianism on the one hand and collaboration, inclusion and respect for democracy and diversity on the other. Having acknowledged this uncertainty, however, there are a number of powerful indications which suggest that the balances in this policy mix will not substantially alter the relevance and validity of the values drift thesis (Gewirtz 2001).

Conclusion

Whether or not credence is given to the idea that the value climate of English schooling is fundamentally changing – moving away from an equal commitment to all – and whether or not the explanation set out in the values drift thesis is a sufficient one, significant changes have clearly taken place since 1988. Changes in the social and political context of schooling and in the control and management of schools have implications for conceptions of schooling: for what is possible, for what is deemed desirable, for whose voices are influential and so on. The way in which the question 'What are schools for?' is answered in practice inevitably changes over time, and the reforms that have been introduced since 1988 are only one – albeit significant – example of this process. Within individual schools the balance that is struck between different educational and schooling perspectives evolves through conflict and adjustment. In some settings aspects of child-centredness and 'social reconstruction' may well be losing out to a new emphasis on economic instrumentalism. In others, schools may be able to harness the more humanistic strands of New Labour's reforms to resist the pressures towards utilitarianism and competitive individualism. It is within the framework of these kinds of value conflicts that an individual teacher has to orient herself or himself both theoretically and practically.

We would argue that, faced with these fundamental questions about values and schooling, the role of professionals – individually and collectively – is not only to take up stances but also to enter into explicit value debate with one another and with the wider community. This debate about the purposes of schooling, and the respective merits of equality, freedom, and other basic principles, is both intellectually and emotionally challenging. There is an understandable temptation to take refuge in forms of scepticism and neutrality. But, as we hope to have illustrated, teachers contribute to changes in their values climate either self-consciously or by default.

Notes

1 Parallel reforms to those made in England in 1988 were introduced in Wales, Scotland and Northern Ireland. However, there are differences in the legislation and in the structure of the educational systems in these countries. In order to be precise, therefore, we refer throughout this chapter specifically to England.

2 Throughout the remainder of this chapter we use 'utilitarianism' as shorthand for this concern with maximizing 'productivity' according to some relatively simple measures of success. It is this current of utilitarianism which, we argue, is built into specific educational policies. There are, of course, other conceptions of utilitarianism and other currents within the utilitarian tradition.
3 In the debate about choice in education at school level, it is the parents who are more often than not described as the consumers, not their children.

References

Angus, L. (1994) Sociological analysis and educational management: the social context of the self-managing school, *British Journal of Sociology of Education*, 15(1): 79–92.

Ball, S.J. (1994) *Education Reform: A Critical and Post-Structural Approach*. Buckingham: Open University Press.

Bottery, M. (1992) *The Ethics of Educational Management*. London: Cassell.

Bourne, J., Bridges, L. and Searle, C. (1994) *Outcast England: How Schools Exclude Black Children*. London: Institute of Race Relations.

Connell, R.W. (1985) *Teachers' Work*. Sydney: George Allen and Unwin.

Daunt, P. (1975) *Comprehensive Values*. London: Heinemann.

Fitz, J., Halpin, D. and Power, S. (1993) *Education in the Market Place*. London: Kogan Page.

Gewirtz, S. (1996) Market discipline versus comprehensive education: a case study of a London comprehensive school struggling to survive in the education market place, in J. Ahier, B. Cosin and M. Hales (eds) *Diversity and Change: Education, Policy and Selection*. London: Routledge.

Gewirtz, S. (2001) *The Managerial School: Postwelfarism and Social Justice in Education*. London: Routledge.

Gewirtz, S., Ball, S.J. and Bowe, R. (1995) *Markets, Choice and Equity in Education*. Buckingham: Open University Press.

Gillborn, D. and Gipps, C. (1996) *Recent Research on the Achievements of Ethnic Minority Pupils*. London: HMSO.

Gillborn, D. and Youdell, D. (1999) *Rationing Education: Policy, Practice, Reform and Equity*. Buckingham: Open University Press.

Hayek, F. (1980) *Individualism and Economic Order*. Chicago, IL: University of Chicago Press.

Housden, P. (1993) *Bucking the Market: LEAs and Special Needs*. Stafford: Nasen.

MacIntyre, M. (1985) *After Virtue: A Study in Moral Theory*. London: Duckworth.

Mulhall, S. and Swift, A. (1993) *Liberals and Communitarians*. Oxford: Blackwell.

Qualifications and Curriculum Authority (QCA)/Department for Education and Employment (DfEE) (1999) *The Revised National Curriculum*. London: QCA.

QCA/DfEE (1999) www.nc.uk.net/about/values (accessed 19 December 1999).

Waine, B. (2000) Paying for performance, in J. Clarke, S. Gewirtz and E. McLaughlin (eds) *New Managerialism, New Welfare?* London: Sage.

Woods, P. (1993) Responding to the consumer: parental choice and school effectiveness, *School Effectiveness and School Improvement*, 4(3): 205–29.

5

School and teacher quality: problem-solving and critical perspectives

Martin Thrupp

Introduction

Perhaps one of the most difficult tasks for beginning teachers is to gain genuine insights into what it means to teach in a 'good' school and to be a 'good' teacher. In part this is because of the inherent complexity of 'quality' judgements in education. However since the 1980s questions of school and teacher quality have also become highly contentious as teachers and schools have been scapegoated by neo-liberals and neo-conservatives for a wide variety of social and economic problems.

The success of the campaign against teachers – which is part of what Stephen Ball (1990) has called the 'discourses of derision' – has led to a framework for teacher education that is increasingly instrumental, focusing, as it does, on the technical dimensions of teaching rather than on wider educational questions. It has also resulted in market and managerial policy measures intended to increase school and teacher compliance to parent-consumers or to government, for instance Open Enrolment, Office for Standards in Education (Ofsted) inspections, target setting and performance-related pay. The resulting competitive and audited climate within schools now places considerable pressure on teachers and headteachers to 'talk themselves up' rather than be frank about quality-related pressures or concerns.

Educational research does not offer any straightforward answers to these issues. A longstanding theme in the sociology of education is that the social class backgrounds of students have such a powerful influence on their achievement that schools are unable to 'compensate for society' (Coleman *et al.* 1966; Bernstein 1970). However since the late 1970s, school effectiveness and school improvement researchers have sought to counter this argument by identifying factors and strategies through which schools and teachers 'can make a difference' (Teddlie and Reynolds 2000). Well-known British studies of this kind include *Fifteen Thousand Hours*

(Rutter *et al.* 1979), *School Matters* (Mortimore *et al.* 1988) and *Success Against the Odds* (National Commission on Education 1996). Yet by the late 1990s school effectiveness and school improvement research was in turn getting criticized for overstating its claims (Slee *et al.* 1998; Morley and Rassool 1999; Thrupp 1999). Thus school and teacher quality remain matters on which educational researchers often disagree.

Given all of this, it would hardly be surprising if beginning teachers retreated to highly pragmatic views of what constitutes school and teacher quality. Yet being able to understand, weigh up and reflect on different perspectives about what it means to teach well and to create a good school goes to the very heart of becoming a good teacher.

This chapter is intended to help you, as a beginning teacher, cut through some of the heat and noise by highlighting a fundamental distinction against which any quality-related views, proposals, policies and practices can be usefully considered. I shall refer to this distinction here as the difference between *problem-solving* and *critical* perspectives on school and teacher quality, although much the same difference has been noted elsewhere as that between 'policy science' and 'policy scholarship' (Grace 1995) or 'sociology for education' and 'sociology of education' (Moore 1996).

Problem-solving perspectives

Problem-solving perspectives on school and teacher quality reflect 'common-sense', functionalist, ahistorical, individuated and often mono-cultural views about the purposes and problems of schooling. Crucially, even when quick fixes are not seen as realistic, there are always thought to be school-based pedagogical or management solutions to school problems such as poor organization, lack of student discipline or low student achievement. Put simply, good/bad schools are thought to develop mostly from the actions of good/bad teachers and headteachers. Such perspectives dominate the media and policy circles as well as the school effectiveness and school improvement research already noted and other related literatures such as those on school change, school leadership, school development, school management, teacher effectiveness, teacher development and teacher quality. Problem-solving perspectives are also widely found amongst teacher educators, headteachers and teachers themselves, even those with considerable experience.

Critical perspectives

By comparison with problem-solving perspectives, critical perspectives on school and teacher quality are less common but more searching. Drawing on sociologically and politically oriented educational research (for instance, Halsey *et al.* 1997; Ball 2000), they hold that schools play a key role in perpetuating social inequality through reproducing the values and ideologies of dominant social groups (for example, middle class, white, male) and the status rankings of the existing social structure. From this understanding the problems faced by schools are often seen as deeply rooted in their social context. As a result those holding critical perspectives tend to be much less convinced than problem-solving colleagues that 'bad' teachers and schools are the problem. The educational solutions of those taking critical perspectives therefore often look quite different from those of problem-solvers and many of the answers are also seen to lie beyond the reach of schools, for instance in the alleviation of poverty and racism (Anyon 1997; Mortimore and Whitty 1997; Gewirtz 1998; Thrupp 1999).

Of course all this is to greatly simplify the state of play: in practice there is a complex and sometimes contradictory spectrum of problem-solving and critical stances. Nevertheless understanding the poles of the debate helps to identify where particular arguments are positioned and where the battlelines over teacher and school quality are being drawn at any particular time. Much of this chapter is therefore concerned with distinguishing problem-solving and critical perspectives around four key issues related to teacher and school quality: why parents choose particular schools and their teachers, what factors make a school and its teachers effective, how schools and teachers should be evaluated and how much disadvantaged schools and their teachers can really be turned around. As a result of this discussion it will become clear that beginning teachers need to look for and favour the critical over the problem-solving because the latter is so inadequate. Indeed I would argue that being critical is the only way to become a genuinely good teacher in the twenty-first century since to take a problem-solving perspective will perpetuate the unfair and anti-educational state of affairs we currently have. While it will also become apparent that being a critically-oriented teacher will not make for an easy life, in a very real sense today's teachers need to choose whether they are going to be part of the problem or part of the solution.

Why do parents choose schools?

From a problem-solving perspective the popularity of a school is regarded as an indicator of school and teacher quality. For instance, throughout the 1990s books have been appearing on how to market one's school to make it more popular. This supposed relationship between a school's popularity and its quality also fits the market-based approach to education brought in by the Conservatives after the 1988 Education Act. This approach was firmly centred on the idea that popular schools were good schools which deserved to thrive while unpopular schools were bad and could safely be allowed to go to the wall (Gewirtz et al. 1995). While New Labour has subsequently backed away from such an overt emphasis on educational Darwinism (the 'survival of the fittest' school), it still emphasizes the importance of parents being allowed to choose the best school to suit their child's educational needs as well as their need for information on student achievement to inform that choice (Whitty 1998; Muschamp et al. 1999).

Yet from a critical perspective, what is going on when parents choose schools is more complicated. The popularity of a school may have precious little to do with how well teachers and headteachers are doing their jobs, meeting the needs of the community and so on. Rather decisions are often dominated by concern about social mobility and the positional advantages that come with getting one's child into a socially elite school setting. Strong evidence for schooling as class strategy comes from studies that have critically investigated parental choice of schools. These have found that amongst parents, especially middle-class parents, low socio-economic schools (low SES schools) are widely considered inferior to middle-class schools (Gewirtz *et al.* 1995; Lauder *et al.* 1999). Although studies of choice also illustrate that there is nothing simple about choice and school mix, intake composition is clearly a key consideration of most parents, although this may often be indirectly expressed through references to school 'safety', 'standards', 'quality' and 'feeling'. One result of the greater popularity of high SES schools is that they tend to be thoroughly oversubscribed, while low SES schools tend to struggle to maintain their rolls. While the preference for higher SES schooling has sometimes been seen primarily as a middle-class phenomenon or as an ethnic issue of 'white flight', working-class families and ethnic minorities also often avoid low SES schools where they can (Reay and Ball 1997; Lauder *et al.* 1999). Overall it seems that most parents, regardless of ethnic or class group, believe that attending high SES schools advantages children, even if their own children are not able to attend such schools.

In part this preference for high SES schooling is likely to reflect the ideological assumption of a relationship between high social status and quality but it also results from the importance of high SES education as a means of social mobility. By keeping out the children of the working-class and ethnic minorities, high SES schools serve parents seeking relative advantage (Ball 1997). That is, parents use socially elite schools to advantage their child's future prospects compared to others. Another way to think about this is to see high SES schooling as a *positional good*. Marginson defines positional goods in education as 'places in education which provide students with relative advantage in the competition for jobs, income, social standing and prestige' (1997: 38). The key point about positional goods is that they are scarce in absolute terms so that only some people can benefit from them. If they were available to all they would lose the relative advantages they bring and hence their positional value.

The fact that high SES schools are seen to offer positional advantage helps to explain why, in Britain and elsewhere, such schools are nearly always more popular than low SES schools, which have little positional value almost irrespective of what they do. This class bias may be an uncomfortable consideration in an era where responding to parents as educational consumers is considered paramount, but it has to be appreciated that parents are often driven to privilege their children's interests above all else in education, including those of other children and their teachers. Moreover the anxieties for parents associated with a market approach to education during the 1990s mean that concern with accessing a high SES school is likely to be growing rather than declining in the UK. Government policy since 1997 may be responding to this concern also. Like the Conservatives, New Labour has hardly sought to discourage parents from the seeking out of elite school settings and indeed it is opening up more potential for this through its promotion of setting and the extension of specialist schools (Whitty 1998; Power and Whitty 1999).

What makes a school and its teachers effective?

Although the class intuition of parents about the superiority of high SES schools may be considered unfair to teachers and students in low SES schools, it is not necessarily irrational. From a critical perspective high SES schools really may be advantageous to attend because they provide their pupils with extra material resources, better pathways to elite tertiary institutions, the effects of the 'old school tie' in the labour market and contextual or 'school mix' effects which push up student achievement.

School mix effects have been highlighted by studies of school processes which suggest numerous advantages that accrue to students who attend middle-class schools over those going to low SES schools (Metz 1990; Gewirtz 1998; Thrupp 1999). These advantages include contact with friends and classmates who have a wider range of curriculum-relevant experiences, higher levels of prior attainment, more experience of school success, more regular attendance, higher academic goals, higher occupational aspirations and less involvement in 'alienated' student subcultures. Students in middle-class schools are also likely to be taught in classes that are more compliant and more able to cope with difficult work so that middle-class schools are able to support more academic school programmes. Finally, it is easier to organize and manage middle-class schools than low SES schools. Day-to-day routines are more efficient and more easily accomplished. They have less pressured guidance and discipline systems with higher levels of student compliance and fewer very difficult guidance/discipline cases. Their senior management teams have fewer student, staff, marketing and fundraising problems and more time to devote to planning and monitoring performance. The net effect is that solidly middle-class schools allow their staff to teach an academic curriculum and organize and manage their schools much more easily than their counterparts at working-class schools can.

The key point to grasp about such advantages is that they do not reflect the calibre of teachers and senior management per se but either stem directly from the other students in the school or from the way school policies and practices of many kinds are supported by high levels of student compliance, motivation and 'ability', which are in turn class-related. Yet this distinction will not be of much consequence to those taking a problem-solving perspective. In particular school effectiveness research (SER) typically claims that, irrespective of the nature of its intake, the teachers and headteacher of any school can be highly effective in a value-added sense (statistical analyses that are supposed to take account of student backgrounds) through implementing particular policies and practices that are characteristic of schools thought to be more effective. Such effectiveness factors typically include certain kinds of leadership, a shared vision, an orderly atmosphere, maximized learning time, careful monitoring of student progress, and so on (Teddlie and Reynolds 2000).

However from a critical point of view, SER exaggerates the extent to which schools can overcome the impact of the social context of schooling. As Morley and Rassool (1999: 6) have put it:

> at a time when social disadvantage appears to be increasing in Britain, school effectiveness theory places less emphasis on poverty, deprivation and social exclusion, and more emphasis on organizational factors such as professional leadership, home/school partnerships, the monitoring of academic progress, shared vision and goals.

Certainly the school mix studies already noted above suggest that the effects of students' social class backgrounds may not be as 'containable' through value-added analyses as SER claims. Many school processes thought to contribute to student achievement might be much less independent of social context than SER typically allows. It also suggests that many effectiveness factors will be hard to replicate because while they may be *school-based*, they may nevertheless not be *school-caused*. They relate to the class backgrounds of students and will therefore be difficult to modify. The overall implication is that the staff of schools with differing SES intake compositions will not be able to carry out similarly effective school policies and practices, even with similar levels of resourcing and after taking 'value-added' account of student backgrounds. The critical literature highlights enduring structural constraints for teachers and school leaders in low SES schools that should lead us to be cautious about problem-solving claims that they and their staff are simply not up to scratch.

How should schools and teachers be evaluated?

The managerial policy package intended to evaluate school and teacher quality in England includes Ofsted inspections, key stage testing and target setting and, most recently, performance-related pay. From a problem-solving perspective the challenge is how to best implement these forms of evaluation or to do well within their terms, for instance getting a good Ofsted report. However for those holding more critical perspectives such approaches to school and teacher evaluation are themselves highly problematic.

A key difficulty that follows from previous points is that such generic frameworks for evaluation are unlikely to adequately capture the impact of context in a way that can justify policymakers' claims of teacher incompetence or school failure. For instance when making judgements on school quality, Ofsted uses its 'Pre Inspection Context and School Indicator' (PICSI) to take some account of the way the social class backgrounds of students impact on levels of student achievement. But since it refuses to concede that the social and political context within which low SES schools are operating makes success in its terms remarkably difficult, Ofsted still does not give nearly enough weight to the social context of schooling (Thrupp 1999). The difficulty here is that it is Ofsted's ability to hold that schools are failing and that school staff are responsible for the decline that provides its power as an agent of managerial accountability. A stronger acknowledgement of school context would muddy the waters in a way that would make its ideological and practical work much more difficult (for more discussion about inspection, see Chapter 7).

A second critical concern has to do with the educational effects of managerial accountability – the risk that the tail will wag the dog – for instance by encouraging teachers to teach to the test and restrict the curriculum to boost their key stage results (Ball 1999). Thus Gillborn and Youdell discuss what they call the 'A-to-C economy' in which 'almost every aspect of school life is re-evaluated for its possible contribution to the headline statistic of the proportion of pupils attaining at least 5 higher grade GCSE passes' (2000: 12). They also note the occurrence of 'educational triage' where decisions are made to focus on some students at the expense of others depending on whether or not they are seen to have the potential to enhance their school's position in the examination league-tables.

This problem in turn raises the further problem, from a critical perspective, that problem-solvers expect working-class and minority students to jump through the hoop of a middle-class schooling system. For example school effectiveness researchers have been oriented towards 'a behavioural, technicist approach in which the vessel of the school is studied rather than the contents', 'a conservative political orientation in which schooling was seen as a "good" which SER was to encourage more children to take up' (Reynolds and Teddlie 2000: 341). In contrast a critical approach to the curriculum does not assume that it is ideologically neutral, rather it sees the need for what Connell calls 'curricular justice', a fundamental shift in curriculum, pedagogy and assessment to suit groups other than the white middle class (Connell 1994). An example might be, say, a programme that provided an authentic history of African Caribbean people, was taught and assessed in a way that gave genuine weight to the language and culture of African Caribbean students in the UK today, and where (crucially) the qualification gained was seen to be of equal standing to that gained in other kinds of courses. This is not just a utopian vision; a critical movement centred on race, gender and social class curricular issues developed in the UK over the 1970s and 1980s and remains an important strand of teacher culture today despite attacks from the Right (Hatcher 1998).

From a critical perspective a further problem with managerial frameworks for evaluation is the opportunity cost they represent in terms of expense, time and energy which could be used elsewhere. It has been estimated that an Ofsted inspection costs a school £20,000 and there are further costs related to local education authority (LEA) inspections and school marketing (Gewirtz 2000; Hood *et al.* 2000). Meanwhile many teachers clearly find Ofsted inspections and key stage testing time-consuming and stressful (Jeffrey and Woods 1998). Gillborn and Youdell (2000: 222) conclude that 'it is time this level of activity was refocused towards the achievement of social justice' (see also Chapter 8).

How much can disadvantaged schools and their teachers really be turned around?

Despite all the problems already noted, New Labour's policymakers and a good many other problem-solvers are adamant that feasible strategies do exist for improving low SES schools 'against the odds' (National Commission on Education 1996). In the case of New Labour this claim is so insistent that researchers who point to weaknesses in its agenda of 'Official School Improvement' (Hatcher 1998) risk being dismissed as 'sceptics', 'cynics', 'energy sappers' and even 'middle class elitists' (Blunkett, cited in the *Times Educational Supplement*, 6 June 1997 and 23 July 1999).

However while the problem-solving belief in school improvement has a common-sense appeal, it is full of holes. Why *should* we expect schools to hold all the answers to wider societal problems? As Anyon (1997: 164–5) has noted in the US context:

> we are aware – and over 30 years of research has consistently demonstrated – that academic achievement in US schools is closely correlated with student socio-economic status. To really improve ghetto children's chances then, in school and out, we must (in addition to pursuing school based reforms) increase their social and economic well-being and status before and while they are students. We must ultimately, therefore, eliminate poverty: we must eliminate the ghetto school by eliminating the underlying causes of ghettoization . . . Unfortunately educational 'small victories' such as the restructuring of a school or the introduction of a new classroom pedagogical technique, no matter how satisfying to the individuals involved, without a long-range strategy to eradicate underlying causes of poverty and racial isolation, cannot add up to large victories in our inner cities with effects that are sustainable over time.

In the UK, Robinson has argued a similar vein, that educational approaches are unlikely to address the impact of social inequality. He has suggested that 'a serious programme to alleviate child poverty might do far more for boosting attainment and literacy than any modest intervention in schooling' (Robinson 1997: 17).

Another key limitation of problem-solving approaches to turning schools around is that they are too generic. All of the literatures related to school and teacher effectiveness and improvement noted earlier and other managerial problem-solving literatures such as Total Quality Management tend to be general rather than context-specific in nature. This is seldom made explicit – it is more the case that the literature is vague about what sort of students, classrooms or schools are actually under discussion. Readers are therefore encouraged to take the view that schools' problems and solutions are essentially the same regardless of their social setting, but this is clearly incorrect. For instance in the school improvement literature, school cultures are variously seen as 'stuck', 'moving', 'individualist', 'collaborative', 'contrived', 'Balkanized', 'wandering', 'promenading', 'formal', 'welfarist', 'hothouse', 'survivalist', 'traditional', 'collegial', 'cruising', 'strolling', 'struggling' and 'sinking' (see Thrupp 1999: 178). What is rarely discussed however are ways in which these various models of school organizational culture might be modified or precluded by the cultural features of different kinds of school social settings such as high and low SES schools, predominantly white schools and schools dominated by ethnic minority students, students for whom English is their second language, children with special educational needs, refugee students and so on.

Problem-solvers also frequently point to inspirational examples of teachers and heads turning low SES schools around and certainly the media offer numerous accounts of heroic teachers and heads winning against the odds in 'tough' schools. Nevertheless, closer inspection usually finds the reality is not as impressive as the story. Test scores turn out to be improved but still low. Impoverished suburbs turn out to be gentrifying in a way that has brought a quite different school intake. Similarly while New Labour has often claimed the success of its programme of 'special measures' for failing schools, where 'special measures' *have* turned schools around, intake changes and the injection of additional resources are often likely to be the cause. Slee notes that 'systematic population cleansing . . . and large injections of funding previously not delivered to the school is not dwelt upon by those chronicling the new histories of schools which are "turned around"' (1998: 107).

It is also important to appreciate that even if some teachers and heads *can* achieve extraordinary levels of achievement with low socioeconomic and minority students, this may not be sustainable over the longer term or useful in policy terms. As Mortimore and Whitty (1997: 6, 8–9) have pointed out:

> we must . . . be aware of the dangers of basing a national strategy for change on the efforts of outstanding individuals working in exceptional circumstances.

> Whilst some schools can succeed against the odds, the possibility of them all doing so, year in and year out, still appears remote given that the long-term patterning of educational inequality has been strikingly consistent throughout the history of public education in most countries.

Nor should it be overlooked that, in many cases, improvement has turned out to be a bridge too far. A development that has highlighted this has been the resignation of a number of 'superheads', bought in to turn around previously failing schools which have been given a 'fresh start', with new names (Mansell 2000). What has been noteworthy about these cases is that even with experienced leadership and additional resources and staffing it has proved so difficult to bring about change. The Fresh Start initiative is unrealistic about both the extent and speed of improvement possible.

Also relevant here is the idea that high teacher expectations of students will bring success against the odds. This idea originates from experimental studies on teacher effects and is a theme frequently stressed in teacher education courses. However it is likely that teacher expectations are also context bound, largely generated in response to the dominant characteristics of the student body in a school. In this respect, teacher expectations may be not so much high or low, as appropriate or inappropriate. Where they are too far away from students' expectations, student resistance will often modify them to a more suitable level (Thrupp 1999).

Towards more critical perspectives on school and teacher quality

Problem-solving discourses on teacher and school quality are seriously challenged by the critical difficulties noted here. After all, if most parents prefer middle-class schools over low SES schools for apparently quite well-founded (if unfair) reasons related to positional advantage, this is hardly a problem for which the staff of 'failing' low SES schools can be blamed. Nor can we reasonably expect generic approaches to school and teacher evaluation and improvement to work in all settings or for all students to succeed in white middle-class terms. Finally the evidence for school improvement is much weaker than problem-solvers usually care to admit. Uncritical optimism is too often substituted for careful analysis.

Nothing much has been said here about the effectiveness of teachers independent of the mix of students they teach, for instance between different teachers teaching the same class of students in the same school. This is because there is likely to be less disagreement between problem-solving and critical stances in this area since those taking critical stances are usually quite happy to concede that there are better and worse teachers in all schools. They would also argue, however, that this is a relatively minor issue which should not serve to distract from the reality that those who are being portrayed as bad teachers in the media and in policy debate are those associated with 'failing' low SES schools which because of their low positional value are not valued by the public or by policymakers. For this reason what it means to be a 'good' or 'bad' teacher cannot be divorced from the issue of school mix, at least not until the differential positional value of high and low SES schools is acknowledged and taken account of in policy.

On the other hand, problem-solvers would often claim that critical arguments on teacher and school quality lead down a slippery slope to cultural deficit and defeatism (see, for example, Edmonds 1979; Barber 1997). The cultural deficit argument is that teachers will be too quick to perceive some inadequacy in the background of students (such as 'bad parenting') and blame student failure on this rather than asking whether their own practice is causing the problem. To counter this argument, beginning teachers need to be very clear about what a deficit perspective really constitutes. It is certainly important not to judge individuals by their backgrounds but when this stance is used to hold teachers responsible for the lack of achievement of students from low SES backgrounds, teachers can become unfairly hoist by their own petard. Moreover there is a world of difference between a deficit approach, which views school failure as resulting from some inherent flaw or inadequacy, 'in' students and critical approaches, which focus on unequal power relations and resources 'for' schools. Nor is defeatism what a critical perspective is about. It is not being argued that schools make *no* difference as one key government adviser claimed (Barber 1997). Rather a critical perspective allows teachers to develop a more sophisticated, sustaining, socially just and genuinely *educational* understanding of good and bad teaching and schools.

What would all this actually mean for beginning teachers? It will clearly vary according to whether you end up teaching in an advantaged or less advantaged school setting. To give a few examples, critical teachers in popular, high SES, schools could

- be modest about the relative popularity of their school, accepting that a school deemed to be of poor quality or failing may, in real terms, have teachers and senior staff who are working harder and smarter than themselves;
- be honest in their public statements about the way in which their schools gain advantage from their high SES intakes;
- refuse to engage in the A–C economy and educational triage;
- build cooperative rather than competitive relationships with other schools;
- ensure that their own school's practices are the least selective or exclusionary possible; and
- support any moves to provide additional resources to disadvantaged schools which need them most.

On the other hand, critical teachers in low SES schools could:

- take heart from knowing that what they are doing is of genuine importance, and that they are probably doing it as well as can reasonably be expected given the circumstances;
- make good use of the gulf between official policy and classroom practice in the service of their students. For instance, when schools are often being asked to impose inappropriate or damaging curriculum or assessment innovations, paying only lip service to what is required may be entirely justifiable;
- commit themselves to improving the learning of the students currently at their school rather than targeting middle-class families as a means of bringing about a change in the positional status of their schools; and
- refuse to engage in the A–C economy and educational triage.

These kinds of activities are admittedly more easily said than done since they will often lead teachers into conflict with local communities, other teachers and senior management, not to mention LEAs and government agencies such as Ofsted and the Department for Education and Employment. Nevertheless it is important not to see the current market and managerial pressures in education as immutable. School life typically presents numerous opportunities for teachers to be politically active in a critical sense without actually losing their jobs. The key thing is to connect with like-minded people in or beyond one's school.

References

Anyon, J. (1997) *Ghetto Schooling: A Political Economy of Urban Education Reform.* London: Teachers College Press.

Ball, S.J. (1990) *Politics and Policymaking in Education.* London: Routledge.

Ball, S.J. (1997) Markets, equity and values in education, in R. Pring and G. Walford (eds) *Affirming the Comprehensive Ideal.* London: Falmer Press.

Ball, S.J. (1999) Labour, learning and the economy: a 'policy sociology' perspective, *Cambridge Journal of Education*, 29(2): 195–206.

Ball S.J. (ed.) (2000) *Sociology of Education: Major Themes*. London: Routledge.

Barber, M. (1997) Hoddle showed us how the White paper can succeed, *Times Educational Supplement*, 7 November.

Bernstein, B. (1970) Education cannot compensate for society, *New Society*, 15: 344–7.

Coleman, J.S., Campbell, E., Hobson, C. *et al*. (1966) *Equality of Educational Opportunity*. Washington: US Government Printing Office.

Connell, R.W. (1994) Poverty and education, *Harvard Educational Review*, 64(2): 125–49.

Edmonds, R. (1979) Effective schools for the urban poor, *Educational Leadership*, 37: 15–27.

Gewirtz, S. (1998) Can all schools be successful? An exploration of the determinants of school 'success', *Oxford Review of Education*, 24(4): 439–57.

Gewirtz, S. (2000) Bringing the politics back in: a critical analysis of quality discourses in education. Unpublished paper, The Open University, Milton Keynes.

Gewirtz, S., Ball, S.J. and Bowe, R. (1995) *Markets, Choice and Equity in Education*. Buckingham: Open University Press.

Gillborn, D. and Youdell, D. (2000) *Rationing Education: Policy, Practice, Reform, and Equity*. Buckingham: Open University Press.

Grace, G. (1995) *School Leadership: Beyond Educational Management*. London: Falmer.

Halsey, A.H., Lauder, H., Brown, P. and Wells A.S. (eds) (1997) *Education, Culture, Economy and Society*. Oxford: Oxford University Press.

Hatcher, R. (1998) Social justice and the politics of school effectiveness and school improvement, *Race, Ethnicity and Education*, 1(2): 267–89.

Hood, C., Scott, C., James, O. *et al*. (1999) *Regulation Inside Government: Waste-Watchers, Quality Police, and Sleaze-Busters*. Oxford: Oxford University Press.

Jeffrey, B. and Woods, P. (1998) *Testing Teachers. The Effect of School Inspections on Primary Teachers*. London: Falmer.

Lauder, H., Hughes, D., Watson, S. *et al*. (1999) *Trading in Futures: Why Markets in Education Don't Work*. Buckingham: Open University Press.

Mansell, W. (2000) Fresh start scheme turns sour, *Times Educational Supplement*, 12 May.

Marginson, S. (1997) *Markets in Education*. St Leonards, NSW: Allen & Unwin.

Metz, M.H. (1990) How social class differences shape teachers work, in M.W. McLaughlin, J.E. Talbert and N. Bascia (eds) *The Contexts of Teaching in Secondary Schools*. New York: Teachers College Press.

Moore, R. (1996) Back to the future: the problem of change and the possibilities of advance in the sociology of education, *British Journal of Sociology of Education*, 17(2): 145–61.

Morley, L. and Rassool, N. (1999) *School Effectiveness: Fracturing the Discourse*. London: Falmer.

Mortimore, P. and Whitty, G. (1997) *Can School Improvement Overcome the Effects of Disadvantage?* London: Institute of Education.

Mortimore, P., Sammons, P., Stoll, L. *et al*. (1988) *School Matters*. Wells: Open Books.

Muschamp, Y., Jamieson, I. and Lauder, H. (1999) Education, education, education, in M. Powell (ed.) *New Labour, New Welfare State?* Bristol: Policy Press.

National Commission on Education (1996) *Success Against the Odds*. London: Routledge.

Power, S. and Whitty, G. (1999) New Labour's education policy: first, second or third way? *Journal of Education Policy*, 14(5): 535–46.

Reay, D. and Ball, S. (1997) 'Spoilt for choice': the working classes and educational markets, in G. Walford (ed.) Special Issue on Choice, Diversity and Equity in Secondary Education, *Oxford Review of Education*, 23(1): 89–101.

Reynolds, D. and Teddlie, C. (2000) The future agenda for school effectiveness research, in C. Teddlie and D. Reynolds *International Handbook of School Effectiveness Research*. London: Falmer.

Robinson, P. (1997) *Literacy, Numeracy and Economic Performance*. London: Centre for Economic Performance, London School of Economics.

Rutter, M., Maughan, B., Mortimore, P. and Ouston, J. (1979) *Fifteen Thousand Hours*. London: Open Books.

Slee, R. (1998) High reliability organisations and liability students – the politics of recognition, in R. Slee, S. Tomlinson with G. Weiner (eds) *School Effectiveness for Whom?* London: Falmer.

Teddlie, C. and Reynolds, D. (2000) *International Handbook of School Effectiveness Research*. London: Falmer.

Thrupp, M. (1999) *Schools Making a Difference: Let's Be Realistic!* Buckingham: Open University Press.

Whitty, G. (1998) New Labour, education and disadvantage, *Education and Social Justice*, 1(1): 2–8.

6

Reforming teachers and their work

Meg Maguire, Justin Dillon and Gill Close

Introduction

This chapter is concerned with charting the reforms which have occurred in schools and in the professional preparation and development of teachers. In many ways, this is an almost impossible task for, since the 1980s, the education system – from early years provision right through to higher education – has been subjected to an unprecedented range of legislation, policy shifts, new requirements and standing orders which are difficult to do justice to in one short piece (but see Maclure 1988; Ball 1993; Mahony and Hextall 2000a). In this chapter, rather than deal with the detail of prescription and legislation, what we want to do is explore the policy landscape in which all these reforms are set down. Our intention here is to consider the scope and shape of these changes and the ensuing consequences for reform and restructuring that are taking place. Perhaps the only thing we can be sure of is that reforms and new requirements will continue to characterize the working lives of teachers for the foreseeable future.

Somewhat contradictorily, as Professor Michael Barber, head of the Standards Team at the Department for Education and Employment (DfEE), noted, 'everything has changed, yet oddly everything, it seems, has stayed the same. Classroom practice would be clearly recognisable to a teacher who had retired in 1975 or 1985 and pupils tend to be organised in similar ways' (Barber 1995: 190). On a superficial level this is true; teachers teach and children and students attend (or not) to their lessons. School days and the school year follow a recognizable rhythm in buildings and classrooms that would certainly be familiar to those who were schooled some time ago. Beyond these reassuringly familiar patterns, however, some substantive changes have occurred: in curriculum, assessment and pedagogy, in the way teachers are prepared for their jobs and in the way they are now held publicly accountable. Why have these changes and reforms taken place?

Background to the reform movement

> The need to raise standards of education for all young people is almost universally recognised. This is partly a matter of economics. The British economy, and indeed the wider European economy, would appear to depend on having a well-educated, adaptable, continuously learning work-force which is able to generate and implement innovation.
>
> (Barber 1995: 189)

No one would challenge the desire and intention to improve schooling. Indeed, in many respects, the liberal history of state maintained educational provision has been one of increased provision, enhanced access to higher education and all-round increases in levels of literacy and numeracy (see Chapter 3). Thus there has always been a school reform movement of some description. More recently, over the last twenty years or so, a formalized movement of school improvement and effectiveness has grown up, concerned to identify processes that facilitate and inhibit educational change (for example, see Stoll and Fink 1996 and Chapter 5 in this volume). Common sense tells us that there will always be a sound case for improving educational provision.

Prior to the Education Reform Act (ERA) of 1988, the most significant Acts of Parliament relating to education and its reform were:

- the 1870 (Forster) Act – which established universal elementary education;
- the 1902 Act – which established secondary education for the 'able', by providing scholarships for grammar school entry;
- the 1944 (Butler) Act – which established universal secondary education, initially a tripartite system (grammar, technical and secondary modern schools).

The ERA was a complex and 'far reaching' act (Maclure 1988: v) because it 'altered the basic power structure of the educational system'. Until 1988 teachers were, in general, left to get on with their jobs, working within the framework created by Parliament. The local education authority (LEA), democratically accountable to its local community, was obligated to manage and organize the provision. The ERA introduced the National Curriculum and a national assessment system and gave increased powers to school governors and, crucially, to the Secretary of State for Education.

'Education influences and reflects the values of society, and the kind of society we want to be' (DfEE/QCA 2000: 100). However, society has changed since the late 1970s. For example, technological changes and globalizing economies have resulted in changes in work and in leisure. It is axiomatic that education needs to be proactive in responding to the challenges these changes represent. Reforming education is an international phenomenon, and, as elsewhere, the impulse for change in the UK has been driven by a desire to overcome some of the key social, cultural and economic dilemmas that have faced the state. These are: the need to reduce public spending, make schooling more responsive to the needs of industry and restore public confidence in state schooling (Gewirtz 1997). The attempts to manage these problems have been seen in the almost constant stream of initiatives that have flowed from Conservative and Labour governments alike.

Briefly, a series of central government interventions have sought to assert control over structure (different types and 'new' schools, such as the city technology colleges), funding issues and curriculum matters (we now have a well established national curriculum, newly revised in 2000, whereas before 1988, this was unheard of). There have been changes in curriculum, assessment and testing, inspection of schools and teachers, initial teacher education as well as the teaching profession itself. We now turn to explore each of these sets of reforms in greater detail through examining systemic reform and the restructuring of the work of the teacher.

Reforms of the school system

The reforms of the school system in England and Wales (but not in Scotland) have been driven by an alleged belief that standards of academic achievement have not been as high as they ought to be. It has been claimed that schools and teachers have, in part, contributed to this national dilemma. It has been alleged that those charged with responsibility for provision in the recent past (the LEAs and educational advisors) have had low expectations of the system, and have been themselves too close to the problems to be able to deal adequately with them. It has also been argued that parents have not always been fully consulted about their children's schooling (Ball 1993). One suggestion has been that (state maintained) education failed because it had become a state monopoly, offering little or no choice to its consumers (parents), unaccountable and opaque in its achievements and procedures, costly and inefficiently managed (Gewirtz *et al.* 1995). One way forward was to make schools more competitive and thus more effective.

What occurred was that a quasi-market form was inserted into education provision (Bartlett 1993). Parents could choose the school they preferred. Schools were funded on the basis of the number of students on their roll. Thus, market choice would drive provision. 'Good schools' – that is to say, popular schools – would survive while 'bad' schools – unpopular ones – would be put out of business. Of course it is a little more complex than this – but not much. The National Curriculum, an entitlement curriculum, would ensure that parents knew what their children were studying; teachers knew what they had to teach. Children would be tested at regular points (at the end of each key stage at 7, 11, 14 and 16) which would give parents accurate information about their child's progress – and the progress of the teachers too! The results of national tests taken at the end of Key Stage 4 (the GCSE), were published in national newspapers (the percentage of students who had gained five or more GCSE examinations at grade C or above). Schools would be regularly inspected to assure that children were being well taught and that standards were being raised. Failing schools would be named so that parents would know which ones to avoid (Ball *et al.* 1994).

Changes to the way in which schools were funded meant that the traditional role of the LEA was eroded. Schools, governors and senior managers now took on responsibility for controlling their own budget, generated by the numbers of children who attended their school. One major problem for schools was this shift meant that the school now had to take over responsibility for staff salaries. The budgets allocated to schools were based on a formula that averaged the costs of paying teachers. Thus, a school with older experienced teachers would have to use more of its budget on salary costs. This shortfall had to be made up from other parts of the budget or schools had to seek alternative methods of raising money. Schools have had to become entrepreneurial, a consequence that raises many concerns. Not all schools are equally placed to raise sums from their local communities; not all schools believe that this is a valid part of their role in society.

It is possible to argue that what these sorts of reforms have achieved is to establish a baseline of provision that gives a guarantee to every parent that their child will receive a sound education regardless of where they go to school. If a family has to relocate, the education of their children will not be disrupted. Parents and children know what to expect in relation to the testing procedures. These are identical all over the country. Every year, GCSE achievements are published, and now, so are the national test results for 11-year-olds at the end of their primary school education. In this way, local communities know what is expected and have transparent information about the achievements of local schools – or do they?

An alternative way of interpreting these policy shifts is to argue that when governments started to believe that they could not control global events (planned economies for example) they looked to intervene else-where. Since the early 1970s the UK's various governments have become more involved in the minutiae of state welfare provision and have become more involved in areas that in earlier times would not have been seen as properly the provenance of national governments, for example parenting, teenage pregnancy, etc. (Hutton 1996). Governments, of what-ever political complexion, have been elected on the basis of their capacity to cut levels of direct taxation. Any government is thus caught in a con-tradictory position: expected to improve state welfare provision while cutting direct taxation. Thus there has been a shift away from welfarist policy-making towards what has been described as a post-welfarist policy complex with a concomitant focus on a 'utilitarian discourse of efficiency, effectiveness, performance and productivity' (Gewirtz 1997: 220).

Yet another interpretation of these reforms would be to suggest that some urgent changes have been long due. While the UK has produced its fair share of Nobel prize winners, there has always been a long tail of underachieving students; currently up to one in 12 of all school leavers lack any formal qualifications (Pearce and Hillman 1998). Any focus on raising attainments for all our young people has got to be a worthwhile enterprise and it is only right that schools should be exhorted to raise standards for all children and that they should be accountable to their local communities and parents. However, the dilemma here is that at a more basic and common-sense level it is also possible to argue that chil-dren from advantaged backgrounds will achieve more than those from less advantaged backgrounds. If a school is to do well in relation to national standards and targets and tests, then what it needs to do is to ensure that it recruits the 'right' sort of parents and children (see Chapters 5 and 9, in this volume). What makes the difference, by and large, may well be intake, nothing more or less.

It is possible to argue that the National Curriculum and its assessment procedures, linked with the requirement to set annual targets for raising attainments, ensure that teachers have high expectations and can really focus on their role as educators. They know what to do (that is, the content to be taught and assessed) and they know how to teach it. As the revised National Curriculum documentation says; 'the National Curriculum secures for all pupils . . . an entitlement to a number of areas of learning . . . necessary for their self-fulfilment and development as active and responsible citizens', and the National Curriculum establishes 'national standards for the performance of all pupils in the subjects it includes' (DfEE/QCA 2000: 12). It adds: 'These standards can be used to set targets for improvement, measure progress towards those targets, and monitor and compare performance between individuals, groups and schools' (DfEE/QCA 2000: 12).

All these changes are having a number of interrelated effects on school management. There is a focus on competition and marketing the school in order to increase recruitment. There is at the same time a preoccupation with target setting and performance monitoring to enhance measured attainment. This means that there is a 'focus on what can be quantified and a particular emphasis on exam results' (Gewirtz 1997: 222).

Reforms of teachers' work and teacher education

Barber has claimed that while all these structural changes have worked to reorganize the 'educational universe', the surprising thing is that 'virtually none of the whirlwind of reforms in the last decade has given priority to teachers, their professional skills or their professional development' (1995: 190). He is interested in 'reconstructing' the profession because 'reform' does not express the strength of the types of changes he wants to see and 'in any case, the word "reform" has been used so much in the last few years that it has almost ceased to have significant meaning' (Barber 1995: 190). He wants to see a revitalized profession where teachers prioritize their own learning and where the status of teachers is enhanced through more professional development and a focus on life-long improvement. While he is talking about a long-term vision for enhancing extended professionalism within the teaching force, perhaps he has somewhat disengenuously ignored the almost continuous attempts to reform and structure initial training and the working lives of classroom teachers and their teacher–manager colleagues.

As with the first part of this chapter, we will not focus on the detail of legislation and policy documentation which has undertaken this particular restructuring. This is well documented elsewhere (Maguire and Dillon 1997; Furlong et al. 2000; Mahony and Hextall 2000a). What is important to note is that any government attempting to reform its educational service needs to pay attention to the way teachers are prepared (to deliver these reforms). As Whitty *et al.* (1998: 75) say:

> One explanation sometimes given for the limited educational impact of the reforms to date is that too many teachers currently in schools are ill-suited to implement them. Either they have been inducted into a system based on different priorities and different practices or they have been actively encouraged during their training to be critical of government priorities. It is therefore not surprising that some attention has been paid to the training of new generations of teachers. In particular, there has been a questioning of the undue influence of university-based teacher educators on people entering the profession.

Broadly speaking, until 1979, teacher training provision was driven by issues of cost as well as the need to match supply to demand – always a tricky consideration. In the main, teacher education courses were built round a consensus on what constituted good practice: considerations of child development, learning theory, teaching styles, issues drawn from sociology and philosophical questions, as well as subject content and teaching methods. The intention was to develop sound professional practitioners who were able to critically reflect on their classroom practice. Changes were usually introduced after a process of public debate. This process provided some important and sometimes influential checks and balances.

However, 1979 marked a significant shift; the traditional policy processes of open debate, consultation and the hammering out of some degree of consensus gave way to a new regime under which policy-making became more clearly political in nature and was ideologically driven. This change was facilitated by a wide range of well publicized, sustained attacks on teacher education. It was argued that teacher education was frequently more concerned with indoctrination than education, more with issues of equality and social engineering than effective education. What was needed was a 'common-sense' approach to teacher training. These promises were realized in the ERA (1988). Standards were to be raised and schools made more accountable to their consumers. From this it followed inevitably that teachers, their pre-service preparation and their in-service development would have to be improved at the same time.

Throughout the 1980s and 1990s, various Conservative governments enacted legislation which asserted controls over teacher education courses specifying subject areas, subject content, time to be devoted to each element as well as insisting that more time be spent in schools (Maguire *et al.* 1998). In September 1993, the Department for Education (DfE 1993) published a Green Paper, *The Government's Proposals for the Reform of Initial Teacher Training*. It proposed that more teacher training should be moved into the school and that the funding for teacher education be managed through a new quango, the Teacher Training Agency (TTA). The development of the TTA, with almost total control over teacher education provision, made up of personal appointees of the Secretary of State for Education, was seen as a move to erode the autonomy and power of higher education and to invest greater control in the central state. In setting up the TTA, the government removed several layers of balances and checks, democratic accountability which in the past had maintained some form of independent stance on initial teacher education (ITE). While the TTA has engaged in consultation exercises as its 'preferred' style of operating, the role of consultation as practised by the agency has sometimes raised concerns in relation to 'the management of consent' (Hextall and Mahony 2000).

In 1996, the government proposed that there should be a national curriculum for teacher training and the TTA, led by Anthea Millett, was charged with producing an initiative on teaching methods to provide, among other things:

> legitimate national standards for teaching and to ensure that teacher trainers, whether in higher education or school-based, are clear – thanks not least to the new national curriculum for initial teacher training – about what teachers have to know, understand and be able to do, and what they as teacher trainers need to know, understand and be able to do in order to prepare the teacher-professionals of tomorrow.
>
> (Millett 1996: 13)

What has actually occurred has been that increasingly schools have been charged with the professional preparation of teachers – a 'learning on the job' approach that clearly has some potential for effective teacher training. (For instance, on a PGCE secondary course of 36 weeks, 24 of these are based in school). However, this responsibility has not been straightforwardly devolved to schools; it has been accompanied by the production of swathes of prescribed competencies that have to be met before qualified teacher status can be attained (Whitty 1997). These competencies, now called 'standards' (DfEE 1998a) refer to levels of competency that have to be met in relation to: knowledge and understanding of subject matter; planning, teaching and classroom management; monitoring, assessment recording, reporting and accountability as well as other professional requirements. Of course these are all good platform attributes for effective teachers, however in the rush to specify, quantify and assess myriads of 'standards' there are a number of unresolved dilemmas.

First, what are we to make of the paradox that allows the government to blame poor schools for poor performances yet at the same time seeks to train teachers in these very institutions? Second, the almost constant allegations of poor quality and low standards in British schools seems unlikely to attract 'able' recruits. After all, who wants to be part of an underperforming service? And while Michael Barber seems not to have recognized that teacher education has been subjected to the same barrage of reforms that have rained down on schools, the weight of legislative change indicates that the opposite is the case. After almost 20 years of reforming teacher education, what is the result? Whitty *et al.* (1998: 77) conclude that:

> School-based initial teacher education, combined with an official list of prescribed competencies, seems likely over time to produce greater consistency of preparation for a narrow set of basic teaching skills alongside increased variation and fragmentation in student experience in other areas.

As evidence of governmental commitment towards enhancing in-school performance and attainment, it has not been enough to reform teachers at source. Strong attempts have also been made to restructure the teaching profession within schools (see Chapter 2, in this volume). This attempt to 'modernize' the teaching profession also draws from market-driven ideology. Thus, performance management techniques which seek to achieve performance improvements (enhanced productivity) through efficiency drives (appraisal, target setting) and rewarding success (performance-related pay or PRP) have patterned this modernizing approach. The key document in all this is the Green Paper of 1998, *Teachers: Meeting the Challenge of Change* (DfEE 1998b).

As Mahony and Hextall (2000a: 1) say, the Green Paper 'looks backwards to a whole swathe of initiatives begun under the previous Conservative administrations, and forwards with the particular orientations of Tony Blair's government'. The Green Paper was quite clear: 'Major reforms are already underway to raise standards. They need to be matched by a new vision of the teaching profession' (DfEE 1998b: 11). The paper talks of the 'imperative of modernisation' where excellent teaching is supported and rewarded and where there is constant improvement. The paper covers issues of leadership, better rewards, training and support for teachers. At the centre of the paper is a new staffing framework for teachers and a new career structure that creates 'incentives' for excellence and 'rewards' high performance. While the paper makes many proposals, it is the move towards performance management – and performance-related pay – which has attracted the most attention (Richardson 1999).

The idea is a straightforward and seductive one; good teachers will be motivated to improve their performance if their efforts are rewarded. It is unfair that unsuccessful teachers should be paid the same as their more successful colleagues. Richardson agrees that 'performance related pay makes a lot of sense in many contexts. It succeeds in motivating people as diverse as taxi drivers, garment assemblers, fund managers and sportsmen' (1999: 29). However, Richardson goes on to state what must seem obvious to many teachers; public sector occupations (like teaching) are complex and not easily reducible to clear and measurable work objectives. Even if student achievement were one measure, there would have to be some way to demonstrate that 'an individual teacher's contribution to pupil performance can be established with confidence' (Richardson 1999: 29). Clearly, it could be that a student did well in a certain aspect of their work – say mathematics at GCSE – because of successful pastoral support or indeed good teaching at an earlier stage. Teaching is a collaborative venture. When the Green Paper does recognize this and suggests that there could be group related performance pay, there are other dilemmas. It could be that one member of the group rode on the backs of colleagues who had to make extra efforts to compensate for this. Thus, group rewards might enhance conflicts and antagonisms in teamwork (Richardson 1999).

Fundamentally though, Richardson has pointed out that there must be a 'suspicion' that performance-related pay is not merely concerned with recruiting, retaining and rewarding good teachers. He suggests that it might be a strategy to attract and reward a minority while doing 'rather little for the large numbers of average performers' (Richardson 1999: 30). In addition, as Mahony and Hextall (2000b) suggest, while PRP may motivate some teachers, it may also have the opposite effect and prove to be counter-productive. The Secondary Head's Association has pointed out that PRP can be demotivating. It might also turn out to be discriminatory in that those who are rewarded are those with the 'valuable' skills, that is to say, information and communication technology or shortage subject teachers. Crucially for this chapter, what is at stake is the way in which the job of the teacher is being reconfigured and restructured. To return again to Mahony and Hextall (2000b: 20), they make the point that while the rhetoric of the Green Paper is couched in terms of modernizing the profession, the teacher is now refigured as 'someone who is both being addressed as a "professional" but whose responsibilities, powers and rights are designated as lying well outside realms of policy reflection and deliberation'. As Lawn has said, the teacher is now positioned as a competent multiskilled (see the TTA standards) worker, who delivers and assesses a regulated curriculum: 'The dominant version is now a notion of individual responsibility and incentive reward legitimated by the Citizen's Charter idea of efficient service and performance incentive' (Lawn 1996: 113, cited in Mahony and Hextall 2000b: 21). The impact of the Green Paper (DfEE 1998b) on the teaching profession remains to be seen.

Concluding comments

Black and Atkin (1996: 199) have pointed up some shortcomings in reforms based on assumptions of failure. They argue that reforms that follow one another at 'breakneck speed' because of perceived shortcomings may be counter-productive. They suggest that evolutionary change that builds on strengths 'capitalises on the accomplishments of the most able professionals in [the] educational system and on their work'. Their point is that 'what needs improvement has not necessarily failed' (1996: 199). Change that demoralizes the teaching profession and 'blames' them for alleged failings is unlikely to be successful. In 1998, a teacher wrote an open letter to David Blunkett, the Secretary of State for Education and Employment, which said 'I have been hectored by the press, badgered by parents, pressured by management and insulted by politicians, just for being a teacher'. It is worth quoting more from this letter as it gives expression to the views of many professionals currently working in education.

> Professionally, I want peace to consolidate and reflect on my job. I've seen too many Government initiatives flower, wither and then die to care about any more targets or aims. White Papers, league tables, curriculum Orders or standing Orders, I've worked through innumerable Secretaries of State for Education and I feel that I can wear my despair and cynicism as the professional equivalent of a long service and good conduct medal. I have earned a privileged insight into my job the hard way and – unlike some politicians – I know exactly what I am talking about. I am a good teacher because I appreciate and like

children. I enjoy my subject, and I admire learning, but I am going to need a lot of help to trust a politician again.

(Teacher writing in the *Times Educational Supplement*,
November 1998)

The ERA marked a revolutionary point in education policy and provision in the UK. At its heart lay two main concerns: to improve and reform education through the insertion of quasi-market forces and thus to raise standards, which, it was argued, had fallen. While it is possible to trace a policy trajectory that originated with the ERA in 1988 and which led to a plethora of curricular changes, assessment developments and the setting up of a wide range of organizations that have been charged with specific responsibilities (for example, the Qualifications and Curriculum Authority, the Teacher Training Agency), perhaps the most important consequence has been that a new political settlement based on a strong state and market freedom has been asserted (Dale 1997). The consequences of this have been to limit the professional autonomy of teachers and teaching while inserting a performance management approach towards their training and their work (DfEE 1998b; Rogers 1999; Furlong *et al.* 2000). It will take time to fully evaluate the effects of these changes, by which point schools and teachers, learning and teaching may have been radically restructured yet again.

References

Ball, S.J. (1993) The Education Reform Act: market forces and parental choice, in A. Cashdan and J. Harris (eds) *Education in the 1990s*. Sheffield: Pavic Publications.

Ball, S.J., Bowe, R. and Gewirtz, S. (1994) Schools in the marketplace: an analysis of local market relations, in W. Bartlett *et al.* (eds) *Quasi-Markets in the Welfare State*. Bristol: School of Advanced Urban Studies, University of Bristol.

Barber, M. (1995) Reconstructing the teaching profession, in H. Bines and J.M. Welton (eds) *Managing Partnership in Teacher Training and Development*. London: Routledge.

Bartlett, W. (1993) Quasi-markets and educational reforms, in W. Bartlett and J. Le Grand (eds) *Quasi-Markets and Social Policy*. London: Macmillan.

Black, P. and Atkin, M. (1996) *Changing the Subject: Innovations in Science, Mathematics and Technology Education*. London: Routledge.

Dale, R. (1997) The state and the governance of education, in A.H. Halsey, H. Lauder, P. Brown and A. Stuart Wells (eds) *Education, Culture, Economy, Society*. Oxford: Oxford University Press.

Department for Education (DfE) (1993) *The Government's Proposals for the Reform of Initial Teacher Training*, Draft Proposals. London: HMSO.

Department for Education and Employment (DfEE) (1998a) *Requirements for Courses of Initial Teacher Training*, Circular 4/98. London: HMSO.

Department for Education and Employment (DfEE) (1998b) *Teachers: Meeting the Challenge of Change*, Green Paper. London: HMSO.

Department for Education and Employment/Qualifications and Curriculum Authority (DfEE/QCA) (2000) *The National Curriculum, Handbook for Secondary Teachers in England, Key Stages 3 and 4*. London: HMSO.

Furlong, J., Barton, L., Miles, S. *et al.* (2000) *Teacher Education in Transition: Reforming Professionalism?* Buckingham: Open University Press.

Gewirtz, S. (1997) Post-welfarism and the reconstruction of teachers' work in the UK, *Journal of Education Policy*, 12(4): 217–31.

Gewirtz, S., Ball, S.J. and Bowe, R. (1995) *Markets, Choice and Equity*. Buckingham: Open University Press.

Hextall, I. and Mahony, P. (2000) Consultation and the management of consent: standards for Qualified Teacher Status, *British Educational Research Journal*, 26(3): 322–42.

Hutton, W. (1996) *The State We're In*, 2nd edn. London: Vintage Press.

Lawn, M. (1996) *Modern Times? Work, Professionalism and Citizenship in Teaching*. London: Falmer Press.

Maclure, S. (1988) *Education Reformed*. London: Hodder and Stoughton.

Maguire, M. and Dillon, J. (1997) Teacher education, in J. Dillon and M. Maguire (eds) *Becoming a Teacher: Issues in Secondary Teaching*. Buckingham: Open University Press.

Maguire, M., Dillon, J. and Quintrell, M. (1998) *Finding Virtue, Not Finding Fault: Stealing the Wind of Destructive Reforms*. London: Association of Teachers and Lecturers.

Mahony, P. and Hextall, I. (2000a) 'Modernising' the Teacher. Conference Paper, Initial Teacher Education Conference, University of North London, March.

Mahony, P. and Hextall, I. (2000b) *Reconstructing Teaching: Standards, Performance and Accountability*. London: Routledge.

Millett, A. (1996) Pedagogy – the last corner of the secret garden. King's College Annual Education Lecture. London: King's College London, July.

Pearce, N. and Hillman, J. (1998) *Wasted Youth: Raising Achievement and Tackling Social Exclusion*. London: Institute for Public Policy Research.

Richardson, R. (1999) *Performance Related Pay in Schools. An Evaluation of the Government's Evidence to the School Teachers' Review Body*, a report prepared for the National Union of Teachers. London: London School of Economics and Political Science.

Rogers, S. (1999) *Performance Management in Local Government*. London: Pitman/Financial Times.

Stoll, L. and Fink, D. (1996) *Changing our Schools*. Buckingham: Open University Press.

Teacher (anonymous) (1998) Dear Mr Blunkett, *Times Educational Supplement*, 6 November.

Times Educational Supplement (TES) (2000) Morale, *Times Educational Supplement* (Friday Magazine), 24 March.

Whitty, G. (1997) Marketisation, the state and the re-formation of the teaching profession, in A.H. Halsey, H. Lauder, P. Brown and A. Stuart Wells (eds) *Education, Culture, Economy, Society*. Oxford: Oxford University Press.

Whitty, G., Power, S. and Halpin, D. (1998) *Devolution and Choice in Education. The School, the State and the Market*. Buckingham: Open University Press.

7

Inspection

Alison Millett, Justin Dillon and Jenny Adey

Introduction

The chances that you will be observed by an inspector during your first few terms are not high. English state-funded schools are inspected on average every six years. However, you will almost certainly be unable to escape the influence that inspection, and in particular the Office of Her Majesty's Chief Inspector of Schools in England (Ofsted), has on schooling. In writing about inspection in schools, it is easy to concentrate solely on Ofsted. Some would argue that Ofsted, particularly in the times when it was under the influence of the then Chief Inspector, Chris Woodhead, has had a major influence on teacher thinking and morale since it was set up in 1992.

It would be a mistake, however, in a chapter on inspection, to ignore other important aspects of the subject. Ofsted is only a recent phenomenon whereas school inspection has been around since the 1830s. Ofsted could change overnight, at the whim of a dissatisfied Secretary of State or with the appointment of a new Chief Inspector with a different philosophy from the former incumbent. Also, as with many aspects of education, there is much to learn from inspection in other countries, not least Northern Ireland, Scotland and Wales.

This chapter looks at several key issues that we believe will still be important in the years to come. These issues will affect your teaching and the schools in which you train and work. They may already have influenced the schools in which you studied. We begin by looking at the background to inspection in schools and at the development of Ofsted. We look at how schools and teachers prepare for inspection and at the responses that inspection can invoke. We move on to discuss some theoretical aspects of inspection. Finally, we look at the links between inspection and school improvement.

One point that we would wish to make is that inspection is not a neutral process. Chris Woodhead refers to it as 'disciplined subjectivity'

(1999: 5). Directly and indirectly, inspection has an impact on many aspects of the lives of those inspected and on those who carry out the inspections week in, week out. The voices of the inspected and the inspectors deserve to be listened to in order to help you to formulate your own opinions and to help you to make sense of your own experiences. However, discussions about Ofsted, and about inspection generally, rarely seem to be conducted with much regard for the evidence or for the complexity of the issues involved. Given the high passions that inspection generates and the degree of personal stress inspection involves, this is understandable. However, it is ultimately unhelpful and counter-productive to argue from emotion and anecdote alone.

The history of inspection

School inspectors were first appointed by the government in 1839 in response to disquiet about the way in which public funds were being spent by some individuals and by some religious societies. A link, which has lasted ever since, was thus established between the receipt of public funding and a requirement to submit to state sponsored inspections (Education and Employment Committee, House of Commons 1999).

Her Majesty's Inspectorate (HMI)

The remit of Her Majesty's Inspectors included reporting on teaching methods, attainment, organization and discipline and on the moral training of children, but their powers of intervention were limited. With the introduction of the system of payment by results in 1862, and a national system of free public elementary education under the Education Acts of 1870 onwards, their numbers and their influence increased. The gradual development of secondary schools, under the 1902 Education Act, led to a system of full inspections for secondary schools and subsequently for elementary schools. The cycle of full inspections was unsustainable however and they began to decline in number.

During the period of broad educational consensus following the 1944 Education Act, HMI 'largely relinquished its inquisitorial role in favour of a more advisory one' (Wilcox and Gray 1996: 26). But HMI inspections were not always seen as advisory and in contrast to local education authority (LEA) inspections, they were viewed as judgemental in nature (Sandbrook 1996). With the growth of the LEAs' own inspectorates it was suggested (DES 1968) that HMI should become explicitly an advisory body, with the job of inspections left to LEAs, but this did not in fact take place. HMI judgements and comments were highly respected by the profession and by policy-makers (DES 1982: 13–14), and in the 1980s their inspections took on a higher profile with the publishing of inspection reports on individual schools.

LEA inspections

Local inspectorates, starting initially in some of the urban school boards in the late nineteenth century, grew in size and status during the first 75 years of the next century. Many LEAs preferred to use the nomenclature of 'adviser' and 'advisory services' to 'inspector' and 'inspectorates' and their monitoring function was downplayed.

During the 1970s, disquiet about educational accountability grew. It found expression in Prime Minister James Callaghan's Ruskin College speech in 1976 (Callaghan 1976). However, LEAs still encouraged schools to evaluate themselves rather than undergo external inspection. The Inspectors Based in Schools (IBIS) approach, introduced in the Inner London Education Authority in 1986 was an attempt to combine accountability with action (Hargreaves 1990); inspection teams went to work on a long-term basis in specific schools where problems had been identified to initiate remedial action.

Following the introduction of the National Curriculum by the Education Reform Act (ERA) 1988 and the provision of financial support to help the development of inspection policies, a critical Audit Commission report (1989) suggested that although evidence was limited, there still appeared to be more advice than inspection. According to Wilcox and Gray (1996), LEAs had in fact responded to being urged to develop effective monitoring and evaluation of school performance, development had taken place, with school self-evaluation being complemented by part or full inspections.

The introduction of Ofsted inspections

By the beginning of the 1990s, political pressure was building for a different sort of inspectorate. HMI was criticized for its lack of published criteria on which judgements were based. The inspectors' independence and objectivity were questioned. They were seen to be pursuing a pedagogical line through published work, inspection reports and advice to politicians and were 'subject to severe strictures from the "new right" as the major proponents of progressivism' (Fitz and Lee 1996: 18). They were described as representing the interests of the provider rather than the consumer, whose rights were set out in the Citizen's Charter (Cabinet Office 1991). Inspection criteria were to be made explicit; accountability to the public was expected; more precise statistical information was required; lay members were to be recruited to keep a check on the excesses of the professionals.

The Education (Schools) Act, 1992 established a new organization, the Office for Standards in Education (Ofsted) headed by Her Majesty's Chief Inspector (HMCI). Ofsted was officially set up as a non-ministerial government department, independent from the Department for Education and Employment (DfEE). Its motto is 'Improvement through inspection' and its remit is 'to improve standards of achievement and quality of education through regular independent inspection, public reporting and informed independent advice' (Ofsted 2000).

In the beginning, full-scale inspections were to be carried out every four years. The number of HMIs was reduced and inspection teams consisted of independent inspectors not employed directly by Ofsted but trained under its auspices, and operating in a competitive market. A range of private firms and LEAs compete for contracts for the inspections. Ofsted sets the framework for these inspections, recruits and trains both Registered Inspectors (RgIs or 'Reggies') and team members including lay inspectors.

Ofsted inspections were originally based on the *Framework for the Inspection of Schools* and the *Handbook* (Ofsted 1992a, 1992b). Inspection of secondary schools under the new system began in September 1993 and of primary schools in September 1994. There have been revisions to both the *Framework* and the *Handbook* with the most recent revision exemplifying the change to a differentiated inspection system introduced in January 2000.

The role of Ofsted

Ofsted is responsible for managing the inspection system of all 24,000 schools in England which are wholly or mainly state-funded. They also inspect nursery education, further education colleges, local education authorities, initial teacher training courses, independent schools, service children's education, LEA funded adult education and youth work. Ofsted produces guidance and frameworks for the benefit of those being inspected. Ofsted reports on many aspects of education and maintains a website of school inspection reports, press releases and other information (http://www.ofsted.gov.uk/).

Ofsted has a statutory responsibility to inform the Secretary of State for Education and Employment about:

- the quality of education provided by schools in England;
- the educational standards achieved by pupils in those schools;
- whether the financial resources made available to those schools are managed efficiently; and
- the spiritual, moral, social and cultural development of pupils at those schools.

(Ofsted 2000)

Preparation for inspection

During the early years of Ofsted inspections, schools could be given as much as four terms' notice or as little as a few weeks. Both of these situations led to considerable stress. In the former the preparations took the school over for months, anxiety was often raised to an unreasonable level and an inordinate amount of time was spent by some schools on preparing documentation. In the latter situation, documentation was rushed, and many schools felt that they had not had time to show themselves at their best (Millett and Johnson 1998). A reduction in the notice period to about six weeks was one of the changes made by Ofsted in response to complaints from schools.

Views of inspection as judgemental or developmental affected the way in which inspection was approached. Some schools took a hostile and uncooperative approach, based on critical views of the Ofsted system and the way in which it had been introduced. Some schools saw their inspection as 'free consultancy while others worked extremely hard to conceal any weakness – they aimed for the "perfect week"' (Ouston and Davies 1998: 14). One headteacher wrote that:

> In my own school I advised teachers to regard Ofsted as a high level audit and to make the best possible use of the inspectors. The music teacher, although closely aligned to the drama department was nevertheless effectively in a department of one, said he had never had better INSET than this knowledgeable music inspector all to himself.
> (ex-headteacher and current Ofsted inspector)

Part 3 of the *Handbook for Inspecting Secondary Schools* (Ofsted 1999) looks at school self-evaluation and provides a useful tool for inspection preparation. Schools are at different stages of self-audit but all should have previous GCSE examination and key stage test results and internal assessments available. The PICSI (Pre-Inspection Context and School Indicator), which is sent to schools prior to an Ofsted inspection, gives national expectations for a range of school types. The PANDA (Performance and Assessment Report) is used for benchmarking – that is comparing the school's key stage results and other factors, such as attendance, with similar schools. Schools with similar percentages of children on free school meals are compared and this can reveal that some advantaged schools which appear to be doing well are not doing well enough. Conversely schools in difficult surroundings can be adding significant value to their pupils' education.

Other data that the school might have, such as baseline testing, CAT (cognitive abilities test) scores, reading tests and ALIS (A level information system) and YELLIS (Year 11 information system) predictions, should all be made available as well as time spent explaining how to use the data. Having been notified of inspection most schools review their policies and practice and make sure that their paperwork reflects these. Many employ the services of their LEA in a consultant capacity to help them in this task (Dimmer and Metiuk 1998); some go through what amounts to a 'mock inspection'.

> Access to information about the inspection is essential and it is helpful to have someone like an LEA inspector who is also a RgI explain the process to staff. In my own school we developed an idea that had been used elsewhere and organised a quiz night in place of a staff meeting for the whole staff including school keepers, dinner staff and administrative staff. The intention was to help everyone find their way around and increase their knowledge of the National Curriculum, school policies and recent legislation. All the relevant documents were arranged around the room and staff divided into mixed teams based on the time served in the school. A small group of senior staff had previously devised the quiz which included photographs of odd angles of the school and tape recordings of middle managers all shouting the ubiquitous 'Oy' to some unsuspecting pupil. Each table

had a joker to play and the prize, in this instance a case of wine, for the winning team was on display. As an exercise in bringing all the staff together, team building and gaining access to a range of material it was deemed an enjoyable success. If noise levels can be taken as an indication it must have been one of our most successful meetings.
(ex-headteacher and current Ofsted inspector)

Although, in some cases, claims were made by schools that inspection had slowed down ongoing development, in others the preparation phase was felt to be useful (Ouston and Davies 1998). Individual classroom teachers were more likely than senior staff to admit to anxieties about the forthcoming inspection (Wilcox and Gray 1996). With changes in Ofsted practice (Ofsted 1997) that initiated the reporting to the headteacher of individual teachers' grades in three bands, pressure on individual performance grew.

Now that all schools have been through the inspection cycle once, the way in which a school prepares for its imminent inspection will depend to a significant extent on its previous experience of Ofsted inspection at both personal and institutional level:

Experience of a previous inspection will be influential. Partly this will be an emotional response – previous experience will either leave a positive or a negative feeling about inspection and this will condition feelings about reinspection. In addition to such general feelings, previous experience will have indicated possibilities that could be exploited to improve inspection from the school's point of view.
(Fidler and Davies 1998: 159)

Most school inspections are now carried out on a six-year cycle. A new *Handbook* has been published to accompany the revised *Framework* which covers the arrangements for 'full' and 'short' inspections (Ofsted 1999). About 20 per cent of schools in the first year (2000) received short inspections – allocated to schools which are 'more successful' (Ofsted 1999: 2). Both short and full inspections must still report on the quality of education provided; pupil achievement; efficiency of the management of financial resources; and pupils' spiritual, moral, social and cultural development. In short inspections, inspectors do not report in detail on each subject taught and inspectors may look at subjects outside their own specialisms. The formal grading system for teaching quality is not used, nor is a profile of teaching quality given to the headteacher at the end of the inspection. Individual classroom teachers must prepare to be observed according to published inspection criteria on a variety of occasions for the whole or part of a lesson. Those holding positions of responsibility are interviewed by inspectors to explore their role in monitoring, evaluating and intervening in the subject or aspect of work for which they have responsibility.

The response to inspection

Responses to the process of inspection vary widely and they can be grouped into two main categories – emotional and social, and methodological.

Inspection can have a major effect on the professional and personal lives of teachers, leading to feelings of professional uncertainty, loss of self-esteem and change of commitment (Jeffrey and Woods 1998). Although some teachers are very positive about their inspection experiences, there are reports of stress-related illness and even suicide following an Ofsted inspection. Some schools have reported a lowering of morale even after positive inspection results.

> During inspection week fear represses the teachers' ability to act and think – they lose their picture of self-worth. They become irritable at home and can suffer from sleeplessness. Before inspection, people feel screwed down, not able to relax. After inspection a huge sense of relief is followed by deflation.
>
> (headteacher, quoted in Williams 1999: 12)

> Many of the worries come from teachers complaining that they have still to be observed, occasionally if staff have a variety of roles, the complaint is that they have been seen too frequently. Non-teaching staff also need to have an opportunity to talk through their experiences. Some schools ask for written feedback from staff following each observation or encounter. I found it useful to have a chart in the staff room on which teachers entered date and time they had been observed. Next to it was a daily sheet on which they entered their funniest moment or worst experience. As well as being a useful log on which to base feedback to the RgI, reference could be made to the most overexposed teacher and funny moments relayed at the daily briefing. I hoped this helped release tension and unite the staff in a common enterprise. We awarded prizes for the best in each category at the staff party at the end of inspection.
>
> (ex-headteacher and current Ofsted inspector)

> Although most staff find the prospect of being observed daunting, in a positive school, after the first observation many are keen to be seen again, as they know they will be more relaxed and confident in future observations. In schools with large departments, teachers that can only be observed for a couple of lessons feel cheated and ask for more observations. It would seem that they want all the work they have put in to be seen and acknowledged.
>
> (Ofsted inspector)

> I have had experience of teachers in inner city schools in small departments, working in isolation and not always recognised by the management, being quite overcome by the positive feedback they receive. This is why it is so important that the head or a senior member of staff is present at the feedback, not just to scribe but to get another overview of the work of the department. At one feedback to the head of a good department in a south London school in a deprived area I asked if I was going slowly enough, he replied that if I went any slower he would probably burst into tears as he had never heard so many nice things said about him. Ofsted can be an opportunity to celebrate good practice.
>
> (Ofsted inspector)

It is certainly the case that many schools do report positive experiences, but these do not necessarily receive the same publicity as negative ones (Fidler and Davies 1998). The quality of the inspection team would seem to be a critical factor here. Ofsted's own monitoring (Ofsted *et al.* 1995) reported a picture of broad satisfaction with the inspection process. Issues that provoked less favourable responses were the match between inspection team members' backgrounds and experience and the profile of the school; the contributions of the lay inspector; lack of professional dialogue with teachers and the quality of subject judgements.

In early inspections, feedback to individual classroom teachers was non-existent or extremely limited, a fact regretted by inspectors as well as teachers (Jeffrey and Woods 1998). Feedback after lesson observation was incorporated into Ofsted guidance (Ofsted 1997), and although sometimes regarded as inadequate, it has generally been welcomed by teachers as an improvement. Teachers appreciate guidance on how to handle feedback. They need to know what form it will take; usually three strengths of the lesson and three weaknesses are given. In terms of feedback at school level, Maychell and Pathak (1997) reported that 94 per cent of secondary headteachers found the oral feedback they had from Ofsted inspectors useful for planning purposes; oral feedback to subject specialists in secondary schools was also popular.

In terms of responses relating to methodology, many writers have questioned the reliability and validity of inspectors' judgements (for example Sandbrook 1996; Wilcox and Gray 1996; Fidler *et al.* 1998). '[The] specification of criteria alone does not guarantee validity. Moreover, criteria can never be so tightly defined as to expel the act of judgement completely' (Wilcox and Gray 1996: 73). Fitz-Gibbon (1997: 19) considers that:

> the aspect of inspection which is the most expensive in inspectors' time, the most costly to schools in staff stress, and the least validated, is the practice of having inspectors sit in classrooms making amateurish attempts at classroom observation and drawing unchallengeable conclusions about effectiveness.

Ofsted's own research claiming a high level of correlation between the judgements of pairs of inspectors (Matthews *et al.* 1998) is not viewed as compelling evidence by many critics (Education and Employment Committee, House of Commons 1999).

Opinions clearly differ about the process of inspection. The Market and Opinion Research International (MORI) survey of primary schools conducted for Ofsted (MORI 1999) found overall satisfaction with the process of inspection. About three-quarters of schools agreed that they were satisfied with the professional knowledge and competence of the inspection team. In cases of disagreement some schools have felt able to negotiate with inspectors over issues of judgement as well as fact (Fidler and Davies 1998). Schools are now able to pursue complaints about their inspection through an extended complaints procedure with an external adjudicator, introduced in 1998 (Ofsted 1998).

The inspection report

The public nature of Ofsted reports has led in some cases to high levels of local interest in the communities in which schools are situated. Public perceptions of the schools drawn from local reporting of Ofsted inspections has resulted in both positive and negative situations regarding pupil recruitment that have affected schools for several years after their inspections.

Research by Maychell and Pathak (1997) indicated that the majority of schools questioned found most of the key issues identified in their reports to be appropriate. On expectations, it seemed that 'their own thinking was close to that of Ofsted inspectors, with eight out of ten secondary headteachers . . . indicating that they had anticipated most of the key issues that came up' (Maychell and Pathak 1997: 22). Ninety per cent of headteachers found the main written report useful for planning purposes. While frequently confirming the results of the school's own self-evaluation, it may have told them nothing new. Headteachers reported finding the results of inspection useful as a management tool to facilitate change, providing a catalyst for action (Millett and Johnson 1998). Key issues were implemented most successfully when they were congruent with the direction already taken by the school (Ouston and Davies 1998).

Inspection as social control, auditing and disciplinary power

Inspectors, school managers, teachers, parents, governors, the public and the media may have a range of views about the purpose of inspection. They may interpret inspection reports in different ways. Messick (1989) has pointed out that it is the use to which assessment information is put – how it is interpreted – that needs to be considered in discussing the validity of the assessment. So too with the results of school inspections. Teachers might fear the process of inspection itself but headteachers might be more concerned about the impact that the final written report, which is a public document, will have on a school's recruitment of staff and on pupil enrolment.

Inspection is wrapped up in issues of social control and accountability. Attempts to understand inspection from theoretical perspectives have been few and far between. Wilcox and Gray (1996) undertook a three-year study of school inspections and examined four theoretical perspectives: inspection as evaluation; inspection as auditing; inspection as a disciplinary power; inspection as a form of social action. There is not space here to examine these ideas in any detail but the point is that the issues surrounding inspection can be examined from a range of perspectives which may be helpful in finding useful questions to ask of the inspection process.

Inspection and development

Ofsted's motto, 'Improvement through inspection' begs many questions. For instance, what kind of improvement takes place and how does the improvement happen? A range of educationalists have challenged the assumption that inspection leads to improvement. This section looks at some of the evidence that has emerged and at some of the claims made for inspection.

Inspection, as with much else in education, cannot easily be evaluated. Some of the research has attempted to gauge schools' and teachers' opinions about the inspection process. Other research has looked at the evidence of a direct impact of inspection on student achievement. Other studies have asked whether inspection provides value for money.

Kogan and Maden (1999) evaluated Ofsted using questionnaires to schools, case studies conducted mainly through interviews; interviews with relevant organizations including unions and associations for inspectors, parents and governors; and financial analyses. They reported that stakeholders identified the main benefits of the Ofsted system as including:

- the process of self-examination which leads up to the inspection week;
- the value of external perspectives on the work and running of schools;
- the increase in mutual support among staff generated by external inspection and a related recognition of improvements in self-esteem which flow from public affirmation of the work of staff, schools and pupils within schools.

Stakeholders identified some weaknesses, too:

- the system is seen as punitive and fault finding and generates a climate of fear which leads to stress and anxiety among staff;
- the summative, judgemental outcomes are not effective in promoting reflective professional development within schools;
- the system is intolerant of alternative approaches to school improvement and effectiveness.

(Kogan and Maden 1999: 20–1)

Kogan and Maden (1999: 25), in a study that the former Chief Inspector, Chris Woodhead, described as a 'reasonably balanced account' (Woodhead 1999: 5) concluded that 'it is hazardous to assume any connection between Ofsted inspection and improved performance'.

Cullingford and Daniels used a predominantly quantitative study in their research. They looked at the impact of the timing of Ofsted inspections on the GCSE examination performance of a representative sample of pupils throughout England. They reported that 'the time of inspections is significant' and that the 'nearer to the exam period that inspections take place the worse the results' (Cullingford and Daniels 1999: 66). They summarize their findings by arguing that 'Ofsted inspections have the opposite effect to that intended. Year on year they lower standards' (Cullingford and Daniels 1999: 66). Woodhead (1999: 5) quoted an unnamed Ofsted statistician as dismissing the research as 'deeply flawed; ineptly executed and poorly argued'.

Fitz-Gibbon and Stephenson-Forster (1999: 115), reporting on a questionnaire study of 159 headteachers, found that Ofsted had 'failed to win the confidence of headteachers' and had 'caused schools considerable expense'. In response to a question asking 'How much information of use to you in improving schooling did you gain from the inspection?', 4 heads (of the 85 who had recently been inspected) reported having learned 'nothing'; 14 reported 'not much'; 34 reported 'some' learning, 28 reported 'quite a lot' and 5 reported 'a large amount'. This points to a wide variation in headteachers' perceptions of the utility of Ofsted.

Surveys conducted by MORI (1999) and by the National Union of Teachers (NUT 1998) when focusing on the long-term effect of Ofsted inspection (rather than on the process and judgements made) came to reasonably similar conclusions. In the MORI survey just 27 per cent of primary schools responding saw inspection as a way to raise standards, and 15 per cent said it helped to improve teaching. In the NUT survey:

> Probably the most significant finding arose from the penultimate question in the survey. Overwhelmingly, head and deputy headteacher members rejected the statement that OFSTED inspections led directly to schools improving. Two-thirds of respondents did not believe that inspections helped school improvement, whereas only 17 per cent agreed with this statement.
>
> (NUT 1998: 3)

Thomas' 1997 survey of the impact of inspection on 80 Welsh secondary schools concluded that 'the weight of evidence indicates that inspection does lead to some improvement in schools; it does not, however, show that inspection brings about large or even medium improvements in many areas' (Thomas 1999: 145). Thomas comments that 'there must be some doubt as to whether [inspection] is a cost-effective method for raising standards' (1999: 146).

In conclusion

Several key questions arise from the research into inspection and its effects on schools. How can inspection be used to improve the dialogue between different sections of the education system? How should inspection be linked to professional development? What is the role of LEAs in school inspection and improvement? These questions, to which there are complex answers, are important. However, for many reasons, they have not been answered to anyone's satisfaction and the whole inspection process has been a political battlefield. Sadly, there is little sign that the fight is over.

References

Audit Commission (1989) *Assuring Quality in Education*. London: HMSO.
Cabinet Office (1991) *The Citizen's Charter: Raising the Standard*, Cmnd 1599. London: HMSO.

Callaghan, J. (1976) The Ruskin speech, *Times Educational Supplement*, 22 October.

Cullingford, C. and Daniels, S. (1999) Effects of Ofsted inspections on school performance, in C. Cullingford (ed.) *An Inspector Calls*. London: Kogan Page.

Department for Education and Science (DES) (1968) *Report of Parliamentary Select Committee: Part 1 Her Majesty's Inspectorate*. London: HMSO.

Department for Education and Science (DES) (1982) *Study of HM Inspectorate in England and Wales (The Rayner Report)*. London: HMSO.

Dimmer, T. and Metiuk, J. (1998) The use and impact of OFSTED in a primary school, in P. Earley (ed.) *School Improvement after Inspection? School and LEA Responses*. London: Paul Chapman Publishing.

Education and Employment Committee, House of Commons (1999) *The Work of OFSTED. Report and Proceedings of the Committee*. London: Stationery Office.

Fidler, B. and Davies, J. (1998) The inspector calls again: the reinspection of schools, in P. Earley (ed.) *Improvement after Inspection? School and LEA Responses*. London: Paul Chapman.

Fidler, B., Earley, P., Ouston, J. and Davies, J. (1998) Teacher gradings and OFSTED inspections: help or hindrance as a management tool? *School Leadership and Management*, 18(2): 257–70.

Fitz, J. and Lee, J. (1996) The early experience of OFSTED, in J. Ouston, P. Earley and B. Fidler (eds) *OFSTED Inspections; The Early Experience*. London: David Fulton.

Fitz-Gibbon, C. (1997) OFSTED's methodology, in M. Duffy (ed.) *A Better System of Inspection?* Hexham: Office for Standards in Inspection.

Fitz-Gibbon, C. and Stephenson-Forster, N.J. (1999) Is Ofsted helpful? An evaluation using social science criteria, in C. Cullingford (ed.) *An Inspector Calls*. London: Kogan Page.

Hargreaves, D.H. (1990) Accountability and school improvement in the work of LEA inspectors: the rhetoric and beyond, *Journal of Education Policy*, 5(3): 230–9.

Jeffrey, B. and Woods, P. (1998) *Testing Teachers: The Effect of School Inspections on Primary Teachers*. London: Falmer Press.

Kogan, M. and Maden, M. (1999) An evaluation of evaluators: the Ofsted system of school inspection, in C. Cullingford (ed.) *An Inspector Calls*. London: Kogan Page.

Market and Opinion Research International (MORI) (1999) *Schools Inspection Survey: Views of Primary Schools in England Inspected in Summer 1998*. London: Market and Opinion Research International (MORI).

Matthews, P., Holmes, J.R. and Vickers, P. (1998) Aspects of the reliability and validity of school inspection judgements of teaching quality, *Educational Research and Evaluation*, 4(2): 167–88.

Maychell, K. and Pathak, S. (1997) *Planning for Action. Part 1: A Survey of Schools' Post Inspection Action Planning*. Slough: NFER.

Messick, S. (1989) Validity, in R.L. Linn (ed.) *Educational Measurement*, 3rd edn. New York: Macmillan and American Council on Education.

Millett, A. and Johnson, D.C. (1998) OFSTED inspection of primary mathematics: are there new insights to be gained? *School Leadership and Management*, 18(2): 239–55.

National Union of Teachers (NUT) (1998) *'OFSTED': The Views of Headteachers and Deputy Headteacher Members of the National Union of Teachers*. NUT: London.

Office for Standards in Education (Ofsted) (1992a) *Framework for the Inspection of Schools*. London: Ofsted.

Office for Standards in Education (Ofsted) (1992b) *Handbook for the Inspection of Schools*. London: Ofsted.

Office for Standards in Education (Ofsted) (1997) *Inspection and Re-inspection of Schools from September 1997*. London: Ofsted.

Office for Standards in Education (Ofsted) (1998) Press Notice 98–7, 10 March. London: Ofsted.

Office for Standards in Education (Ofsted) (1999) *Handbook for Inspecting Secondary Schools*. London: The Stationery Office.

Office for Standards in Education (Ofsted) (2000) Press Notices for July 21. http:www.ofsted.gov.uk/.

Ofsted, Keele University and Touche Ross (1995) *Inspection Quality 1994/1995*. London: Office for Standards in Education/Central Office of Information.

Ouston, J. and Davies, J. (1998) OFSTED and afterwards? schools' responses to inspection, in P. Earley (ed.) *School Improvement after Inspection? School and LEA Responses*. London: Paul Chapman.

Sandbrook, I. (1996) *Making Sense of Primary Inspection*. Buckingham: Open University Press.

Thomas, G. (1999) Standards and school inspection: the rhetoric and the reality, in C. Cullingford (ed.) *An Inspector Calls*. London: Kogan Page.

Wilcox, B. and Gray, J. (1996) *Inspecting Schools: Holding Schools to Account and Helping Schools to Improve*. Buckingham: Open University Press.

Williams, E. (1999) Sleeplessness? Irritability? Low self-esteem? You must have Ofsteditis, *Times Educational Supplement* (Mind and Body Supplement), 26 March.

Woodhead, C. (1999) An inspector responds, *The Guardian Education*, 5 October.

8

Social justice in schools

Brenda Gay

Introduction

This chapter sets the discussion of social justice in a philosophical, historical and sociological framework. The philosophical stance enables us to examine critically the values and assumptions embedded in the British education system, so that we might reflect on issues of social justice in order to inform our classroom teaching and policy-making at both departmental and school levels. The historical and sociological perspectives indicate shifts in emphasis in attempts to achieve social justice and the implications for different groups of pupils.

Conceptualizing social justice

The concept of justice has long been an area of philosophical discourse. Plato in the fifth century BC made the link between justice and education. In *The Republic*, Plato used a debate on justice to describe a highly differentiated and meritocratic education system, based on selection at an early age through the recognition of innate quality. The system was aimed at producing the three classes required by society: rulers, whose education would equip them to govern justly, warriors and workers. Although Plato's language is in places metaphorical and the content of his education system reflects his own times, we can discern seminal influences on today's education system.

Embedded in the concept of social justice are such concepts as equity and equality. To say 'all men and women are equal' is nonsense. Individuals vary in physical characteristics, abilities, personality, ethnic origin and their range of cognitive, cultural, linguistic and affective experiences. Instead we might say 'equal in some respect'. We might say that all men and women are equal in the sight of God. Yet this concept of equality has been used to justify societies in which there exist gross inequalities in income, lifestyle and treatment. We might say 'all men and women are equal in the eyes of the law', meaning that our justice system treats all people in the same way. However, this is not always the case. Definitions of what counts as deviant behaviour and subsequent ways of dealing with it may vary according to the status and class of the perpetrator and different social classes have differential access to ways of dealing with law enforcement agencies.

We might say that equality means giving all people the same. Yet individuals' needs vary considerably and treating people differently may be more appropriate, following the principle 'from each according to his abilities to each according to his needs' (Marx 1875, quoted in Partington 1992). For example, how are equality and equity reflected in a departmental policy that sets pupils according to ability? Should all sets in a particular year be of equal size, enabling all pupils to benefit from being in smaller sets or should pupils who have greater need of individual attention be placed in significantly smaller sets leading to larger sets for the rest of the year group?

For a discussion of the importance of recognizing different individual needs see Dewey (1966), who talked in terms of equality of concern for each individual in the community to develop as a person. Dewey viewed education as the means whereby personal qualities are liberated to enable human beings to achieve their maximum distinctive growth. However, equality of concern does not mean equality of treatment. Thus, there are some things everyone needs to know but not everything needs to be known by everybody and teachers should be concerned with objectives appropriate to each individual.

Gewirtz (1998: 470) argues that 'within recent studies of education policy, social justice has been an under-theorized concept' and within empirical studies that show how inequalities are produced and reproduced in education policy there is little explicit discussion of the meaning of the concept. Gewirtz distinguishes between two dimensions of social justice – the distributional, which is the way in which material and non-material goods are distributed in society, and the relational, which refers to the 'nature of the relationships that structure society' (1998: 470). Notions of distributive justice fall into two categories – equality of opportunity and equality of outcome. Equality of opportunity emphasizes equal access, formal rights and participation, whereas equality of outcome 'seeks to ensure equal rates of success for different groups in society through direct intervention to prevent disadvantage, for example via positive discrimination or affirmative action programmes' (Gewirtz 1998: 472). The issues discussed in this chapter will show how policy-making has been influenced by a concern with both equality of opportunity and equality of outcome.

Social justice and access to secondary education

In the nineteenth century British education was starkly divided on class lines. In the public schools and endowed grammar schools the curriculum, centred on the classics, was designed as an education for leadership and, in the public schools, to produce the 'Christian gentleman'. In the elementary schools for the mass of the population, the emphasis was on the acquisition of the basic skills of numeracy, reading and writing. The curriculum was designed to produce a labour force with sufficient skills for the factory and an electorate who had some basic skills of literacy and numeracy. The elementary school curriculum was intended also to inculcate the values of obedience and respect for property. In an attempt to widen access to secondary education the Balfour Act of 1902 set up grammar schools in every town. However, a child's chances of taking up a place at a grammar school were largely dependent on parental means, as only 25 per cent of the places were allocated free to elementary school pupils on the basis of a highly competitive scholarship examination.

The 1944 Education Act made significant changes in the structure of the education system in an attempt to redress some of its inequalities. The old arrangement of 'elementary' and 'higher elementary' education was replaced by primary, secondary and further education. Behind the Act lay the assumptions that pupils could be divided by age, aptitude and ability and that individuals possessed an underlying intelligence, which could be determined by specifically designed objective tests. Therefore it set up a tripartite system of secondary education with grammar, secondary modern and technical high schools which would enjoy parity of esteem. Access to each type of school was based on the results of the eleven-plus examination. The curriculum in each type of secondary school reflected the supposed different abilities and aptitudes of their intakes. The curriculum in the grammar schools was more traditionally academic and in the modern schools less academic for the more practical child, while the curriculum in the technical schools, very few of which were built, concentrated more on science and technical subjects. Until 1951, with the introduction of the GCE examination, secondary modern schools did not provide the opportunity for pupils to take public examinations and the expectation was that children in these schools would leave school at 15. Equity was seen in terms of equality of access within a differentiated system and was based on the notion of sponsored mobility whereby meritocracy of ability replaced selection based on birth and social position.

Social justice and the tripartite system

Despite the good intentions of the Act, concerns soon arose about the equity of the selection process and the differences in the educational opportunities available in grammar and secondary modern schools. A series of reports and research studies uncovered significant inequalities. *Early Leaving: a Report of the Central Advisory Council for England* (CACE 1954) found that working-class children were underrepresented and middle-class children, despite forming a smaller proportion of the population, overrepresented in the grammar schools. The Crowther Report (1959) found wide social class differences in the age of leaving school among national service recruits. Many working-class pupils were not achieving as highly as they should in the light of their measured intelligence at age 15 for reasons of home background and family attitudes. The Robbins Report (1963) found social class differences in higher education and highlighted the existence of 'large reservoirs of untapped ability in the population, especially among girls'. Variations among local authorities in the percentage of grammar school places available were as extreme as 40 and 8 per cent. When it was seen that girls performed better in the eleven-plus examination, boys' scores were adjusted so that boys with lower scores than girls gained grammar school places (Bignell and Maguire 1997: 66).

Material and non-material factors in the home, some of which were linked to social class, were found to lie behind disparities in achievement. These included parental aspirations and willingness to make sacrifices for their children (Jackson and Marsden 1962), differences in child-rearing practices (Newson and Newson 1963), the use of toys and attitudes to play (Jones 1966), access to different linguistic codes (Bernstein 1958), continuity between home and school values (Bernstein 1973) and parents' interest in their children's schooling as evidenced *inter alia* by attendance at parents' meetings and willingness to provide facilities at home for study (Dale and Griffiths 1965).

Differences among schools were also identified. The Newsom Report (1963) showed that 80 per cent of the schools in which the average and below average child was taught were seriously deficient in respect of buildings, resources and teacher turnover. Hargreaves (1967) found a wide disparity in resources between grammar and secondary modern schools in Manchester. More subtle inequalities were identified, such as the social distribution of knowledge (Young 1971), the access by different groups in society to different forms of cultural capital (Bourdieu 1974) and the tendency of schools to reproduce the status quo in society by offering different learning experiences to different groups of pupils (Willis 1977). The two-tier system of public examinations, with GCE for the top 20 per cent and the Certificate of Secondary Education (CSE) for the next 40 per cent of pupils was inherently unequal and led to 40 per cent of pupils leaving school without formal qualifications.

Cumulative evidence therefore suggested that the tripartite system was not as egalitarian as had been hoped and reorganization on comprehensive lines was seen as a way of removing some of the inequities. Some local authorities took initiatives in advance of government directive to establish a comprehensive system. In 1965 the Department of Education and Science issued *Circular 10/65* inviting local education authorities to submit plans for reorganizing education on comprehensive lines in order to end selection at age 11 and eliminate separatism in secondary education (DES 1965). Over the next decade the majority of local authorities proceeded with plans for comprehensive organization. The comprehensive system was 'intended not to offer the same education to all, but the same educational opportunities to all' (DES 1977: 8).

Comprehensive education and social justice

While some structural inequalities were removed as a result of the organization on comprehensive lines, inequalities still remained. In local authorities where grammar schools continued to exist the comprehensive schools were perceived by many parents as second best. Banding and streaming policies within comprehensive schools often perpetuated the divisions of the grammar and secondary modern schools. In some areas comprehensive schools catered for a broad social and ability mix, but schools in other areas became neighbourhood comprehensives. Middle-class parents became adept at gaining places for their children in 'better' schools, rather than using their local comprehensive. Schools in inner cities particularly found it difficult to recruit and retain staff. The defer-ment of the raising of the school leaving age to 16 until 1972 meant that large numbers of pupils continued to leave school at age 15 without any formal qualifications. Furthermore some schools serving similar catch-ment areas were seen to be more effective than others (Rutter *et al.* 1979).

The late 1970s and 1980s saw mounting concern on the part of success-ive Labour and Conservative governments about standards in education and the need to ensure that all pupils were given opportunities to max-imize their potential. The introduction of the GCSE in 1986, with the first examinations in 1988 to replace O-levels, and the CSE aimed to give access to public examinations to 80–90 per cent of all 16-year-olds. De-spite the concern to promote greater equality of opportunity via access to a common examination, inequities began to emerge, particularly in rela-tion to coursework, which in some subjects could amount to 100 per cent of the examination. Coursework was perceived to advantage certain groups of pupils. Pupils who had greater access to resources at home were more likely to achieve higher grades. Girls appeared to respond better than boys to coursework, partly because of the consistent effort required, whereas boys tended to do better in terminal examinations because of their prefer-ence for leaving work until the last minute (Arnot *et al.* 1996). The de-mands of coursework for extended pieces of writing disadvantaged children with language difficulties and the amount of support in school varied among schools and within subjects in the same school (Smithers, quoted in Charter 2000a).

The Education Reform Act (1988) and social justice

The Education Reform Act of 1988 brought a major shift in the control of the curriculum by central government and in the management of schools. Behind the Act lay a concern to raise standards; to give all children the right of access to a worthwhile curriculum (an entitlement curriculum); to give equality of access to educational chances on a national basis and to minimize local differences in the quality of education. Hence the National Curriculum orders prescribed three core and seven foundation subjects to be taken by all pupils with programmes of study for each. The monitoring of standards through national tests at the end of each of the Key Stages 1, 2 and 3 and regular school inspections were designed to min-imize differences in performance among schools. The concept of equality shifted to that of giving all pupils the entitlement to the same curriculum. The National Curriculum Orders reinforced this by requiring schools to implement an equal opportunities 'policy to which the whole school subscribes and in which positive attitudes to gender, equality, cultural needs and special needs of all kinds are actively promoted' (NCC 1990: 2).

However, the National Curriculum Orders for the year 2000 shifted slightly towards the principle of equality of concern for individual needs and differences as schools were now able to disapply up to two National Curriculum subjects:

> to allow pupils making significantly less progress than their peers to study fewer National Curriculum subjects in order to consolidate their learning across the curriculum . . . or to respond to pupils' individual strengths and talents by allowing them to emphasise a particular curriculum area by exchanging a statutory subject for a further course in that curriculum.
>
> (DfEE and QCA 1999: 17)

The 1988 Education Act passed greater control for financial management from the local authorities to schools and gave the opportunity for schools to opt out of local authority control entirely and have grant maintained status, allowed greater parental choice of school and provided for the setting up of city technology colleges. These provisions however have resulted in an unintended widening of the gap between the educational opportunities of children from different social class and ethnic backgrounds.

The publication of schools' examination results in the form of league tables was intended to produce greater transparency and reduce inequalities by encouraging schools to aim for the best possible results. Yet this, coupled with greater parental choice of school, has resulted in what Ball (1994) described as an education marketplace which reproduced relative social class and ethnic advantages and disadvantages for children from certain types of background. Ball suggested that in an education market the strategic processes of choice systematically disadvantage working-class families and the link between choices and resources (via per capita funding) disadvantages working-class schools and communities. 'The market is not neutral. It presumes certain skills, competencies and material possibilities (access to time, transport and childcare facilities which are unevenly distributed across the population' (Ball 1994: 118).

Responsibility for their own budgets meant that schools increasingly had to raise additional money, which has also widened disparities. A survey by the Directory of Social Change found that schools in affluent areas were:

> enjoying a growing advantage over others by raising the lion's share of £230 million a year in private funding . . . 20 per cent of primary and 5 per cent of secondary schools raise less than £1,000 a year from parents. At the other end of the scale 3 per cent of secondary schools supplement their budgets by more than £250,000.
>
> (O'Leary 2000)

In their case study on parental choice of schools Gewirtz et al. (1995) showed how open enrolment policy extended the ways in which middle-class parents were able to take advantage of the system. The authors identified a strongly class-related typology of choosers – 'the privileged/

skilled', 'the semi-skilled' and the 'disconnected'. Privileged choosers are able to interpret information about schools, match the school to their child's perceived intellectual and other needs and strategically plan in order to gain a place at the school of their choice. The disconnected choosers, by contrast, tend to be constrained in their choice by both material and non-material factors.

The same study highlighted ways in which league tables and per capita funding have made schools sensitive to the images that they present and to the types of pupil that they wish to attract. In some cases the policies of the more successful schools have led to undersubscribed schools taking a disproportionate number of pupils with learning or other difficulties. Certain categories of pupils are seen to be desirable: girls, pupils with musical interests and some groups of South Asian students who are strong on science subjects. Other groups are seen as undesirable: children with emotional or behavioural problems; working-class children whose parents are viewed as not valuing education and children with learning difficulties or special educational needs. Such pupils are regarded by some as expensive to educate and they may threaten balanced intakes and lower the school's ranking in league tables.

Gender and social justice

Our discussion on social justice has mainly focused on social class. However other forms of inequality exist. The Sex Discrimination Act (1975) brought an increased awareness of gender inequalities in society as a whole and in school. In the 1970s and 1980s attention concentrated on the differential treatment and achievement of boys and girls and the underachievement of girls relative to boys in public examinations despite their higher performance on tests at age 11. Kelly (1988) from an analysis of 81 studies concluded that girls received less of the teachers' attention in class than boys. Paechter (1998), summarizing evidence from a number of studies, suggested boys dominated the classroom; they claimed more teacher time, resources and control over the lesson content and classroom talk and displayed more disruptive behaviour. Equal opportunities policies were targeted on raising girls' expectations and encouraging them to take traditional male subjects at A-level such as physics and mathematics. Initiatives were taken such as the Women into Science and Engineering Project and attempts were made to make textbooks and examinations more girl-friendly. From the 1970s onwards the majority of Oxford and Cambridge colleges became co-educational.

By the late 1980s it was clear that positive interventions to increase girls' achievements had been effective and girls began to overtake boys in their performance at both GCSE and A-level. In 1989, girls were 6 percentage points ahead of boys in achieving five or more GCSEs at grades A* to C. Ten years later that lead had grown to 10.6 per cent. Since 1993 girls have performed better than boys in the boys' traditional stronghold of mathematics. Furthermore, as Arnot *et al.* (1996) noted, the gender gap in subjects taken at GCSE decreased in most subjects from the mid-1980s to the mid-1990s with exceptions such as physics, design and technology and economics, which were male-dominated, and home economics and social studies which were female dominated. The results of the A-level examinations taken in 2000 showed that, for the first time, girls had overtaken boys not only in their number of passes at all grades but in the percentage of passes at the top two grades. Girls gained 18.1 per cent and boys 17.8 per cent of the A grades. According to Smithers (quoted in Charter 2000a, 2000b) the widening gap can be attributed to girls' greater expectation of a good university place and their greater determination to use their results as a springboard to successful careers. Other factors include girls' greater verbal abilities at a young age which leads them to master English faster than boys, giving them an edge in all subjects and the emphasis on coursework in both A-level and GCSE which seems to favour the more consistent efforts of girls.

Evidence that girls were performing better at all levels shifted the focus to the underachievement of boys. National Curriculum assessment tests in 1991 and 1992 had shown that at the age of 7, girls performed better than boys in reading, writing and spelling. The Ofsted report on boys' performance in English at secondary school (1993) painted a similar picture; the majority of pupils who experienced difficulty in learning to read and write were boys; boys' results in public examinations at 16 were not as good as girls', and many more girls than boys continued to study English beyond 16. The report linked boys' poorer performance to 'attitudes to writing and reading which are less positive than girls'' and suggested that social and cultural pressures helped to create these attitudes (Ofsted 1993: 27).

The reasons for the widening gender gap lie not only in the raising of girls' motivation and achievement and with the anti-academic and anti-reading culture into which many boys are drawn, but in wider social problems. For 'the question of gender and performance is more complex, affecting different sub-groups of boys and girls in different ways and often reflecting the influence of social class and ethnicity' (Arnot *et al.* 1998: 1). The decline of many traditional working-class occupations has meant that many working-class boys cannot see a future direction for employment. The lack of a male role model for boys living in single parent households with their mothers is compounded at primary school by the preponderance of female teachers. Research on peer group culture (Mac an Ghaill 1994) has shown that the response of some working-class boys to their lack of achievement in school and the changed economic circumstances has led to a 'laddish culture' which despises learning.

National and local initiatives have been taken to improve boys' performance. The introduction of the literacy hour in primary schools was partly a response to the need to raise standards of literacy amongst boys in particular who, it was believed, would respond to its more structured approach. The results of the 1999 National Curriculum Tests, the first following its introduction, indicate the literacy hour may have had some effect as the proportion of boys reaching the reading level expected of an 11-year-old rose by 14 per cent to 78 per cent but that of girls by 5 per cent to 86 per cent. However, fewer than half of all boys reached the target level in writing compared with almost two-thirds of girls. As part of its Raising Achievement in Shropshire Schools programme, the LEA has run a Boys and English project. Shenfield High School in Essex has been teaching boys and girls separately at Key Stage 3 for all subjects and for mathematics, English and science at Key Stage 4 since 1994. This has resulted in an improvement in the performance of both boys and girls at GCSE. In the wake of the A-level results in summer 2000, the Secretary of State for Education, David Blunkett, announced that he intended to ask Ofsted to assess how single-sex lessons could help boys at all ages. This would include experiments in single-sex lessons for 8–11-year-olds in primary schools, although the emphasis would be on secondary schools.

Race and social justice

The Race Relations Act (1976) resulted in policies in schools to redress racial inequality. The concern in the 1980s was to promote both anti-racist policies to combat racism and multicultural education, which celebrated diversity. Schools acknowledged the cultural heritage of other nations in their curricula with the inclusion, for example, of world faiths in religious education and literature from other cultures in English syllabuses. However, according to Blair and Arnot (1993) the National Curriculum has reduced multiculturalism in the classroom. The languages spoken by many children are not recognized and already overcrowded programmes of study restrict opportunities for teachers to introduce other cultural heritages.

Studies on racial inequality in education have shown that the situation is highly complex; the picture is different for boys and girls; pupils from some ethnic groups are more disadvantaged than others and socioeconomic factors combine with ethnicity. Of particular concern are African-Caribbean boys. Gilborn (1990) and Mac an Ghaill (1988) concluded that African-Caribbean boys receive disproportionately more control and criticism compared to other ethnic groups when committing the same offence. Wright (1987) found that African-Caribbean pupils were placed in examinations well below their ability on the basis of their behaviour. By contrast, Mirza (1992) found that African-British girls were doing better than white working-class girls. Figures of the applications to higher education courses in autumn 1999 showed that although non-white people are still underrepresented in higher education there was a rise of 3.3 per cent in black and 2.6 per cent in Asian applicants.

Teachers' perceptions may disadvantage some groups of African-Caribbean students. Watson and Maguire (1997: 78) argue that there is 'overwhelming evidence that black children and school students are subjected to low expectations on the part of their teachers, that they are on the receiving end of demeaning stereotyping and that racial harassment is a common part of daily life in the schools in the UK'. A more controversial explanation is given by Sewell (1997) who claims that many African-Caribbean boys are burdened with a representation of themselves centred on the 'body not the mind'. The media has perpetuated this image so that it is no longer racism but youth culture that is the main obstacle to the achievement of certain groups of black students (Sewell, quoted in Lightfoot 2000).

Conclusions

Children are not born equal. They are born into different environments and have different innate characteristics. Education can reduce some of the inequalities both through providing equal opportunity of access and by positive intervention on behalf of certain groups. Levels of prosperity have risen; access to educational opportunities has been considerably widened, as evidenced by the fact that over 40 per cent of 18-year-olds go on to higher education. Nonetheless there are groups in society who are disadvantaged and the education system must ensure it is not compounding but ameliorating these disadvantages. A holistic approach is needed in view of the complex links between social class, ethnicity and education.

References

Arnot, M., David, M. and Weiner, G. (1996) *Educational Reform and Gender Equality in Schools*. Manchester: Equal Opportunities Commission.

Arnot, M., Gray, J., James, M., Ruddock, J. with Duveen, G. (1998) *Recent Research on Gender and Educational Performance*. London: HMSO.

Ball, S.J. (1994) *Education Reform: A Critical and Post-Structural Approach*. Buckingham: Open University Press.

Bernstein, B. (1958) Social class and linguistic development: a theory of social learning, in A.H. Halsey, J. Floud and C. Anderson (eds) *Education, Economy and Society*. Glencoe: Free Press.

Bernstein, B. (1973) *Class, Codes and Control, Vol. 2*. London: Routledge and Kegan Paul.

Bignell, K. and Maguire, M. (1997) Diversity and social justice, in J. Dillon and M. Maguire (eds) *Becoming a Teacher*. Buckingham: Open University Press.

Blair, M. and Arnot, M. (1993) Black and anti-racist perspectives on the National Curriculum, in A.S. King and M.J. Reiss (eds) *The Multicultural Dimension of the National Curriculum*. London: Falmer Press.

Bourdieu, P. (1974) The school as a conservative force: scholastic and cultural inequalities, in J.S. Eggleston (ed.) *Contemporary Research in the Sociology of Education*. London: Methuen.

Central Advisory Council for Education (England) (CACE) (1954) *Early Leaving*. London: HMSO.

Charter, D. (2000a) A-level girls triumph over laddish culture, *The Times*, 16 August.

Charter, D. (2000b) Work ethic puts girls top of class, *The Times*, 16 August.

Crowther, G. (1959) *A Report of The Central Advisory Council for Education England* (The Crowther Report). London: HMSO.

Dale, R.R. and Griffiths, S. (1965) *Downstream*. London: Routledge and Kegan Paul.

Department for Education and Employment (DfEE) and Qualifications and Curriculum Authority (QCA) (1999) *The National Curriculum: Handbook for Secondary Teachers in England and Wales*. London: DfEE and QCA.

Department of Education and Science (DES) (1965) *Circular 10/65*. London: HMSO.

Department of Education and Science (DES) (1977) *The Growth of Comprehensive Education*. DES Report on Education No.87. London: HMSO.

Dewey, J. (1966) *Democracy and Education: An Introduction to the Philosophy of Education*. New York: Free Press.

Gewirtz, S. (1998) Conceptualizing social justice in education: mapping the territory, *Journal of Education Policy*, 13(4): 469–84.

Gewirtz, S., Ball, S.J. and Bowe, R. (1995) *Markets, Choice and Equity in Education*. Buckingham: Open University Press.

Gilborn, D. (1990) Student roles and perspectives in antiracist education: a crisis of white ethnicity? *British Educational Research Journal*, 22(2): 165–81.

Hargreaves, D. (1967) *Social Relationships in a Secondary School*. London: Routledge and Kegan Paul.

Jackson, B. and Marsden, D. (1962) *Education and the Working Class*. London: Routledge and Kegan Paul.

Jones, J. (1966) Social class and the under fives, *New Society*, 221: 935–6.

Kelly, A. (1988) Gender differences in teacher–pupil interaction: a meta-analytic review, *Research in Education*, 39: 1–23.

Lightfoot, L. (2000) Black culture 'holding back' boys, *The Daily Telegraph*, 21 August.

Mac an Ghaill, M. (1988) *Young, Gifted and Black: Student–Teacher Relations in the Schooling of Black Youth*. Milton Keynes: Open University Press.

Mac an Ghaill, M. (1994) *The Making of Men: Masculinities, Sexualities and Schooling*. Buckingham: Open University Press.

Mirza, S. (1992) *Young, Female and Black*. London: Routledge.

National Curriculum Council (NCC) (1990) *NCC Curriculum Guidance 3: The Whole Curriculum*. London: HMSO.

Newsom, J.H. (1963) *Half Our Future: A Report of the Central Advisory Council for Education England* (Newsom Report). London: HMSO.

Newson, J. and Newson, E. (1963) *Infant Care in an Urban Environment*. London: Allen and Unwin.

Office for Standards in Education (Ofsted) (1993) *Boys and English*. London: DfEE.

O'Leary, T. (2000) Gap between rich and poor schools widens, *The Times*, 12 May.

Paechter, C. (1998) *Educating the Other: Gender, Power and Schooling*. London: Falmer Press.

Partington, A. (ed.) (1992) *The Oxford Dictionary of Quotations*. Oxford: Oxford University Press.

Plato (1961) *The Republic*. London: Penguin Books.

Robbins, G.H. (1963) *Higher Education: A Report of the Great Britain Committee on Higher Education* (The Robbins Report). London: HMSO.

Rutter, M., Maughan, B., Mortimore, P. and Ouston, J. (1979) *Fifteen Thousand Hours*. London: Open Books.

Sewell, T. (1997) *Black Masculinities and Schooling*. Stoke on Trent: Trentham Books.

Watson, B. and Maguire, M. (1997) Multi-cultural matters, in J. Dillon and M. Maguire (eds) *Becoming a Teacher*. Buckingham: Open University Press.

Willis, P. (1977) *Learning to Labour*. Farnborough: Saxon House.

Wright, C. (1987) Black students – white teachers, in B. Troyna (ed.) *Racial Equality in Education*. London: Tavistock.

Young, M. (ed.) (1971) *Knowledge and Control: New Directions for the Sociology of Knowledge*. London: Collier-Macmillan.

9

Parents and schooling

Diane Reay

Introduction

This chapter is about parental involvement in education. It provides a brief history of home–school relationships in the UK and gives a short overview of the existing literature before discussing the current 'state-of-play' in relation to parents and schooling at the beginning of the twenty-first century. Much of the parental involvement literature works with an homogeneous notion of 'the parent'. In contrast, in this chapter I intend to focus on the differences which permeate parental involvement in order to convey some of the persistent inequalities that continue to shape relationships between home and school.

Most of the existing texts concentrate on the primary stage of schooling (Lareau 1989; David *et al.* 1993; Vincent 1996; Reay 1998) and this is partly because relationships with parents are often seen to play a more minor role in secondary school teachers' working lives. Apart from parents' evenings, contact is still likely to be an extraordinary rather than an ordinary event in which communication takes place when there are problems rather than when things are going well. However, lack of direct contact does not translate into lack of influence or impact on secondary teachers' working lives (Crozier 2000). Parents have been key in both the Conservatives' and now the Labour government's efforts to drive up educational standards. In the Conservative government report *Choice and Diversity* (DfE 1992) one of the four conditions for school success was a high level of parental and community involvement, while David Blunkett promised in the New Labour White Paper *Excellence in Schools* (DfEE 1997) that Labour's partnership approach to education would be committed to involving parents fully.

A brief history of home–school relationships

There have been enormous changes since the beginning of the 1950s in the relationship between home and school. Where once there was a clearly defined separation in which schools made very few educational demands of parents, we now have a situation in which it is the expectation that parents will become involved in their children's schooling. The importance of close links between teachers and parents in promoting children's achievement was first recognized in the 1960s. The Plowden Report (1967) promoted parental involvement as an aspect of children's education that was in need of further development, but it still remained an 'optional extra' for both schools and for parents. One direct consequence, however, was the establishment of Education Priority Areas. These initiatives, set up in the late 1960s, saw the appointment of home–school liaison teachers with explicit responsibility for promoting home–school links (Halsey 1972). The Plowden Report also recommended initiatives to inform parents about school, such as written reports and parents' evenings.

More recently, partnership between parents and teachers has become enshrined in educational policy (DES 1985, 1986, 1988). The 1985 White Paper *Better Schools* emphasized the importance of home–school links, arguing that schools could be more effective if they could rely on the cooperation and support of parents in the pursuit of shared objectives. The White Paper went on to urge schools to explain their aims and policies to parents and associate parents with their work. Three years later the 1988 Education Reform Act promised parents much more information about the performance of schools and individual pupils. A recurring theme throughout the Act was that of accountability to parents – so that parents would be able to judge their children's progress against agreed national targets for attainment and assess the effectiveness of their school. The Conservative government's aim with these changes was to produce better educational standards, based upon individual parents' demands (David 1993). Parents were to be encouraged to become consumers within education. A further aspect of this consumer orientation lay in the promotion of parental choice. Parents were to be allowed to choose the best school to suit their children's educational needs. The reality, however, has been somewhat different to the policy rhetoric. Since the inception of the policy there has been a growing body of research which demonstrates that educational markets are class and race-biased. 'Parents seem to make choices on the basis of the perceived class and, in some instances, racial composition of schools' (Gewirtz *et al.* 1995: 184). (For a further discussion of the consequences of parental choice see Chapter 5.)

The growing consumer-orientated perspective was particularly evident in the 1991 *Parent's Charter* (DES 1991). Under the charter, parental access to information about schools and their own children's progress and results, in the context of wider performance, would be mandatory. Parental rights to know were to be enlarged through five key documents: a report about each individual child; regular reports from independent inspectors; a performance table for all local schools; a prospectus about individual schools; and an annual report from a school's governors (1991: 7). In addition the charter also made clear to parents that they too had responsibilities. By

1991, the whole approach to parent–school relations had shifted from one about how to ensure some measures of equity to how to ensure parental rights and responsibilities in order for individual parents to be able to influence each child's educational success in formal examination situations (David 1993). Perhaps the best summation of the state-of-play in relation to parental involvement, at the beginning of the 1990s, was provided by Philip Brown (1990: 66–7) who wrote that:

> We are entering a 'third wave'...which is neither part of a final drive to 'meritocracy', nor the result of a socialist victory for educational reform. To date, the 'third wave' has been characterized by the rise of the educational parentocracy, where a child's education is increasingly dependent on the wealth and wishes of parents, rather than the ability and efforts of pupils...the ideology of parentocracy involves a major programme of educational privatization under the slogans of 'parental choice', 'educational standards' and the 'free market'.

Since then there has been an increased emphasis on the accountability of both teachers and parents. During the 1990s parental involvement was officially recognized as a key factor in school improvement and effectiveness (Reynolds and Cuttance 1992), and in 1994 became a requisite part of a school's development plan (Ofsted 1994). Ofsted guidelines issued the following year (1995: 98) encouraged inspectors to explore how well schools help parents to understand the curriculum and the teaching it provides, and how this can lead to parents and teachers working together to provide support at home.

Existing literature on parental involvement

Until recently, nearly all the literature on parents and schooling has focused on the 'how to do it' issues (for example, see Macbeath 1989; Merttens and Vass 1993; Hughes *et al.* 1994; Topping 1996), rather than considering the relationship between parents and schools and the complex range of influences on parental involvement. As Gill Crozier points out, while there are a large number of texts outlining models of 'good' parental involvement, few pay attention to whether parental involvement is 'either useful, desirable or indeed viable at secondary level from the perspectives of parents, teachers and the students themselves' (Crozier 2000: 29). Furthermore, like the policy documents, the literature has assumed that all parents share an identical experience of involvement in their children's schooling. This 'universal' parent operates to render invisible inequalities between the sexes but also those existing between parents. Structural constraints of gender, race, class and marital status are missing except when they emerge reworked as 'problems to be dealt with'. As Miriam David (1993: 99) points out in her discussion of the typologies of parental involvement which permeate the literature:

> What none of the typologies or schemes paid attention to, however, are the definitions of and changing practices with respect to the

notion of parent. In particular, the gendered and racialised notions of parent were not acknowledged.

When subjected to scrutiny it rapidly becomes apparent that most of the texts on parental involvement are premised on the unexamined assumption that parental involvement is a shared, equal task – between parents and between parents and teachers. The term 'partnership', which regularly appears in the texts, acts discursively to imply reciprocity and equality between parents and school. According to Stephen Ball (1998), home–school relationships are homogenized and reduced to the anodyne rhetoric of partnership in books on school effectiveness, while Carol Vincent points out the reliance on consensual language, such as 'partnership', 'involvement' and 'dialogue' which feature strongly in the home–school literature, edits out of the relationship tension and conflict, and the inequalities underlying them (1996: 73). Despite assumptions of equal, harmonious relations between teachers and parents, parents are often positioned as the subordinate party (Vincent and Warren 2000). Because most of the texts overlook disparities in the material, cultural and social resources different groups of parents have access to, they fail to recognize the inequalities that arise when certain groups of parents are better at presenting themselves and framing their concerns and opinions in ways that many teachers recognize as valid.

Behind assumptions of partnership between teachers and parents in the literature lies a second implied partnership – one between both parents in relation to their child's schooling. Both the home–school literature and the large body of work on school effectiveness mirror government and official policy documentation in working with an homogeneous notion of 'parent' which fails to recognize the gendered division of labour operating in the home with respect to parental involvement. This failure to recognize gender continues despite the recent empirical research demonstrating that it is predominantly mothers who are 'the most involved parent' (Crozier 2000; Vincent 2000). Fathers are far more likely to be 'helping hands' rather than equal partners in their child's education. A number of research studies (David et al. 1993; Reay 1998) also found a class difference in paternal involvement. Middle-class fathers often act as public personae, taking a high profile in the public sphere of home–school relations but leaving the day to day management to female partners, while working-class fathers are less involved than their female partners either in school or at home.

So we can see how important issues of gender, race and social class are hidden by normative constructions of 'partnership' and 'parent'. The 'universal parent' we find throughout the parental involvement literature renders invisible inequalities between the sexes, between social classes and between different ethnic groupings. The importance of teachers recognizing not only difference and diversity, but the ways in which they are rooted in inequalities is vital. Despite the homogeneity reigning in the texts on parental involvement, some teachers still continue to adopt deficit conceptions of certain parent groups, based on assumptions relating to ethnicity, gender, marital status and social class. Critically interrogating such taken-for-granted assumptions, as well as textual constructions which deny difference, is becoming increasingly important within a contemporary context in which increased parental involvement and parental choice are invariably presented as beneficial for all.

Contemporary policy

We have now reached a point at the beginning of the twenty-first century when parental involvement is no longer the optional extra it was considered to be in the days of Plowden. Instead, it has become a central plank in British government educational policy. Under the Labour government, elected in May 1997, there has been an intensification of the move from parental rights to increased parental responsibilities initiated under the previous Conservative administration (Whitty *et al.* 1998). Edwards and Warin (1999) go as far as to argue that collaboration between home and school seems to have been superseded by the colonization of the home by the school.

Certainly schemes like PACT (Parents and Children with Teachers) and IMPACT (Maths for Parents and Teachers), which are devised to ensure parents support their children's reading and numeracy development, are widespread (Merttens and Vass 1993), while in 1999 home–school agreements became a statutory requirement, despite considerable disquiet from both educationalists and parent groups. According to the Government White Paper *Excellence in Cities* (DfEE 1998a): 'all schools should, in discussion with parents develop a home–school contract. These agreements will reflect the respective responsibilities of home and school in raising standards, stating clearly what is expected of the school, of the parent and the pupil'. The home–school agreement policy is an initiative which many educationalists fear will move beyond parental obligations into regulation. As Joan Sallis (1991) argues, the concern is that the emphasis of agreements will shift to lecturing parents on inadequacies they may be unable to remedy, and that those feelings of inadequacy will only be increased.

The notion of the 'good parent' that we find in the home–school literature is just as pervasive within contemporary educational policy. The 'good parent' is deemed to be one who will support their child's school curriculum and provide an array of stimulating learning activities for the child out of school time. Implicitly, all those other parents who lack the material resources, educational knowledge and confidence to meet the ideal are positioned as 'deficient' in some way. Furthermore, the intensification of educational reform since 1988 has also repositioned parents and teachers in relation to each other, generating processes of mutual surveillance. 'The policies in relation to parents and school are two-pronged: firstly to create a structure whereby parents monitor the teachers' work and call them to account and secondly to ensure that parents take on their own responsibilities' (Crozier 2000: 7).

Crozier writes about a 'new' blame culture within which parents are frequently criticized for lack of sufficient commitment to their children's education and are seen to be partially responsible for both children's poor

educational performance and their poor behaviour. The rest of the responsibility, she argues, is seen to lie with teachers. We need to question
whether new policy initiatives such as the Home–School Agreements Policy (DfEE 1998b) and the Homework Policy (DfEE 1998c) are creating
conditions for a productive, harmonized partnership between parents and
teachers, or whether they are generating a situation of antagonistic relationships. There is some evidence that the latter scenario is the more likely
one and that having to deal with confrontational parents and those who
challenge schools' decisions is a developing role for schools in contemporary
Britain (Barnard 1999; Crozier 2000).

The impact of social differences on involvement in schooling

The current enthusiasm for yet more and more parental involvement
among policymakers has failed to take into account the dangers some kinds
of parental involvement pose to pupils' equal opportunities for educational
resources. Aspects of parental involvement and schools' accountability to
parents may work against equal opportunities. First, teachers need to bear
in mind that parents' personal histories and their educational experiences
influence their involvement in their children's schooling, particularly their
effectiveness in dealing with teachers, and that such differences are rooted
in social class, ethnicity and race. Where children's class and cultural background bears little resemblance to that of their teachers, connections
between home and school may be minimal and tenuous.

Second, the concerns of involved parents are often narrow and aimed
primarily at gaining advantage for their own children. While the new
century has seen growing angst about educational achievement that
cross class and race, it is primarily middle-class mothers who are juggling
intense anxieties about their children's education alongside the pursuit of
their educational advantage (Jordan *et al.* 1994). The combination of relative affluence, educational expertise and higher levels of confidence and
entitlement in relation to children's schooling gives middle-class mothers
options most working-class mothers do not have. Many middle-class
mothers are able to compensate for what they perceive to be gaps in the
state provision through the employment of tutors alongside attempting
to modify the provision the school makes for their child, all the while continuing to complement the school site offerings through mothering work
in the home (Reay 1998). In both the UK and the US there has been a history of middle-class parental action directed at controlling both teachers
and working-class parents (Cohen 1981; Sieber 1982). Currently, middle-
class parental action in the UK is leading to increasing class and racial
segregation between and within schools, from pressure for streaming on
the presumption that their children will be allocated to top sets (Gewirtz
et al. 1995) to the avoidance of schools with a sizeable cohort of black
and/or white working-class pupils who might hinder their own child's
learning (Bagley 1996).

The differential impact of social class positioning and ethnicity means
that parents are dealing with different layers of continuity and discontinuity

between their own, and their children's, educational experiences. Where parents are positioned on this continuity/discontinuity spectrum has important consequences for both the quantity and quality of involvement in children's schooling. Unlike the harmonious, anodyne relationships presented in many of the parental involvement texts, in reality parent–teacher relationships are characterized by a struggle for control and definition. Teachers have two broad sets of relationships to manage: 'with the assertive, demanding middle class parents on the one hand and with the seemingly passive, disengaged working class parents on the other' (Crozier 2000: 123). One consequence is that school–parent links, even in predominantly working-class schools, are dominated by middle-class parents. Schools tend to offer their scarce resources to those who demand them most vociferously rather than to those in the greatest need.

It is important to remember that there exists a significant minority of parents whose own negative experiences of schooling makes involvement in their children's schooling difficult, even painful (McNamara *et al* 2000). As one of the working-class, minority ethnic mothers in my research study asserted:

> You need parental involvement. You need parents to be able to complement what you're doing but that's all it should be. It shouldn't be any more. You see not all people speak English, not all parents read and write so how can they help their children at home? They're at a disadvantage anyway so when they come to school they've got to get the help there . . . there's a lot of parents who can't, just can't do it.
>
> (Josie, quoted in Reay 1998)

Levels of separation and connection between home and school in parents' own educational experience influence current patterns of involvement. In particular, the merging of history and geography in parents' lives gets played out in the school involvement practices of parents, like Josie, who are migrants to Britain. It can be argued that often their cultural capital is in the 'wrong' currency because the experience of attending schools in other countries undermines their capacity to engage productively in the contemporary British educational market (Gewirtz *et al*. 1995).

However, ethnicity has consequences for home–school relations that extend beyond differences in cultural capital. Although it is a difficult area for teachers to confront, research suggests that institutional racism still operates within schools (Gillborn and Youdell 2000), while some studies argue that teachers do not always appreciate the cultural conflict existing between schools and minority ethnic families in the context of values, beliefs and behavioural norms (Bastiani 1997). The significance of race is also highlighted through evidence that shows that black working-class mothers feel a greater need to compensate for perceived deficits in state education than their white counterparts. In particular, insufficient attention to both black culture and racism within schools results in many black families sending their children to supplementary schools (Reay and Mirza 1997). Research in both the UK and the US suggests not only that parental involvement is dominated by white middle-class mothers but that at times such mothers operated, perhaps unintentionally, in ways that tended to exclude black mothers (McGrath and Kuriloff 1999).

What can be done?

How do you set up dialogue with parents whose own negative experiences of schooling make contact with teachers difficult? At teachers we belong to a section of society who have largely been successful in education and feel relatively at home in school contexts. It is often difficult to understand why certain groups of parents are disengaged from their children's schooling. The 'common-sense' reaction is to feel that they do not care about their children's education. Yet, all the research evidence points to these parents caring just as much as more privileged, confident parents. Rather, they lack the resources, economic, cultural and psychological, of more socially advantaged parents. What can teachers do then to facilitate fairer, more equitable relations between home and school?

There are no easy answers when it comes to attempting to address the inequalities embedded in parental involvement. Many schools expend lots of effort in making schools more welcoming places for all parents. At the same time, schools have often had to deal with the paradox that facilitating parents' groups and providing space for parents within the school has often exacerbated inequalities of class and race rather than alleviating them. Higher levels of confidence and a greater sense of entitlement contribute to white middle-class parents feeling more at home within schooling than black or white working-class parents, and, as Vincent (2000) has demonstrated, they will tend to dominate parents' groups and associations. As a consequence, extra resourcing to encourage greater involvement will always be taken up disproportionately by them. At a time when educational policy is preoccupied with school effectiveness and school improvement, both ideologies that locate responsibility for change firmly with schools and their staff, I would suggest a need to remember Basil Bernstein's (1970) caution that 'schools cannot compensate for society'. That is not to say that school cannot enact changes that will make a difference, only that the wider social context always impinges in complex ways that are often ignored within both the school effectiveness and the home–school literature.

Practices that make parents genuine partners rather than recipients of any assessment of their child are one way of breaking down boundaries between home and school, while regular information to parents about school policies and teaching methods may make all parents feel they are being consulted. Having a regular time every week when the form tutor or class teacher is available to speak to parents and frequently reminding parents through a newsletter that this is a time they are welcome to raise concerns will not result in a flood of parents who have a history of rarely coming into school. However, it may convince a few that they are entitled to discuss issues that are worrying them with their child's tutor and give the school a more inviting, friendly feel. As McNamara et al. (2000: 482) point out, 'personal contacts meant a great deal to some parents and a single telephone call could be remembered for a long time'. Many predominantly middle-class schools now have informal class telephone lists so that parents can regularly contact each other regarding both social and educational issues. While it is the parents who have been proactive in establishing such networks, schools with predominantly working-class intakes could take the initiative in encouraging their parents to network in similar ways. Alistair Macbeath (1995) suggests that setting up parent–teacher organizations that function at the level of the tutor or class group are less intimidating for white and minority ethnic working-class parents.

Although I recognize that it may be difficult to find the resources, providing support for parents' own learning is often a powerful draw for white and minority ethnic working-class parents. One of the schools in which I carried out research held an afterschool computing club which initially was dominated by children who had access to computers at home. When the staff realized that all these children were ones with the opportunity to develop computing skills at home they targeted children without such opportunities and then arranged for their parents to come and see what the children were learning. As a consequence there is now a parents' computing club which runs solely for parents without computing facilities at home. Such a policy may initially appear incidental to improving parental involvement, but as the headteacher asserts, 'It has made a number of parents we don't normally see in school feel far more at home and that's had a positive impact on their interaction with their children's teachers'.

Conclusion

In this brief overview of the key issues in relation to parents and schooling, I have tried to highlight a range of social justice issues often overlooked in the rhetoric around partnership with parents. Parental involvement continues to be characterized by two fundamental inequalities that are deeply problematic for schools committed to establishing more equitable relationships with their students' families. Home–school relationships both privilege already advantaged parents and reinforce existing power imbalances between teachers and minority ethnic and white working-class parents. However, as I have tried to indicate above, there are many school-based initiatives that seek to address these inequalities, but they are inevitably costly in terms of both resources and teacher time. It is important for teachers to do all they can to combat the problem within existing resource constraints, while remembering Bernstein's dictate that they cannot compensate for society. World-shattering changes in the direction of increased social justice may not come about because teachers are being proactive, but certainly at the level of their own tutor group there is much that individual teachers can contribute towards making dialogue with all their students' parents more equitable and positive.

References

Bagley, C. (1996) Black and white unite or fight? The racialised dimension of schooling and parental choice, *British Educational Research Journal*, 22(4): 569–80.

Ball, S.J. (1998) Big policies/small world: an introduction to international perspectives in education policy, *Comparative Education*, 34(2): 119–30.

Barnard, N. (1999) The challenge of confrontational parents, *Times Educational Supplement*, 23 April.

Bastiani, J. (1997) *Home School Work in Multi-Cultural Settings*. London: David Fulton.

Bernstein, B. (1970) Education cannot compensate for society, *New Society*, 26 February.

Brown, P. (1990) The 'third wave': education and the ideology of parentocracy, *British Journal of Sociology of Education*, 11(1): 65–85.

Cohen, G. (1981) Culture and educational achievement, *Harvard Educational Review*, 51(2): 270–85.

Crozier, G. (2000) *Parents and Schools: Partners or Protagonists?* Stoke on Trent: Trentham Books.

David, M.E. (1993) *Parents, Education and Gender Reform*. Cambridge: Polity Press.

David, M.E., Edwards, R., Hughes, M. and Ribbens, J. (1993) *Mothers and Education: Inside Out? Exploring Family-Education Policy and Experience*. London: Macmillan Press.

Department of Education and Science (DES) (1985) *Better Schools: A White Paper*. London: HMSO.

Department of Education and Science (DES) (1986) *Education Act*. London: HMSO.

Department of Education and Science (DES) (1988) *Education Reform Act*. London: HMSO.

Department of Education and Science (DES) (1991) *The Parent's Charter: You and Your Children's Education*. London: DES.

Department for Education (DfE) (1992) *Choice and Diversity*. London: HMSO.

Department for Education and Employment (DfEE) (1997) *Excellence in Schools*. London: HMSO.

Department for Education and Employment (DfEE) (1998a) *Excellence in Cities*. London: HMSO.

Department for Education and Employment (DfEE) (1998b) *Draft Guidance on Home–School Agreements*. London: DfEE.

Department for Education and Employment (DfEE) (1998c) *Homework Guidelines for Primary/Secondary Schools, Draft Consultation*. London: DfEE.

Edwards, A. and Warin, J. (1999) Parental involvement in raising the achievement of primary school pupils: why bother? *Oxford Review of Education*, 25(3): 325–41.

Gewirtz, S., Ball, S.J. and Bowe, R. (1995) *Markets, Choice and Equity*. Buckingham: Open University Press.

Gillborn, D. and Youdell, D. (2000) *Rationing Education: Policy, Practice, Reform and Equity*. Buckingham: Open University Press.

Halsey, A.H. (ed.) (1972) *Educational Priority, Vol 1: EPA Problems and Policies*. London: HMSO.

Hughes, M., Wikeley, F. and Nash, T. (1994) *Parents and Their Children's Schools*. Oxford: Blackwell.

Jordan, B., Redley, M. and James, S. (1994) *Putting the Family First: Identities, Decisions, Citizenship*. London: UCL Press.

Lareau, A. (1989) *Home Advantage*. London: The Falmer Press.

Macbeath, A. (1989) *Involving Parents: Effective Parent–Teacher Relations*. Oxford: Heinemann Educational.

Macbeath, A. (1995) Partnership between parents and teachers in education, in A. Macbeath, D. McCreath and J. Aitchison (eds) *Collaborate or Compete? Educational Partnerships in a Market Economy*. London: Falmer Press.

McGrath, D.J. and Kuriloff, P.J. (1999) 'They're going to tear the doors off this place': upper-middle class parent school involvement and the educational opportunities of other people's children, *Educational Policy*, 13(5): 603–29.

McNamara, O., Hustler, D., Stronach, I., Rodrigo, M., Beresford, E. and Botcherby, S. (2000) Room to manoeuvre: mobilising the 'active partner' in home–school relations, *British Educational Research Journal*, 26(4): 473–90.

Merttens, R. and Vass, J. (1993) *Partnership in Maths: Parents and Schools*. London: Falmer Press.

Office for Standards in Education (Ofsted) (1994) *Reporting Pupils' Achievements*. London: HMSO.

Office for Standards in Education (Ofsted) (1995) *Guidance on the Inspection of Nursery and Primary Schools*. London: HMSO.

Plowden Committee (1967) *Children and their Primary Schools*. London: HMSO.

Reay, D. (1998) *Class Work: Mothers' Involvement in their Children's Primary Schooling*. London: University College Press.

Reay, D. and Mirza, H. (1997) Genealogies of the margins: researching black supplementary schooling, *British Journal of Sociology of Education*, 18(4): 477–99.

Reynolds, D. and Cuttance, P. (1992) *School Effectiveness: Research, Policy and Practice*. London: Cassell.

Sallis, J. (1991) Home–school contracts: a personal view, *Royal Society of Arts News*, 4: 7.

Sieber, T.R. (1982) The politics of middle class success in an inner-city public school, *Boston University Journal of Education*, 164(1): 30–47.

Topping, K. (1996) The effectiveness of family literacy, in S. Wolfendale and K. Topping (eds) *Family Involvement in Literacy*. London: Cassell.

Vincent, C. (1996) *Parents and Teachers: Power and Participation*. London: Falmer Press.

Vincent, C. (2000) *Including Parents?: Education, Citizenship and Parental Agency*. Buckingham: Open University Press.

Vincent, C. and Warren, S. (2000) Class, race and collective action, in J. Salisbury and S. Riddell (eds) *Gender, Policy and Educational Change: Shifting Agendas in the UK and Europe*. London: Routledge.

Whitty, G., Power, S. and Halpin, D. (1998) *Devolution and Choice in Education: The School, the State and the Market*. Buckingham: Open University Press.

10

Excellence in cities

Meg Maguire and Justin Dillon

Introduction

The majority of new teachers work in urban environments – many in inner cities. What is so special about inner cities? Why is it that they continue to attract the attention of policymakers? Our intention here is to provide an account of and a background to the urban school that is essential in any attempt to understand and 'to improve the education of the urban poor' (Grace 1994: 45). We argue that teaching in inner-city schools offers a particular set of challenges, that these have been constructed over time and that they have fundamental implications for society at large. This challenge has been recognized in a range of contemporary policy innovations which will also be outlined briefly in the second part of what follows.

First, we want to explore what is meant by urban education and in order to do this it is necessary to locate the urban in its historical context. The nineteenth-century modern industrial form was distinguished by a 'great movement of population from the land to the towns, from village to factory' (Hall 1977: 8). During the century, a developing awareness of the brutalization and inhumanity of urban life and the oppression of the industrialized factory system 'pointed clearly to the limits of the market as a mechanism for "invisibly" securing the greatest good for the greatest number' (Hall 1977: 8). It was recognized that some form of political intervention was essential; issues of urban sanitation, the amelioration of poverty, disease and child labour were all regarded as critical causes for social improvement. Education was not initially regarded as a fundamental concern. Gradually it was recognized that some form of basic schooling needed to be provided by the state. This idea was based on two main justifications. First, the urban masses needed some form of minimal literacy to sustain the growth and expansion of capital. Educational provision in other European (competitor) nations was far in advance. An uneducated mass workforce was no longer economically viable. Second, and just as important, it was recognized that an unruly inner-city 'mob' had the potential for revolution (as had been the case in France). Thus, as Hall (1977: 9) puts it, while the cities had to be improved, they also had to be controlled and 'civilized'.

> Some way had to be found to create, within the ranks of the urban-industrial masses, an inner attachment to society's goals, a positive commitment to the social order. Respectability, thrift, sobriety, self-discipline were required, to form – as it were from inside – an impulse, a 'formed sentiment', among the masses to adapt to the logic, rationale and mores of industrial capitalism. Thus, education took its place, alongside chapel, tract, self-improving societies, temperance movements, improving popular fiction, as a major cultural force reshaping the inner sentiments and aspirations of the masses. Like other missionary crusades, it was only a partial success.

The urban schools, the old elementary schools, whose wonderful buildings are still present in our cities, were set up specifically to school the urban working class. They were set up to 'gentle' the masses but not to 'gentrify' them. Their curriculum was basic and their intention straightforward enough. Schooling was used, as it still is, to reproduce society; education distributes life chances and education legitimates 'failure'. After all, if everyone has the opportunity to succeed in a meritocratic system, then 'failure' can be individually constituted. Throughout the first half of the twentieth century, a pattern of limited provision persisted. A small minority of working-class people climbed the ladder of success. As one of this small group recalls:

> In practice the school unconsciously orientated its teaching to the exceptions among us . . . who were going to be lifted up into a higher social class. How many of these? That was the point . . . Always the pride that prevailed in this working class school was that it succeeded in turning out less recruits for the working class than any other of its kind in the district. That less was still the majority, mind you . . . but the school's official boast was not of them.
>
> (Common 1951, cited in Hargreaves 1982: 75–6)

The majority of working-class youngsters were not so 'successful'. In many ways, their compulsory schooling – for education it was not – seemed almost irrelevant. When work was plentiful, educational achievement was not important; when work was scarce, education was used to keep them off the streets (the compulsory dole schools of the late 1920s and early 1930s, forerunners, perhaps, of current youth 'training' projects such as the New Deal). The coercion to attend school was not always met in a compliant way. Grace has recorded some incidents of schoolroom life in the nineteenth century which do not seem so distant from contemporary experiences:

> I had occasion to punish a boy slightly this morning: he swore most horribly and rushed from the school . . . I was suddenly startled by a

large stone passing my ear. I got out of the reach of stones thrown through the window and continued the lesson.

(Grace 1978: 32)

Compare that with:

Paper planes, knobs of chewing gum and once a gravel filled condom (apparently looted empty from a pastoral studies class) just miss my head as I attempt to write a French irregular verb on a ravaged black-board pitted with holes.

(Owen 1990)

Inner-city schools have *always* served a distinct section of society; the working-class urban poor. Their schools 'in and around the inner city stand' as 'beacons and landmarks of working class education' (Hall 1977: 11). In contrast, the privileged schools have in the main remained out-side the city, while in the city, some grammar schools have developed in either the middle-class suburbs or within middle-class areas of urban gentrification. As Hall (1977: 11) presciently put it:

there has never been, in England, anything remotely approaching a 'common' or 'comprehensive' school experience for all classes of chil-dren. Each kind of school has been absorbed into its socio-geographic segment, and taken on something of that imprint.

Some 'urban' issues have persisted over time. What sort of education should be on offer in our inner-city schools? Is the current curriculum, at which so many have persistently 'failed,' an appropriate offer? If some children were to be offered a different curriculum, what would this do for their chances? Do teachers (mainly white middle-class) hold reduced aspirations and expectations of working-class and minority children? What can be done to support and motivate inner-city young people in the current situation of high youth unemployment? What can be done to ensure that New Labour's vision of an inclusive society is achieved so that, in the words of Tony Blair (1997: 4), we become 'one nation, in which each citizen is valued and has a stake; in which no one is excluded from opportunity and the chance to develop their potential; in which we make it, once more, our national purpose to tackle social division and inequality'?

The contemporary city

It is now argued that if post-war Britain was characterized by profitable manufacturing industries providing high levels of employment and good salaries, homes, health and schooling for its citizens, then Britain in the twenty-first century is undergoing the trauma of deindustrialization. Manu-facturing jobs have declined. Employment is becoming fragmented by short-term contracting and by a move to part-time rather than full-time jobs. However, deindustrialization does not occur in a uniform manner or in isolation from other structures. Regions and cities experience its effects differentially (Ball *et al.* 2000). Some cities have experienced significant overall decline while others have experienced localized outer-city growth set alongside inner-city decay. Particular communities have experienced the differential effects of post-Fordist labour market restructurings. For example, a Labour Force Survey has estimated that 62 per cent of black young men in London were unemployed as contrasted with 20 per cent of white men in the same age cohort (TUC 1995).

Thus the urban setting makes visible some of the fundamental contradictions within the wider society (Grace 1978: 3). In London, the impact of deindustrialization is significant. From the city business zone which contains empty office buildings through Docklands, where investments have been made in bricks and mortar with almost no job creation for local people, to areas of new settlement like Tower Hamlets or Stoke Newington; from housing ghettos like Thamesmead, with no local amenities for recreation to gentrified housing locales such as parts of Islington and Hackney, the poorest live across the road from some of the richest in the country. Maden (1996) has argued that this polarization was exacerbated by post-war urban planning through which skilled workers were resettled in new towns and greenfield developments outside metropolitan areas; what Newsam (1996) has described as the 'planned dereliction of the inner city'.

Hutton (1995) has characterized the UK as the 'thirty, thirty, forty society' where the bottom 60 per cent are 'disadvantaged', 'marginalized' and 'insecure'. He describes a society where 'segmentation of the labour market . . . is sculpting the new and ugly shape of British society' (Hutton 1995: 108). He underlines the fact that more than half of the people in the UK are 'living either on poverty incomes or in conditions of permanent stress and insecurity' and so it has been much harder to sustain relationships, let alone parent children adequately in contemporary society.

While these conditions are not unique to urban settings, it is in inner cities where the highest concentrations of the marginalized and dispossessed are to be found (Davies 1998; Rutter and Jones 1998). Between 1981 and 1991 'the degree, intensity and extent of poverty increased markedly in inner London and other large metropolitan areas' (Maden 1996: 20) and 'in the list of England's thirty most deprived areas, all inner London boroughs are there' (Maden 1996: 21). Six London boroughs are listed in the worst 10 areas of deprivation in the UK – where deprivation is measured in relation to employment, housing, education credentials, race, crime, lone caring, and so on. London thus provides a cockpit in which to view, in a concentrated manner, many of the inequities of contemporary policy-making writ large (Grace 1978).

Welfare spending and the 'culture of contentment'

It has sometimes been argued that as deindustrialization has impacted on western societies in consequence of global capitalism, individual nation-states are unable to resist this change. However, western democratic capital states do have some options at their disposal. One of these is in relation to social welfare spending for the public good (Whitty *et al.* 1998). In the UK, successive governments have dealt with the economic shifts of deindustrialization through appropriating a neo-liberal ideology which has underpinned social and economic policy until relatively recently.

Essentially there has been a massive disruption in national ethics and values, an attempt to shift from 'a culture of commitment to relative public good to a defence of relative private interest' (Grace 1994: 53). Grace argues that this shift is characterized by the reification of private and individualized self-interest. For some time, a belief in the 'justice' inherent in a meritocratic society has been asserted. If an individual has achieved in school for example, the acquisition of this cultural capital is regarded as an individual asset that can be exchanged for material advancement. For example, the traditional elite higher educational system (as opposed to the 'new' universities) which richly rewards its students with access to higher salaries (and 'satisfying' careers as opposed to tedious jobs) is paid for by the majority and provides for (in the main) a rich and powerful elite who justify their claim to privilege, and low cost higher education, on the basis of merit.

At the same time a powerful constituency, which Galbraith (1992) has called the 'contented electoral majority' or the 'culture of contentment' actively resists the 'burden' of redistributive taxation. Individuals have the right to hold onto as much of their money as possible, it is argued, while ensuring that they maximize their capacity to access state provisions – health, welfare and education. This can be done through moving house to access a good state school, or activating cultural capital to interview successfully and obtain a place in a suburban selective school (see Rosen 1996). All these individual measures are less available to inner-city working-class families. As Grace (1994: 46) says, the constituency of contentment contains within itself a 'relative unwillingness to look at longer term social, economic, or environmental planning, if these threaten present contentment'. With Grace, we believe that it is the urban poor who are on the losing side of this value shift and it is to their education that we now turn.

Schooling in the city

As long ago as 1991, the HMI recognized the distinctiveness of inner-city schools where 'a higher than average proportion of pupils were disadvantaged'. They acknowledged the 'extra challenge' of teaching in the city, particularly London, and highlighted a number of professional dimensions which they believed to be particularly relevant to teaching in urban schools. These were: multicultural education; language development, including English as an additional language (EAL); class management, behavioural problems and absenteeism; low expectations and achievement (HMI 1991). However, we would want to suggest that all this exemplifies a 'problem' or 'deficit' approach which neatly hides the structural underpinnings that support and frame urban disadvantage. So it is the family who does not value education that is to blame for its own 'failure to succeed' (see also Chapter 9).

In many ways urban schooling has always been mythologized through individualized 'deficit' rather than structural disadvantage. Our initial examples of dissent and disruption capture the sense of crisis and panic that surrounds the inner-city school. 'Inner-city' does not mean the gracious boys' grammar school set well in the heart of the city – simply, it stands as a signifier for the schools that are attended by black and white working-class 'difficult and disruptive' children. Therefore the 'solution' has frequently been to improve these schools, through tactics like the effective schools movement, specific strategies such as 'assertive discipline', the use of 'positive role models' or to close them down. These tactics have not significantly impacted on inner-city schools. As Grace (1994) has argued, what is needed is a stronger conceptualization than one of mere 'deficit' as well as the political will to tackle structural disadvantage.

As we have already argued, the most drastic effects of deindustrialization, recession and social restructuring, such as cutbacks in social welfare, housing and health, have been disproportionately experienced by those who are most vulnerable: the unemployed, the single parent, the refugee, the recent migrant. Children who go to school 'in the most economically deprived areas of the inner cities will be faced with declining resources, a scarcity of experienced teachers, poorer plant facilities, reduced educational support, and in some cases their local school will close' (Ball 1990: 99). In the 'culture of contentment' who will defend these schools, now often constructed as 'failing' or 'underachieving' schools? Who will want to teach in them? Whose children will attend them?

Some schools serve a community composed mostly of recent migrants and refugees who may well still be traumatized by their experiences. Other schools serve the needs of one local community, perhaps white working-class or British Bengali. The range of differences and the range of needs is enormous, yet patterns of inequality persist and have become reinforced by the social policies of the 1980s and 1990s. For example, parental choice at primary/secondary transition has not yet delivered school improvement. In the inner city, choice becomes a subtle form of 'discriminatory sorting' (Moore and Davenport 1990: 221). It is worth quoting Maden (1996: 22) at length in relation to this issue.

> Peter Newsam has shown how secondary schools in the inner London area have increasingly moved beyond a simple first and second class division to a much more hierarchical and qualitatively polarised system. In his analysis, over three quarters of children in the top 25 per cent of the ability range are now in half the available schools, including the selective independent schools (which represent a third of this favoured half). The other half represents schools which contain very few and sometimes no pupils who are in the top 25 per cent of the ability range. These are best classified as 'other' and 'secondary modern' schools and, as Sir Peter comments 'such schools are no more failed comprehensives than a Brussels sprout is a failed cabbage'. Over half of inner London's secondary age pupils are in such schools.

In a small study of classroom life in London urban primary schools (Pratt and Maguire 1996) teachers reported a wide range of difficulties. They argued that non-attendance at school was sometimes caused by factors such as family difficulties or illness due to poor housing conditions. They stated that inadequate sleeping facilities and overcrowding resulted in tired children who came late for school. Lack of money at home resulted in children coming to school hungry. 'A child comes to school having slept ten to a damp room with no breakfast, telling me the electricity has been cut off and petrol poured through the letter box. How would you feel? Could you concentrate on learning?' (teacher cited in Pratt and Maguire 1996: 24).

The teachers did make positive suggestions that could help resolve some of the difficulties resulting from home circumstances, for example, providing breakfast facilities in schools. They suggested strategies to support parents and local communities – all of which had resource implications. Teachers believed overwhelmingly that the main work needed to be done through improved government policies on education, employment, housing and health: 'Deprived areas need more resources' as one teacher said.

What to do?

The school effectiveness research highlights the key attributes of a 'good' school which, it is argued, can be reproduced elsewhere. In this way it is possible to 'blame' individual schools for their failure to succeed (where success is measured in relation to GCSEs obtained or scores in the national tests – see Chapters 3, 5 and 9). However, there are some contradictions involved in relation to urban schools.

> Inevitably however, any school improvement that takes place is likely to benefit those from advantaged families – those better able to make use of the new opportunities – more than those from families which are facing difficulties ... Thus, though overall national standards may rise, the difference between the most and the least advantaged will probably also increase.
>
> (Mortimore 1995: 17)

In addition, less attractive poorer areas in the inner cities may find it harder to attract and retain teachers. Indeed, in October 2000, it was reported in the national press that two inner-city schools had to offer a four day week as a consequence of staff shortages (*Times Educational Supplement*, 6 October 2000). Schools in suburban settings or middle-class urban enclaves are able to draw on parental financial support in a way that is closed to urban schools. 'Those living in the inner cities may increasingly become the only groups in society receiving merely the basic state provision' (Whitty 1990: 113).

These dilemmas have been recognized by Tony Blair's New Labour government who have set themselves the goal of national renewal where 'the power of the market is harnessed to serve the public interest' (Blair 1998:

7). While there is not enough space here to do justice to the project of the Third Way, essentially it is an attempt to 'balance economic realities against social justice in a world in which the old-style welfare state is no longer sustainable or necessarily desirable' (Bullen *et al.* 2000: 442). Specifically in relation to inner cities, two major projects have been designed to tackle disadvantage and spur social inclusion. These are the Education Action Zone (EAZ) projects and the Excellence in Cities initiative. The Labour government also pledged to transform inner-city schooling through the provision of city academies, which will partly be privately funded and will have greater freedoms than other schools in relation to the curriculum and staffing. The first academies are due to open in September 2001.

EAZs were set up in 1997 (DfEE 1997) in order to raise standards in areas of high disadvantage through drawing on the expertise and funding of local businesses in partnerships with schools. The government invited interested groups to bid for matched funding in order to support their proposals. Successful partnerships then started to set up breakfast clubs and homework support classes. Some EAZs focused on ICT skills and management training. Others worked on core skills and 14–19 transitions. Initially some schools were reluctant to bid for EAZ money. Concerns were expressed that education was drifting away from being a welfare provision, towards becoming a profit-making concern for the business partners (Hatcher 1998). Other concerns were expressed: those who have made successful bids might not be in the most needy areas – they may simply be the best consortia at preparing and writing the bids. However, it is still too early to assess the success or otherwise of this initiative (Jones and Bird 2000 – but see Hatcher and Le Blond 2000).

Excellence in Cities (DfEE 1999) has been far more focused and specific in its intentions. The strategy has specified six large conurbations – London, Birmingham, Manchester, Liverpool, Leeds and Sheffield – where a wide range of tactics will be deployed. These include some new and smaller EAZs as well as a commitment to provide a learning mentor for 'every young person who needs one, as a single point of contact to tackle barriers to pupils' learning' (DfEE 1999: 3). There is an emphasis on literacy and numeracy skills, a network of learning centres and a strengthening of school leadership. Again, while it is impossible to fully describe this initiative, it is useful to highlight some of the distinctive features of this strategy compared with the EAZs. Whitty (2000) has argued that one of the potential strengths in Excellence in Cities is that it is attempting to include *all* children in its remit. Thus tactics such as streaming and extending opportunities for gifted and talented children might work to keep middle-class families and their children in city schools. It may be that this social mix will enhance school success for all and stem the (middle-class) flight from public provision of schooling. Time will tell.

Urban schools and trainee teachers

In conclusion we want to make two main points in relation to the contemporary reforms of teacher education as these have specific impact on the inner-city experience (see Chapter 6 for a discussion of recent reforms in teacher education). If trainee teachers are spending the majority of their time in schools, coping and surviving in difficult circumstances, without much more than a cursory appreciation of the urban context, it may well be that they 'blame' their school students for the difficulties they face in their teaching (which could indirectly contribute towards low expectations and achievement). 'The urban poor, however they are constituted in ethnic, gender or class terms in various societies, and wherever they are located, are a challenge to established institutions' (Grace 1994: 45). This 'challenge' is not always easy for teachers to manage but perhaps more importantly, without any knowledge or theoretical exploration of the urban context, it is perhaps understandable that some schools may 'blame' the students for the disruptions they sometimes pose.

Perhaps the most intractable and contradictory dilemma that faces teachers in the inner city is the paradox of recognizing the social and material realities in which the school is placed, while at the same time ensuring that aspirations and expectations are not reduced by these challenges. But the greatest challenge lies beyond individual and localized responses:

> Adequate human and material resources are fundamental to the renaissance of effectiveness and of hope in urban education. Only those who have not taught in the inner city assert otherwise. With such resources the capacity of urban schools to respond to the new informational economy and its consequences could be greatly enhanced. The children, youth and adults of the inner city and of other deprived urban locations could realise the skill and knowledge capacities which they undoubtedly have.
>
> (Grace 1994: 52)

It is still too early to assess the impact of recent innovations such as the Education Action Zones and the major policy thrust on inner-city education in Excellence in Cities. The government has argued that 'an individual's educational opportunities should not depend solely on the school they happen to attend' (DfEE 1999: 27) and that their 'mission is to bring about a step-change in standards in the inner city' (DfEE 1999: 2). Our fears are that without a strong multiagency response to alleviate childhood poverty or without the long-term commitment of resources, we may still continue to do more to 'express regret than we have [done] to resolve the problems of our inner city schools' (DfEE 1999: 4).

References

Ball., S.J. (1990) Markets and ERA, *The Urban Review: Issues and Ideas in Public Education*, 22(2): 85–99.

Ball, S.J., Maguire, M. and Macrae, S. (2000) *Choice, Pathways and Transitions Post 16. New Youth, New Economies in the Global City*. London: Routledge Falmer.

Blair, T. (1997) Bringing Britain Together. 8 December (URL; http://www.cabinet-office.gov.uk/seu/index/more.html).

Blair, T. (1998) *The Third Way: New Politics for the New Century*. London: The Fabian Society.

Bullen, E., Kenway, J. and Hey, V. (2000) New Labour, social exclusion and educational risk management: the case of 'gymslip mums', *British Educational Research Journal*, 26(4): 441–56.

Common, J. (1951) *Kiddar's Luck*. London: Turnpike Press.

Davies, N. (1998) *Dark Heart*. London: Vintage.

Department for Education and Employment (DfEE) (1997) *Excellence in Schools*, Cmnd 3681. London: HMSO.

Department for Education and Employment (DfEE) (1999) *Excellence in Cities*. Nottingham: DfEE.

Galbraith, J.K. (1992) *The Culture of Contentment*. London: Sinclair-Stevenson.

Grace, G. (1978) *Teachers, Ideology and Control*. London: Routledge and Kegan Paul.

Grace, G. (1994) Urban education and the culture of contentment: the politics, culture and economics of inner-city schooling, in N.P. Stronquist (ed.) *Education in Urban Areas: Cross-National Dimensions*. London: Praeger.

Hall, S. (1977) Education and the crisis of the urban school, in J. Raynor and E. Harris (eds) *Schooling the City*. Glasgow: Ward Lock in association with The Open University.

Hargreaves, D. (1982) *The Challenge for the Comprehensive School: Culture, Curriculum and Community*. London: Routledge and Kegan Paul.

Hatcher, R. (1998) Profiting from schools: business and Education Action Zones, *Education and Social Justice*, 1: 9–16.

Hatcher, R. and Le Blond, D. (2000) Education Action Zones and Zones d'Education Prioritaires. Conference paper, European Conference on Educational Research, University of Edinburgh, 20–23 September.

Her Majety's Inspectorate (HMI) (1991) *Training Teachers for Inner City Schools*. London: HMSO.

Hutton, W. (1995) *The State We're In*. London: Jonathan Cape.

Jones, K. and Bird, K. (2000) 'Partnership' as strategy: public–private relations in Education Action Zones, *British Educational Research Journal*, 26(4): 491–506.

Maden, M. (1996) Divided cities: 'dwellers in different zones, inhabitants of different planets'. The TES/Greenwich Education Lecture 1996. London: University of Greenwich and The Times Educational Supplement.

Moore, D. and Davenport, S. (1990) Choice: the new improved sorting machine, in W.L. Boyd and H.J. Halberg (eds) *Choice in Education: Potential and Problems*. Berkeley, CA: McCutchan.

Mortimore, P. (1995) Better than excuses, *Times Educational Supplement*, 7 July.

Newsam, P. (1996) Take the terminology to task, *Times Educational Supplement*, 22 March.

Owen, M. (1990) School for scandal, *The Guardian*, 1 May.

Pratt S. and Maguire, M. (1996) Inner city children and their schooling, *Primary Teaching Studies*, 9(2): 22–8.

Rosen, M. (1996) The old school lie, *New Statesman*, 26 January.

Rutter, J. and Jones, C. (eds) (1998) *Refugee Education: Mapping the Field*. Stoke: Trentham Books.

Trades Union Congress (TUC) (1995) *Young People in the Labour Market in 1995*. Report prepared for the 1995 Youth Conference. London: TUC.

Whitty, G. (1990) Creeping privatization and its implications for schooling in the inner city, *The Urban Review*, 22(2): 101–13.

Whitty, G., Power, S. and Halpin, D. (1998) *Devolution and Choice in Education*. Buckingham: Open University Press.

Whitty, G. (2000) Education, exclusion and social class. Seminar Paper. Annual Seminar of the Centre for Public Policy Research. Education Policy and Social Class. King's College London. 12 July.

Further reading

Gewirtz, S., Ball, S.J. and Bowe, R. (1995) *Markets, Choice and Equity in Education.* Buckingham: Open University Press.

Grace, G. (1984) *Education and the City: Theory, History and Contemporary Practice.* London: Routledge and Kegan Paul.

11

Teachers and the law

Dylan Wiliam

Sources of law

There are two main sources of law in England and Wales: statute law and common law. Statute law is created by Parliament when it passes acts like the 1988 Education Reform Act. Common law, on the other hand has been built up over the centuries from tradition. A teacher's responsibility for children (and by extension that of a student teacher) derives largely from common law, not statute law. The crucial part of this responsibility is the notion of a *duty of care*.

Everyone has a duty of care to everyone else. If a person runs down a busy street and knocks someone over causing injury, that person might well be held liable in a court of law for the injury caused. However, this general duty of care extends only to what one does, rather than what one does not do. If someone has been knocked over in the street, a passerby has no obligation to help the injured person.

However, the role of teachers (and student teachers) in school is different, because they have taken on what is called a 'special relationship' in respect of the children in the school. If a child is hurt in the school playground, teachers have a duty to help the child because of the special relationship. Being in a special relationship with someone else places a duty of care that includes what one does not do (acts of omission) as well as what one does (acts of commission).

Whether a special relationship exists or not depends on what a person professes to be, rather than what they are. So for example, if someone says 'Let me through, I'm a doctor' in a crowd of people surrounding a person injured in a road traffic accident, that person assumes a special relationship with the injured person, whether they are, in fact, a doctor or not, and is responsible for what they do not do as well as what they do.

A student teacher taking a class is also responsible for acts of omission as well as commission because the student is implicitly assuming a special relationship with the individuals in that class. A qualified teacher from another school who happened to be visiting, however, would only be responsible for what they did, because they have no such special relationship (that is to say, they are not there as a teacher).

The interpretation of particular laws, whether derived from common law, or brought about by statute, is built up over time by referring to what has been determined in similar cases in the past. This is *case law*. The 'ground rules' of case law are that if a higher court decides a case in a particular way then a lower court must follow that ruling and any court at the same level should have regard to it, but a higher court does not have to. So, for example, the High Court would have to follow a ruling decided by the Court of Appeal, but the House of Lords does not. A selection of the most important cases relating to the teacher's role is included at the end of this chapter.

There is a third kind of law called 'delegated legislation'. This is a means by which an Act of Parliament does not specify the details of the legislation, but instead grants powers to some other person or organization to specify the details of the law. For example, the part of the 1988 Education Reform Act that relates to the National Curriculum covers only three pages. The National Curriculum is brought into being by a statement in section 4 of the Act which states that 'The Secretary of State may by order specify in relation to each of the foundation subjects such attainment targets, such programmes of study and such assessment arrangements as he considers appropriate for that subject'. That is all that is in the Act, but it grants power to somebody else to make law. In this case, it is the Secretary of State for Education, who, by signing his or her name to an Order, makes it statutory.

The reason for such 'delegated' legislation is very sensible. For example, teachers' pay is revised every year. The framework for this process is established in statute law but without some mechanism for delegated legislation, the actual details would have to be dealt with by Parliament every year, taking up parliamentary time.

What is very disturbing is the number of such legal powers that have been given to secretaries of state. The 1988 Education Reform Act, for example, gave over *200* new powers to the Secretary of State to make statutory regulations and orders. As a consequence, it is very difficult to keep up with the current state of the law. Furthermore, the speed and lack of opportunity to debate and examine legislation before it becomes law in recent years means that the regulations that are made are sometimes flawed. For example, the Education (School Performance Indicators) regulations which were published in August 1993 contained three substantial errors, which had to be rectified by publishing the Education (School Performance Indicators) No. 2 regulations!

The good news for beginning teachers is that hardly any of the recent legislation (more acts in the last 10 years than in the previous 50) impacts directly on the classroom teacher. The impact of almost all recent educational legislation has been at a management or a policy level. The task of the ordinary teacher is to carry out any reasonable instruction from the headteacher (this is a part of teachers' standard conditions of service in state schools; in independent schools, conditions are laid down by the governors or equivalent, but invariably include such a requirement). Even where certain tasks are not necessary in law, if it is a reasonable instruction, then it is part of a teacher's contractual duty to carry it out. If a teacher is given an instruction that she or he considers unreasonable, then they could, of course, refuse to carry it out, but they would risk being formally disciplined, either by the headteacher or the governors of the school. Because of this, a teacher's job really comes down to two things: carrying out the headteacher's instructions, and discharging a duty of care to the pupils in the school.

Duty of care

The earliest definition of what a duty of care might mean in the context of schools and teaching was established in Williams v Eady: 'The duty of a schoolmaster is to take such care of his boys as a careful father would take of his son'. This creates the clear impression that there were neither girls nor female schoolteachers around in these days, but then it is a very old judgement (1893). That was the earliest definition of what exactly that duty of care amounted to in the educational setting – a careful father. Over the intervening years – and certainly over the past 50 years – the duty of care has been interpreted more precisely. That is the strength of common law established through case law: as public perceptions change, interpretations of the law can shift, without changing the 'letter' of the law.

In September 1993, for example, a schoolteacher was suspended for sticking masking tape over a pupil's mouth. Now, that in itself is not surprising because local authorities have the power to suspend people for a range of disciplinary offences, very few of which relate to the law. What was unusual in this case is that the police were involved, because in the past, they have been rather unwilling to act unless the level of harm to the child was relatively serious. Such action would certainly not have been regarded as a matter for the police (or probably even the education authority) in 1893.

In 1938 the notion of a careful parent was reaffirmed in a judgement that held that 'the courts [would] not put on the headmaster [sic] any higher standard of care than that of a reasonably careful parent'. However, two decades later the requirement had shifted somewhat. Because of the way that case law is built up (as described above), the central notion of a reasonable, prudent or careful parent cannot be overturned, but more recent judgements have provided a gloss on the original judgement. By 1962, the common law duty of a schoolmaster [sic] is held to be that

> of a prudent parent bound to take notice of boys [sic] and their tendency to do mischievous acts, not in the context of home but in the circumstances of school life, and extends not only to how pupils conduct themselves but also to the state and condition of the school premises.

There is an implication here that there are more risks at school than at home and therefore a teacher needs to be aware, and take account, of this. In 1968, it was held that

> it is a headmaster's duty, bearing in mind the propensities of boys and girls [at last!] between the ages of 11 and 18 to take all reasonable and proper steps to prevent any of the pupils under his care from suffering injury from inanimate objects, from actions of their fellow pupils or from a combination of both.

So while the *standard* of care required is the same for teachers and for parents, teachers are expected to take account of the special circumstances pertaining in school in discharging this duty.

The same standard of duty of care applies to student teachers, but the law does recognize that by virtue of their lack of training and experience, they are less able than their colleagues to anticipate events and to take appropriate action. If while a student is teaching a class, something goes wrong and their inexperience leads to a pupil being injured, it could well be the case that the student would not be found negligent whereas an experienced teacher acting in exactly the same way could be. While teachers are in training the law does not expect as much as it does when they are qualified, provided, of course, that they do exercise an appropriate level of responsibility.

Negligence

In practice, most court cases relating to duty of care come under the general heading of negligence. To prove negligence one has to establish that there was a duty of care, that it was breached, that there was damage, that the breach caused the damage, and that the damage was reasonably foreseeable. The last of these has been very important in the past. In 1984 a pupil brought an action against a teacher who had tackled the boy round the neck in a 'staff vs students' rugby game, causing the boy severe injuries. The teacher was found to have been negligent because the court held that it *was* reasonably foreseeable that a 14-stone teacher tackling an eight-stone pupil around the neck would cause injury. As a result, the boy was awarded substantial damages. These were paid by the local education authority (LEA), because although it was the teacher and the school who were actually being taken to court, all local education authorities are exposed to what is known as *vicarious liability* as regards the negligence of their employees. Even if a teacher has acted against local authority guidance, the authority can still be liable, and since they tend to have more money that most teachers, most actions are brought against the LEA in addition to the school or an individual teacher.

However, as can be seen from the dates of the important cases relating to negligence, actions against schools and teachers are rare. Very few actions actually reach the courts. In this sense, teaching is not a 'high-risk' activity (unlike medicine where malpractice suits are much more common). It is important to remember that most teachers never find themselves accused of anything in their whole teaching career. However, it is also important to know what one's professional duties are.

Of the responses that a teacher can make to claims of negligence, the two most important are a) that there was no breach of duty, or b) that what happened would have happened anyway. For example, if one pupil suffers injury as the result of an assault from another pupil during morning break would the school be held to be negligent? If the attack was unpredictable or completely unexpected, then it is likely that an action for negligence would not succeed – the courts have always held that something that would not have been prevented had there been supervision is not negligence. However, if the attacker was known by the school to be a bully and given to random and unprovoked attacks, then an action for negligence could well succeed, especially if teachers who should have been on duty at break time were not at their allotted posts.

Another response to an action for negligence is illustrated by the following case. A primary school teacher was going to take two young girls out, and had them dressed ready to go when another child came along with a cut hand. The teacher attended to the child with the cut hand during which time one of the two other little children ran out of the school gates and into the road. The driver of a passing car swerved to avoid the child and was killed. The family of the driver sued the teacher and the LEA for negligence. In this case, the teacher was found *not* to be negligent, because the court held that the teacher had behaved reasonably in dealing with the injury to the other child first. The fact that a teacher is distracted by a more serious or urgent incident is a defence. Although the law places a higher burden on the teacher than on the proverbial person 'on the Clapham omnibus', it still only requires that the teacher behaves reasonably in the circumstances. But even in this judgement, the court was careful to point out that the ruling depended on the fact that it was an *infant* child with a cut hand. A 15-year-old with the same small cut would probably not be grounds for leaving younger children alone, and an action against whoever left the school gates open so that the child could run out into the road might still succeed. The important message here is that the law only requires you to act reasonably – provided you do so, you won't be held liable.

The criterion of reasonableness also governs whether student teachers can teach classes without a qualified teacher present. It would probably not be held to be reasonable to leave a student on her or his own with a class during the first week of teaching practice. A court might also hold that it was unreasonable to leave a teacher on her or his own with a class known to be particularly difficult even towards the end of teaching practice. However, it is widely accepted that there are times when student teachers have to be left alone in the classroom to establish that they can manage a class effectively. The courts have generally followed the principle that the test of what is reasonable in ordinary, everyday affairs may well be answered by experience arising from 'practice adopted generally and followed successfully for many years' (Wright v Cheshire County Council [1952] All ER 789).

Sanctions

The most important remaining aspects of educational law – or at least the ones that everybody seems to want to know about – are sanctions: discipline, confiscation, punishments and such matters. Can a teacher confiscate cigarettes from a pupil? The important thing about confiscation is that one must not permanently deprive someone of something – that is theft. So confiscating cigarettes from a pupil may be quite reasonable, but smoking them oneself later is not.

The duty of care also plays a part here, however. If, for example, one discovered that a student had a flick-knife, which was subsequently used to injure another pupil, it is quite possible that one would be found negligent if one had *not* tried to confiscate it, or at least reported the matter to someone else (because of the responsibility for omission as well as commission in a special relationship, and one's duty of care to all the pupils at a school).

Most schools have a procedure laid down for what to do with confiscated items. Personal stereos might be kept in the headteacher's office until the end of the day and then returned, cigarettes might be returned only to parents, and flick-knives would probably be handed over to the police. The important thing here is to find out what your school's policy is and follow that.

The same applies to detention. Section 550A of the 1996 Education Act clarified the existing case law that a school may detain pupils after school whether the parents approve of this or not, provided 24 hours' notice has been given. Since this period of 24 hours starts when the parents receive the notice, this means, in effect, that a detention notified on Monday cannot take place until Wednesday. However, the important point is that all teachers at a school must follow the school's policy on detention. Find out what it is, and stick to it.

Use of physical force

The use of physical force is again covered by common law. In simple terms, the use of reasonable force is permissible to prevent a pupil causing injury to themselves or to others, and to prevent damage to property. However, Section 550A of the 1996 Education Act allows teachers, and others authorized by the headteacher of a school to have control of pupils, to use reasonable physical force to restraining a pupil when a pupil is:

- committing a criminal offence (including behaving in a way that would be an offence if the pupil were not under the age of criminal responsibility);
- injuring themselves or others;
- causing damage to property (including the pupil's own property);
- engaging in any behaviour prejudicial to maintaining good order and discipline at the school or among any of its pupils, whether that behaviour occurs in a classroom during a teaching session or elsewhere.

The first three of these derive from common law, but the fourth is a specific power available to teachers, and whoever in a school the head-teacher authorizes to be 'in control' of students. Whether these additional powers apply to student teachers in a school depends on whether the headteacher has included student teachers in the list of those author-ized to be in control of pupils. As with all these issues, it is essential to find out what the school's policy is. It is also important to remember that the definition of 'reasonable' in this context is that it is the minimum force necessary to achieve what is required. Even for an experienced teacher, a good rule of thumb is never to touch a pupil in anger.

The courts have also held that schools' supervision of pupils extends to the pupils' journey to and from school. This principle was reinforced in a ruling concerning the case of two boys who were caught smoking on the way to school and were caned (this was before the use of corporal punish-ment in schools was banned). One of the parents took action against the school but the court decided that from the moment that the pupils left home, then they were under the school's jurisdiction, and could be pun-ished for deeds committed on the way to and from school.

Corporal punishment

Until relatively recently, the law regarding corporal punishment treated teachers looking after students in the same way as a parent. The teacher was *in loco parentis* or 'in the place of the parent'. Common law in Eng-land and Wales condones a parent hitting a child as 'proper chastisement' provided it is not excessive, although this may well change as a result of European legislation and the adoption of the Convention on Human Rights.

The first definition of what was reasonable in terms of corporal punish-ment in schools was given in 1860: 'Punishment must be reasonable and moderate and not for the gratification of passion or rage or excessive in its nature or degree or protracted beyond the child's endurance'.

Until 1986, decisions regarding corporal punishment in state schools were delegated to local education authorities. Some LEAs had banned all corporal punishment; those that had not were required to set up proced-ures for administering corporal punishment. For example, in most schools only a small number of teachers were allowed to administer corporal punishment and it had to be entered into a punishment book. It is im-portant to remember, however, that even in schools that allowed the use of corporal punishment, the kind of 'clipping across the ear' that used to happen informally was probably illegal, and certainly a breach of the teacher's contract. As far as most teachers were concerned, the changes made in 1986 did not change the position of individual teachers with respect to corporal punishment, but only whether one could send a pupil to somebody else to be beaten.

The change in the law came because two Scottish parents wanted the right to exempt their children from corporal punishment in school. Hav-ing lost their case at every level of the domestic legal system the action went before the European Court of Human Rights where the judgement was overturned. The British government's original response was to allow a situation in which individual parents had the right to withdraw their children from corporal punishment. There was a great deal of concern that this would create a situation in which two students guilty of exactly the same offence in school might receive very different punishments because of what their parents had said. For this reason, sections banning the use of corporal punishments in state schools were tagged onto the end of the 1986 Education (no 2) Act – an act largely concerned with the governance of schools – which happened to be going through Parliament at the time.

Defamation

Most people are familiar with the distinction between slander and libel. Defamatory speech is slander but if it is in any kind of permanent form (writing, audiotape, etc.) it is libel. Interestingly enough if someone writes something defamatory on a blackboard, even though it is easily removed, that technically is probably libel rather than slander. The distinction between slander and libel is important, because in order to succeed with an action for slander one generally has to prove some financial loss as a result of the untrue remark, whereas in libel it is necessary to prove only that one's standing in other people's eyes would be lowered. Although actions for defamation are very rare, the safest course is to avoid saying anything 'that would be calculated or likely to reduce somebody's standing in the eyes of their peers', and it is worth remembering that pupils have exactly the same rights under this law as teachers.

Copyright

The area in which teachers are most likely to break the law or run into trouble is copyright. A new agency set up as a result of the 1988 Copyright Designs and Patents Act insists that its poster is displayed by all photocopiers in schools that have signed an agreement permitting limited copying of copyright documents. The poster specifies exactly what one can and cannot copy. One can for example, make class sets of certain materials for use in teaching provided both the school or the LEA and the author of the work are signatories to the agreement. Certain kinds of publications are designed to be photocopied, in which case the copyright agreement might, for example, allow unlimited photocopying within the purchasing institution.

The traditional length of copyright has been 50 years from the death of the author. So, for example, the work of Alfred Lord Tennyson came out of copyright 50 years after the end of the calendar year in which he died. However, published editions have a copyright of 25 years irrespective of the date of the author's death so if one photocopied a page of a book of Tennyson's poems one would not be infringing the author's copyright, but one could be infringing the *publisher's* copyright. This aspect of copyright is particularly important in areas such as music publishing because of the expense of typesetting pieces of music.

However, recent attempts to harmonize copyright legislation across the European Union is likely to increase the copyright period to at least 70 years after the death of the author. How this will work out in practice is not clear, because it could mean that a work written by an author who died in 1940, and has been out of copyright in the United Kingdom since 1990 could become copyright again until 2010. Nevertheless, the implications for teachers are clear, and similar to the advice on other topics in this chapter: find out what the local circumstances are in your institution.

The area in which schools break copyright laws most frequently would appear to be that of computer software, simply because most commercial business software is not copy protected. Computer games that are bought predominantly by adolescent males have very extensive precautions to prevent them being copied because the manufacturers know that this is the sort of thing that adolescent males do. However, the business market has, in recent years, put a great deal of pressure on the software manufacturers not to impose 'copy-protection' on business software because it makes the software more difficult to use, and as a result most business software is not copy protected. A single copy of such software can be used on more than one machine quite easily. Schools often reason like this: 'Why should I spend £5,000 buying multiple copies of a desk-top publishing package when it's only going to be used by one class for two weeks in the whole year?' Nevertheless, what they are doing is illegal and some LEAs have been 'raided' and, where they have been found to be using software illegally, have been fined.

As far as the new teacher is concerned, the only safe course of action is to ask the member of staff at the school responsible for ICT (information and communications technology) before using any software, and certainly you should not install any software on a school computer without asking the network manager first.

Health and safety at work

Another important piece of legislation is the Health and Safety at Work Act of 1974. This Act makes provision concerning the health, safety and welfare of employees and the health and safety of visitors to any work premises. Strangely, for the purposes of law, pupils count as visitors, rather than workers in educational institutions. This law is important in that it gives the duty of care some 'criminal teeth'. If, for example, there was a nail sticking out of a table, which the teacher knew about, and one day a pupil walked past it cutting their leg, the teacher would be in breach of their duty of care and there would be a possibility of successful civil action against the teacher and the school or LEA. However, the Health and Safety at Work Act would also allow the Health and Safety Executive to bring a *criminal* prosecution against the school and the individual teacher for having dangerous premises.

There is sometimes a reluctance to report health and safety issues because they can be disruptive. For example, if a classroom has window catches that do not work properly, the teacher might be unwilling to make too much of a fuss, because the response of the senior management at the school is likely to be to move the teacher to another classroom. Nevertheless, one does have to provide for the health and safety of pupils in one's classes and if one knows about anything that is likely to cause a risk then one must do something about it. Inconvenience is no excuse, and it is certainly no defence in law.

Summary

Inevitably, this chapter has focused on the 'pathology' of school teaching. As a teacher you will have important responsibilities, but it is important to keep things in perspective. As long as you use physical force only to prevent injury to students, damage to property or other crimes, or to maintain good order, and then only the minimum necessary; as long as you think the consequences of your actions through; as long as you act reasonably, then you will be OK. No one will sue you or take you to court, and it is extremely unlikely that you will be assaulted in any way. And you will, like most teachers, enjoy the job.

Relevant case law

The extracts from legal judgements given below are taken from Barrell (1970).

Punishment

- Punishment must be reasonable and moderate and not for the gratification of passion or rage or excessive in its nature or degree, or protracted beyond the child's endurance (R v Hopley [1860] 2 F&F 202).
- A teacher acts in loco parentis and detention of a parent of his/her own child is unlawful if it is for such a period or in such circumstances as to take it out of the realm of reasonable parental discipline (R v Rahman [1985]).

Negligence

- The duty of a schoolmaster is to take such care of his boys as a careful father would take of his son (Williams v Eady [1893] 10 TLR 41).
- The courts will not put on a headmaster any higher standard of care than that of a reasonably careful parent (Hudson v Rotherham Grammar School and Johnson [1938] *Yorkshire Post*, 24 March 1938, 25 March 1938).

- The common law duty of a schoolmaster is that of a prudent parent bound to take notice of boys and their tendency to do mischievous acts, not in the context of the home but in the circumstances of school life, and extends not only to how the pupils conduct themselves, but also to the state and condition of the school premises (Lyes v Middlesex County Council [1962] 61 LGR 443).
- It is a headmaster's duty, bearing in mind the propensities of boys and girls between the ages of 11 and 18, to take all reasonable and proper steps to prevent any of the pupils under his care from suffering injury from inanimate objects, from actions of their fellow pupils, or from a combination of both (Beaumont v Surrey County Council [1968] 66 LGR 580).
- A defendant who through training or experience, may have grounds to visualize more clearly the results of his acts in a particular sphere than would be expected of the proverbial man in the street owes a higher duty of care (Baxter v Barker and others [1903] *The Times*, 24 April 1903, 13 November 1903).
- School authorities must strike some balance between the meticulous supervision of children at every moment when they are under their care, and the very desirable objects of encouraging the sturdy independence of children as they grow up; such encouragement must start at quite an early age (Jeffery v London County Council [1954] 52 LGR 521).
- The mere fact of the fall of a blackboard is not evidence of negligence (Crisp v Thomas [1890] 63 LT756).
- It is negligence for a teacher to order a child to undertake a dangerous operation (Foster v London County Council [1928] *The Times* 2 March 1928).
- It is, I think, impossible to avoid the conclusion that it was a most unfortunate, unforeseeable and quite unpredictable thing which occasioned the accident on this day . . . It appears that this was the first time such a thing had happened. In those circumstances, I find it is impossible to say on the facts than any negligence was shown on the part of the defendant (Wright v Cheshire County Council [1952] 2 All ER 789).
- The test of what is reasonable in ordinary everyday affairs may well be answered by experience arising from practices adopted generally and followed successfully for many years (Wright v Cheshire County Council [1952] All ER 789).
- Where a course of action follows general and approved practice an action of negligence will not lie (Conrad v Inner London Education Authority [1967] *The Times*, 26 May 1967).
- An action for negligence cannot succeed if it is founded on an event which is simply an accident (Webb v Essex County Council [1954] *Times Educational Supplement*, 12 November 1954).
- A schoolmaster is not liable for a sudden act which could not have been prevented by supervision (Gow v Glasgow Education Authority [1922] SC 260).
- Where there is no evidence of lack of supervision or that, assuming there was supervision, it would not have prevented an accident, there is no liability (Langham v Wellingborough School Governors and Fryer [1932] 101 LJKB 513).

- It is not incumbent upon a local education authority to have a teacher continuously present in a playground during a break (Ricketts v Erith Borough Council and Browne [1943] 2 All ER 629).
- The duty of a schoolmaster does not extend to the constant supervision of all the boys in his care all the time; only reasonable supervision is required (Clarke v Monmouth County Council [1954] 52 LGR 246).
- Even if there is failure of supervision, the question arises whether the best supervision could have prevented the accident (Price v Caernarvonshire County Council [1960] *The Times*, 11 February 1960).
- When a class of nine or ten are using pointed scissors, it is not necessary to wait until after a lesson, or to make sure that the rest of the class put their scissors down before giving individual attention to one child (Butt v Cambridgeshire and Isle of Ely Council [1969] *The Times*, 27 November 1969).

Reference

Barrell, G.R. (1970) *Legal Cases for Teachers*. London: Methuen.

Part 3 | Teaching and learning

John Head

Introduction

There is little doubt that adolescents often receive a bad press, with lurid tales of blackboard jungles in schools, and car theft, drug use and sexual promiscuity outside school. For reasons such as these adolescence has been described as a time of 'storm and stress'. Is this reputation justified?

The first point to note is that there is nothing new in these criticisms. Even in classical Greece there were complaints about unruly youth failing to respect their elders. In *The Winter's Tale*, Shakespeare wrote, 'I would that there were no age between ten and three-and-twenty, or youth would sleep out the rest.' Since the early 1950s in Britain we have experienced rockers and mods, punks, and a whole series of youth cults and fashions which have aroused adult disapproval.

What is the contemporary evidence? It is mixed. On many criteria, for example, of physical health, adolescents are a favoured group (Heaven 1996), but there are some problems. Among boys the high crime rates for those in their late teens is disturbing, with over 8 per cent of the 18-year-old cohort being convicted or cautioned for an indictable offence (that is an offence sufficiently serious to attract the possibility of a prison sentence). One-third of males have such a finding of guilt by the age of 30. The crime rates for females are much lower, in the range 10 to 20 per cent of that for males, at all ages. In addition, suicide rates among young men aged 15 to 24 more than doubled between 1971 and 1992, from less than seven per 100,000 of the population to over 15, despite the fact that the overall rate for the general population had gone down in that time. The suicide rate for females aged 15 to 24 remained under four per 100,000 throughout this period (Coleman and Hendry 1990). Among girls, eating disorders are common, but it is difficult to give a precise estimate of the extent of the problem as only the most severe cases get notified to the authorities. Clearly it is possible to gather data to support either argument, that adolescents are, or are not, undergoing storm and stress.

Modern psychologists (for example, Coleman and Hendry 1990) tend to argue that each phase of life presents certain characteristic challenges and problems, and adolescence is not unique, it just presents a particular set of such challenges. That thesis leaves open the question whether the passage through adolescence has become easier or more difficult in recent years.

We can attempt to sort out what these issues might be by considering four major ideas related to adolescence: physical development, the age between, cognitive and emotional growth, and gaining a personal identity.

Physical development

Adolescence is usually taken to start with puberty. This phase of life not only involves development of the genitalia but several other associated physical changes. Prior to puberty, both boys and girls grow at about the same rate – about 5 cm per annum. Girls experience puberty first and enter a spurt phase when they grow at about 8.5 cm per year. Boys experience puberty later, but their growth spurt is more dramatic (height increase of about 9.5 cm p.a.) and it lasts longer. Consequently in about Year 8 girls tend to be bigger than their male contemporaries. Later on the boys overtake them.

These body changes can produce side-effects, such as reduced coordination and fatigue (muscular growth occurs before a corresponding growth of the heart and lungs). There are not only these external changes but also internal ones, arising from the hormonal environment changing. Occasionally boys experience short-term problems, for example, breast enlargement, but it is the girls who suffer most, with the majority of young adolescents reporting considerable distress from menstruation (Prendergast 1992).

Alongside the purely physical effects of puberty there are the psychological effects. The adolescents know that they are now capable of parenthood and hence issues such as one's sexual orientation become important. In the past some psychoanalysts, notably Anna Freud (1937) and Peter Blos (1962), suggested that prior to puberty children enjoyed a latency period, in which they had overcome the problems of childhood and they were able to cope with all the demands that life placed on them. Puberty brought about a new set of problems, physical and psychological, and adolescence was a period of crisis until solutions had been found to these new concerns. Maybe they made this argument too strongly. For many adolescents puberty presents few major problems, but we should be sensitive to the possibility that for some there are real concerns. In western Europe in the past century the age of puberty has dropped by about three years, and, as a result, the period of adolescence has been extended.

The age between

The second major idea comes from sociology. It is argued that with both children and adults we have a clear idea about appropriate roles and functions, but with adolescents the situation is confused. They receive alternate messages telling them to grow up and yet reminding them that they are not yet adult.

Adolescents tend to envy adults for their perceived freedoms, for example, to drive a car, drink alcohol, or to stay out late, and they will tend to pester adults to be allowed more freedom for themselves. This battle for independence can strain relationships with parents and teachers. It may not be easy for parents to abandon their role of a protector.

Part of the problem is that adolescents do not always appreciate the constraints placed on adults. If we did just what we liked we would probably lose all our friends because of our selfish, anti-social behaviour and some may even end up in prison. Adolescents may fail to recognize the constraints implied in adult behaviour. They may carry the battle for independence too far, for example taking the rule that they can do what they like within their own bedroom as a licence to play their radio and CDs as loudly as they want, regardless of the others in the house.

Probably the wisest course for parents and teachers is to negotiate a progressive position, that is to say one in which the adolescent gains increasing freedoms year by year. Certainly, in an 11–18 age range school I would expect the Year 12 and 13 students (sixth formers) to be treated very differently from 11-year-old pupils.

Sometimes adults may despair but there is evidence that even disadvantaged adolescents, those in residential homes and with experience of abuse, do listen to adults. The youth culture is such that adolescents cannot be seen to be too submissive to adult authority. In school you may find students seemingly hostile in front of their peer group but in reality they are listening and responding to what you are saying.

This period of detachment from adult control can generate anxieties of its own, and it is in early adolescence that boys and girls conform most closely to the norms of their peer group, in respect to such matters as dress and leisure interests (Montemayor *et al.* 1994; Cotterell 1996). Membership of the group provides security and gives the basis for a recognizable teenage culture and lifestyle. In many respects, membership of the peer group can be a positive experience, leading to the formation of lifelong friendships, but there is a negative side. Teenage groups sometimes develop an ethos which demands that members demonstrate that they are cool by taking risks, including some which involve criminal behaviour. Those who do not conform to the group ethos can be bullied or marginalized.

Cognitive and emotional growth

One of the rewarding aspects of teaching in secondary schools is witnessing the students suddenly 'take off'. Students who recently did the very minimum of work necessary to avoid trouble develop a new enthusiasm for ideas and ideals. They may wish to challenge your beliefs, to ask searching questions, and express commitment to various causes. They want to read books and want to hear your opinion on issues. It might be noted that the commonest age for religious conversion is 16.

One model of thinking, that of Jean Piaget, suggests that there is a qualitative difference in thinking occurring in adolescence. Children tend to be concerned with the real immediate world. In adolescence an interest in abstract notions develops. A child will feel unhappy about something tangible – pain, loneliness or hunger. An adolescent may feel unhappy when listening to music or seeing a beautiful sunset. This inexplicable emotional response may be puzzling to the adolescent.

Another aspect is that adolescents are very self-conscious. Children tend to live in their own world and are not too concerned about others. As adolescents decentre (to use the jargon term) they may do so in a lopsided way (Elkind 1967). They realize that other people have their own ideas but adolescents feel that they are the focus of these ideas. They believe that they are being observed and judged by others. A more adult stance would be to recognize that other people have their own agenda of interests and concerns, and we probably only feature in a very minor way in most of them.

Gaining a personal identity

The fourth major idea is that adolescents need to gain a sense of identity (Erikson 1950, 1968; Kroger 1996). It is difficult to define personal identity, but I have spoken of it as being a *life-script* (Head 1997). Individuals are both the authors of their scripts, as it reflects their self-image, and also they are like actors, using the script to decide what to say and do.

Identity development occurs at all stages of life, but is particularly important in adolescence. A child's sense of self is largely determined by others. The social class is that of the parents. Where one lives and goes to school, and how one spends one's leisure time, is determined by others. In becoming adult they have to carve out their own lifestyle, to decide on their own career and to develop their own sexual and social relationships (Moore and Rosenthal 1993). The main areas of identity include career plans, personal relationships, and having some beliefs which give a sense of purpose and worthwhileness to life.

A successful identity comes from matching a sound sense of oneself, what one is like and what one is good at, with a sound sense of the world, what opportunities exist. It is necessary to have some goals but these need to be realistic. In essence, there are two processes involved in gaining a sense of identity. The first is to think about the issues, trying to match oneself against the possibilities available in life. The second is to make the decisions necessary for planning the way forward.

Within one class you may find some immature students who have not yet started on these processes while others have already gained an adult sense of self. There are also two intermediate positions. Some adolescents may be fully aware of all the issues but cannot decide what they should do. They will debate issues at length but show no settled commitment. Career plans and expressions of belief may change day by day. The other intermediate position can be found when the adolescent makes firm decisions without much thought. They do so in order to avoid the discomfort of self-examination. The problem that might then arise is that they make decisions which later on prove unsatisfactory. Sometimes they make career choices that later they regret. Sometimes someone who is predominantly homosexual goes into denial and enters marriage and then finds the situation intolerable. The key point is that it is much easier to sort out these options in adolescence than later on in adulthood.

This process of identity achievement can only be directly undertaken by the individual concerned, it is something occurring within their mind. As teachers, we can help, partly by informing students about the world, the range of careers and lifestyles available, and partly by helping them recognize their own qualities and limitations. Possibilities should be debated. We should not force teenagers to rush into making decisions as adolescence should provide space and time for this process of identity acquisition to occur.

Gender differences

Consideration of gender differences is important in itself and also because it reminds us that adolescents are not a uniform homogeneous group. There will be both individual diversity and social diversity, defined by race, class and gender (see Chapter 8).

It is in adolescence that gender differences become most marked (Wolpe 1988). In part this is due to the earlier maturation of girls. In addition, boys and girls have a very different experience of puberty. For most boys it does not in itself present a problem, in fact it adds to life's pleasures. As noted earlier, for girls puberty introduces physical discomfort. It is believed that one cause of anorexia is an attempt to reverse the effects of puberty. The main problem for boys is in not experiencing puberty. The boy who is a late developer tends to have a low status as he cannot compete effectively in sports or in looking after himself in a fight (Askew and Ross 1988).

Boys and girls tend to approach sexual relationships with different agendas (Lees 1986). For boys, sexual activity is seen to be solely a source of pleasure and is undertaken for selfish reasons. From my experience, girls tend to be more socially mature and see sexual experience leading on to the possibility of pregnancy, a prospect that produces mixed feelings (for girls of 14 it is both what they dread most and look forward to most in life).

These differences in maturity and attitudes towards sexual experience, combined with the effects of belonging to same-sex peer groups in early adolescence, tend to bring about a short-term separation or hostility between the sexes. Girls at this age complain of the sexual harassment they receive from boys and that they are in a no-win situation. A girl who consents to sex may be labelled a 'slag' and those who refuse are seen to be frigid. Later in adolescence individuals break away from the same-sex group and the seeing of the other gender in terms of stereotypes in order to form stable one-to-one relationships.

Until recently we have tended to see girls underachieving in education, for example, in 1980 about 40 per cent of the places in higher education were taken by women. Recently there has been a change. Females are participating more (and are now a majority in higher education) and achieving more (in 1999 51 per cent of the girls in state schools gained at least five Grades A–C in the GCSE examinations; only 39.9 per cent of boys did so).

There are debates about what is seen as a male malaise, but the decline of employment prospects in traditional male areas, such as mining, engineering and the military, is widely believed to be a major factor (Winefield et al. 1993). Boys can confirm their masculinity by gaining employment in such traditionally male areas; in so doing they gain both income and status. The loss of well over a million jobs in manufacturing since 1980 has been accompanied by increases in opportunities in the service industries and fields such as information technology. Girls have been quicker in moving into these new areas of employment. Boys seem to have lost the incentive to succeed.

Another factor might be that about 20 per cent of families with children are now headed by a single mother so that boys lack a father around the home to act as a mentor. Boys know that masculinity involves being different from a woman, so they may rebel against the mother without having a clear sense of what it is they are trying to achieve.

Schools can help address these matters. Boys seem to be more disorganized in lessons and so need clear instructions about what is needed and how they are to proceed. The school pastoral system should seek to minimize undesirable behaviours, such as bullying, and promote opportunities for boys to overcome their reluctance in talking about their difficulties. More detailed suggestions for teachers can be found in Head (1999).

What worries adolescents?

I have encountered four main areas of concern. About one-third of those surveyed reported a reasonable degree of unhappiness about one of the following four issues. The first is with the family, sometimes about a split home, more usually about arguments relating to money and staying out late at night. The second is the school. Complaints are mainly about the disciplinary procedures, which seem unnecessary, but complaints about the workload are common, too. The third concern is a feeling of lacking an aim in life, in fact in not seeing much purpose in life at all. As already noted, these feelings tend to be labile, and are indicative of the continuing search for a sense of identity. Finally there is concern about social and sexual relations. There is a conflict between the wish to assert individuality and to be popular with others. In addition there are concerns about sexual orientation and being sexually successful. Within the competitive ethos of the peer group success with a partner of the other sex confers a high status.

It is difficult to generalize about how one responds to these expressions of unhappiness. Remembering their self-consciousness, it is essential to respect confidence and not do or say anything to embarrass the individual. Ultimately choices have to be made by the individuals about their own lives. Our role is to listen, to provide factual information, if appropriate, and to help the students think through for themselves what it is they really believe in and want to do.

Sometimes the problems will be beyond your competence. You should be able to call upon the school pastoral and PSE (personal and social education) staff to help you. There are also various agencies which deal with specific issues, for example, drug abuse and pregnancy, and it would be sensible to know the names and contact telephone numbers of such agencies so that the pupils can gain specialist advice.

At the beginning of this chapter the question whether adolescence is harder nowadays was left unanswered. It is true that society has become more labile in recent years. There is less job security and families are breaking up more commonly, with current divorce rates being about one-third of marriage rates. Factors like these may make the adult world appear more difficult to enter.

Working with adolescents is challenging, but it can also be most rewarding, and in outlining some of the problems you might encounter I would not wish the difficulties to obscure the sense of achievement, and even the fun, you should enjoy.

References

Askew, S. and Ross, C. (1988) *Boys Don't Cry*. Milton Keynes: Open University Press.

Blos, P. (1962) *On Adolescence*. New York: Free Press.

Coleman, J.C. and Hendry, L. (1990) *The Nature of Adolescence*. London: Routledge.

Cotterell, J. (1996) *Social Networks and Social Influences in Adolescence*. London: Routledge.

Elkind, D. (1967) Egocentrism in adolescence, *Child Development*, 38: 1025–34.

Erikson, E.H. (1950) *Childhood and Society*. New York: Norton.

Erikson, E.H. (1968) *Identity, Youth and Crisis*. New York: Norton.

Freud, A. (1937) *The Ego and the Mechanisms of Defence*. London: Hogarth Press.

Head, J. (1997) *Working with Adolescents: Constructing Identity*. London: Falmer Press.

Head, J. (1999) *Understanding the Boys: Issues of Behaviour and Achievement*. London: Falmer Press.

Heaven, P.C.L. (1996) *Adolescent Health*. London: Routledge.

Kroger, J. (1996) *Identity in Adolescence*. London: Routledge.

Lees, S. (1986) *Losing Out: Sexuality and Adolescent Girls*. London: Hutchinson.

Montemayor, R., Adams, G.R. and Gullotta, T.P. (1994) *Personal Relationships During Adolescence*. Thousand Oaks: Sage.

Moore, S. and Rosenthal, D. (1993) *Sexuality in Adolescence*. London: Routledge.

Prendergast, S. (1992) *This Is the Time to Grow Up: Girls' Experience of Menstruation in School*. Cambridge: Health Promotion Trust.

Winefield, A.H., Tiggemann, M., Winefield, H.R. and Goldney, R.D. (1993) *Growing Up with Unemployment*. London: Routledge.

Wolpe, A.M. (1988) *Within School Walls*. London: Routledge.

<table>
<tr><td>13</td><td># Learning in the classroom</td></tr>
</table>

| 13 | # Learning in the classroom |

Martin Monk

Introduction

As a beginning teacher you are in the process of going through one of the periods of most rapid learning in your life. The places in which you are learning most rapidly are the classrooms in which you are doing your teaching practice. In those rooms you are looked upon by the others – the pupils – as the one person who is not learning. However, at the moment, in any lesson you teach you are the most important learner because you are responsible for planning, coordinating, managing and assessing the learning of up to 30 or so others in the class. In spite of these responsibilities, you have yet to develop the skills, repertoires of actions and knowledge base to do that effectively and efficiently. The chances are that you are reading this in the knowledge that you have a lot to learn. So what is learning all about?

In this chapter different ideas about learning will be reviewed and discussed briefly. Some of those ideas have pedigrees that have dignified them with grand names, like constructivism, cognitivism or behaviourism. Some of those ideas are common sense and are part of our everyday language. The discussion will focus on you learning to be a teacher. However, what is true for your learning will also be true for the learning of your pupils. In the classroom everyone is a learner.

The most important lesson of all

Schools are places where people come to know about their futures. You have embarked on a course that will help you know if your future is as a teacher. How will you decide? The decision is shaped by the success and failure you 'enjoy' as you plan lessons, organize and manage classes, and evaluate. If you are successful in these activities the chances are you will see yourself as a future teacher. If you are not successful then you will not. This seems obvious, but there is a lesson about learning that goes beyond you and your immediate concerns. What is true of you, is true for your pupils.

In school pupils learn about their futures. Those who enjoy success will see themselves as being good at school learning. They will want to carry on and further their formal education. Sadly, those who do not enjoy success learn quite quickly that schools and school-type learning is not for them. The most important lesson pupils learn in school is how good they are at learning in school. As the teacher in charge of the learning of your pupils you need to plan activities that will enable the pupils to enjoy success. Without that success your pupils will learn that they cannot learn. From then on your work with them will turn from delight to drudgery. So the most important lesson on learning for you is to be found in an everyday phrase: nothing succeeds like success.

Human beings are self-reflective animals. We are able to use our minds to reflect on our actions, rather than just act. We can mentally model our actions and reflect on them. We develop a mental model of who we are as an individual human being by reflecting on our actions and their outcomes. Out of the successes and failures of our biographies we have an idea of what type of person we are compared with others, what we are good at doing and what we are appallingly bad at doing. Each of us has a view of ourselves, or a self-image.

At the same time we also carry an image of the person we would like to be, or our ideal-self. In choosing to act, or not, we can close the gap between our ideal-self and our self-image. Success in our chosen actions provides a reward that is not external, in the experimental psychology sense of laboratory rats with food pellets, but internal and subjective. The reward, in that it belongs to us subjectively, directly reinforces our view of ourselves as being a particular type of person with particular skills and talents. Failure challenges our view of ourselves and is therefore distressing.

Much of what we do is what we think is appropriate to bring about closer congruence between our self-images and our ideal-selves. How successful we are in closing the gap between our self-images and our ideal-selves adds to our self-esteem. A small gap between one's self-image and ideal-self is indicated through high self-esteem. We value ourselves because we are able to do those things we think we ought to be able to do.

If part of our self-image is that we are good at mathematics we will try to do well at it. If we think we cannot learn French we will not bother to try. The effort we put into learning depends upon the degree of success we expect to achieve. This can lead to a self-fulfilling prophecy. If part of our self-image is that we are poor at games and sports and therefore we do not put much effort into playing sports, we will probably not be successful. That lack of success can be used to reinforce the original judgement. Not only does 'nothing succeed like success', but also there is nothing like failure for providing that 'I told you so' rationalization of our incompetence.

Moral components may be worked into our self-images and ideal-selves but the process itself is amoral. Pupils who are consistently disruptive in class may be closing the gap between their self-image and ideal-self as pupils who do not get on in school.

Such knowledge places a heavy responsibility upon your shoulders, for the responsibility is yours, and not that of your pupils. You are their teacher and not the other way about. Common staffroom talk, particularly after a lesson that went poorly, is of the lack of motivation of certain pupils. It is easy to blame the pupils for a lesson going adrift. As a beginning teacher, however, the professional responsibility for the lesson will be with your planning, organizing and managing. Pupil motivation can only be a scapegoat. All pupils are motivated – in the sense that they have needs and drives. Those needs and drives may not align with yours. The chances are that the principal reason they do not align with yours is because the pupils have not enjoyed success in their learning experiences before you taught them. Your professional responsibility is to set aside ideas of pupils' motivation and to plan, organize and evaluate lessons where pupils will be successful.

Read Chapter 12 on adolescence to follow up some of these issues. Ideas about who you are as a person, your self-image and self-esteem have developed out of the early work of people like George Herbert Mead. More about this can be found in psychology and social psychology books under the heading of symbolic interactionism. To find out more about ways of categorizing people's traits – such as motivation – you need to look for psychometrics and particularly the psychometrics of personality.

Pedagogical content knowledge

How can one plan activities for lessons so that pupils are successful? The two chief sources of information available to you – other than the suck it and see of actual classroom teaching – are your own biography and the wisdom of others. Your own biography is likely to be a poor guide. You are being trained as a teacher because you enjoyed some degree of academic success in school. To have been awarded a degree in the UK puts you amongst the top 30 per cent of the people in your year. This means there is a massive 70 per cent who did not achieve as you did. So your personal success is unlikely to be a reliable guide for how to plan lessons for a mixed performance group in a comprehensive school.

More experienced teachers that you will work with have built their own repertoires of strategies. It is possible these may have been shaped by cycles of variation and selection. They may have tried one way of teaching. If it worked they tried it again. If not they modified the strategy and tried the modification. In extreme cases this may have been blind variation and selective retention. Such a mechanism you may recognize. Psychologists call it operant conditioning. Operant conditioning involves trying things out and seeing what happens. It is very effective in producing single well ingrained ways of behaving, but it can be a slow and painful way to learn if you have to run every trial in practice.

Of course, experienced teachers do not run every trial in practice, for they have built up a mental model of how to teach their subject. With a well developed mental model it is possible to run the trials in one's head and never set foot over the classroom threshold. Disasters may be avoided rather than lived. With very well developed models the operation of the mental model may even become subconscious. That degree of subconscious operation may be such as to allow a great deal of fluency in the repertoire and choices of classroom action. What one witnesses is the skilled behaviour of a professional.

The particular mental model of how to teach your subject is sometimes referred to as pedagogical content knowledge (PCK). Now PCK is not the same as knowing your subject. This is a silly mistake that politicians make when they want to win parental votes. The idea that just because you know some subject means you can teach it is a nonsense. Of course the opposite is a nonsense too: just because you know how to teach one subject does not mean you can teach anyone anything.

At its crudest, PCK is tips for teachers – tips for your own teaching. It combines knowledge of your subject with knowledge of learning activities, knowledge of the resources in your department and school, and, of course, knowledge of your pupils. It is largely idiosyncratic through a biographical component and is not easily transferred as it evolves through your experience in a given school. Change schools and you will once again have a lot to learn – but nowhere near so much as the first time – as you rebuild and repair your PCK.

Pedagogical content knowledge is specific knowledge of how to teach your subject so your pupils enjoy success. One of the quickest ways to gain such knowledge is through working alongside experienced successful teachers while taking responsibility for small parts of their lessons. When they are teaching you watch what they do – and ask questions later. When you are teaching they watch you – and make points later. The exchange between mentor and beginning teacher can be very fruitful if you can persuade your mentor to share the teaching and not just to abandon you. Through shared experience and conversation you can quickly appropriate your mentor's mental model and make it your own.

Poor mentors still 'throw their student teachers in at the deep end'. Swimming to survive, one has to rely on operant conditioning to build a mental model. As mentioned before, this can be a slow and painful way to learn.

To find out more about mental models you need to look under cognitivism and constructivism in the index of a psychology book. For ideas on trial-and-error learning, both classical and operant, you need to look for behaviourism.

Scaffolding pupils' learning

If sharing experiences and talking about them is the quickest way for you to develop your skills as a teacher then it is doubtlessly going to be the case that the same activity will enhance the learning of your pupils. Showing learners what to do while talking them through the task is sometimes referred to as scaffolding. The idea is that learners are supported in carrying out a task by the use of language to guide their action. The next stage in scaffolding is for the learner to talk themselves through the task. Then that talk can, in turn, become an internalized guide to the action and thought of the learner.

In planning learning activities at which your pupils are to be successful, you will need to allow time in your lessons to show the pupils what to do. You will need to allow time for them to do things for themselves with your support; you will need to allow time for a discussion of difficulties and progress, weaker and better performances.

Pupils often complain that poor teachers just come into the classroom and start an activity while the pupils do not know what is going on. Better teachers, so pupils say, talk with them about the work they are doing and how it all fits together. That is, they allow the opportunity for the pupils to work on their own mental models for the topic in hand. This does not mean you personally have to work with each and every pupil. This sharing of mental models can be done by pupils discussing tasks in small groups. The small groups can then report back to the whole class (not every one, but a selected two to three) so the class shares the same vision of what it is they are trying to achieve.

Ideas about scaffolding are often associated with the work of Jerome Bruner and Lev Vygotsky. You can find out more about these ideas in a plethora of modern psychology books.

Progression

Mass public education is a relatively new idea in the history of education. It is only recently that we have attempted to treat all adults as equals in political life. Universal adult suffrage, with voting rights for women at age 21, did not come in the UK until 1928; that is just within living memory. In economic and social life our consumerist society is still a long way from being egalitarian. It is therefore not that surprising that until the late 1960s the emphasis in educational provision was not on devising programmes of study, schemes of work and learning activities that would help all children learn more effectively and more efficiently. Instead the emphasis was very much on sifting and sorting so as to find the right people for sponsorship and advancement.

Psychological models, in being socially, politically and economically located, work symbiotically to support the grouping and training practices of the society in which they are embedded. In a society that is built on difference, legitimation of that difference is part of the burden by psychological theories. From this perspective, the rise of the intelligence quotient (IQ) as a means of sifting and sorting pupils for different educational destinations can be seen as entirely appropriate. In such a situation it makes sense to try to match educational opportunity to educability, particularly in a climate of parsimonious resourcing. Placing some pupils along some scale of IQ fixes them so they can become a suitable case for treatment rather than a messy human being who does well on some things and not on others, who has good days and bad days. In the decades after the Second World War the measure of a person's IQ came to have the popular interpretation, erroneous from a psychological point of view, of being fixed for all time. A measure once made, a decision once taken was not troublesome if this viewpoint was adopted.

As economic, political and social circumstances ebb and flow over the course of history so our attitudes to similarity and difference shift. Chapter 2 illustrates how education is circularly underwritten by the social, political and economic. From the 1960s onwards a definite and gradual shift has been taking place. Amongst professionals involved in education, pupils are now seen as having equal potential, and thereby equal value, even though they may not have equal performance. Pronouncements of politicians, the press and even on occasions the former Chief Inspector of Schools should be set against this background.

In developing your PCK you will need to develop your ideas on what it means to say that pupils are making progress in their learning. Rarely is there one viewpoint because within any school subject the subject itself is multifaceted. Getting better at running 100 metres has a simple criterion by which progress can be judged: the time to do it gets less. But learning a foreign language, mathematics, history or science, for example, is not such a unitary act (PE teachers will be quick to point out that physical well-being cannot be measured simply by the 100 metre dash either).

Within any one subject area there is a professional consensus, although one that rarely goes uncontested, about what it means to say one learner has progressed more than another. You should be familiar with the attainment targets and the eight levels of progression that are to be found in the National Curriculum documentation for your subject. These provide a rough and ready guide, but they are by no means exhaustive. Alternative viewpoints are possible. One of the things you must develop to qualify as a professional, rather than an interested amateur, is a well-grounded knowledge of the pathways of progress that pupils can make as they become more skilled and more knowledgeable in your subject. If you do not have a clear view of what progress means, how will you help your pupils along the path to success?

Again, what is true for your pupils' learning is true for your own. Setting aside the politics of the Department for Education and Employment's (DfEE) attempts to codify 'high standards', you should nevertheless be thinking about your own progress in the classroom. To help you develop your personal sense of progression you should keep asking yourself 'What does a better performance as a teacher look like?' It may be useful occasionally to sit down and write out your own account. If you are brave enough, show it to your mentor and take note of the reactions you get.

If you look up developmental psychology you will find studies on both the biological and interactional aspect of maturation. You will also come across the work of Jean Piaget and his studies of how children's thinking changes as they mature. You might find the cognitive psychology literature on expert systems of interest in connection with your own practice.

Activities and objectives

Often commentators on learning distinguish content knowledge from skills, that is declarative knowledge – things you can say – from operational knowledge – things you can do. This in itself is not such a clear-cut distinction because to monitor mental operations rather than physical ones can require a declaration in speaking or writing to demonstrate the outcome of your invisible thought processes. How can we tell if people are making progress in their thinking?

What is in anyone's head is only available to the rest of the world if that person produces some output. The variety of outputs is quite limited. These are various actions including demonstrating, telling orally, writing and drawing, and finer derivatives of these like calculating, tabulating, plotting and graphing. As these are the only actions by which you will be able to judge the progress of your pupils, they are also a guide to the activities your pupils should be working on in your lessons. Your pupils will learn most effectively in the lessons by being active and not passive. You will need to plan activities for the pupils in your lessons.

Learning by observation is another way of learning. However, it is perhaps best thought of as a way to update your mental model(s) rather than to develop skills. You have probably been keen to start teaching yourself and may have been frustrated by watching teachers at work in lesson observation tasks. You feel that doing it for yourself is the best way to learn to teach. The same must also be true for your pupils in learning your subject. They too need to practice to make progress. They will make slow progress by only watching you at work all the time. If they do need to watch you, then you need to talk through what you are doing to scaffold changes to their mental models.

As you plan activities for lessons you will continually need to ask yourself why the pupils are going to carry out that particular task. It is always worth reflecting on what the pupils will be able to do at the end of the lesson that they could not do at the beginning. As a beginning teacher, first your college tutor and then your school mentor will ask you what the objectives are for the learning activities you plan for your pupils. Being clearer about learning objectives will help you help the pupils. If you are confident in what it is they will be able to do after learning then you can share the objective with them and shepherd them along the way to achieving the learning objective.

Shepherding will be necessary as pupils' concentration can drift, particularly when their skills or memories fail them. Evidence from experimental psychology suggests that even in adults the attention span is no more than 20 minutes. This means that during lessons pupils' activities need to be short and varied.

Experimental psychology is the source of a wealth of ideas on organizing more efficient and effective learning. Because the studies have generally been laboratory based, however you will need to be careful in extracting general principles and rules to guide you in your own classroom. Differentiation and progression are the reverse and obverse of the same coin (see Chapter 15 for more on this issue).

Personal relationships

For your pupils, you are their teacher not a student teacher. Pupils will react to the symbolic you – the professional teacher you are to become – rather than the personal you – the novice teacher you know yourself to be. This means you have to learn to slip into the role of 'a teacher' in order to function effectively in the school. At first you may feel uneasy about not being true to yourself, or you may want to be more friendly than the teachers who taught you. With any luck, these thoughts will pass. The irony is that you become a teacher by playing the role of the teacher. Gradually that role becomes who you are – like putting on some favourite clothes. How you will behave again depends upon a mental model – the mental model of what you think it is to be a teacher and to be a good teacher. You need to discuss this with your mentor. Not only are there personal components to these models of teacherly behaviour but there are school components in terms of the school's practices, norms and rituals. To be effective you have to absorb these so you can work with and within them.

Dramaturgical social-psychology, particularly associated with the writings of Irving Goffman, provides a useful place to start exploring further this aspect of learning and teaching.

One parting shot on relationships and learning in the classroom. If you want to be successful then a good place to start is to learn all the names of the children you teach. At the end of the day, you will be less effective in teaching your subject if you do not also remember you are teaching your pupils.

Books that will give you more on psychology and the classroom

Driscoll, M.P. (1999) *Psychology of Learning for Instruction.* London: Allyn and Bacon.

Entwhistle, N.J. (1996) *Styles of Learning and Teaching (An Integrative Outline of Educational Psychology for Students, Teachers and Lecturers).* London: David Fulton Publishers.

Gagne, E.D. (1993) *The Cognitive Psychology of School Learning.* Harlow: Longman Higher Education.

Howe, M.J.A. (1998) *Principles of Abilities and Human Learning. Principles of Psychology.* London: Taylor and Francis.

Howe, M.J.A. (1999) *Teachers' Guide to the Psychology of Learning.* Oxford: Blackwell Publishers.

Schwartz, B. (1995) *The Psychology of Learning.* New York: W.W. Norton & Co. Ltd.

Schwartz, B. and Robbins, S. (1995) *Psychology of Learning and Behavior.* New York: W.W. Norton & Co. Ltd.

Siefert, K. (1999) *Constructing a Psychology of Learning and Teaching.* New York: Houghton Mifflin.

Walker, J.T. (1995) *The Psychology of Learning.* New York: Prentice Hall.

Zelan, K. (1991) *The Risks of Knowing: Developmental Impediments to School Learning.* Amsterdam: Kluwer Academic.

| 14 | # Managing effective classrooms |

Sheila Macrae and Mike Quintrell

Introduction

Teachers need a wide range of organizational and managerial strategies to maintain the order necessary for students to learn well. Interestingly, and perhaps paradoxically, these tactics can be difficult to learn while observing successful teachers in action, because such teachers can make the whole process appear so easy. However, when good classroom organization is set against less good organization, it becomes possible to compare and contrast the different strategies used and, in this way, come to understand what works and what does not.

In this chapter we explore issues concerning classroom organization and management and offer some theoretical and practical advice. The chapter differs from some of the other contributions to this book in that many of the issues covered may seem to be technical ones. What we aim to do is to show how a range of personal, social, psychological and philosophical issues underlie much classroom activity. For human beings, there is no such thing as practice without an underlying theory.

What is classroom organization and management?

Ask a group of student teachers before their first teaching practice to describe any anxieties they may have, and before long someone will mention discipline or class control. It is the source of greatest unease amongst student teachers.

(Wragg 1981: 4)

Studies of teacher behaviour (Rutter *et al.* 1979; Wragg 1984) have identified specific skills which are demonstrated by effective teachers and which can be learned and applied by those new to the profession.

The work that goes on in the classroom does not, and should not, take place in a vacuum. Instead, it can be viewed as one of four layers (the institution, classroom, individual teacher and local community) in the overall structure of the school (Watkins 1995). The first three layers, that of the institution, the classroom and the individual teacher, play the most important parts but these are impacted upon by the fourth layer, which is the community the school serves. It is the successful interweaving of organizational and management strategies at all four layers that maximizes a school's well being and enables teachers to teach and students to learn in a supportive, enabling environment (Watkins 2000).

The whole-school approach

To promote coherence across all four layers it is widely recognized that a whole-school approach is the most effective (DES 1989). The aim of a whole-school approach is to identify and deal with, in a proactive, systematic, supportive and open way, the sorts of inconsistencies that can lead to confusion or cause problems. For example, under what circumstances are students allowed to leave class during lessons? It is essential for less experienced teachers to have a forum in which they feel safe to discuss issues without fear of ridicule. Some issues may be more appropriately discussed in a departmental setting, for example, how to improve the pass rate at GCSE within the constraints of a decreased budget and fewer staff. Yet other topics may best be organized within whole-school in-service training when a helpful way of discussing issues is to use hypothetical rather than actual events. For whole-school guidelines to be effective, the role played by all concerned needs to be made explicit and procedures need to be clear, concise and consistent (Watkins and Wagner 2000). Since governors have responsibility for appointing staff and for school policy, their support must be sought.

In the 1997 Government White Paper, *Excellence in Schools* (DfEE 1997), the use of assertive discipline was recommended as a way of improving behaviour in schools. Assertive discipline is a commercial classroom management package based on the work of Canter and Associates, a US corporation. It adopts a neo-Skinnerian behaviour modification approach and is based on rewards and punishments as a way for teachers to 'take charge' of their classrooms (Hill 1990: 72). While assertive discipline has its proponents, Rigoni and Walford (1998) see it as inflexible and argue that it works against progressive personal and social education which encourages listening skills, problem-solving and conflict resolution through discussion.

Successful schools

There are several organizational features that appear to characterize 'successful schools' (see Charlton and David 1990; Cooper 1993; Fontana 1994). These include: school rules that are few, realistic and open to change and development; clear and efficient lines of communication within the school; and decisions that are never arbitrary but are related to the procedures, standards and values that the school is seen to operate and all concerned are seen to support (O'Brien 1998) (but see Chapter 5 for a critique of simple ideas about school effectiveness). Successful schools have classrooms that reflect their ethos.

Some teachers begin the academic year by encouraging their students to draw up most of their own class rules. These can then be displayed on a notice-board and referred to when necessary. Teachers also might like to list rules that they will attempt to keep (Sinclair 1999). For example, they may promise to mark students' work promptly or have to explain reasons for any delay. Neill and Caswell (1993) state that good teachers present rules as something both they and the students must keep in order to promote the efficient running of the classroom. In this way, confrontations between teachers and students can be avoided if both sides are seen to be bound by the terms and conditions of rules they have had a hand in drafting. The emphasis is on 'we' rather than on 'you' and 'me'. For example, in dealing with anti-social behaviour, it is more convincing to argue that 'in this classroom *we* don't expect people to behave like that' rather than simply saying 'don't *you* do that'.

A US study conducted by Wayson *et al.* (1982) identified 13 characteristics of a successful school. Among these were that the type of leadership role adopted by the headteacher is a major determinant in how the school operates and that this role needs to be balanced by complementary leadership qualities in the senior management team (SMT). The causes of problems, as opposed to the symptoms, are focused on and, for the most part, individual teachers deal with the problems they encounter. Specifically, practices are adapted to meet the school's own identified needs and to reflect their particular styles of operation rather than trying to use other institutions' methods and processes (O'Brien 1998). In addition, these schools have well-developed links with both parents and community agencies, are open to comment and criticism from sources within and outside the school and practise well-tried methods rather than untested and sometimes insubstantial procedures (for a discussion of the parent–school relationship, see Chapter 9).

The role of the teacher

The classroom is a small, dynamic, social arena in which the teacher's and each student's performance is open for all to see. To operate effectively within such a vital environment calls for a special awareness and sensitivity from teachers in order that students do not feel threatened and defensive:

> Being constantly exposed to things that you cannot understand (like Maths) or required to attempt actions that you cannot do (like gym) is itself threatening for many people: unable to run away, every moment is fraught with the danger of being exposed, yet again, as incompetent. And this in its turn threatens to bring the public humiliation that we would do almost anything to avoid.
>
> (Claxton 1984: 215)

Students need to feel secure in the knowledge that things are under control, despite many of their apparent efforts and ploys to disrupt the smooth running of lessons. Whether, in fact, a teacher actually feels confident is almost immaterial; if they can appear in control they may be halfway there. It is important from the start to try to present an image of being in charge. This includes being clear about what is acceptable and where the boundaries lie. While this may seem self-evident, it can be difficult for beginner teachers who need time to find out not only what is acceptable to the school but also what they are willing to tolerate.

Some time ago, Hargreaves (1975) suggested that most teaching sessions follow a pattern: the entry phase, settling down, the central part where teachers present their main points and set the students tasks, followed by clearing up prior to the exit. Smith and Laslett (1993) describe this pattern as the 'four rules of classroom management': get them in, which has two components: greeting and seating; get on with it, which includes lesson content; get on with them, which means knowing who is who and what is going on; get them out, which has two phases: concluding the lesson and dismissing the class. We shall look now at each of these four phases of the lesson.

Greeting and seating

Classroom management begins as soon as the students start to arrive for their lesson and the whole tone of what follows can be set before the students have even crossed the threshold. The teacher should try to be in the classroom before the students begin to arrive. If the school likes students to line up outside the room, teachers can use this opportunity to create a serious, firm and business-like atmosphere. Dean (1996) suggests that beginner teachers should avoid individual questions at this stage and concentrate on watching the students as they line up, calling attention to any who seem slow to do so in an orderly manner. Dean (1996) does advise however, that a few friendly comments might be made to some students. Once inside the classroom, students should be encouraged to settle quickly and quietly.

The lesson begins

When the teacher is happy that everyone has settled they then need to indicate that work is ready to begin. Good teachers make use of eye contact in such a situation, making clear by gestures that they are waiting for certain individuals to give their attention. The teacher should try to look relaxed and confident as they wait for silence. Fontana (1994: 108) gives some advice about how this confidence might be demonstrated, including:

- talk quietly and slowly;
- maintain relaxed and non-threatening eye contact with the class in general and certain individuals in particular;

- avoid nervous gestures and mannerisms;
- do not be afraid to smile at the class where appropriate and do join in any reasonable classroom laughter;
- avoid unjustified antagonism or overreaction to students' behaviour.

The lesson content

Speaking clearly without shouting and using eye contact to engage the attention of the whole class are skills that can be practised. Under stress, all of us subconsciously make ourselves smaller, hiding away in the corner. Try to see yourself as others see you. Another strategy is to realize that you are actually engaged in 30 one-to-one conversations rather than being outnumbered by a uniform mass of faces. If someone is not concentrating, it is often sufficient to stop for a moment and watch them to regain their attention (Merrin 1998).

Good teachers pre-empt bad behaviour by constantly scanning the classroom and noting those who are not working and then moving towards them, maintaining eye contact. Kyriacou (1998) refers to this as 'withitness', adding that efficient teachers are skilful at noting cues that indicate what is going on. They can thus nip potential bad behaviour in the bud. Good teachers also move around the classroom, looking for those having problems and for those becoming restless with the work they have been given and either trying to re-engage them or changing the task (Watkins 2000). A key issue here is that we are defining the behaviour as 'bad' rather than labelling the pupil as 'bad' – a critical distinction.

Get on with them

Gray and Richer (1988) found that relationships were more positive when teachers emphasized rewards rather than punishments, acted immediately on any indiscipline, were approachable about students' personal problems, involved students in leadership activities and arrived punctually for lessons. Fontana's research (1994: 78) indicated that the 'effectiveness of non-material rewards depends closely upon the prestige and status in which the person giving the rewards is held. If a teacher is liked and admired by the class, then generally individuals will value his or her praise and encouragement'.

Concluding the lesson and dismissing the class

Keep track of time in order to allow enough time to tidy up, collect books, give homework, answer any questions students might have and to pass on any other instructions or information to the class. While this should be done in good time, it is necessary to ensure that students do not start to pack away before being told to do so by the teacher. The lesson might end with some words of praise about the work done and a summary of what was covered. In some schools, a very formal lesson structure is used across all subjects, in which teachers write down the lesson aims at the start of the lesson (for example, on a flip chart) and then refer to them at the end of the lesson.

The leaving of the classroom should be well ordered and if necessary, controlled. The beginner teacher may need to dismiss students in groups rather than permitting a rush for the door. Only when the teacher is sure the class can leave the room in an orderly fashion should they be allowed to do so.

Reflection

When the lesson is over it is advisable to try to find some time to run over how it went and to determine ways in which it might be improved. Dean (1996: 103) suggests that beginner teachers might ask themselves the following questions:

Did the lesson start well?
How satisfactory was the organization?
Did changes of activity go smoothly?
Were there any behaviour problems?
If so, were they dealt with in a satisfactory way or could they have been handled better or differently?
What was the context of any problems?
Could they have been avoided with different planning?
Were there some students who did not benefit from the work in the lesson?
How could they be dealt with differently on another occasion?
Was the balance of time about right?
Did the lesson ending go smoothly?
Were the objectives of the lesson achieved?

Many beginning teachers are asked during their training to observe lesson phases in order to chart what experienced teachers do to move the teaching session from one stage to another in an orderly, effective manner. It is frequently the case that disruption occurs at the point where the lesson moves from one phase to the next. Trainee teachers are usually asked to focus on 'starts and finishes', the language used, the ways in which experienced teachers respond to early signs of trouble, whether teachers plan for fast workers and slow learners, whether teachers give clear signals of movement from one phase to the next ('Right, we are going to pack up in five minutes') and what actions teachers take with disruptive students.

It might be advantageous for beginner teachers and those who are more experienced to reflect on and identify the sorts of professional skills they think are necessary for themselves and their colleagues. Wragg (1993) suggests this might take the form of a hierarchical list of dimensions with levels appropriate to beginners and more experienced teachers:

In class management, for example, a notion like 'organize the handing out and collection of materials' might be a fairly basic matter,

involving a teacher thinking about how this can best be organized . . .
On the other hand, 'judging the right language register, appropriate
response to and suitable activities for a student bewildered by a new
mathematical or scientific concept' clearly exerts a much higher level
of intellectual and practical demand.

(Wragg 1993: 57)

Smith and Laslett (1993) describe the 'four Ms' needed for effective
classroom organization: management, mediation, modification and
monitoring. The management of lessons includes their organization and
presentation, which requires the ability to analyse the various phases
and elements of a lesson, select and deliver appropriate material and reduce sources of friction. Mediation, they argue, is about ways to enhance
self-concepts and avoid damaging confrontation in the classroom. Modification is about understanding learning in order to devise programmes
for shaping and rewarding behaviour. Monitoring involves checking the
effectiveness of school policies on discipline and pastoral care as well as
how senior management can help colleagues avoid stress and cope with
problems in classroom management.

Many transactions that take place are immediate and unpredictable
and coping with the idiosyncratic and peculiar demands of classroom life
sets school teaching apart as a distinctive professional activity. Essentially,
teachers have to create, organize and promote learning in a forum that
does not offer ideal conditions, very often with limited resources and in
which they must maintain order and be responsive to students' different
temperaments, abilities and social relationships. Smith and Laslett (1993)
compare teaching with a game of chess in which experienced teachers
understand opening moves and their effects on subsequent moves. It can
also be argued that learning, both academic and social, follows the same
rules.

In the course of a day, teachers are frequently called upon to make
rapid, informed judgements that are shaped by a number of factors. These
include, among other things, their own values about how students should
be treated, their own physical and mental state and their intuition about
the current classroom climate. This means that they may react differently
to similar sets of circumstances from day to day (Watkins 2000). Essentially teachers need to be encouraged to understand and develop different
styles of management and organization according to the work being
undertaken as well as the age and ability of the students. Clearly, different
strategies apply according to whether the teaching is aimed at the whole
class, a group or an individual.

Therefore, although teachers need to be consistent, paradoxically they
also need to be flexible and adaptable and the ways in which they operate
with one group may not be appropriate with another (Watkins 2000).
There is no one remedy for every problem and teachers must identify
those strategies and techniques that work best for them and fit their own
philosophy of teaching. Successful teachers operate a series of bargains
and accommodations that are essential to maintain a healthy learning
environment. The resolution of these tensions is described by McNamara
(1994: 67) as 'practical pedagogy'. 'The teacher's practical pedagogy should

be based upon informed choices so that she [*sic*] is aware of the costs and benefits entailed in pursuing one course of action rather than another'. These informed choices are part of a collection of strategies that teachers build up and can draw upon and the development of these is a career-long task (Chase and Chase 1993).

As we have indicated, the teacher's job is largely about maintaining order, which does not necessarily mean dealing with discipline problems and disruptions. Rather, it is about allocating attention and 'orchestrating the flow of people, events and materials in a confined space with few resources' (McNamara 1994: 22). Although the focus of maintaining order is not disciplinary, it can be argued that teachers who successfully achieve this, have fewer discipline problems.

Managing behaviour

The sort of misbehaviour that teachers deal with most regularly is of a persistent, low-grade nature such as 'talking out of turn', 'calculated idleness or work avoidance', 'hindering other students' and 'making unnecessary (non-verbal) noise' (DES 1989). These repetitious patterns of bad behaviour can result in student underachievement as well as teacher and student stress. They can also lead to habitual negative responses from teachers, which do nothing to improve the situation and can actually exacerbate it.

As Watkins and Wagner (1987: 9) warn, 'Whether a student's action is seen as a "breach of discipline" will depend on who does it, where, when, why, to whom, in front of whom and so on'. One teacher's interpretation of deviancy may be another's idea of liveliness and creativity. This is where a whole-school policy is essential so that behaviours can be evaluated and responded to in a socially just and fair manner (Lund 1996). One of the first questions to ask of problem behaviour is, 'how can we try to ensure it does not arise?' or 'how do we understand it?' An inability to understand the other side is frequently at the root of classroom dissonance:

> It is all too easy for both sides to set up the other as a cardboard cut-out: a caricature of lawlessness on the one side, of oppression on the other. Neither opponent acts alone. For the adolescent boy angrily confronting his teacher, the endorsement, the admiration of his watching classmates is crucial. To the teacher trying to contain the potential violence, at stake is his [*sic*] own professional reputation: the approval or the contemptuous pity of his colleagues. Both sides have to win. It has become necessary to fight to the death.
>
> (Salmon 1995: 79)

Watkins (1995) suggests that it is advisable to take a broad problem-solving approach which sees behaviour in terms of the constructive engagement of students. The sort of language used to describe disruptive incidents can carry interesting messages and it is important to remain focused on the behaviour and not the person. Salmon (1995) warns against the 'language of complaint':

Instead of focusing on the unpleasant effects which a particular action may have for others, it becomes necessary to step into the aggressor's shoes, to try to see what he or she may be attempting to achieve by such behaviour. Rather than seeing hostile behaviour as an in-built problem of particularly difficult individuals, it becomes possible to look for what is essentially at stake for young people who behave in this way. The situation may then be resolved, without either side 'winning', by means which allow students to keep face, to retain their vital sense of dignity.

(Salmon 1995: 79)

In addition, as Watkins (1995: 3) points out, 'by talking about patterns of behaviour, diagnostic thinking can be improved and a better range of interventions considered'. Schools with well-articulated behaviour policies are likely to deal more confidently with issues of discipline and individual teachers, in the knowledge they will be supported, can feel empowered to try to handle all or most of the routine discipline problems themselves. For instance, in a study by Maxwell (1987) it was suggested that there were lower suspension rates in schools where teachers felt empowered to deal with behaviour problems. As a first strategy, it is useful to ask students whom you consider to be misbehaving 'what are you doing?', followed by 'why are you doing it?' rather than simply diving in with 'stop doing that'. It is also advisable to offer students a choice – 'if you do that again then this will be the consequence' so it is *their* action that triggers any punishment rather than simply being *you* punishing them.

The role of the student

On examining student–teacher relationships, Hargreaves (1975) found that students take particular interest in three aspects of teachers' behaviour: their discipline style; their instructional style; and their personal characteristics. Other studies show that students prefer teachers who: are respectful to them; listen to their concerns; consult them; and enhance their self-esteem. According to Morrison and McIntyre (1969) and Nash (1976) students prefer teachers who: maintain a disciplined atmosphere; are cheerful; give interesting lessons; take an interest in students as individuals; and present an amicable learning situation. Students expect to learn and to be taught and those teachers who fail to be friendly, firm and fair in their dealings are frequently 'punished' by students for refusing to be 'proper' teachers. The punishment usually takes the form of bad behaviour as a way of 'getting their own back' but may also take the form of 'bunking off'. In extreme cases students may stop coming to school altogether. For those students who have been long-term absentees or truants it is important that teachers realize their return to school may be very difficult and may be on a very fragile footing (Reid 1987). Teachers would be advised not to make an issue of their return but to welcome them back unobtrusively, aware that academic and social reintegration may be necessary.

School procedures and ways of operating should be made explicit for students in order to encourage them to take responsibility, make decisions, organize themselves and control their own behaviour. By setting high standards for themselves, teachers can encourage students to do likewise (Charlton and David 1993; McManus 1994). It should be kept in mind, however, that students come from a variety of backgrounds with a wide range of experiences and what is understood by 'high standards' and what is attainable may vary between students and for students at different times in their school career.

Bryk and Driscoll (1988: 89) found that students were better behaved in schools with a well-developed community spirit. Such schools, 'attend to the needs of students for affiliation . . . provide a rich spectrum of adult roles, engage students personally and challenge them to engage in the life of the school'. Relations between staff and students can be further developed and deepened when they are given the opportunity to see each other in different roles; for example, in a drama production, in organizing a school fair, or on a school journey. There is a tendency for both teachers and students to ascribe to each other narrowly prescribed roles and it can be a revelation for both parties to observe different and often unimagined facets of the other, outside the teacher/student situation.

Conclusion

Although teachers' lessons should challenge the students academically, Bereiter (1972) argued that much lesson content is not always academically demanding and the organization of students is a fairly straightforward activity. However, the integration of these activities is far from straightforward and to orchestrate them into a coherent performance presents teachers with an enormous challenge. It is this notion of practical performance that is central to the teacher's pedagogical expertise – the ability to keep the plates spinning while attempting to promote learning in the dynamic, social arena of the classroom. Teaching can feel rather like giving four or five improvised plays in a single day. Good classroom organization and management liberate teachers from many of the daily hassles and confrontations and enable them to establish the order without which the classroom can become a battleground (Watkins and Wagner 1987).

For teachers to feel comfortable in the classroom it is advisable that they try to develop their own professional philosophy, to think about the sort of teacher they would like to become and decide what they need to do to actualize this aim. They might also like to consider the sorts of relationships they would like to develop with both colleagues and students and identify where compromises might be necessary. These issues are crucial as they relate to the sort of person the teacher is and to their reasons for being a teacher. It is the willingness continually to reflect on these concerns that will enable teachers to grow, develop, enjoy and make a success of their teaching.

References

Bereiter, C. (1972) Schools without education, *Harvard Educational Review*, 42(3): 390–413.

Bryk, A.S. and Driscoll, M.E. (1988) *An Empirical Investigation of the School as a Community*. Chicago, IL: University of Chicago School of Education.

Charlton, T. and David, K. (1990) Towards a whole school approach: helping to ensure pupils are fit for the future, *Links*, 3(15): 20–4.

Charlton, T. and David, K. (eds) (1993) *Managing Misbehaviour in Our Schools*. London: HMSO.

Chase, C.M. and Chase, J.E. (1993) *Tips From the Trenches*. Lancaster, PA: Technomic Publishing Co.

Claxton, G. (1984) *Live and Learn*. London: Harper and Row.

Cooper, P. (1993) *Effective Schools for Disaffected Students: Integration and Segregation*. London: Routledge.

Dean, J. (1996) *Beginning Teaching in the Secondary School*. Buckingham: Open University Press.

Department of Education and Science (DES) (1989) *Discipline in Schools*, The Elton Report. London: HMSO.

Department for Education and Employment (DfEE) (1997) *Excellence in Schools*. London: HMSO.

Fontana, D. (1994) *Managing Classroom Behaviour*. Leicester: British Psychological Society.

Gray, J. and Richer, J. (1998) *Classroom Responses to Disruptive Behaviour*. Basingstoke: Macmillan Educational.

Hargreaves, D. (1975) *Interpersonal Relations and Education*, 2nd edn. London: Routledge and Kegan Paul.

Hill, D. (1990) Order in the classroom, *Teacher Magazine*, 1(7): 70–7.

Kyriacou, C. (1998) *Essential Teaching Skills*, 2nd edn. Cheltenham: Stanley Thornes.

Lund, R. (1996) *A Whole-School Behaviour Policy: A Practical Guide*. London: Kogan Page.

McManus, M. (1994) Managing classes, in B. Moon and A. Shelton-Mayes (eds) *Teaching and Learning in the Secondary School*. London: Routledge.

McNamara, D. (1994) *Classroom Pedagogy and Primary Practice*. London: Routledge.

Maxwell, W.S. (1987) Teachers' attitudes towards disruptive behaviour in secondary schools, *Educational Review*, 39(3): 203–16.

Merrin, C.S. (1998) Managing Students with Difficult and Challenging Behaviour in a Mainstream Secondary School and the Implications for Staff Development. Unpublished MA dissertation. London: Institute of Education.

Morrison, A. and McIntyre, D. (1969) *Teachers and Teaching*. Harmondsworth: Penguin.

Nash, R. (1976) *Teacher Expectations and Pupil Learning*. London: Routledge and Kegan Paul.

Neill, S. and Caswell, C. (1993) *Body Language for Competent Teachers*. London: Routledge.

O'Brien, T. (1998) *Promoting Positive Behaviour*. London: David Fulton.

Reid, K. (ed.) (1987) *Combating School Absenteeism*. Sevenoaks: Hodder and Stoughton.

Rigoni, D. and Walford, G. (1998) Questioning the quick fix: assertive discipline and the 1997 Education White Paper, *Journal of Education Policy*, 13(3): 443–52.

Rutter, D., Maughan, B., Mortimore, P. and Ouston, J. (1979) *Fifteen Thousand Hours: Secondary Schools and Their Effects on Children*. London: Open Books.

Salmon, P. (1995) *Psychology in the Classroom*. London: Cassell.

Sinclair, A. (1999) *How to Succeed in an Inner-City Classroom: A Guide for New Teachers*. London: Bell Publications.

Smith, C.J. and Laslett, R. (1993) *Effective Classroom Management*. London: Routledge.

Watkins, C. (1995) *School Behaviour. Viewpoint No. 3.* London: Institute of Education.

Watkins, C. (2000) *Managing Classroom Behaviour: From Research to Diagnosis.* London: Institute of Education, University of London in association with the Association of Teachers and Lecturers.

Watkins, C. and Wagner, P. (1987) *School Discipline: A Whole School Approach.* Oxford: Blackwell.

Watkins, C. and Wagner, P. (2000) *Improving School Behaviour.* London: Paul Chapman Publishing.

Wayson, W.W., Achilles, C., Pinnell, G.S. *et al.* (1982) *Handbook for Developing Schools with Good Discipline.* Bloomington, IN: Phi Delta Kappa Educational Foundation.

Wragg, E.C. (1981) *Class Management and Control: A Teaching Skills Workbook.* Basingstoke: Macmillan Education.

Wragg, E.C. (1984) *Classroom Teaching Skills.* London: Croom Helm.

Wragg, E.C. (1993) *Class Management.* London: Routledge.

15

Differentiation in theory and practice

Christine Harrison

Introduction

Differentiation, progression and coverage of the curriculum were the three main sources of concern for teachers cited in the evaluation of the implementation of the Science National Curriculum by Russell *et al.* (1995). That this continues to be the case with the implementation of yet another version of the National Curriculum in 2000 and that the concerns are not confined to science is also evident. The purpose of this chapter is to consider not only what differentiation is, and how some schools have responded to it, but to suggest teaching and learning styles that allow for effective differentiation.

In the Collins English dictionary, the verb 'to differentiate' is explained as 'to make different; to distinguish; to classify as different'. The mystery lies in what it is that has to be made different, distinguished or classified. It is not about the differences between pupils; these manifest themselves anyway. The difference is in the types of action taken by schools and teachers, rather than in the abilities of the pupils or the structure of the system. This fits Dickinson and Wright's (1993) description of the purpose of differentiation as 'intervening to make a difference'.

Differentiation is not a new idea within education, but simply one that has gained more prominence in recent years. The 1986 Department of Education and Science (DES) document, *Better Schools*, lists differentiation as one of the four indicators of an acceptable curriculum. A previous DES document, in 1981, states that the teacher's professional role is to:

> recognise and develop the potential of individual pupils. All pupils should be encouraged throughout their school careers to reach out to the limits of their capabilities. This is a formidable challenge to any school since it means that the school's expectation of every pupil must be related to their individual gifts and talents.
>
> (DES/WO 1981: 9)

Maximizing an individual's potential hinges on creating learning experiences for children that will allow each of them to progress, from the stage where they currently are, towards where each has the capability to be. It is about identifying what a pupil can do and deciding on the subsequent experience, encouragement, support and advice that will further develop the knowledge, ideas and skills of that pupil. The Warnock Report (DES 1978) emphasized this by stating that 'The purpose of education for all children is the same: the goals are the same. But the help the individual children need in progressing towards them will be different'.

Dickinson and Wright (1993) defined differentiation in a pragmatic way as 'the planned process of intervention in the classroom that maximizes potential based on individual needs'. Thus differentiation requires teacher strategies that recognize pupil capabilities and provide for educational development. These strategies require the teacher to utilize formative assessment practices to gather information about learners and act upon it (see Chapter 17). Since a collection of assessment information of this sort is certain to reveal heterogeneity (Black 1998), then any action that ensues that is likely to be effective involves differentiation. For some teachers, this will require a change in teaching style, while others will adapt and strengthen their present pedagogy to develop differentiation in their classrooms.

The 1982 Cockcroft Report (DES 1982) drew attention to the 'seven year difference' in mathematical understanding of children entering secondary school and there is every reason to suppose that a similar range exists within other curriculum areas. The task facing teachers in developing a differentiated curriculum is neither simple nor easy. In some situations, teachers choose to ignore formative assessment and the need to differentiate because they feel that it is better not to know the details of the problem if they think that there is little that they can do to rectify it (Perrenoud 1991). There is no miracle remedy but there are recognizable ways of differentiating and within each of these there are a number of strategies that can be identified. By selecting, practising, developing and honing these strategies, teachers can evolve their own systems of differentiation that suit their teaching style and provide for their pupils' needs.

Strategies for differentiating

There are three main approaches to differentiation: by task; by outcome; and by support. These approaches are not exclusive and it is possible that all three may be working concurrently within a single learning environment. A common response of some schools and teachers is to try and differentiate by organization. These schools have dealt with the wide range of needs by organizing the pupils into narrow bands of abilities for all their lessons (streaming or banding) or for specific subjects (setting). Within classrooms, some teachers place pupils into working groups of similar ability, so that the range of needs in each group is reduced. However these systems of organization are not in themselves a means of differentiating. The range of pupil needs and abilities within one classroom might be reduced by organizational methods but this only limits the range to which the teacher needs to respond. Organization may reduce the number of strategies that a teacher needs to employ or reduce the preparation time in planning and preparing for a reduced number of needs, but it is not differentiation per se.

'Differentiation by organization' is simply a mechanism to begin making differentiation manageable. There are a number of teachers, schools and educationalists who would consider the implications of setting, streaming and banding intolerable, mainly because they 'label' pupils and limit the expectations of both pupils and teachers (see Chapter 16). Rowntree (1988) discusses this 'self-fulfilling prophecy' by considering that pupils generally have been led to believe that they cannot all achieve a worthwhile level of learning. Those that exhibit that they can learn early on are recognized by both their teachers and peers and continue to progress with their learning. Other pupils, who have not had the opportunity or confidence to demonstrate some competency or other, remain unrecognized in the social context of the classroom and possibly continue unchallenged and perhaps unsuccessfully in their learning. In extreme cases, pupils in bottom sets may opt out of the system, claiming that they cannot do a particular subject and refuse to try to engage in classroom activities. Dweck (1986) refers to such behaviour as 'learned helplessness' and highlights the fact that this is more common in mathematics and science than elsewhere in the curriculum. While there is not time and space to pursue this here, it is a complicated issue that teachers and schools need to unravel, evaluate and consider. The concern that I have about 'differentiation by organization' is that some may believe that this action at the organizational level removes the need to differentiate, rather than realizing it simply reduces the range of response required.

Some teachers view differentiation as a system that caters for the extremes of the range, for pupils who are viewed as 'special' and not typical (Naylor and Keogh 1998) and as such either delegate responsibility to special educational needs departments or support teachers. They therefore do not differentiate for the majority of the class because they do not feel that such an approach is needed and do not cater for the very able or statemented pupils because they consider this an extra burden, outside their area of expertise and not their responsibility.

Differentiation by task

This strategy involves offering different activities to individuals or specific groups of children where the learning outcomes may be similar or different. At the simplest level, the teacher finds or develops a number of tasks that will match the learning needs of each of the pupils in the class. However the practicalities of lesson planning usually limit the number of tasks to around three; yet the range of needs that reflects the capabilities and past learning experiences of the pupils in the class will undoubtedly warrant a larger number than this. Three tasks within one lesson are a beginning however and, if care is taken to match tasks to students' abilities, aptitudes and interests, then it is possible for the system to work and evolve.

The manner in which the teacher introduces a task to pupils can be used to fine-tune the task to individual needs. The choice of stimulus activity, depth of detail, clues given, ways in which links with previous learning are highlighted and, most importantly, which outcomes are stressed, can all be used to hone a task to suit an individual or group of pupils.

Allowing students a choice in tasks will enable them to develop their differing aptitudes and interests. Giving pupils a shared role in the responsibility for their learning fosters good practice for future learning and creates a sense of motivation and trust. The effectiveness of this will depend even further on the teacher giving explicit outcomes and instructions to pupils, so that pupils are aware of all the tasks to be undertaken and therefore make a sensible choice. Discretion will obviously need to be used by the teacher to ensure suitable choices are made.

If resources such as worksheets are used within activities, the selection or production of these might focus on appropriate readability levels, ease of use and good design to ensure accessibility for pupils. The appearance of a worksheet must invite a pupil to interact with it, removing any barriers to learning by its clarity, interest and attractiveness. It may be beneficial to replace text-based materials with other sources, such as video or audiotapes, CD ROMs or concept keyboards (see Chapter 18). An alternative delivery may stimulate interest and fit in with the preferred learning style of certain pupils.

In some schools and within some published courses, learning modules are designed that cater for different abilities. Within a topic that lasts several weeks, teachers map predetermined routes for different ability groups (for example, average, above average and below average pupils). This is a form of differentiation by task. However, there are drawbacks with such approaches, which teachers must overcome if such schemes are to be effective. This approach may reinforce teacher expectation of individuals and limit the opportunities available for pupil learning. It may also label pupils and create a poor work ethos with some pupils. Unless a regular monitoring system is built into the scheme, pupil progress during the topic will not be recognized and mismatches of work with pupil capabilities may occur. The formative assessment role of the teacher is vital in this approach to differentiation, as with other differentiated approaches, because the teacher is the link between the materials and the learner that can mediate and encourage the learning. Published schemes might save the teacher time in terms of devising activities but they still require the teacher to judge the appropriateness of each activity, to adapt activities to allow access or to extend pupil learning and also to match the challenges of an activity with the capabilities of individual pupils. The most worrying aspect of implementing a prescribed system, such as published material, is that it may cause some teachers to shift the responsibility for differentiation from their own planning and delivery to that of the scheme, instead of adapting the resource to meet the context of their classroom situation.

Differentiation by outcome

This strategy involves organizing an activity from which several outcomes may emerge. Such activities are often called 'open-ended', but it is important that the teacher anticipates and identifies learning routes that particular pupils might take within the activity so that the necessary support can be given. It may be that the knowledge or skills developed in the activity are common to most pupils but the activity allows for different products. This will cater for students' differing aptitudes and interests and preferred learning styles, particularly if the products can be created within different media.

Differentiation within an activity that starts from a common point may develop the learning so that there are differences in the knowledge or skills that are acquired by individuals. This often requires an exploration of what ideas and skills pupils bring to the learning situation by such techniques as brainstorming or concept maps, or simply encouraging pupils to ask questions about some stimulus material that reflects their ideas, knowledge and background interests. From this starting point, different ideas can be developed within the planned activity and the final products and outcomes match with pupil capabilities.

It is important to ensure that all pupils achieve at their highest capable level when working on a task where the outcomes are differentiated. Pupils will be more likely to compare their product with others in the class if the task seems, on the surface, a common one, and such comparisons can be demotivating. The way in which progress is recognized for each pupil may be an essential factor in overcoming such problems. In helping pupils recognize what they have learned, how they have progressed over recent weeks and in negotiating targets for future learning situations, an anxiety-free and supportive learning environment can be established. Such an atmosphere would benefit any mode of differentiation, but is especially important when differentiating by outcome, as this system can expose the capabilities of pupils to a wider audience than differentiation by task.

Differentiation by support

This form of differentiation is probably the most important and yet least recognized of the three described. Teachers know that some pupils require more help than others to complete a set task and, in giving or organizing this help, teachers are differentiating by support. Many teachers do this intuitively in their classrooms, seeing it as simply part of their teaching role. It exists as a variety of strategies, which I have grouped as resources, group work and interventions.

Within a task, pupils might need help getting started, staying on task or completing specific sections. Poor readers can be helped by providing audiotaped versions of the worksheet. Alternatively, hint sheets, planning sheets or study guides may cue pupils in to what they should do. The use of icons on worksheets, spelling lists or keywords can also be helpful for some pupils.

Vygotsky (1978), a psychologist whose work underpins a number of recent educational projects and research ideas, believed that human development is 'intrinsically social and educational' and that 'children undergo profound changes in their understanding by engaging in joint activity and conversation with other people'. Group work not only overcomes the problems shy pupils have in one-to-one conversations, but presents a forum in which all pupils can voice their ideas. The language and analogies used allow pupils to reveal to themselves and others their thoughts and ideas, and also to compare these with the views of other learners. Group work can provide a supportive background that benefits all the learners within the group. However, there is more to group work than a number of pupils sitting around a table or the teacher arranging who should go in which group. The Oracle project (Simon and Willcocks 1981) which looked at interactions in primary classrooms, found that the majority of pupils worked as individuals within groups and so the effect of grouping did not actually benefit their learning. Getting children to work collaboratively and creating group identity are essential prerequisites to group work.

Support by intervention requires the teacher to observe individuals or groups of pupils engaged in activities and, from the responses or actions witnessed, to enter into an interaction with the pupils to direct the learning forwards. It is an on-the-spot assessment of where the learning has reached and then a decision about which direction it should now take. It is a difficult task because the teacher must judge carefully when to intervene, so that their words and actions do not hinder the flow of ideas between group members. The teacher must create time to do this because it performs two essential services; it provides a direct feedback message system on pupil progress and also shapes the learning programme for the pupils to ensure a close match with their capabilities. In order to do this, teachers must free themselves of the 'housekeeping' role that may occur when activity-based learning takes place. The organization and management of resources need to be carefully planned to give the teacher time to interact with pupils during the lessons.

Differentiation in action

The following three scenarios are descriptions of differentiation in action within different types of classroom. They have been adapted from good examples of differentiated practice that I have witnessed or have been told about in schools. They represent lessons in mathematics, English and science for which I apologize to readers from other disciplines. While the problems and solutions for differentiation may differ between subjects, I am convinced that the messages, hints and ideas that they generate are not domain-specific, and, as such, are easily transferable or adaptable to all subject areas.

The mathematics classroom

Kim's department uses an individualized scheme called SMILE to provide for the needs of pupils in mathematics. SMILE has a plethora of workcards, and the teacher regularly negotiates packages of one or two weeks' work with individual pupils. Kim spent most of her first year of teaching sitting at her desk, with a line of pupils waiting for their books to be marked or for Kim to tell them what to do next. Some pupils rarely spoke to the teacher but worked on at a steady, though not necessarily determined pace, while others were constantly demanding the teacher's attention. Kim had the resources for differentiated learning, but not the teaching and learning style to make it effective.

In order to overcome these problems, she introduced a learning contract. At the start of each topic of work she negotiated with pupils what work they were going to do, how long they anticipated each part of the work should take and how they were going to carry it out. She also asked each pupil to select a weekly target for improving some aspect of their learning, which was also included in the contract. The contracts were drawn up and signed by both the pupil and Kim, and pupils were encouraged to show and discuss their contracts with a mentor, who might be another pupil, a relative or form tutor. While initially the introduction of the contract procedures took up valuable class time, the pupils eventually became more expert in deciding what they were capable of achieving and in reflecting on their progress and previous learning, so that contract setting became a fast and efficient task. The contracts also engendered a sense of responsibility for their own learning amongst the members of the class and a more cooperative and collaborative work ethos. It also freed Kim to move around the class more, enabling her to interact better with the pupils by witnessing the activities as they occurred, rather than in the product they formed.

Kim made use of the differentiation potential of the SMILE scheme by making the pupils focus on their own learning strategies and capabilities. In carefully negotiating appropriate work and routine, she encouraged pupils to be more receptive to the learning experience and fostered a willingness to learn and respond to the experience. As a consequence of this, she created time within her classroom where she could begin to assess formatively and also, in helping individuals, to differentiate by support.

The science classroom

Rahana's department produced a detailed work scheme of the topic she was to teach. It had a number of activities, each with National Curriculum references and comprehensive apparatus and resources lists, and some of the activities had worksheets to support them. Rahana started her lesson using an idea taken from some developed by Bentley and Watts (1992). She placed a drawing on the overhead projector of an astronaut on the moon who had just let go of a hammer, and asked the class to think what would happen next to the hammer. After a few minutes, she asked for suggestions. Three possibilities were suggested by pupils:

- the hammer will remain where it is;
- the hammer will fall (slowly) to the moon's surface;
- the hammer will float upwards into space.

Rahana then asked the pupils to raise their hands for the one of these possibilities they believed to be correct. She then separated the class into three different groups, using the criteria of similar preconceptions to decide the appropriate grouping. Each group then had a different task to carry out before returning to the astronaut drawing and deciding whether their initial idea was upheld with the new evidence acquired from completing their activity.

One activity was based on a worksheet and a short video which the pupils took away to the resource corner and watched, using the remote control to stop or review sections of film that seemed interesting or important to the work they had been asked to do. The video focused on the effects of gravity and the pupils were required to answer a number of questions and then to write a paragraph explaining what gravity is and where can it be experienced.

Another activity was worksheet based and required pupils to discuss, in groups, events in a diary supposedly written by a space scientist living in the future on a moon station. Pupils had to list all the events on the moon that were linked with the moon's gravity and explain how these would be experienced differently on Earth.

The third activity was textbook based. Pupils read and discussed, in pairs, a section from the text that dealt with the difference between mass and weight, and then answered some questions and calculations from the book.

Rahana spent the first five minutes or so following the lesson introduction with the pupils attempting the diary activity, listening and helping each group list their first few ideas. She then moved to the video group and asked them to review for her how far they had got with the questions on the worksheet and any sequences on the video that were surprising for them so far. This took around 10 minutes, and Rahana then spent a further 10 minutes discussing with pairs from the textbook group what they had found from their reading.

This lesson demonstrates differentiation on many different levels. The teacher started with a stimulus activity that revealed something of pupils' current understanding of the work. She then geared the activity to build on their current understanding by providing three different tasks to direct their future learning. Her classroom organization and management meant that pupils were quickly and efficiently engaged in their appropriate tasks, leaving the teacher the freedom to move from group to group and differentiate by support. At the end of the lesson, she created an opportunity for both the pupils and the teacher to judge whether the learning had been developed by reviewing the final products and returning to the initial stimulus activity.

The homework asked pupils to use their ideas and notes from the lesson to either describe what would happen if a sport of their choice was played on the moon, or to invent a sport that would be better played on the moon than on Earth. This provided homework that was differentiated by outcome, where pupils could apply their developing ideas about gravity and the moon to explain sporting events.

The English classroom

Steven introduced an assignment on poetry by reading three short poems by different poets; Hughes, McGough and Owen, and asked pupils to state what they liked or disliked about each poem. He then divided the class into groups of four and gave each 10 cards that had statements concerning the nature of poetry. Each group was asked to discuss and select three statements that they either agreed with or felt were interesting. They then had to find a poem that they considered best illustrated their chosen statements. They were told to use the teacher as a resource for guidance and to look through the numerous poetry books that had been organized in four different areas in the classroom.

As each poem was selected, the group had to explain to the teacher what had led them to decide both on the statement and the choice of poem. Steven moved round the groups, checking on the progress pupils were making and encouraging pupils to remain on task. He started with a group who had been restless during the stimulus activity and who, by their body language, were initially disinterested in the task. He managed to answer questions from one group, while observing other groups working, and so was able to judge which groups were in need of direction and help. This work was developed in subsequent lessons to produce a class display on the 'Essence of Poetry', and also as the stimulus material for pupils writing their own poetry.

In this lesson, the teacher again begins with considering and sharing pupils' interests and ideas and by the use of prepared cards allows pupils some choice in the direction that their learning will take. The differentiation is undoubtedly by outcome, but in the selection of one statement rather than another, and in the degree of guidance and direction given to each group by the teacher, the learning routes are both different and supported as they develop. The organization of the books into four areas gave the pupils some space to work in and adequate resourcing and so further supported the work. The teacher also showed how he valued the work that was produced by creating a wall display that was subsequently used as a further learning stimulus. This strategy motivates pupils and allows them to see some of the markers in their progress as they complete one learning stage and use it to set off on the next.

Final thoughts

The classroom scenarios show three approaches to differentiation but what has not been considered is why these should be different from one another. It may be related to individual preferences with regard to teaching style or to the structures and constraints of a particular domain. Indeed, the problems and solutions to differentiation in the English classroom may be markedly different to those encountered in science, which again will differ in mathematics, classics or history. However the difference in differentiated approach seems to be governed more by the features of the learning group than that of the teacher or the subject. There is clearly considerable research potential within the realms of differentiation and a great deal of it could be well served by action research, where we can gain invaluable insights into teacher beliefs and practices with differentiation.

The difficulty for both new and experienced teachers is that they must decide which track to tread. The difference is only that experienced teachers have probably considered, tried and witnessed a greater range of teaching strategies and used a more extensive range of teaching resources. Charting the progress of your own attempts at scaling some of the complex routes of differentiation may be one way of analysing and evolving suitable techniques for future use, and will also provide a starting point for discourse with other colleagues, who may be seeking their own pathways.

References

Bentley, D. and Watts, M. (1992) *Communicating in School Science: Groups, Tasks and Problem Solving 5–16.* London: Falmer Press.

Black, P. (1998) *Testing: Friend or Foe?* London: Falmer Press.

Department of Education and Science (DES) (1978) *Special Educational Needs: Report of the Committee of Enquiry into the Education of Handicapped Children and Young People* (The Warnock Report). London: HMSO.

Department of Education and Science (DES) (1982) Mathematics Counts: Inquiry into the Teaching of Mathematics in Schools (Cockroft Report). London: HMSO.

Department of Education and Science/Welsh Office (DES/WO) (1981) *The School Curriculum.* London: HMSO.

Department of Education and Science (DES) (1986) *Better Schools.* London: HMSO.

Dickinson, C. and Wright, J. (1993) *Differentiation: A Practical Handbook of Classroom Strategies.* London: National Council for Educational Technology.

Dweck, C. (1986) Motivational processes affecting learning, *American Psychologist,* 41: 1040–8.

Naylor, S. and Keogh, B. (1998) Differentiation, in M. Ratcliffe (ed.) *ASE Guide to Secondary Science Teaching.* Hatfield: ASE.

Perrenoud, P. (1991) Towards a pragmatic approach to formative evaluation, in P. Weston (ed.) *Assessment of Pupils' Achievement: Motivation and School Success.* Amsterdam: Swets & Zeitlinger.

Rowntree, D. (1988) The side-effects of assessment, in R. Dale, R. Fergusson and A. Robinson (eds) *Frameworks for Teaching.* London. Hodder and Stoughton.

Russell, T., Qualter, A, McGuigan, L. and Hughes, A. (1995) *Evaluation of the Implementation of Science in the National Curriculum at Key Stages 1, 2 and 3. Volume 3: Differentiation.* London: SCAA.

Simon, B. and Willcocks, J. (eds) (1981) *Research and Practice in the Primary Classroom.* London: Routledge and Kegan Paul.

Vygotsky, L. (1978) *Mind in Society: The Development of Higher Psychological Processes.* London: Harvard University Press.

Further reading

Covery, A. and Coyle, D. (1999) *Differentiation and Individual Learners: A Guide for Classroom Practice.* London: Centre for Information on Language Teaching and Research.

Hart, S. (ed.) (1996) *Differentiation and the Secondary Curriculum: Debates and Dilemmas.* London: Routledge.

Harrison, C., Simon, S. and Watson, R. (2000) Progression and differentiation, in M. Monk and J. Osborne (eds) *Good Practice in Science Education: What Research Has to Say*. Buckingham: Open University Press.

James, F. and Brown, K. (1998) *Effective Differentiation*. London: Collins Educational.

Kerry, T. (1999) *Learning Objectives, Task-setting and Differentiation*. London: Hodder and Stoughton.

Naylor, S. and Keogh, B. (1995) Making differentiation manageable, *School Science Review*, 77(279): 106–10.

Postlethwaite, K. (1993) *Differentiated Science Teaching*. Buckingham: Open University Press.

Quicke, J. (1995) Differentiation: a contested concept, *Cambridge Journal of Education*, 25(2): 213–24.

Simpson, M. (1997) Developing differentiation practices meeting the needs of pupils and teachers, *The Curriculum Journal*, 1(8): 85–104.

Sotto, E. (1994) *When Teaching Becomes Learning: A Theory and Practice of Teaching*. London: Cassell Education.

Stradling, R. and Saunders, J. (1993) Differentiation in practice: responding to the needs of all pupils, *Educational Research*, 35: 127–37.

Teare, B. (1997) *Effective Provision for Able and Talented Children*. Stafford: Network Educational Press.

Waterhouse, P. (1990) *Classroom Management*. Stafford: Network Educational Press.

Waterhouse, P. (1990) *Flexible Learning: An Outline*. Stafford: Network Educational Press.

16

Setting, streaming and mixed ability teaching

Jo Boaler and Dylan Wiliam

Introduction

How should students be grouped for teaching? Should they be placed in groups according to some notion of general ability and taught in the same differentiated groups for every subject (streaming), in different 'ability' groups for different subjects (setting), or should classes include the whole ability range (mixed ability)? Are some methods of grouping more appropriate to older or younger children, and do different subjects lend themselves more to one sort of student grouping than another?

In this chapter, we review the research that has been conducted on ability grouping in the UK, the US and elsewhere. We look at the impact of different forms of ability grouping on achievement, on attitudes, and on the ways that young people develop their perceptions of who they are within the school system.

The history of ability grouping in the UK

For much of the twentieth century, it was widely believed that individuals had a certain amount of general 'ability' that was fixed (if not at conception or birth, at least very early in life) and could be measured accurately. This belief underpinned the selective system of secondary schooling which allocated children either to grammar or secondary modern schools on the basis of their scores on the eleven-plus test. The same belief underpinned the internal organization of schools. In the early 1960s, Jackson (1964) found that 96 per cent of junior schools used streaming for older students (10 and 11-year-olds) and 74 per cent had placed children into different classes based on their supposed 'general ability' by the time they were aged 7. Jackson's study also identified some of the negative effects of streaming, including the tendency of teachers to underestimate the potential of working-class children, and the tendency for the lower streams to be given less experienced and less qualified teachers. Jackson's report contributed towards an increasing public awareness of the inadequacies of streamed systems and in 1967 the Plowden Report (DES 1967, a major report on primary schools) recommended the abolition of all forms of ability grouping (Bourne and Moon 1994).

In the 1970s and 1980s there was an increase in the use of mixed ability grouping in both primary and secondary schools. This was partly driven by the evidence that setting and streaming created and maintained inequalities but was also prompted by evidence that 'ability' was not fixed, and that measures of a child's general ability at the age of, say, 11, typically accounted for less than half of the variability in students' achievements at age 16.

However, the 1990s witnessed a reversal of this thinking, with a number of schools reconsidering their policies on mixed ability teaching. This change was caused in part by the requirements of the end of key stage tests and the changes brought about in GCSE examinations as a result of the Education Reform Act (1988). In some subjects, the Key Stage 3 tests (often called SATs[1]) and the GCSE examinations are tiered so that which levels or grades are available depends on which tier the student sits, and the different tiers cover different subject matter. Even in subjects that do not use tiered tests and examinations, there are different requirements for different levels and grades, so preparing students within the same class for different tiers creates additional difficulty for the teacher. There is no doubt that many teachers regard mixed ability grouping as incompatible with the requirements of the National Curriculum (Gewirtz et al. 1993).

However, probably the major impetus for a move away from mixed ability grouping was another consequence of the Education Reform Act – the creation of an educational marketplace, in which schools are required to compete for students, so that schools have become much more concerned to create images that are popular with local parents:

> Mixed ability is also on our agenda. We're reviewing it at the moment . . . The National Curriculum has made us review it really. I think it may well have an offshoot though, it may make us attractive to parents . . . The staff are finding it more and more difficult, you see, resources have been cut, there's no doubt about it. With the National Curriculum coming in there are more and more subjects which are saying, 'coping with that ability range within the classroom, without the kind of support you need is very difficult'.
>
> (headteacher, quoted in Gewirtz et al. 1993: 243)

As a result of these twin pressures – a national curriculum that many teachers see as incompatible with mixed ability teaching, and the perception that ability grouping was popular with parents – the early 1990s saw significant numbers of secondary school subject departments returning to policies of setting (that is, subject-specific grouping by ability). Primary schools have faced overt pressure to group their students according to ability, at least for certain subjects, from both the Department for Education and Employment (DfEE) and the Office for Standards in Education

(Ofsted), and the new Labour government made its position clear in its 1997 White Paper *Excellence in Schools*: 'Unless a school can demonstrate that it is getting better than expected results through a different approach, we do make the presumption that setting should be the norm in secondary schools' (DfEE 1997).

Reasons for and against ability grouping

The main reason given for the use of setting has been that teachers can adapt their pace, style and content to particular ability groups. Ability grouping is believed to create greater homogeneity amongst students and enable more whole-class teaching. There is also a widespread notion amongst the education community that setting increases attainment, particularly for high ability students (Ball 1981a, 1981b; Dar and Resh 1986). This is a particularly relevant argument given that secondary schools are now ranked according to their GCSE results. On the other side of the argument, those who oppose setting generally do so because they are concerned that it creates inequality. Many proponents of mixed ability teaching also believe that there are significant advantages in giving students the opportunity to progress at different rates using differentiated learning materials (see Chapter 15 for a discussion of differentiated learning materials).

In one of the most significant studies of mixed ability and streamed teaching conducted in the UK, Ball (1981a) found that subject teachers in secondary schools differed in their preferences for ability grouping and that these preferences were formed in relation to a number of ideologies. The proponents of mixed ability grouping represented what he termed an 'idealist perspective'. They viewed mixed ability classes as an important part of comprehensive education that offered students a greater degree of equality of opportunity. At the other extreme he identified a group of teachers as belonging to the 'academic perspective'. This group were concerned about maintaining academic excellence and they viewed mixed ability classes as a threat to this concern. The third and largest group of teachers he placed within the 'disciplinary perspective'. These teachers were in favour of mixed ability teaching because they believed that the abolition of streams would reform the social atmosphere of the school and eliminate 'troublesome low stream anti-school classes' (Ball 1981b: 162).

Ball's three categories provide a useful summary of some of the issues and concerns that UK researchers have found influence decisions about mixed ability and setting or streaming in schools. The debate about ability grouping was well summarized by Slavin (1990: 473):

> In essence, the argument in favour of ability grouping is that it will allow teachers to adapt instruction to the needs of a diverse student body and give them an opportunity to provide more difficult material to high achievers and more support to low achievers. The challenge and stimulation of other high achievers are believed to be beneficial to high achievers. Arguments opposed to ability grouping focus primarily on the perceived damage to low achievers, who receive a slower pace and lower quality of instruction, have teachers who are less experienced or

able and who do not want to teach low-track classes, face low expectations for performance and have few behavioural models.

The debates about setting and mixed ability teaching have important implications, not only for the way in which students learn and develop, but for the ideological conflicts and resolutions that affect teachers in schools. What does research have to say about these issues, however? Does it support the notions that setting creates inequality or that setting diminishes or enhances attainment for certain students? In the next section we consider the way in which research findings support, contradict and, more generally, inform these various notions.

The outcomes of setting and streaming

Focus on equality

Most of the research that has been conducted in the UK into setting, streaming and mixed ability teaching has focused upon issues of inequality and on the effects of ability groupings upon students' development. Many of these studies have been of a qualitative nature, often focusing on a single school, in which students have been observed, interviewed and followed over long periods of time. The first of these to have a major impact on the educational community was conducted by Brian Jackson (1964). He found that children whose fathers were in professional jobs had a lower chance of being placed in a low stream than children with similar IQs whose fathers were in unskilled jobs. He also found that teachers were likely to underestimate working-class children and place these children in low streams.

In Ball's study of Beachside Comprehensive – a school that was moving from streaming to mixed ability teaching in the 1970s – he found that social class was an important factor in the allocation of students to different streams (Ball 1981a). Subsequent studies have found a range of other factors apart from 'ability' that have been shown to influence placement in ability groups:

> Although ability is supposedly the major criterion for placement in subject and examination levels, ability is an ambiguous concept and school conceptions of ability can be affected by perceptions that pupils are members of particular social or ethnic groups and by the behaviour of individual pupils. Factors related to class, gender, ethnicity, and behaviour can be shown to affect the placement of pupils at option time, even those of similar ability.
>
> (Tomlinson 1987: 106)

Ball concluded from his study that streaming does not allow the ideals of comprehensive education to be fulfilled, because although children from different social classes enter and share the same building, they are not given equal access to opportunities and they are inhibited from mixing with each other. Ball (1981a), Hargreaves (1967) and Lacey (1970) all found that placing students into high and low streams also created a polarization of students into pro- and anti-school factions. Thus, students who ended up in high sets or streams became pro-school whereas those who ended up in low sets or streams became anti-school and suffered all of the disadvantages associated with this. In a more recent study Abraham (1995) set out to investigate whether the polarization of pupils according to their social class occurred as a result of setting as well as streaming. He investigated a comprehensive school that made extensive use of setting, and found that students were also polarized into pro- and anti-school factions, based partly upon their social class, in response to the groups in which they were placed.

The various studies that have been conducted in the UK provide conclusive evidence that setting and streaming create and perpetuate social class divisions amongst students. They have also shown that students of similar ability are frequently placed in different sets or streams according to their social class, their gender or their ethnic origin (and presumably this is why low sets and streams in schools are often made up of disproportionate numbers of students who are black, working-class, male and who have behavioural problems). The studies have also shown that the experience of being placed in a low set or stream can create anti-school feelings that derive from diminished perceptions of self-image and worth. Indeed it was in response to some of these studies that many schools abandoned setting and streaming in the 1970s and 1980s.

Focus on attainment

As noted above, most of the studies of ability grouping conducted in the UK have primarily focused upon issues of equality and fairness (Abraham 1994) rather than on whether ability grouping does indeed improve learning. In contrast, research in the US has provided a wealth of empirical evidence concerning the relative achievement of students in academic, general and vocational tracks (what would be called streams in the UK). Slavin (1990) produced an important review of the most significant of these investigations, from the US and elsewhere.

Slavin included in this analysis every research study conducted in the field as long as they were relevant and methodologically sound. His review included the results of six randomized experiments, nine matched experiments and 14 correlational studies that compared ability grouping to heterogeneous groupings. Across the 29 studies reported Slavin found the effects of ability grouping on achievement to be essentially zero for students of all levels and all subjects (the median effect size was +0.01 for high achievers, −0.08 for average achievers and −0.02 for low achievers, none of which are significantly different from zero).[2] The four British studies that were included in Slavin's analysis found no differences in achievement between streamed and unstreamed classes.

One of the most carefully constructed series of studies into ability grouping was conducted in Israel (see Linchevski and Kutscher 1998). In one of the studies Linchevski and her colleagues compared the eventual attainment of students in 12 setted schools with their expected attainment, based upon entry scores. This showed that ability grouping had no effect on attainment in 10 of the schools and a small negative effect in the other two. A second study examined the thinking and performance of students of similar attainment who were on the borderline between two different ability bands and were thus assigned to different groups. While the differences in attainment between the highest-scoring students in the lower band and the lowest-scoring students in the upper band were very small, the subsequent attainment differed greatly, with the students assigned to the higher groups attaining significantly more than students of a similar ability assigned to lower groups. Linchevski concluded from this that the achievements of students close to the cut-off points were largely dependent on their arbitrary assignment to either the lower or higher group. Another study compared the achievements of two groups of students at the same school assigned either to setted or mixed ability groups. This study showed that the average scores of the most able students placed in setted groups were slightly, but not significantly, higher than the able students placed in mixed ability groups. However the scores of students in the two lower setted groups were significantly lower than similar ability students in the mixed ability classes. Linchevski found that low ability students in the mixed ability classes coped well with tests because they were used to high demands and high expectations.

Other studies that have found differences in achievement between homogeneous and heterogeneous groupings have tended to replicate Linchevski's finding with some small, statistically insignificant increases for students in high tracks gained at the expense of large *statistically significant* losses for students in low tracks (Hoffer 1992; Kerckhoff 1986). Readable reviews of the research on setting and streaming can be found in Hallam and Toutounji (1996), Harlen and Malcolm (1997) and Sukhnandan and Lee (1998). However, most studies of ability-grouping are limited in that they look at what happens to high or low attaining students *on average*, rather than on whether ability grouping or mixed ability grouping is more or less effective for particular students (what is sometimes called 'aptitude-treatment interaction').

In a UK research study, Boaler (1997a, 1997b, 1997c) combined aspects of the UK and US studies reported by performing an in-depth study of students over three years that focused upon the students' attainment, in addition to their beliefs and values. This revealed some surprising results. The research included case studies of two cohorts of students, matched in terms of ability, gender and socioeconomic status. One of the cohorts was taught mathematics in a mixed ability environment, the other in a highly differentiated, setted environment. The study showed that a significant number of *high ability* students were disadvantaged by setting arrangements, more specifically by their placement in the top set. These top set students developed negative attitudes and demonstrated considerable underachievement in class-based assessments and GCSE examinations. The students related their negative responses to the pressure, high expectations and fast-paced lessons they experienced (Boaler 1997b). In a comparison of the high ability students taught in the setted group with the high ability students taught in mixed ability groups, the students with the highest eventual achievement were those taught in mixed ability groups

(Boaler 1997a). One of the important differences between this study and many previous studies was that it considered individuals, rather than average scores reported across groups. It was this focus upon individuals that revealed that only *some* students were suited to a top set environment; many students reacted against it and underachieved because of it, particularly the most able girls.

Conclusions

There is a widespread belief, within and outside the UK education community, that setting is an advantageous way of grouping students – particularly high ability students. In an Ofsted survey, 94 per cent of schools were found to use setting in the upper secondary years for mathematics (*Guardian* 1996). The support for setting generally derives from a view that setting and streaming confer academic advantages, which are believed to outweigh the potential disadvantages for 'low ability' students as well as any discriminatory practices affecting disadvantaged groups of students of a particular ethnic group, class or gender. However there is little, if any, research that supports the notion that setting enhances achievement for students. Indeed, in bringing together the different research studies on ability grouping the general conclusion is that streaming has no academic benefits whatsoever, while setting confers small academic benefits on some high-attaining students, at the expense of large disadvantages for lower attainers. In terms of attitude and motivation, both setting and streaming appear to be damaging to the majority of students, and these findings appear to hold true across the age range and across different subjects. Research has also shown conclusively that implicit and explicit prejudices result in decisions being made about the grouping of students according to their ethnicity, social class and gender, which almost certainly contribute towards long-term underachievement and disaffection.

One of the reasons that students in setted and streamed groups do not achieve more than students in mixed ability groups, as many think they should, may be that teachers often do not acknowledge the mixed ability nature of setted groups. One of the general aims of setting is to reduce the spread of ability within the classroom. This often results in teachers believing that all of the students in an ability group can be taught at the same pace, using the same style and method. Teachers tend to teach towards a 'reference group' (Dahllöf 1971) in each class, at a pace to which all students are assumed to be able to adjust. This model has serious drawbacks for students who deviate from the reference group.

In an ongoing study of approximately 1000 students in six schools, as they moved from mixed ability to setted grouping, we found that teachers catered effectively to mixed ability groups in Year 8, using a variety of strategies for differentiation but adopted much more limited teaching styles when teaching setted groups (Boaler *et al.* 2000). These styles were associated with severe disaffection amongst students.

One advantage of setting and streaming, of course, is that many teachers are more comfortable with such systems. Teachers of subjects such as mathematics and languages in particular often have strong beliefs about the hierarchical nature of their subjects which they think preclude the use of differentiated materials with mixed ability classes. However, even teachers of these subjects have devised successful mixed ability approaches, such as the SMILE mathematics scheme and materials developed by individual mathematics departments (Boaler 1997a). Unfortunately, many of the schools and teachers that favour setting do not acknowledge the personal nature of their preference but reflect upon notions of academic attainment that research suggests are misguided.

The consequences of setting and streaming decisions are great. Indeed, the set or stream into which students are placed, often at a very young age, will almost certainly dictate the opportunities they receive for the rest of their lives, and 'opportunity to learn' is consistently found to be the most important factor influencing academic achievement in international comparisons (Bursten 1992). It is worth noting that England makes more use of ability grouping than *any* of the countries that outperform England in international comparisons.

Slavin (1990) points out that as mixed ability teaching is known to reduce the chances of discrimination, the burden of proof that some sort of grouping by ability is preferable must lie with those who claim that it raises achievement. Despite the wide range of well-conducted research studies in this area, this proof has not been forthcoming.

Notes

1 The effect size is the difference in group means, divided by the standard deviation, resulting in a measure of effect in standard deviations. Effect sizes less than 0.2 are generally regarded as small or negligible.

2 When the first national curriculum assessments for seven-year-olds were introduced in 1991, the external assessments were called 'standard assessment tasks' or SATs, following the recommendation of the TGAT report [see Chapter 3, this volume]. However, following representations from Educational Testing Services, the New Jersey-based developers of the American Scholastic Aptitude Test, which is known by the same acronym, the term Standard Assessment Task was changed to Standard Tasks. Furthermore, when the format for the first assessments at Key Stage 3, held in 1992, was changed from that originally prescribed by Kenneth Clark, then Secretary of State for Education, the name of the external component of Key Stage 3 national curriculum assessment was changed to 'national curriculum tests', as was that for the first Key Stage 2 assessments when they were introduced two years later. The external components of Key Stage 2 national curriculum assessment have therefore never been called 'SATs', but teachers, students and parents continue to refer to them in this way.

(Reay and Wiliam 1999: 353)

References

Abraham, J. (1994) Positivism, structurationism and the differentiation–polarisation theory: a reconsideration of Shilling's novelty and primacy thesis, *British Journal of Sociology of Education*, 15(2): 231–41.

Abraham, J. (1995) *Divide and School: Gender and Class Dynamics in Comprehensive Education.* London: Falmer Press.

Ball, S.J. (1981a) *Beachside Comprehensive.* Cambridge: Cambridge University Press.

Ball, S.J. (1981b) The teaching nexus: a case of mixed ability, in L. Barton and S. Walker (eds) *School, Teachers and Teaching.* Lewes: Falmer Press.

Boaler, J. (1997a) *Experiencing School Mathematics: Teaching Styles, Sex and Setting.* Buckingham: Open University Press.

Boaler, J. (1997b) When even the winners are losers: evaluating the experience of 'top set' students, *Journal of Curriculum Studies,* 29(2):165–82.

Boaler, J. (1997c) Setting, social class and survival of the quickest. *British Educational Research Journal,* 23(5): 575–95.

Boaler, J., Wiliam, D. and Brown, M.L. (2000) Students' experiences of ability grouping – disaffection, polarisation and the construction of failure, *British Educational Research Journal,* 27(5): 631–48.

Bourne, J. and Moon, B. (1994) A question of ability?, in B. Moon and A. Mayes (eds) *Teaching and Learning in the Secondary School.* London: Routledge.

Bursten, L. (ed.) (1992) *The IEA Study of Mathematics III: Student Growth and Classroom Processes.* Oxford: Pergamon.

Dahllöf, U. (1971) *Ability Grouping, Content Validity and Curriculum Process Analysis.* New York: Teachers College Press.

Dar, Y. and Resh, N. (1986) *Classroom Composition and Pupil Achievement.* New York: Gordon and Breach.

Department for Education and Employment (DfEE) (1997) White Paper, *Excellence in Schools,* Cmnd 3681. London: HMSO.

Department of Education and Science (DES) (1967) *Children and their Primary Schools* (The Plowden Report). London: HMSO.

Gewirtz, S., Ball, S.J. and Bowe, R. (1993) Values and ethics in the education market place: the case of Northwark Park, *International Studies in Sociology of Education,* 3(2): 233–54.

Guardian (1996) Blair rejects mixed ability teaching, *The Guardian,* 8 June.

Hallam, S. and Toutounji, I. (1996) *What Do We Know About the Grouping of Pupils by Ability? A Research Review.* London: University of London Institute of Education.

Hargreaves, D. (1967) *Social Relations in a Secondary School.* London: Routledge and Kegan Paul.

Harlen, W. and Malcolm, H. (1997) *Setting and Streaming: A Research Review.* Edinburgh: Scottish Council for Research in Education.

Jackson, B. (1964) *Streaming: An Education System in Miniature.* London: Routledge and Kegan Paul.

Kerckhoff, A.C. (1986) Effects of ability grouping in British secondary schools, *American Sociological Review,* 51(6): 842–58.

Lacey, C. (1970) *Hightown Grammar.* Manchester: Manchester University Press.

Linchevski, L. and Kutscher, B. (1998) Tell me with whom you're learning and I'll tell you how much you've learned: mixed ability versus same-ability grouping in mathematics, *Journal for Research in Mathematics Education,* 29(5): 533–54.

Reay, D. and Wiliam, D. (1999) I'll be a nothing: structure, agency and the construction of identity through assessment, *British Educational Research Journal,* 25(3): 343–54.

Slavin, R.E. (1990) Achievement effects of ability grouping in secondary schools: a best evidence synthesis, *Review of Educational Research,* 60(3): 471–99.

Sukhnandan, L. and Lee, B. (1998) *Streaming, Setting and Grouping by Ability: A Review of the Literature.* Slough, UK: National Foundation for Educational Research in England and Wales.

Tomlinson, S. (1987) Curriculum option choices in multi-ethnic schools, in B. Troyna (ed.) *Racial Inequality in Education.* London: Tavistock.

17 | Assessing pupils

Bob Fairbrother and Christine Harrison

Introduction

Assessment is one of the most important aspects of teaching yet it is often treated as unproblematic – simply a set of technical issues. However, the main thrust of this chapter is that the technical aspects are interconnected with a range of other issues that affect all teachers in one way or another. There are important questions to be asked about why we are assessing as well as what we assess. The chapter also concentrates on the more neglected aspects of teacher assessment rather than on the formal, high stakes assessments such as end of key stage tests and the GCSE and A-level examinations.

A complete assessment of pupils covering all their achievements in school will involve more than just a collection of scores and comments for each of the subjects they are taught. Constructing records of achievement which attempt to build up a profile of each pupil is an important, whole-school exercise in which you are likely to be involved. We say something about profiles, and about records and reports, but we do not have the space to deal fully with the subject.

Why assess?

Many teachers test their pupils regularly, often in the form of end-of-topic tests, believing that these actions inform their pupils, and other interested parties such as parents. Such action is not usually formative for most pupils in that the feedback is either absent or too ambiguous because it is coded into marks or grades and occurs too late to remedy any shortfall in the learning.

Testing can have other effects on the way that pupils learn. Poor results in tests can lead to low self-esteem and, with some pupils, result in lack of motivation and refusal to participate actively in future learning. Such pupils prefer to opt out of tasks because they feel that failure is inevitable, whatever effort they put in (see Holton 1995 for an account of this in a school). Pupils tell you that they 'can't do maths' or that 'it's no good teaching me French when I can't even spell in English'. Dweck (1986) categorizes the behaviour of such pupils as 'learned helplessness' and while this behaviour can begin in primary school, it becomes much more striking in its negativity as pupils reach adolescence. Effective assessment should provide an opportunity to motivate pupils to improve their work by providing clear feedback and an opportunity to see how they are progressing. To be effective, assessment has to be both reliable and valid.

Reliability and validity

Increasing the length of a test can increase its reliability, but more complex marking and misinterpretation of the questions can contribute to greater uncertainty (or unreliability) in the marks or grades which pupils are given. An examination is said to be reliable if a candidate gets the same mark in different circumstances, such as a different examiner marking the questions or the examination being held on a different day. In your informal assessments you can accept some unreliability because you can talk to the pupils about the meaning of the questions and about their answers and your marking. In public examinations such as the GCSE, discussion with pupils is not possible. Furthermore, when a lot is at stake, it is important that the examination is fair to all the candidates. This means that the examination boards put a lot of emphasis on reliability.

Validity is the most important characteristic of a test or examination. A simple way of describing it is to say that a test is valid if it does what you want it to do. There is a conflict between achieving high reliability and high validity. Probably the most reliable test you can devise is a single multiple-choice item. The limitations of this are obvious. A highly reliable measurement of something you do not want is not only a waste of time, it can be damaging if wrong decisions (inferences) are made using the information.

Increasing the validity of your assessment of pupils' performance in your subject involves increasing the variety of your questions. There are several consequences of doing this, for example:

- questions and hence tests become longer;
- marking becomes more difficult and time consuming;
- pupils can interpret the same question in different ways and so give different answers.

Wiliam (1993) suggests the validity of an assessment should be defined as a property of the inferences made on the basis of the assessment. It can be seen as the extent to which inferences within and outside the domain of assessment are warranted. So, for example, inferences made about the effectiveness of a school based on the proportion of students achieving five A–C grades in the GCSE is an inference that goes beyond the domain assessed. That is to say, the GCSE examiners compose their examinations (the domain of assessment) with the aim of assessing what pupils can do in their subject; they do not do it in order to use the results to measure school effectiveness. This is something that others do. There is not the space here to rehearse the arguments for and against the validity of that particular inference but you should read Wiliam (1993) if you wish to know more.

Wiliam (1996) uses the work of Messick (1980, 1989) to take the validity argument further. As well as an assessment being used to make inferences, it can also have consequences. These might or might not be desirable and might or might not be foreseen. Undesirable consequences reduce the validity of an assessment. For example, if you want to test pupils' ability to recall factual information, a series of simple short-answer questions is valid for that purpose and can be highly reliable. However the use of such a test would have some undesirable consequences if the pupils then concentrated on learning only that kind of information.

Summative assessment

Probably the biggest influences on your assessment practices and your assessment material are the key stage tests and the GCSE and A-level examinations. You have a duty to prepare your pupils for these tests and examinations, and it makes sense to incorporate the questions in your end-of-unit and end-of-year tests. The examination boards issue instructions and guidance for conducting assessments of practical work, and these will influence how you do your assessments further down the school.

You should realize, however, that these tests and examinations are constrained by time and space so that they cannot assess everything that your pupils should have mastered. For the key stage tests you are required to give a teacher-assessed level, and this can, and should, be based upon more than a repetition of what is assessed by these formal means. Furthermore these formal tests and examinations are endpoint assessments. Their results are used to produce a single grade or level which attempts to summarize the standard reached by a pupil at a particular point in time. For this reason they are often referred to as summative. The results are given to the pupils but they are also given to other people who use them for a variety of purposes such as selection for jobs and for further and higher education (see Swain 2000 for a more detailed discussion of summative assessment). Because they occur at an endpoint it is difficult to use the results to guide the future teaching and learning of the pupils involved. Some schools analyse the results of the tests to help improve the teaching of other pupils. For example, if a group of pupils taking a test did less well in questions on one topic than in questions on another, you can try to analyse the reasons for this and perhaps change your teaching.

Profiles, records and reports

If students perform differently in the various parts of an examination, then combining the different results into a single mark or grade represents a loss of information. A *profile* is a way of attempting to overcome this problem by setting out what is known of someone under separate headings. It is not a method of assessment but a record of information about someone. You are likely to contribute to profiles as a part of your job as a teacher; the most common is probably the school report sent home to parents at the end of the year. At a minimum this will contain marks or grades about test performance, about the effort a pupil has put in and, typically, some comments from the teachers.

It is important for you to distinguish between a *record* and a *report*. You should be keeping a *record* of each pupil you teach. It will contain information about marks given for classwork, homework and tests, but it will also give other details of what a pupil has done without attempting to mark or grade, or interpret it in any way. The record is for your own personal use when talking to pupils, parents and other teachers. Another person might not be able to make much sense of a record because you will probably use your own shorthand and rely on it to jog your memory. A record is flexible, continually being updated, and very informative (for you).

A *report*, on the other hand, interprets information before presenting it. You, for example, will interpret your records before making a report on a pupil. This makes a report shorter and easier to use but it is subject to the idiosyncrasies of the interpreter; you might see a pupil's behaviour as showing independence of mind but another teacher might see it as argumentative. A good record will enable you to talk knowledgeably about your pupils and to support your comments with specific examples.

Formative assessment

As teachers, you can use the assessment information that you gain to tailor the future learning experience of your pupils, both in terms of plans for the whole group and for individuals within the group. Assessment can also be used to chart pupil and group progress and inform you about the effectiveness and appropriateness of your teaching programme. This type of assessment is described as formative since there is a feedback mechanism for channelling the information gained into actions that modify future teaching and learning activities (see Sadler 1989 for more discussion of the interrelationship of formative assessment and teaching, and Black 1993 and Wiliam and Black 1996 for a detailed discussion of formative and summative assessment).

Self-assessment

While you might set up formative assessment situations, your pupils have a vital role to play in using the evidence to bring about improvement and in assessing themselves. However, self-assessment is not an easy behaviour for pupils to acquire. Broadfoot *et al.* (1988) discovered that pupils in secondary school found self-assessment difficult, partly because clear assessment criteria were not provided (see page 188 on subjective marking) but mainly because pupils tended to make judgements by comparison with peers (norm referencing) rather than with performance criteria (criterion referencing).

If you incorporate self-assessment and peer assessment (assessment by pupils of each other) into your classroom repertoire, you and your pupils will need to focus on the performance criteria for a piece of work. You can do this by discussing with the pupils work from the previous year or you can concoct pieces that emphasize particular problems or qualities that might occur in the piece of work that is about to be done by the class. Recognizing how certain criteria are displayed in someone else's work and which criteria are not met is a valuable exercise for the pupil which can ultimately help them in assessing their own work and in developing an awareness of how they themselves might improve on future tasks (see Fairbrother 1995 for a description of how this has been done with pupils).

Where teachers have concentrated on developing self-assessment techniques in their pupils, significant learning gains have been made. Fontana and Fernandes (1994) investigated the effect of daily self-assessment on achievement in mathematics. Teachers were given training in self-assessment methods on a 20 week part-time course which enabled them to teach their pupils to understand both learning objectives and assessment criteria. Pupils in these classes came to learn, over time, how to target their learning, and were allowed to select their own tasks from a range provided by their teacher. A control group was set up of pupils taught by teachers who had attended a similar length training course on a different aspect of education. The achievement gains of the pupils who used self-assessment techniques were significantly higher than those of the control group. An important message from this study is the necessity for training and for the inclusion of opportunities in the classroom for self-assessment creating individualized action.

Grades and comments

The necessity to concentrate on performance criteria is also evident in Butler's (1988) work. She found that when pupils were given performance criteria for specific tasks, followed by comment on the match, or not, of their individual performance, then their subsequent achievement was higher than pupils who were given grades or comments plus grades. This is interesting in that not only do grades not improve achievement, but they can override the positive effect of constructive comments related to task performance.

Many teachers find Butler's study difficult to deal with in that they cannot envisage an assessment system in their school that does not regularly grade work. The problem here seems to be that of emphasis. In a recent UK study, science and mathematics teachers attempted to put into action formative ideas developed from Black and Wiliam's (1998) review that led to the paper *Inside the Black Box*. Some of these teachers decided to mark all work by writing comments rather than grades in their pupils' books. Many of these teachers still graded work and recorded the grades in their mark books but the emphasis during feedback to pupils was on comments. Not only were pupils accepting of this behaviour but many reported that it helped them much more in understanding what they needed to concentrate on in future learning situations.

Workload

One of the big problems with writing comments on pupils' work is the amount of time it takes. Commenting on all the work of every pupil you teach is an ideal that needs to be tempered with judgement, otherwise everything else in your school life and your personal life might suffer. Different strategies can reduce the pressure. You can take advantage of periods of time in the classroom when pupils have been given work to do on their own for you to talk to one or two pupils about their work and write comments in their book. You can write comments on *some* of the work of all of your pupils. You can spread the load by writing comments on one-quarter of the pupils one week, another quarter the next week, and so on, so that in a four-week period all the pupils have received written comments. You need a good record keeping system so as to keep track of what you are doing. Yet another way is to write comments every month, say. In this way you can summarize progress and point out strengths and weaknesses. A month is a reasonable time – it is long enough for pupils to be able to show progress but short enough to be in the memory span of most pupils. You could require pupils to respond, in writing, to your comments so that you know they have read them.

Involving pupils in self-assessment can be a way of reducing your workload. Brown (1998) describes how pupils on the Graded Assessment in Mathematics project (GAIM) successfully maintained their own assessment records, with many pupils taking a proactive role in claiming which criteria they could fulfil. This allowed the teachers' role to be reduced to that of checking evidence and so diminished the idea of excessive workloads that teachers foresee as one of the barriers to adopting formative practices.

Technical issues

In the course of your teaching you assess your pupils many times. You can use some of the material from the formal, external examinations for your own internal purposes but you will also need to make up your own questions, particularly for your day-to-day teaching. You have three main ways of getting information from pupils – written, oral and practical. Which method you use will depend on what information you want and on what you are going to do with it. We deal here only with aspects of written and oral assessment since the assessment of practical work is rather more specialized and tends to be subject specific.

Objective marking

In objective marking (often called criterion-referenced) you are looking for specific points, and you award a mark (or marks) for each point. For example, the solution to a numerical question could have one mark for a statement of the correct theory, two marks for the method used in applying the theory, and one mark for the correct answer. You can usually decide for yourself how you divide up the marks, and it will depend on the relative importance that you attach to each part of the answer. Some guidance about this can be obtained from the specimen material which the examination boards issue as well as from the staff of your school.

Extended (prose) writing can often be broken down into its different parts such as, in geography, mention of weather conditions, local resources, and historical development in an explanation of why places are like they are. You might give three marks for each part and an additional three marks for the way everything is put together. This is less atomistic in the way marks are allocated and begins to move towards subjective marking.

Subjective marking

Subjective marking is usually more applicable to extended prose. You read what the pupil has written and make a holistic judgement on the quality of the answer. While objective marking lends itself to the award of numerical marks, subjective marking often results in a letter grade.

It would be wrong to dismiss subjective marking as unreliable. Teachers and examiners can be consistent in their subjective judgements particularly when the qualities that constitute a piece of work are clearly understood. A big advantage of subjective marking is that it is quick. Even five minutes spent on each of 30 essays represents two and a half hours of marking. However, you must know what you are looking for in the work – and so must the pupils. 'Please Miss,' says Mary, 'you gave me a C but Amanda got a B'. What must Mary do to improve? When setting the work you should make clear to the pupils what you want them to do. While fundamentals such as spelling, punctuation and grammar will always be present, frequently you will be concentrating on particular bits of the National Curriculum, for example:

- the social, cultural, religious, and ethnic diversity of a particular society (history);
- identify and describe characters and events in a story (English);
- use scientific knowledge and understanding to explain observations, measurements or other data or conclusions (science).

Perhaps Mary got a C because she neglected the religious aspects in her description of Victorian society. You must be able to tell her this. So marking pupils' work involves much more than simply giving a mark or a grade. You will write comments, follow up on what you write, keep records, and generally incorporate assessment as an integral part of your teaching.

Norm referencing and criterion referencing

Subjective marking is more easily norm-referenced than criterion-referenced. In a norm-referenced approach pupils are judged in relation to the performance of others. This means the same standard of work can be given a low grade if it comes from a pupil in a high ability group (because it is at the bottom end of the range), but a higher grade if it comes from a pupil in a low ability group (because it is at the top end of the range). In a criterion-referenced approach pupils are judged in relation to stated criteria, and all pupils will get the same mark if they meet the same criteria. You can read more about norms and criteria in many books, for example Rowntree (1987).

Attempts to make GCSE grades more criterion referenced ran into difficulty because candidates reached the same overall standard in a subject in many different ways. This has resulted in graded *descriptions* rather than grade *criteria*. Early versions of the National Curriculum used a criterion-referenced approach to decide on levels of attainment. Teachers were ticking hundreds of boxes in order to keep a record of which criteria their pupils had achieved. They were then using rules for adding up the ticks to decide on the level. Apart from any reservations about the validity of the final result, the system was unmanageable. The National Curriculum attainment targets now use 'descriptions of increasing difficulty', and a particular level 'describes the types and range of performance that pupils working at that level should characteristically demonstrate' (DfEE/QCA 1999). They are sometimes said to be domain referenced rather than criterion referenced because a level represents a domain of performance rather than the simple addition of several criteria. The advice given in the National Curriculum for using the descriptions to decide on a pupil's level of attainment at the end of a key stage is that 'teachers should judge which description best fits the pupil's performance' (for example, DfEE/ QCA 1999: 19). This involves a combination of subjective and objective information.

The subject department in your school, and even the school itself, might have a common marking policy so that heads of department, senior managers and pupils are able to interpret marks from different teachers in the same way. In addition most schools involve their teachers in discussions about standards so that the same standard of work is given the same mark or grade by different teachers.

Oral assessment

The most common oral assessment is the questioning you do as a part of your normal teaching. There are several reasons why you would do this, for example:

- introduction – finding out what pupils already know, creating interest in a new topic;
- revision – recalling the main points of the last lesson or of a period in the current lesson;

- monitoring – checking the understanding of pupils as teaching takes place.

There are some guidelines which you should keep in mind when asking questions:

- use pupils' names;
- do not allow pupils to call out answers;
- call upon pupils who have *not* put up their hands;
- spread questions round the class;
- do not always accept the first correct answer; ask other pupils if they agree or if they have more to add;
- allow time for pupils to absorb the question and to compose an answer (wait time).

Some of the above are obvious but are important enough to emphasize. For example, knowing and using pupils' names is more than showing the pupils you know them as individuals. After the lesson you can relate the names in your mark book and on pupils' exercise books to the individuals who put their hand up and answered questions in class. You can talk about pupils to other teachers and to parents, and so get a better understanding of the individuals you are teaching.

There are two types of wait time: the time between asking a question and calling on a pupil to give an answer and the time between receiving an answer and commenting on the answer yourself. Pupils need to think what a question means and then to compose an answer. This can take quite a long time depending on the kind of question that is asked. Even if pupils know the answer, they might not bother to respond if they know that you are going to give the answer anyway (see Budd-Rowe 1974).

Concluding remarks

There would be very little support for banning tests in schools. The issue really is more to do with the emphasis that you give to tests and the way in which you feed back test information to pupils. It is therefore essential that you plan opportunities to use test information in a formative way within your teaching programme. This can be achieved by placing the test slightly earlier than the end of the topic. The test can then be used to identify specific areas of learning that need more support from you and more work from the pupil. The time after the test can be used to rectify the shortfall. In this way tests are used not to show how different children perform at a specific point in time but what learning needs they have. Rather than hear pupils claim that they have 63 per cent or a B, we need to hear pupils say, 'Well I did okay in English, but now I need to work on getting a better balance between dialogue and description in my essays' or 'In maths, I need to improve my graphing skills and check again through multiplication of decimal numbers before I am tested again'. Knowing what to do next in the learning should be the goal, and progress should be monitored by comparing a pupil's current performance with their previous one rather than ranking them against others in the class. Summative norm-referenced comparison of the performance of individuals can then be left to the public examination system, with teachers and pupils concentrating on assessing to help target future learning opportunities.

References

Black, P.J. (1993) Formative and summative assessment by teachers, *Studies in Science Education*, 21: 49–97.

Black, P. and Wiliam, D. (1998) *Inside the Black Box*. London: King's College London.

Broadfoot, P., James, M., McMeeking, S., Nuttall, D. and Stierer, B. (1988) *Records of Achievement, Report of the National Evaluation of Pilot Schemes*. London: HMSO.

Brown, M. (1998) Formative assessment for learning: general issues illustrated by examples from England, in B. Black and A. Michel (eds) *Learning From Pupil's Assessment: International Comparisons*. Los Angeles, CA: University of California.

Budd-Rowe, M. (1974) Relation of wait-time and rewards to the development of language, logic and fate control: part II – rewards, *Journal of Research in Science Teaching*, 11(4): 291–308.

Butler, R. (1988) Enhancing and undermining intrinsic motivation; the effects of task-involving and ego-involving evaluation on interest and performance, *British Journal of Educational Psychology*, 58: 1–14.

Department for Education and Science/Qualifications and Curriculum Authority (DfEE/QCA) (1999) *The National Curriculum Handbook for Secondary Teachers in England Key Stages 3 and 4*. London: HMSO.

Dweck, C.S. (1986) Motivational processes affecting learning, *American Psychologist* (Special Issue: Psychological Science and Education), 41: 1040–8.

Fairbrother, B. (1995) Pupils as learners, in B. Fairbrother, P. Black and P. Gill (eds) *Teachers Assessing Pupils: Studies from Science Classrooms*. Hatfield: Association for Science Education.

Fontana, D. and Fernandes, M. (1994) Improvements in mathematics performance as a consequence of self-assessment in Portuguese primary school pupils, *British Journal of Educational Psychology*, 64: 407–17.

Holton, J. (1995) Pupil assessment without stress: a study of assessment in an EBD school, in B. Fairbrother, P. Black and P. Gill (eds) *Teachers Assessing Pupils: Studies from Science Classrooms*. Hatfield: Association for Science Education.

Messick, S. (1980) Test validity and the ethics of assessment, *American Psychologist*, 35: 1012–27.

Messick, S. (1989) Validity, in R.L. Linn (ed.) *Educational Measurement*, 3rd edn. New York and London: Macmillan and American Council on Education.

Rowntree, D. (1987) *Assessing Students: How Shall We Know Them?* London: Kogan Page.

Sadler, R. (1989) Formative assessment and the design of instructional systems. *Instructional Science*, 18: 119–44.

Swain, J. (2000) Summative assessment, in M. Monk and J. Osborne (eds) *Good Practice in Science Teaching: What Research Has to Say*. Buckingham: Open University Press.

Wiliam, D. (1993) Validity, dependability and reliability in national curriculum assessment. *The Curriculum Journal*, 4(3): 335–50.

Wiliam, D. (1996) National Curriculum assessments and programmes of study: validity and impact, *British Educational Research Journal*, 22(1): 129–41.

Wiliam, D. and Black, P. (1996) Meanings and consequences: a basis for distinguishing formative and summative functions of assessment, *British Educational Research Journal*, 22(5): 537–48.

<table>
<tr><td>18</td></tr>
</table>

18 | Special educational needs – becoming more inclusive

Chris Abbott

It is important to recognize that this report is based on the belief that
special educational needs and handicaps are relative to the contexts in
which children and young people are educated . . . The aims of
education are the same for all and the common human needs of
children and young people are of greater significance than individual
abilities or difficulties.

(Committee to Review Special Educational Provision 1985: 211)

Introduction

This chapter examines the recent history of the response of the educational system to learners with special educational needs (SEN). It considers
a range of responses from teachers, policymakers and other relevant groups.
All teachers need to be aware of SEN issues, and they have particular duties
laid out in the SEN Code of Practice. The code is discussed in order that
you can consider its implications for your teaching.

The report quoted above (known as the Fish Report, after its chair)
followed the highly influential Warnock Report (DES 1978), and the 1981
Education Act (DES 1981) both of which came down firmly in favour of
inclusive education. At the time when the Fish Report was published, the
arguments for inclusive education seemed compelling and any opposition
to them risked being labelled as divisive and inequitable. The authors of
the Fish Report were unequivocal:

> [I]ntegration in society is a process not a state. It is not simply a
> question of placement in the same groups and institutions as others.
> It is a process which requires continued and planned interaction with
> contemporaries and freedom to associate in different groups. The
> potentially adverse effects of isolation and segregation, in whatever
> context, including comprehensive institutions, are now well-known,
> including the risks to social competence and to the development of a
> positive self-identity.

(Committee to Review Special Educational Provision 1985: 5)

Many special needs teachers, particularly those in inner London (the focus of the Fish Report) expected that within a few years most special schools would be closed, almost all children would be educated together and segregated schooling would become an historical anomaly. That almost none of this has yet happened is explained by several factors, particularly the arrival of the National Curriculum and, subsequently, league tables of schools.

In parallel to the policy changes, there has been a developing awareness among educators of the need to aim not just for integration but for inclusion. Integration too often implies that the person concerned should change in some way in order to become integrated. Others (Clough 1998; Allan 1999; Daniels and Garner 1999; Lunt and Norwich 1999) have considered inclusion in far greater depth than is possible in this chapter.

Prior to the publication of the Fish Report, the 1981 Education Act had led to increasing numbers of young people being considered as having special educational needs at some point during their school career. A figure of 20 per cent of all children, quoted in the Warnock Report (DES 1978), was highly influential in changing attitudes, freeing resources and ensuring that serious attention was paid to the issue. At the time, special schools were educating approximately 2 per cent of the school population.

The mid-1980s was a time of great expectations for those involved in special needs education. The old barriers were to be swept away, young people were to be educated together and mainstream schools would have to become more inclusive. Inclusion, however, was overtaken by events, more particularly by one event: the publication of the 1988 Education Reform Act and all that followed from it. Suddenly, schools and local education authorities were faced with fundamental changes, changes that carried the force of law and the insistent voice of a timetable of implementation, neither of which were true of the 1981 Act.

Withdrawal or in-class support?

Prior to the events of the mid-1980s, the fundamental controversy regarding special needs provision in mainstream schools had been the one that has since reappeared: is it more desirable to educate young people with special needs by withdrawing them from the lessons where they are experiencing difficulty and educating them elsewhere, or should support teachers be provided to enable such young people to learn alongside their more able peers in ordinary schools? The support system approach has much more in common with the aims and beliefs of the 1981 Act than does the practice, formerly widespread, of withdrawing children and educating them in small groups with specialized resources in the care of a teacher whose only role is to work with those children. Implicit in the latter approach is an assumption that children can be categorized.

Categories of need

Teachers entering the profession in the 1970s would have met terms such as 'mentally handicapped', 'maladjusted' and 'physically handicapped'.

These terms, stark though they may seem, replaced others that were even more uncompromising. The British education and health systems have a long history of placing people in categories and until the turn of the century, the categories in general use were terms that would today be entirely inappropriate:

Idiots
[P]ersons so deeply defective in mind from birth . . . [as to be] unable to guard themselves against common human dangers . . .

Imbeciles
[M]ental defectiveness not amounting to idiocy . . . incapable of managing themselves or their affairs . . .

Feeble-minded
. . . require care, supervision and control for their own protection . . .
. . . permanently incapable of receiving proper benefit from the instruction in ordinary schools . . .

Moral imbeciles
. . . some permanent defect coupled with strong vicious or criminal propensities on which punishment has had little or no effect . . .

Acute lunacy
. . . has been excluded from the definitions.

(Great Britain 1886)

The categories in use today are based on a belief that special educational need is a product of context rather than an innate state situated within the child. Teachers still talk about categories of need, however, and it may be useful to consider these before discussing the influence of context. The categories of need referred to since the first version of the SEN Code of Practice (DfE 1994) was published include:

• learning difficulties;
• specific learning difficulties;
• emotional and behavioural difficulties;
• physical disabilities;
• sensory impairment: hearing difficulties;
• sensory impairment: visual difficulties;
• speech and language difficulties.

The tendency to adopt labelling children as a strategy for meeting need has been described by Feiler and Gibson (1999) as one of the four main threats to the inclusive movement (the others being lack of precision in definitions of inclusion, the lack of research evidence and the tendency for some children to be excluded even if they are within the school environment). The draft 2000 Code takes the process of generalizing and grouping rather further and 'does not assume that there are hard and fast categories of special educational need' (DfEE 2000: 60). This echoes the point made above that an understanding of special educational needs should be focused on the context in which a child is educated rather than on an innate deficit within that child.

Children will have needs and requirements which may fall into at least one of four areas, although many children will have inter-related needs which encompass more than one of these areas. The impact of these combinations on the child's ability to function, learn and succeed should be taken into account. The areas of need are:

- communication and interaction;
- cognition and learning;
- behaviour, emotional and social development;
- sensory and/or physical.

(DfEE 2000: 60)

The next sections examine each of these four areas in more detail.

Communication and interaction needs

It has become increasingly clear that difficulties with speech and language, if noted early enough in a child's school career, need not be a life-long difficulty. Language units have been set up, often in schools, to provide early intervention during a child's first years at school and these have often been remarkably successful. It is unlikely that many secondary teachers will have to deal with this range of needs.

Categories of need tend to change regularly and new ones sometimes appear. A relatively recent arrival from the USA is the notion of attention deficit disorder (ADD), sometimes linked to hyperactivity (ADHD). This is an area of controversy in the USA, where many young students have been prescribed drugs to control the disorder. Drug therapy has been seen as a last resort in Britain but is now on the increase. ADD and ADHD seem to be gaining acceptance among professionals and are terms that teachers will meet; criticism of their use tends to be similar to that of the notion of dyslexia, that the term signifies a model of special educational need as a medical condition for which a cure, or at any rate relief, can be prescribed. Others (Place et al. 1999) have argued that ADHD may be a root cause of some of the behaviour difficulties observed in schools.

Cognition and learning needs

By far the largest group of children defined as having special educational needs are those defined as having learning difficulties. These difficulties may be minimal, moderate or severe, depending upon the context in which the young person is being taught and the task involved. All teachers will have students with learning difficulties in their classrooms, although it is unlikely that these difficulties will be of a severity that causes the young person involved to be unable to speak or communicate. Children with such needs are still most likely to be found in special schools.

Some children display a range of difficulties with learning that seem at odds with what also appears to be a high level of understanding in other contexts. They are able to learn in other ways very quickly, but reading, writing and spelling in particular appear to give them great difficulty.

Many people have regarded this collection of difficulties as a specific trait and have termed it 'dyslexia'; others resist the notion of one kind of difficulty and prefer to use the general term 'specific learning difficulties'. Whatever the personal perspective on this argument, it is true that some young people do appear to have particular difficulties with language, especially in its non-verbal forms, and teachers need to be adept at dealing with this. It is unfortunate that the many different agencies seeking to support people with dyslexia are not able to agree on the most appropriate action for teachers to take.

Behaviour, emotional and social development needs

Perhaps above all other categories of need, this is the one that is most affected by context. It is also probably the area of need which classroom teachers feel is more difficult to meet within the mainstream classroom than any other. Children can appear to be extremely disruptive, unmotivated or withdrawn, and a whole range of behaviours can be seen as falling within this area. At the present time, many young people whose needs relate to this area are educated separately, often within a school that operates a behavioural management ethos. Recent government initiatives, particularly *Excellence in Cities* (DfEE 1999; see also Chapter 10), are seeking to address this issue and to find ways of enabling mainstream schools to meet this range of needs.

Sensory and/or physical needs

The assumption too easily made about physical disability is that children can be included in mainstream provision provided that physical alterations are made to the building. This is too simplistic and fails to take account of the psychological and sociological hurdles that are involved in the successful inclusion of such young people into mainstream schools.

It is often those young people who have hearing difficulties or who are deaf who have the greatest difficulties with inclusion into mainstream education. Where children have developed a confident grasp of signing they are likely to feel much more comfortable talking to others who are similarly bilingual. Talking to a hearing person may involve learning to lip-read and this can be very difficult for some young people. Technology is beginning to offer support in this area and it is likely that speech-to-text hand-held devices will become available soon.

Some children with visual difficulties have been successfully included in mainstream schools for many years. This has sometimes been achieved through the sensible use of computers and other specially adapted aids, but in many cases a willing teaching force and a well-prepared group of students are the most important factors. Children with colour vision difficulties may not be able to cope with certain colour combinations when reading; with many computer programs this can be amended, but printed materials present insuperable problems. Science teachers, in particular, need to be sensitive when dealing with the topic of colour vision difficulties. Other children may suffer from a narrowing of their field of vision; they may not need to sit near to the board but they may need to be directly opposite it, or, in some cases, to one side.

Children and their needs in context

The issue of context-related need was mentioned earlier and it is the issue that has dominated thinking about SEN since the mid-1980s. To reiterate: it is generally accepted that special educational needs arise often from the contexts in which we place children, rather than from the child itself. A child who exhibits signs of emotional and behavioural disturbance in a mainstream school may be entirely calm and at ease in another setting such as a small special school or an off-site unit. Factors such as the size of a school, the pressure of being one of such a large student body or a bewildering variety of tasks and directives when joining a new school, can cause the special educational need to become noticed, or cause it to become so important that it cannot be ignored. It follows from this argument that an essential requirement for schools is to create contexts that do not aggravate or form special educational needs among the student body. This is a task not only for the senior management of the school but also for all staff (teaching and support) and students.

Differentiation – strategies for support

Tasks given to learners should always be capable of differentiation to meet the different needs and capabilities of those students. Chapter 15 of this book covers differentiation in depth but it is appropriate here to pick out the key points as they apply to the topic of special educational needs. In too many cases teachers use the strategy of differentiation by outcome; at its simplest level this means that one task is given to all students so that some of them produce a range of responses while others struggle to produce anything at all.

A more appropriate strategy involves differentiation by task; a careful teacher will allow for a range of tasks to be offered. There are many ways in which this can be done, and the use of a variety of strategies is likely to be more effective than an overreliance on the same methodology. Some teachers prepare alternative versions of a task, particularly where an activity is based around the use of worksheets. Others may prepare different tasks for different groups in the classroom, although this has the built-in danger of leading to a permanent setting within the classroom that is unlikely to be appropriate (see Chapter 16). Students who find difficulties with one task will not necessarily react in the same way to another; as with special needs in general, the difficulty will be related to the context – in this case, the learning activity – rather than to the learner. It is unrealistic to expect that teachers will always be able to provide a differentiated range of activities, but it should be the aim of a good teacher to do so whenever possible and as often as possible.

The SEN Code of Practice

Following a wide-ranging consultation exercise, a Special Educational Needs Code of Practice (DfE 1994) was introduced and now affects all schools and teachers. It is to be updated and superseded in late 2001 by a revised version, and the following comments are based on the draft version of this new code produced in July 2000. It is useful to consider here the fundamental principles quoted in the Code of Practice which underpin the proposals it contains:

- a child with special educational needs should have their needs met;
- the special educational needs of children will normally be met in mainstream schools or settings;
- the views of the child should be sought and taken into account;
- parents have a vital role to play in supporting their child's education;
- children with special educational needs should be offered full access to a broad, balanced and relevant education, including the Foundation Stage Curriculum and the National Curriculum.

(DfEE 2000: 3)

The draft Code of Practice recommends a two-stage process of identification of special educational needs by schools and teachers, a reduction from the previous five stages in the 1994 Code. The proposed reduction was suggested in the hope that it would streamline the process of needs identification and avoid some of the delays inherent in the previous system.

Subject teachers have a particular role in the first of these stages, as the draft code indicates that one of the triggers for *school action*, the first phase, could be 'the teacher's or others' concern, underpinned by evidence, about a child or young person' (DfEE 2000: 46). This comment suggests that not only should subject teachers be sensitive to such situations as they arise, but that they should share their concerns with others and that they should also be ready to make the necessary evidence available that will demonstrate the nature of the difficulty.

If a particular student seems to be experiencing difficulties and is not known to have special educational needs, it is the responsibility of that child's subject teachers to spot the difficulty, contact the special educational needs coordinator (SENCO) and attempt to describe the nature of the needs that have been noted. Following their consultations with the SENCO, subject teachers then need to take the action agreed, and this may form part of the written IEP (individual education plan) for that student. It may be that a move to a different part of the classroom has been suggested, or that the teacher should speak more clearly and face the child concerned. This can lead to a dramatic improvement in communication where a child with a hearing difficulty is concerned. The SENCO may wish to attend a lesson in order to make an informal assessment of the situation prior to any formal process that the school may have developed.

A particular focus during the school action phase of identifying special needs is the collection of information and evidence. This proposed process will be extremely valuable if it is necessary to progress to the second phase, *school action plus*. The main responsibility for action lies with the SENCO, though it is essential that the subject teacher gives enthusiastic support and cooperation without which there is less hope of improving the situation. The school may decide to provide support in the form of technology, a support teacher or an assistant, if these are available. Extra help may be given by learning support teachers where they exist, and their job is made much easier when subject teachers keep them fully informed about the work in hand and offer to assist them in devising suitable teaching programmes. It may be that, following this process of gathering information, the school decides to seek outside assistance and consider the need for a statement of special educational needs, but this will not always be the case.

SEN statements were an outcome of the 1994 code and have become widely used, although there has been criticism of the number of statements written, the length of time taken to prepare them and the differing patterns of statementing in various local education authorities (LEAs). The revised code contains clear expectations that statements will in future be much fewer in number and will be in place for shorter periods of time.

Information and communication technology and SEN

The 1994 Code of Practice highlighted the ways in which information technology (IT) could assist schools and students in the meeting of special educational needs. IT in this case usually means computers and the various pieces of hardware that can be attached to them. The 2000 draft code is much less specific in this area but includes a number of general statements implying the use of information and communications technology (ICT) as it is now generally described, and there is a growing literature in this area (Blamires 1999).

Children with learning difficulties can use overlay keyboards or onscreen keyboards to access an activity that for other students involves the use of a standard keyboard. An overlay keyboard is a device on which paper sheets containing words or pictures are placed. Pressing on the words or pictures sends commands to the computer, since the overlay has an associated file containing the instructions devised by the teacher. There are over 100 keys on a normal computer keyboard, and the choice of the correct one can be daunting for children with learning difficulties, even at secondary age. A paper overlay or an onscreen selection area with a choice of eight or 10 actions is a much more appropriate tool in this situation. Many teachers also use overlay keyboards to speed up the writing process for learners whose writing is slowly and laboriously produced. In a science lesson, for example, some teachers might use overlays that create the phrases and concepts frequently included when writing up an experiment. Pressing on the area concerned will cause these to be written to the screen, and the student can then concentrate on the novel parts of the activity.

Children with visual difficulties may be helped by magnification software, or by the use of other magnification technology to deal with printed material. Such devices are very portable and make it possible for a student with a visual difficulty to be placed on an equal footing with others. Screen readers can offer access to a wide range of information sources including the Internet, and Web browsers can easily be set to display text in large formats.

Children with hearing difficulties sometimes communicate using electronic mail, and the rapid increase in the number of schools with Internet access continues to open up wonderful possibilities. Children who become very ill and have to spend long periods in hospital or at home can keep in touch with their schools through electronic mail, and be set homework in this way too. Many children are able to keep up with their coursework in this way, and the ready availability of computers may sometimes result in a vastly improved amount of work being done during a period as an in-patient than was previously the case.

There are some difficulties, though, that arise from the use of a computer itself which can be a source of stress or frustration. This is often the case when a child has a slight loss of fine motor control and finds that the mouse is very difficult to control. In such cases, it is possible to substitute a trackerball, sometimes described as an upside-down mouse, which enables the two mouse actions of clicking and moving to be separated rather than having to be done simultaneously. More importantly, the trackerball itself remains stationary – the movement being controlled by the large ball on top.

Many other devices can be substituted for a mouse, and children with physical disabilities are then able to use head switches, puff switches (controlled by blowing) or even control the computer with eye movements. Where the degree of difficulty is not so great, the perceptive teacher will use the inbuilt control facilities of the software to alter the mouse tracking speed and rate at which double clicks must be made. Such small changes, which take only a few seconds and are reversible for the next user, can transform a frustrated student into one who is able to become increasingly confident.

Although all these uses of ICT, and many others, have always been explored by inventive teachers in enlightened classrooms and schools, the impetus has sometimes come from outside agencies. This support can no longer be relied upon, as the major change in this area since the Code of Practice came into being has been the requirement that schools investigate the use of ICT for a particular need before outside experts are called in. This means that all teachers, but special educational needs coordinators in particular, must become familiar with the different ways in which IT, which may not only mean computers, can offer support. It is to the SENCO that a teacher should turn if advice is needed about meeting a particular need, or if a teacher has concerns of any kind about the progress or lack of it made by particular students.

Conclusion

The two concepts that teachers should bear in mind with regard to SEN are context and differentiation. Teachers must be able to plan activities that can be offered in a range of different forms to meet the needs of all the students in their classrooms. They need to be perceptive observers of their students, noticing where they have difficulties, and attempting to record and describe those situations so that, in consultation with colleagues, they can attempt to improve the situation. Where difficulties are obvious, they must not focus on why the student cannot do something, but on whether the learning environment provided is appropriate for that student's needs. Some aspects of that environment may be outside your control, but important factors such as your attitude, the provision of differentiated work and your awareness of student reaction, may not.

Inclusive education should not just be a worthy aim or a statement of policy, but a goal towards which teachers, parents and other agencies are striving. The LEA, in particular, has an important role to play, and it has been shown that inclusive practices must become a 'corporate priority which is reflected in global targets within the LEA' (Ainscow *et al.* 1999: 137). It will never be easy to make an education system inclusive but it will always be indefensible to accept that it should be otherwise. Inclusion 'trips easily off the tongue but can be without meaning or substance' (Wade 1999: 81), but this must be avoided if education is to be a benefit which is truly available to all.

References

Ainscow, M., Farrell, P., Tweddle, D. and Malki, G. (1999) The role of LEAs in developing inclusive policies and practices, *British Journal of Special Education,* 26(3): 136–40.

Allan, J. (1999) *Actively Seeking Inclusion.* London: Falmer Press.

Blamires, M. (ed.) (1999) *Enabling Technology for Inclusion.* London: Paul Chapman Publishing.

Clough, P. (ed.) (1998) *Managing Inclusive Education: from Policy to Experience.* London: Paul Chapman Press.

Committee to Review Special Educational Provision (1985) *Educational Opportunities For All: Report of the Committee Reviewing Provision to Meet Special Educational Needs* (The Fish Report). London: Inner London Education Authority.

Daniels, H. and Garner, P. (eds) (1999) *Inclusive Education (World Yearbook of Education 1999).* London: Kogan Page.

Department for Education (DfE) (1994) *Code of Practice on the Identification and Assessment of Special Educational Needs.* London: DfE.

Department for Education and Employment (DfEE) (1999) *Excellence in Cities.* Nottingham: DfEE.

Department for Education and Employment (DfEE) (2000) *SEN Code of Practice on the Identification and Assessment of Pupils with Special Educational Needs.* London: DfEE.

Department of Education and Science (DES) (1978) *Special Educational Needs: Report of the Committee of Enquiry into the Education of Handicapped Children and Young People* (The Warnock Report). London: HMSO.

Department of Education and Science (DES) (1981) *Education for All.* London: HMSO.

Great Britain (1886) *Classification of Defectives Under the Mental Deficiency, Lunacy, Idiots and Education Acts.* London: HMSO.

Feiler, A. and Gibson, H. (1999) Threats to the inclusive movement, *British Journal of Special Education,* 26(3): 147–52.

Lunt, I. and Norwich, B. (1999) *Can Effective Schools be Inclusive Schools?* London: Institute of Education.

Place, M., Wilson, J., Martin, E. and Hulsmeier, J. (1999) Attention Deficit Disorder as a factor in the origin of behavioural disturbance in schools, *British Journal of Special Education,* 26(3): 158–63.

Wade, J. (1999) Including all learners: QCA's approach, *British Journal of Special Education,* 26(2): 80–3.

English as an additional language: challenges of language and identity in the multilingual and multiethnic classroom

Roxy Harris and Constant Leung

The demographic context

Becoming a teacher in contemporary Britain means developing effective practice with regard to pupils who come from ethnic and linguistic minority families. According to Department for Education and Employment (DfEE) figures, in 1999, approximately 12 per cent of pupils in primary and secondary schools in England were described as belonging to minority ethnic groups, with roughly 8 per cent of them said to use English as an additional language (EAL). These figures have major implications for all teachers that we will discuss in more detail in the chapter.

The figures, though, need to be treated with some caution since they contain some inadequacies. However, we will first look at the way the broad figures disguise striking regional variations. For example, 2.6 per cent of pupils in maintained primary schools in the North East of England and 2.7 per cent in the South West are described as belonging to ethnic minorities, while comparable figures for Inner London are 56.5 per cent, Outer London 31.2 per cent and the West Midlands 15.9 per cent. Similarly, the figures for the number of pupils for whom English is an additional language in maintained primary and secondary schools are 5.3 per cent for the North West and Merseyside and 3.7 per cent for the South East, but 29.4 per cent for Greater London. Even within regions themselves, broad figures may conceal major local variations. For example, the overall West Midlands figure of 10.7 per cent of pupils for whom English is an additional language masks the fact that the figures for specific localities in the region are 27.4 per cent for Birmingham and 17 per cent for Sandwell.

Once you have developed an awareness of the demographic picture, you can begin to seek out information that will build a more specific local awareness. For instance, a study of the languages of London's school-children (Baker and Eversley 2000: 5), found that in Greater London the range of home languages spans more than 350 language names, with English dominant at 67.9 per cent of the 850,000 schoolchildren surveyed. Of the remaining languages, the top 10 are Bengali and Sylheti, Panjabi, Gujarati, Hindi/Urdu, Turkish, Arabic, English-based Creoles, Yoruba, Somali and Cantonese. Again, these overall figures do not reveal the particularly heavy weightings of languages other than English in specific London local education authority areas such as Brent (Gujarati 23.9 per cent), the City of London (Bengali and Sylheti 56.4 per cent), Ealing (Panjabi 20.1 per cent), and Tower Hamlets (Bengali and Sylheti 53.8 per cent) (Baker and Eversley 2000: 12).

The historical context

The EAL issue arose as a result of the inward migrations and settlement of peoples and languages since 1945, particularly in the 1950s, 1960s and 1970s. Martin-Jones (1989) usefully characterizes these movements principally of people entering Britain as either migrant workers or as refugees. Martin-Jones sees a significant divide between those entering from other parts of Europe and those from former colonies and Third World nations. It has been the languages of people from these latter nations which have had the greatest impact on EAL policy and practice in Britain (see ILEA 1989; Alladina and Edwards 1991; Peach 1996).

Unfortunately, the entrance into the UK of migrants from former colonies and so-called developing countries was accompanied by a considerable amount of racial hostility and contempt for their languages. This led to an official assimilationist approach (DES 1971), based on the idea that schools should set about erasing the languages and cultural practices of the children of new migrants as a precondition for their educational success. This position was later modified following the Bullock Report (1975: 286), which stated that:

No child should be expected to cast off the language and culture of the home as he [sic] crosses the school threshold [and] . . . the school should adopt positive attitudes to its pupils' bilingualism and wherever possible should help maintain and deepen their knowledge of their mother tongues.

Despite this declaration, the Bullock Report did not indicate how schools were to give practical expression to this aspiration. A decade later, another official document, the Swann Report (1985), while generally reaffirming a positive attitude to the home and community languages of ethnic minority pupils, firmly ruled out any role for the mainstream school in relating these languages to the learning process and to the official curriculum:

We find we cannot support the arguments put forward for the introduction of programmes of bilingual education in maintained schools
in this country. Similarly we would regard mother tongue maintenance, although an important educational function, as best achieved
within the ethnic minority communities themselves rather than within
mainstream schools.

(Swann Report 1985: 406)

However, one principle upon which the Swann Report insisted was that
ethnic minority pupils for whom English was an additional language
should at all times be educated in the mainstream classroom alongside
their peers to avoid segregated provision and to guarantee equal access to
the curriculum. In the contemporary educational world, access to the curriculum means access to the National Curriculum. It is to the relationship
between English as an additional language and the National Curriculum
that we now turn.

English as an additional/second language (EAL/ESL) and the National Curriculum

Many of the ethnic minority pupils whom we have described so far are in
the process of learning to use English for both social and academic purposes. At present, with the possible exception of some short-term English
language induction courses, all pupils with EAL are expected to follow the
National Curriculum (CRE 1986; NCC 1991; SCAA 1996).[1] This expectation means that additional language learning opportunities, particularly
for academic purposes, are to be provided in mainstream classes or subject
lessons. Hence, 'the teaching of English is the responsibility of all teachers'
(SCAA 1996: 2).

Within the National Curriculum, EAL, unlike English or science, is not
regarded as a discipline in its own right; therefore there is no dedicated
curriculum specification for it. EAL is seen as a pupil phenomenon with
implications for teaching and learning. At the same time, for all intents
and purposes, the curriculum specifications and assessment criteria for
(the National Curriculum subject) English are used for both mother tongue
English speaking pupils and those who are still in the process of learning
EAL.[2] It is emphasized that:

English is the area of the curriculum in which pupils have the
opportunity to learn English and learn about language in many
ways ... Throughout the programme of studies for Key Stages 1–4
there are examples of work related to words and their meanings, to
grammar, style and idioms, which are essential for the development
of English.

(SCAA 1996: 8)

Teachers concerned with EAL are advised that effective planning 'ensures
a range of language experiences, including different audiences and purposes' (SCAA 1996: 13).

A glimpse of professional reality

In order to understand how EAL provision is organized in schools, it is important to know something about funding and staffing issues. EAL provision is non-mandatory (unlike subjects such as English and mathematics) and from 1966 until the end of the 1990s EAL funding came from a special grant, commonly known as 'Section 11'. Section 11 funding was earmarked 'to support the cost of employing additional staff to help minority ethnic groups overcome linguistic and other barriers which inhibit their access to, and take up of, mainstream services' (Ofsted 1994: 1). Since 1998 the monies have been administered under a DfEE grant scheme known as Ethnic Minority and Travellers' Achievement Grant (EMTAG). This grant is time-limited, often two or three years at a time. The funding available to a school, via the local education authority, can vary from one grant period to another depending on the total size of grant and competing demands from other schools. A vast majority of EAL teachers, often referred to as language support teachers, are employed through this funding. Although since the 1960s funding has been regularly renewed, the time-limited nature has meant instability for schools in terms of even medium term curriculum response, and for individual EAL staff in terms of their career and professional development. The shortage of funds has also meant that generally EAL staff are very thin on the ground.[3]

Given that EAL is not a curriculum discipline with its own programme of study and timetable slots, EAL teachers are expected to work alongside their mainstream colleagues in the classroom and in the school in a variety of ways. Broadly speaking, the roles EAL teachers are expected to play include the following: classroom teacher; curriculum adviser and developer; day-to-day adviser and in-service professional development provider and liaison person (for a fuller account, see Bourne and McPake 1991).

The extent to which any one EAL teacher can contribute to the above roles depends on a number of individual and school circumstances. Professional experience has shown that, given the shortage, EAL teachers can only meet some of the teaching and curriculum development demands in school. Many teachers working in classrooms with a high number of EAL pupils receive no assistance from EAL specialists. It is therefore important for all teachers to have some knowledge about some of the key concepts and principles that have been influential in shaping EAL teachers' classroom strategies. A knowledge of these principles may enable non-EAL teachers to begin to understand the teaching and learning issues involved.

Pedagogic principles and classroom strategies

Earlier we pointed out that EAL is a cross-curricular teaching concern. Within this perspective, two linked pedagogical principles can be identified in the professional literature. The first principle is concerned with making learning activities and tasks personally meaningful and understandable through curriculum planning (Bourne 1989; Travers 1999; see Chapter 3 in Edwards and Redfern 1992 for a more detailed discussion).

The second principle focuses on using learning activities that encourage active engagement. This principle is important because 'Children's second language skills develop well when . . . they have opportunities to model the second language used by peers in small group collaborative activities, where talk and interaction are central to the learning going on' (Hampshire County Council 1996: 2). Another rationale for adopting this principle is that:

> Learning is best achieved through enquiry-based activities involving discussion . . . To learn a language it is necessary to participate in its meaningful use . . . The curriculum itself is therefore a useful vehicle for language learning . . . A main strategy . . . for both curriculum learning and language learning is the flexible use of small group work.
>
> (Bourne 1989: 63)

These principles are consistent with a constructivist view of education which puts a great premium on hands-on experiential learning (see Chapter 13 for more details). They also require the teacher to have a very clear understanding of at least two language development issues in the classroom context:

- the link between curriculum knowledge and the language used to express that knowledge;
- the link between spoken and written English (and other languages) used for interaction in the classroom, including teacher talk and teacher writing, and the development of spoken and written English for assignments, assessments and tests in different subject or curriculum areas.

In the classroom, both EAL and other teachers have to interpret these broad principles with reference to their EAL learners who may be at different stages of English language development. Some possible strategies are outlined below.

Contextual support using physical movements/actions, visual/audio material and realia

Unfamiliar concepts and complex ideas can often be made more comprehensible by using pictures, diagrams and visual and other sensory representations. For instance, the central ideas in the topic of paper making may be visually supported by a series of pictures or drawings showing the process involving tree logging, making pulp and so on. Even ephemeral and often domain-specific concepts such as cynicism and sarcasm in a particular narrative context may be exemplified by drama activities. In many ways the value of this kind of contextual support is quite well understood. An important issue here is not to assume that contextual support of this kind can be understood by all pupils. It is possible that sometimes even the most obvious picture, to the teacher, may not make any sense to some pupils. For some very young pupils, the picture of an inkwell or the image of a vinyl record may mean nothing. The usefulness of any contextualization material and activity has to be constantly evaluated in relation to the pupils involved. A further issue is that while contextual support may lead to a degree of understanding, this understanding of the content meaning does not automatically mean understanding or even being aware of the associated language.

Opportunities for language development by teaching and modelling language in context

Cummins' (1992) distinction between basic interpersonal communication skills (BICS) and cognitive academic language proficiency (CALP) has been useful in helping teachers see how to analyse language demands for their pupils. A teacher asking pupils to choose a colour by holding up a colour chart, is a classroom example of BICS. From the EAL pupil's point of view, even if they do not understand the question or the names of the colours, the immediate meaning of the activity can be worked out by observing others. The physical context of the activity and the active engagement in the activity (by having to choose a colour) can provide an opportunity for highly focused language modelling by the teacher, and conscious noticing and active use by the pupil. The value of this observation can be made more obvious if we picture a different scenario – this time the teacher asks the same question but without holding up the colour chart. This kind of use of highly contextualized language supported by visual and other materials can be helpful for pupils at all stages of developing listening, speaking, reading and writing in EAL, but its benefits are immediately obvious to those teachers who are working with pupils at an early stage of learning English.

Opportunities to move from the here-and-now language to academic genres

Meaning in speech in social situations can be interactionally built up. Imagine the following:

Pupil 1: What are we doing?
Pupil 2: Miss said we have to write down what we said.
Pupil 3: Like what we did on Monday.
Pupil 1: What, like we write down the things we made up?

Classroom conversations, even when they are curriculum-related, are full of examples of this kind of joint focus forming and meaning making. This is indeed one of the main characteristics of everyday spoken language. Furthermore, spoken language is often informal in that it is not necessarily made up of well-formed sentences; the phrase or the clause is more likely to be the unit of utterances (Kress 1994). The ability to read and write effectively in an academic style cannot be assumed, even when a pupil appears to be able to handle here-and-now spoken English, and can read and produce some everyday texts such as simple stories and factual accounts.

The ability to read and understand academic texts, especially in the senior years of schooling, requires more than a knowledge of curriculum-related vocabulary and grammar. Pupils have to develop a knowledge of text types or genres. That is, they need to know something about the conventionally established ways of selecting and structuring information in specific formats for different purposes, for example, a narrative, instructions for games, a letter of complaint, a technical report. They also have to know the specific features of language expression involved, for example, the use of slang in a play dialogue or technical terms in a report. Furthermore, pupils need to be able to go beyond the literal meaning. Some texts, and not just literary texts, cannot be fully appreciated without an ability to understand and decipher humour, cynicism, sarcasm, irony and other culturally supported meanings. In face-to-face situations some of these implied meanings may also be signalled by physical actions, contextual clues and facial expressions that can assist interpretation.

Some of the knowledge and skills involved in the process of writing are sometimes 'hidden'; only the outcomes are visible. In the school, curriculum writing tasks tend to be about representing ideas or events, for example, telling a story or reporting on the results of an experiment. The purpose of a great deal of writing in school is to show that one can communicate one's ideas and thoughts without the benefit of either contextual support or immediate contributions and feedback from others (as in a conversation). This strategy involves pupils drawing on their existing knowledge and expertise to package ideas and produce a piece of text by themselves.

Gibbons (1998: 101) provides a highly illuminating example of how language features change as pupils move from group talk to individual writing:

Text 1 (spoken by three 10-year-old students with accompanying action)
S1: This . . . no it doesn't go . . . it doesn't move . . .
S2: Try that . . .
S3: Yes it does . . . a bit . . . that won't . . .
S2: Won't work it's not metal . . .
S1: These are the best . . . going really fast.

Text 2 (spoken by one student about the action, after the event)
We tried a pin . . . a pencil sharpener . . . some iron filings . . . the magnet didn't attract the pin . . .

Text 3 (written by the same student)
Our experiment was to find out what a magnet attracted. We discovered that a magnet attracts some kinds of metal. It attracted the iron filings, but not the pin . . .

The above discussion shows that a great deal of the academic use of written English in school is different from classroom spoken English in a number of ways. Some of the differences are related to vocabulary and grammatical choice; some are concerned with information structuring; and others are related to the properties and constraints of the different modes of language. These differences often reflect the different purposes served by spoken and written language in different contexts. Thus harnessing the knowledge and understanding achieved through classroom activities mediated by the spoken language provides a mere starting point (for a fuller discussion on developing reading and writing in EAL, see Leung in press).

A need for caution

In educational practice, questions concerning EAL are inextricably connected to questions of ethnicity, which themselves are far from simple.
Earlier reference was made to the need to treat collected figures for the
number of ethnic minority pupils in the school system in England with
caution. There are a number of reasons for this. In the first place, according to the DfE (1995: 1), 'There are serious weaknesses with the quality
and usefulness of data provided by the current Ethnic Monitoring Survey'.
One immediate problem was that as far as ethnic origin was concerned
'there is a significant proportion of pupils shown in the unclassified category' (DfE 1995: 2). The ethnic origin of 35.9 per cent of pupils was left
as 'unclassified' because either the parent or the school failed to complete
the survey. It is possible to argue that this failure reflected an ideological
objection to supplying the requested information. However, a more likely
explanation is that it has become increasingly difficult to fit real pupils in
real schools into neat, tidy and discrete ethnic categories. The complexities involved were fully reflected in a number of commentaries following
the 1991 UK Census. For instance, among ethnic minority males aged 16
to 34, 40 per cent of those designated as Black-Caribbean, 7 per cent of
Indians, 6.2 per cent of Pakistanis, 16 per cent of Chinese, 18 per cent of
Other-Asian, 19.2 per cent of Black-African and 60 per cent of Black-Other
stated that they were 'currently living with a white partner' (Berrington
1996: 199–200). Furthermore, as Peach (1996: 24) states:

> A significant proportion of the ethnic minority population is derived
> from mixed unions and new ethnic identities are being forged which
> will be increasingly difficult to capture within the existing census
> categories . . . Indeed, one of the lessons to be derived from the 1991
> Census, is that new ethnicities are emerging in Britain.

Later, we will examine this question of new ethnicities a little more, but
first it is necessary to look at the second reason for exercising caution
concerning figures on the ethnic origins of pupils. In the DfEE's 1999
figures, the ethnic group categories used are as follows: White, Black Caribbean Heritage, Black African Heritage, Black Other, Indian, Pakistani,
Bangladeshi, Chinese, Any Other Minority Ethnic Group. The inadequate
nature of these categories lies in the way that the different labels appear
to be trying to measure different things. There is a colour category –
White, Black Caribbean Heritage, Black African Heritage, Black Other.
There is a nationality category – Pakistani, Bangladeshi. There is also an
ethnic category – Indian, Chinese.[4] In addition there are the problems associated with what the catch-all category 'White' hides and oversimplifies.
Finally, there is no guidance as to what the practising teacher is to do with
the category of apparently unclassified pupils represented by labels such
as Black Other, or Any Other Minority Ethnic Group.

For anyone becoming a teacher there is a need to find ways of thinking
about these issues that have some practical utility for day-to-day interactions with pupils. There are a number of central problems that require
attention. First of all schools and teachers have experienced some
difficulty in accommodating the idea that pupils belonging to 'visible'

minority groups are members of ethnic formations which, far from being fixed, stable, homogeneous and comfortably knowable, are instead complex, fluid and heterogeneous. Second, there has been a difficulty in envisioning these ethnic minority pupils as cultural and linguistic insiders rather than permanent outsiders living in the UK. Third, many schools and teachers have struggled to see how these pupils might be at one and the same time aligned to *both* UK/English/British ethnic identities *and* those associated with other global locations.

Some help is available in making sense of the situation in the work of theorists operating generally in the field of what has come to be known as British Cultural Studies. Gilroy (1987) depicts the refusal to allow for change and variation in representations of broader British and minority ethnic identities as ethnic absolutism. Hall (1988) suggests that minority individuals, rather than seeking to preserve their ethnic identities unchanged, are actively and continuously engaged in a process of creating new ethnicities. Mercer (1994), amongst others, sees significant numbers of young members of UK-based 'visible' minority groups as being intimately connected *both* with the everyday mores of their UK locations *and* wider African, Caribbean and Asian derived diasporas. Hall provides a useful summary of the general position being described here when he identifies the concept of translation which:

> describes those identity formations which cut across and intersect natural frontiers, and which are composed of people who have been *dispersed* forever from their homelands. Such people retain strong links with their places of origin and their traditions, but they are without the illusion of a return to the past. They are obliged to come to terms with the new cultures they inhabit, without simply assimilating to them and losing their identities completely. They bear upon them the traces of the particular cultures, traditions, languages and histories by which they were shaped. The difference is that they are not and will never be *unified* in the old sense, because they are irrevocably the product of several interlocking histories and cultures, belong at one and the same time to several 'homes' (and to no one particular 'home'). People belonging to such *cultures of hybridity* have had to renounce the dream or ambition of rediscovering any kind of 'lost' cultural purity, or ethnic absolutism. They are irrevocably *translated* . . . They are the products of the new *diasporas* created by the post-colonial migrations. They must learn to inhabit at least two identities, to speak two cultural languages, to translate and negotiate between them. Cultures of hybridity are one of the distinctly novel types of identity produced in the era of late-modernity, and there are more and more examples of them to be discovered.
>
> (Hall 1992: 310, original emphasis)

To put it briefly, the essential point for new teachers to grasp is that the majority of young ethnic minority pupils in England are daily engaged in the active construction of what Back (1996) terms 'new forms of working class Englishness'. Linked with this endeavour is a specifically linguistic dimension.

One of the factors with which any teacher needs to come to terms, is that there are two aspects of the actual patterns of language use of many pupils for whom English is an additional language, which are little commented upon:

1 Many such pupils with EAL are more linguistically comfortable with a local urban spoken English vernacular than with an ethnic minority 'community' language which they might encounter in family contexts (see Harris 1997, 1999; Leung *et al.* 1997, for examples of this phenomenon).

2 Even where these pupils begin their school careers in England with very limited English language proficiency, their entry to English tends to be connected with a local urban spoken vernacular English, learned informally, rather than with the spoken or written Standard English associated with the formal aspects of the school curriculum.

Hewitt made a number of perceptive observations on the significant ways in which urban youth, in their routine language use, participate in the 'destabilisation of ethnicity' (1991: 27). He suggested that an important but often overlooked part of their language use is what he describes as a 'local multi-ethnic vernacular' or a 'community English'. This language use is 'the primary medium of communication in the adolescent peer group in multi-ethnic areas' (Hewitt 1991: 32). For Hewitt (1995: 97), the sources of this language use are diasporic and global as well as local, and contribute to:

> the obliteration of pure language forms deriving from a single cultural source, evident in some inner city areas [in the UK] and . . . the diasporic distribution of communicative forms which, whilst generated from and based in local communities, nevertheless reach out and extend lines of connection in a global way. The local penetration and mixing of language forms evident in some urban settings in the UK should, in fact, be seen perhaps as a reflex of the broader linguistic diasporic processes.

The view of reality sketched by Hewitt tends not to have been shared by very many schools and teachers in England, who have preferred to project onto pupils with EAL, what Harris (1997) has called a 'romantic bilingualism'. This phrase refers to the practice 'of attributing to pupils drawn from visible ethnic minority groups an expertise in and allegiance to any community languages with which they have some acquaintance' (Harris 1997: 14).

In preference to this approach it might be useful for new teachers encountering pupils with EAL to begin to work with a framework offered by Harris (1999) as a prelude to developing effective classroom pedagogies suited to differing linguistic needs of individual pupils. In this framework there may well be three broad groups of pupils with EAL.

1 The 'new' arrivals

These pupils may be relatively recent arrivals in the UK possessing a limited acquaintance with, and low levels of expertise in, the English language, together with little familiarity with contemporary British cultural and educational practices.

2 *The low-key British bilinguals*

- pupils born and brought up in a multilingual home in a British urban area. They have regular routine interaction with family and community languages other than English without claiming a high degree of expertise in these languages. They are entirely comfortable with the discourse of everyday English, particular local vernacular Englishes and with contemporary British cultural and educational practices. They have, however, along with fellow pupils of all ethnic backgrounds, including white British ones, difficulty in reproducing accurate and fluent written Standard English in the preferred written genres favoured in specific school subject disciplines.
- pupils born and brought up in British urban areas who enter early years schooling with a dominant spoken language proficiency in a home/ community language originating from outside the UK, but not in English.
- pupils born in another country who enter the British schooling system sometime between the ages of 5 and 16 and appear to gradually move from the 'new' arrival to the low-key British bilingual category.
- pupils of Caribbean descent who perhaps constitute a special case of the first category of British bilingual in terms of their patterns of language use. That is, they may have substantial experience and expertise in a Caribbean Creole language such as Jamaican Creole, which while having a lexical relationship with English is often not intelligible to English-speaking outsiders.

3 *The high-achieving multilinguals*

These pupils have a good level of expertise or an untapped potential to rapidly acquire expertise in (a) 'home'/'community' language(s) other than English. At the same time they also have a high degree of proficiency in the kinds of written Standard English required for school success.

It should be evident that each of these distinct groups of pupils will require distinct approaches to language and learning developed by sensitive teachers. The pedagogic principles discussed earlier should be translated into classroom strategies and teaching activities with reference to the actual pupils in the classroom. To sum up, for many teachers, as Garcia (1996: vii) has commented from a North American standpoint:

> it has become necessary to cope with a process of change whereby the ethnolinguistic identity of children is itself undergoing rapid change . . . The greatest failure of contemporary education has been precisely its inability to help teachers understand the ethnolinguistic complexity of children, classrooms, speech communities, and society, in such a way as to enable them to make informed decisions about language and culture in the classroom.

Notes

1 For a detailed discussion of the development of this approach to EAL, see Mohan *et al.* (2001); suffice it to say at this point that a number of official documents have

argued for the mainstreaming of EAL provision. For instance, in a landmark invest-igation into the EAL provision and practice of the Calderdale education authority, the CRE (1986) found the practice of providing separate non-mainstream school-ing for pupils with EAL to be racially discriminating and contrary to 'the prevailing educational view' and recommended that 'provision for second language speakers is made in conjunction with mainstream education' (CRE 1986: 6, 16). The term EAL itself is of relatively new coinage; previously it was referred to as ESL (English as a second language). Indeed in other parts of the English-speaking world, the term ESL is still preferred. For some the notion of an 'additional' language is generally held to be ideologically more positive than 'second' language which might encourage a deficit view of pupils' linguistic repertoire. For this reason, some-times pupils with EAL are also referred to as bilingual pupils. Also see relevant parts of Swann Report (1985) and Bullock Report (1975).

2 For details of pre-Level 1 and adapted Level 1 EAL assessment descriptors see QCA (2000).

3 Specific staffing statistics in local education authorities are generally not reported in the public domain but most professionals would agree that there is a shortage of EAL specialists. For instance, in one London borough the EAL teacher to EAL pupils ratio is reported to be 1: 200.

4 Although 'Indian' and 'Chinese' could also indicate nationality, referring to India and mainland China, in British educational discourse they are just as likely to be ethnic markers referring to a wide variety of people of Indian or Chinese extraction including, say, those from East Africa or Hong Kong and Vietnam respectively.

References

Alladina, S. and Edwards, V. (1991) *Multilingualism in the British Isles*, vol. 2. Lon-don: Longman.

Back, L. (1996) *New Ethnicities and Urban Culture*. London: UCL Press.

Baker, P. and Eversley, J. (2000) *Multilingual Capital: The Languages of London's Schoolchildren and their Relevance to Economic, Social and Educational Policies*. Lon-don: Battlebridge Publications.

Berrington, A. (1996) Marriage patterns and inter-ethnic unions, in D. Coleman and J. Salt (eds) *Ethnicity in the 1991 Census*, vol. 1. London: HMSO.

Bourne, J. (1989) *Moving into the Mainstream: LEA Provision for Bilingual Pupils*. Windsor: NFER-Nelson.

Bourne, J. and McPake, J. (1991) *Partnership Teaching: Co-operative Teaching Strategies for English Language Support in Multilingual Classrooms*. London: HMSO.

Bullock Report (1975) *A Language for Life*. London: HMSO.

Commission for Racial Equality (CRE) (1986) *Teaching English as a Second Language*. London: Commission for Racial Equality.

Cummins, J. (1992) Language proficiency, bilingualism and academic achievement, in P.A. Richard-Amato and M.A. Snow (eds) *The Multicultural Classroom*. New York: Longman.

Department of Education and Science (DES) (1971) *The Education of Immigrants: Education Survey 13*. London: HMSO.

Department for Education (DfE) (1995) *Ethnic Monitoring of School Pupils: A Consulta-tion Paper*. London: DfE.

Department for Education and Employment (DfEE) (1999) *Minority Ethnic Pupils in Maintained Schools by Local Education Authority Area in England* – January 1999 (Provisional). DfEE Statistical First Release (SFR 15/1999). www.DfEE.gov.uk. Gov-ernment Statistical Service.

Edwards, V. and Redfern, A. (1992) *The World in a Classroom: Language in Education in Britain and Canada*. Clevedon: Multilingual Matters.

Garcia, O. (1996) Foreword, in C. Baker, *Foundations of Bilingual Education and Bilingualism*, 2nd edn. Clevedon: Multilingual Matters.

Gibbons, P. (1998) Classroom talk and the learning of new registers in a second language, *Language and Education*, 12(2): 99–118.

Gilroy, P. (1987/1991) *There Ain't No Black in the Union Jack*. London: Routledge.

Hall, S. (1988) New ethnicities, in A. Rattansi and J. Donald (eds) (1992) *'Race', Culture and Difference*. London: Sage/The Open University.

Hall, S. (1992) The question of cultural identity, in S. Hall, D. Held and T. McGrew (eds) *Modernity and its Futures*. Cambridge: Polity Press/Open University.

Hampshire County Council (1996) *Bilingual Learners Support Service: Service Guidelines*, 2nd edn. Hampshire: Hampshire County Council.

Harris, R. (1997) Romantic bilingualism: time for a change? in C. Leung, and C. Cable (eds) *English as an Additional Language: Changing Perspectives*. Watford: NALDIC.

Harris, R. (1999) Rethinking the bilingual learner, in A. Tosi and C. Leung (eds) *Rethinking Language Education: From a Monolingual to a Multilingual Perspective*. London: CILT.

Hewitt, R. (1991) Language, youth and the destabilisation of ethnicity, in C. Palmgren, K. Lovgren and G. Bolin (eds) *Ethnicity and Youth Culture*. Stockholm: Stockholm University.

Hewitt, R. (1995) The umbrella and the sewing machine: Trans-culturalism and the definition of surrealism, in A. Alund and R. Granqvist (eds) *Negotiating Identities*. Amsterdam: Rodopi.

Inner London Education Authority (ILEA) (1989) *Catalogue of Languages: Spoken by Inner London School Pupils: RS 1262/89*. London: ILEA Research and Statistics.

Kress, G. (1994) *Learning to Write*. London: Routledge.

Leung, C. (in press) *Developing Reading and Writing in English as an Additional Language*. Cheshire: United Kingdom Reading Association.

Leung, C., Harris, R. and Rampton, B. (1997) The idealised native-speaker, reified ethnicities and classroom realities, *TESOL Quarterly*, 31(3): 543–60.

Martin-Jones, M. (1989) Language education in the context of linguistic diversity: differing orientations in educational policy making in England, in J. Esling (ed.) *Multicultural Education Policy: ESL in the 1990s*. Toronto: OISE Press.

Mercer, K. (1994) *Welcome to the Jungle*. London: Routledge.

Mohan, B., Leung, C. and Davison, C. (eds) (2001) *English as a Second Language in the Mainstream: Teaching, Learning and Identity*. Harlow, Essex: Longman.

National Curriculum Council (NCC) (1991) *Circular Number 11: Linguistic Diversity and the National Curriculum*. York: NCC.

Office for Standards in Education (Ofsted) (1994) *Educational Support for Minority Ethnic Communities*. London: Ofsted.

Peach, C. (1996) Introduction, in C. Peach (ed.) *Ethnicity in the 1991 Census*, vol. 2. London: HMSO.

Qualifications and Curriculum Authority (QCA) (2000) *A Language in Common: Assessing English as an Additional Language*. London: QCA.

School Curriculum and Assessment Authority (SCAA) (1996) *Teaching English as an Additional Language: a Framework for Policy*. London: SCAA.

Swann Report (1985) *Education for All*. London: HMSO.

Travers, P. (ed.) (1999) *Enabling Progress in a Multilingual Classroom: Towards Inclusive Education*. London Borough of Enfield: Language and Curriculum Access Service.

Part 4 | Across the curriculum

Bethan Marshall

Literacy is at the top of the political agenda. The Labour government, elected in May 1997, suggested that its educational track record should be judged four years later by the proportion of pupils attaining the minimum standard in English (80 per cent of pupils at level 4 by the end of Key Stage 2). To enable schools to reach this target they introduced *The National Literacy Strategy* (NLS) (DfEE 1998). At first glance such an action would appear uncontroversial. That schools should teach children to read and write is incontestable. But there the consensus ceases. For the whys and wherefores, the ways and means of enabling pupils to become literate lie behind one of the most publicly contested issue in education.

It may be that the very centrality of literacy to the curriculum is responsible for the lack of neutrality in the way in which the subject is discussed. For beneath the common aim of most state education systems to encourage a literate society lie deeper, more problematic, questions. What, for example, does it mean to be literate? What kind of literacy do we need in the twenty-first century and perhaps most importantly, what kind of society do different types of literacy encourage? Our view of education is intimately connected with our view of society. While tabloid headlines would have us believe that this last remark is solely a preoccupation of those on the Left, T.S. Eliot, whose views were well to the Right, made a similar connection. In his essay, 'On Modern Education and the Classics', Eliot describes education as:

> A subject which cannot be discussed in a void: our questions raise other questions, social economic, financial, political. And the bearings are on more ultimate problems even than these: to know what we want in education we must know what we want in general, we must derive our theory of education from our theory of life.
>
> (Eliot, cited in Tate 1998: 3–4)

When we apply Eliot's observation to the literacy debate it becomes clearer that for some this will include a moral dimension. This point lends any discussion an emotive edge that it might not otherwise have had (see also Ball 1984 and Street 1997). For example, John Rae, a former headmaster of Westminster School, wrote in the *Observer* in February 1982:

> The overthrow of grammar coincided with the acceptance of the equivalent of creative writing in social behaviour. As nice points of grammar were mockingly dismissed as pedantic and irrelevant, so was punctiliousness in such matters as honesty, responsibility, property, gratitude, apology and so on.
>
> (Rae, cited in Graddol *et al.* 1991: 52)

In identifying progressive teaching so closely with the permissive society, Rae appears to locate a problem with literacy developing somewhere around the mid-1960s. As we shall see his observation is misplaced. Yet such an opinion has found credence with more recent social commentators including the journalist Melanie Phillips. In her book *All Must Have Prizes*, written as an invective against what she saw as the failings of the liberal educational establishment, she comments, 'The revolt against the teaching of grammar becomes a part of a wider repudiation of external forms of authority' (Phillips 1996: 69). In a chapter ironically subtitled 'Proper literacy' she lays the blame at the door of radical English teachers:

> English, after all is the subject at the heart of our definition of our national cultural identity. Since English teachers are the chief custodians of that identity we should not be surprised to find that revolutionaries intent on using the subject to transform society have gained a powerful foothold, attempting to redefine the very meaning of reading itself.
>
> (Phillips 1996: 69)

Yet both Rae's and Phillips' analyses of the problem are almost certainly more to do with their view of society than of literacy standards in schools. There is a subtle but significant elision between rules of language and standards of behaviour where anxiety about the latter requires greater emphasis on the former. Grammatical rules become societal laws. Any suggestion that these might be redefined or abandoned becomes a threat to civil order. Their contention, however, that others besides themselves have politicized the teaching of literacy is not without foundation. Yet whereas for Phillips and Rae literacy is to be taught as a set of rules in order to reinforce an orderly society, for those on the Left its prime aim is to liberate:

> Literacy becomes a meaningful construct to the degree that it is viewed as a set of practices and functions to either empower or disempower people. In the larger sense, literacy must be analysed according to whether it promotes democratic and emancipatory changes.
>
> (Freire and Macedo 1987: 41)

For such writers, the type of literacy required by Phillips is simply 'schooled literacy' (Street and Street 1991), that is, an ability to decode the print on the page but little else. They demand what has become known as 'critical literacy':

> Critical literacy responds to the cultural capital of a specific group or class and looks to ways in which it can be confirmed, and also at the ways in which the dominant society disconfirms students by either ignoring or denigrating the knowledge and experiences that characterise their everyday lives. The unit of analysis is social and the key concern is not individual interests but with the individual and collective empowerment.
>
> (Aronowitz and Giroux, cited in Ball *et al.* 1990: 61)

Others, such as Shirley Bryce Heath, have problematized the issue still further by examining the literacy of different social groups and noting how children from certain communities are disadvantaged by narrow definitions of 'schooled literacy' (Heath 1983). As Gee notes, such a perception of what it means to be literate means that 'the ability to talk about school based sorts of tasks is one way in which Western-style schools empower elites: they sound like they know more than they do' (Gee, cited in Corden 2000: 27).

Even those with a less overtly radical agenda use the term 'critical literacy' to describe a form of literacy that goes well beyond the basics. Richard Hoggart, in his essay, 'Critical literacy and creative reading', writes:

> The level of literacy we now accept for the bulk of the population, of literacy unrelated to the way language is misused in this kind of society, ensures that literacy becomes simply a way of further subordinating great numbers of people. We make them literate enough to be conned by the mass persuaders . . . The second slogan has to be 'Critical Literacy for All'. Critical Literacy means . . . teaching about the difficulties, challenges and benefits of living in an open society which aims to be a true democracy.
>
> (1998: 60)

For all these writers, albeit to varying degrees, literacy becomes a means of 'reading' the society in which we live. Integral to this task is a demand that we do not take 'authority' at face value but question and challenge it as part of the democratic process. They do not want passive subjects but active citizens.

Perhaps the arguments about what constitutes a literate society would not be so acute, however, if the debates were not transferred into the classroom. For our notions of education become entwined with our pedagogy. Again the battle lines are well defined, and it is easy to see why when we read John Dewey's definition of the differences between traditional and progressive education. To digress for a moment, John Dewey, with his definitive book, significantly entitled *Democracy and Education* (1916), is seen by many as the father of progressive education although its antecedents go well back beyond the eighteenth century. Writers such as Phillips (1996) see the origins of progressivism in the work of Rousseau who emphasized the centrality of the child. Yet in England it owes as much to the prevalence of the dissenting academies of the late eighteenth century, as it does to the work of Rousseau.

But to return to Dewey's definitions. While not specifically writing about literacy, his analysis of the differences between traditionalists and progressives explains once more some of the reasons behind the debates surrounding its teaching. He sees 'the main purpose and objective' of traditional education as the preparation of

> the young for future responsibilities and for success in life, by means of acquisition of the organised bodies of information and prepared forms of skill which comprehend the material instruction. Since the subject matter as well as standards of proper conduct are handed down from the past, the attitude of the pupils must, upon the whole, be one of docility, receptivity, and obedience.
>
> (Dewey 1966: 18)

You can see echoes of Phillips' arguments in such a definition, yet there would appear to be a general acceptance of such a description in the way in which literacy is currently discussed. Commenting on the introduction of the new national curriculum for initial teacher training in English and mathematics, a *Guardian* leader wrote that 'All major political parties are now agreed that there has to be more focus on "tried and tested" teaching methods' (*Guardian* 1997). Like Dewey, they contrast this approach with 'progressive education' which for them has become synonymous with a 'child centred' approach. They see the introduction of the 'new compulsory national curriculum for teacher training courses' as the 'the culmination of the move away from child centred learning' (*Guardian* 1997).

A similar attitude can be found in the then Secretary of State for Education, David Blunkett's, remarks in a *Daily Mail* article, written in response to those who would question elements of the NLS: 'I still encounter those in the education world who would prefer the quiet life of the past, where education was "progressive"' adding, 'that it ends the ill disciplined "anything goes" philosophy which did so much damage to a generation' (Blunkett 1999). Yet writing over 50 years before, Dewey argued against precisely this perception of his work:

> Just because traditional education was a matter of routine in which plans and programs were handed down from the past, it does not follow that progressive education is a matter of planless improvisation . . . Revolt against the kind of organisation characteristic of the traditional school constitutes a demand for high organisation based upon ideas.
>
> (Dewey 1966: 28–9)

Central to his philosophy was the notion that it was insufficient to consider *what* the child needed to learn but to understand *how* they learned. The challenge is 'to discover and put into operation a principle of order and operation which follows from understanding what educative experience signifies' (Dewey 1966: 29). He acknowledges, however, that 'It is accordingly a much more difficult task to work out the kinds of materials, of methods, and of social relationships that are appropriate to the new education than is the case with traditional education' (Dewey 1966: 29).

At the risk of oversimplifying what is a much researched and highly complex issue, it is possible to see this binary opposition in the recent reading debates – characterized by the terms 'phonics' and 'real books' – with the traditionalists supporting the former and the progressives encouraging the latter. Those involved in the debate, particularly those who advocate 'real books', have understandably complained that such oversimplistic headlines traduce the complexity of their method. It is, however, symptomatic of their position that they view the teaching of reading as irreducible to a simplistic set of skills. You will not find such niceties from advocates of phonics, such as Chris Woodhead, the former Chief Inspector of Schools, who is known to believe that we have overcomplicated the problem to the detriment of the pupils. Give teachers the information, he has contended, and they will simply 'transmit' that knowledge to the pupils.

In contrast, perhaps the best known advocate of 'real books', Margaret Meek, argues that she has always taken what is called a 'constructivist' view of teaching children to read (see for example Meek 1988, 1991). In other words, she has sought to build on what they already know, which includes their knowledge of how books work and how print conveys meaning. In this way, reading and writing are always taught within a clearly defined context.

Meek's work has never precluded the teaching of phonics, indeed she acknowledges its use and importance, but she has been a stern critic of those who, like Woodhead, would teach it as a system of isolated blends of sound from which words can be formed. This method, as we have seen, is much closer to Dewey's definition of traditional education in that it requires the 'acquisition of the organized bodies of information and prepared forms of skill which comprehend the material instruction' (Dewey 1966). Evidence of the notion that the teaching of reading can be parceled up into sets of skills can be found in any commercial scheme based on teaching reading and writing through phonics.

On the other hand, as Dewey acknowledges, Meek's approach demands considerable skill on the part of teachers who need to be aware of the progress of the individual child and adjust their teaching accordingly. Some publishers, most notably the Oxford Reading Tree (see Rowsell 2000), have attempted to provide a scheme that builds both on the work of those using the 'real books' approach as well as the phonics research of Usha Goswami (Goswami and Bryant 1990). This blend of methods is still by far the most common strategy for most primary schools (Raban *et al.* 1994). But the concern over such an apparently pragmatic amalgam, from those who advocate a strict phonics regime, can only be understood if we consider the underlying model of learning implied in either approach and its potential social significance. While the former demands an actively engaged pupil, the latter requires an 'attitude of the pupils [which] must upon the whole, be one of docility, receptivity, and obedience' (Dewey 1966).

A superficial glance at the *National Literacy Strategy: Framework for Teaching* (DfEE 1998) might suggest that it is a document that readily conforms to Dewey's definition of traditional education. While it has no statutory force, the inspection regime and the rhetoric accompanying it has meant, in effect, that most schools have adopted it in its entirety. It details the content or subject knowledge that children should be given term by term, year by year in each year of the primary school to develop their literacy skills. The approach at Key Stage 3 is very similar (DfEE 2000).

Underpinning the strategy is the notion that there are three elements in the development of literacy in children – word level, which to a greater or lesser extent involves the teaching of phonics; sentence level, which looks at grammar and, third, text level. While the developers of the strategy insist that these are integrated, the term 'levels' implies a hierarchy or rather a teaching order and it is this, along with the sheer weight of the content that must be delivered, that has given the NLS its traditionalist feel.

But before we discuss the NLS in more detail, it is worth examining what motivated the production of this document. Part of the rationale of the NLS involves a third strand of the literacy debate that we have not thus far considered – that of the economic imperative for a literate society. Here again, however, we find the divisions following a very similar pattern to those already explored.

Concern about falling standards in literacy is a common feature of almost every official report throughout the twentieth century (see Marshall 2000) and one of the most frequently cited sources of those concerns are employers. The almost annual complaints from the Institute of Directors about falling standards echo much earlier reports such as the Newbolt Report of 1921. Citing Boots Pure Drug Company, it commented that, 'The teaching of English in present day schools produces a very limited command of the English language' (Departmental Committee of the Board of Education 1921: 72). In the same report, all but a few employers complained that they had found difficulty in 'obtaining employees who can speak and write English clearly and correctly' (Departmental Committee of the Board of Education 1921: 72). Successive reports make similar observations. Yet despite such stark evidence to the contrary, research comparing standards over a 30 year period carried out by the National Foundation for Educational Research (Brooks 1997) showed that no such decline in standards had occurred.

Part of the explanation for such apparent discrepancies between perception and evidence must in part be attributable to that view of society which sees evidence of moral decline and gives such an anxiety educational expression. As we have seen, writers like Rae and Phillips are all too willing to accept a terminal decline in standards even though they assume a golden age (which cannot have existed if the reports are to be believed) occurring sometime before the 1960s, at which point they believe the rot set in. Yet this is insufficient. It would appear also that politicians utilize, and so give credence to, the notion that standards are declining to lend support for educational change and here the economic arguments become significant.

The Labour government, elected in 1997, confirms the rule. Part of its undoubted concern in introducing the NLS was rightly to raise levels of literacy among the population for its own sake. At the beginning of the NLS framework, David Blunkett wrote: 'All our children deserve to leave school equipped to enter a fulfilling adult life. If children do not master the basic skills of literacy and numeracy they will be seriously disadvantaged later' (DfEE 1998). As Henrietta Dombey points out, however, this was not their only motivation. 'It seems that higher scores on literacy and numeracy for the country's eleven-year-olds are expected to reverse the tide of economic decline, unemployment and national uncertainty' (1998:

128). Here again the familiar divisions occur. For while the literacy hour, with its apparently prescriptive solution, might appeal to the more conservative, others use the economic argument to press for a more radical agenda. For example, Gunther Kress (1995, 1997) argues that the model of literacy implicit in the NLS will not fit pupils for the economy of the future. Part of his contention is that traditional 'schooled literacy' does not pay sufficient attention to the demands of the new technologies. But Kress's argument is more significantly dependent on the notion that the new economies, built on 'fast capitalism', demand adaptable and flexible workers:

> The question I am posing is simply this: in relation to the economic and social futures such as these, what is the English curriculum doing? . . . If jobs are moveable with the speed of global fiscal markets, then certain requirements of a fundamental kind follow the kind of person whom we are preparing for that world. Somehow they will have to be prepared not just to cope, but to control their circumstances.
>
> (Kress 1995: 18)

Yet Kress's agenda is most clearly seen when he attempts to define the literacy necessary to achieve this end. In terms that clearly echo Dewey, he writes:

> If we represent literacy, in the curriculum, as a matter of fixed, immutable rules, we encourage a different attitude to the one suggested by a representation of literacy as a set of resources shaped by society and constantly reshaped by each individual reader and writer. The former encourages an acceptance of what is; a certain attitude to authority; a limitation accepted and internalized by the individual. The latter encourages curiosity about how things have come to be as they are; a certain attitude to individual responsibility and agency; and an internalization of the individual as active, creative and expansive.
>
> (Kress 1995: 75)

In other words, to produce the flexible worker of the future, to create the learning society we need to cope with an ever changing economic landscape, we need a theory of literacy that incorporates a vision of an active participant rather than a passive receiver of predetermined rules. It is this notion of the active individual that governs his view both of the way in which we need to learn and the beginnings of literacy in preschool children. He does not assume, however, that all children will engage in the process in the same way, but wants to understand what they are doing in order to develop them further: 'My preference is for intervention, for aiding and abetting, for making sure that children have to hand what will make that possible' (Kress 1995: 37).

There is one element that the literacy debate has so far omitted and that is the role of language in learning. The NLS does state, near the very beginning of the document that: 'Literacy unites the important skills of reading and writing. It also involves speaking and listening which, although they are not separately identified in the Framework, are an essential part of it' (DfEE 1998: 3). Yet it moves away from understanding language as a vehicle for learning in the following comment by narrowly focusing on knowledge about language itself: 'Good oral work enhances pupils' understanding of language in both oral and written forms and of the way in which language can be used to communicate' (DfEE 1998: 3).

The idea that language is essential to the learning process gained currency through the writing, amongst others, of James Britton, Douglas Barnes and Harold Rosen in books such as *Language, the Learner and the School* (Barnes *et al.* 1972) and *Language and Learning* (Britton 1974). Their work built on the writing of the Russian psychologist Lev Vygotsky. Although Vygotsky's research was carried out in the 1930s, it was not translated in the West for nearly 30 years. Vygotsky argued that language was an essential cognitive tool.

> [By] focusing attention on the interaction between speech and the child's social and cultural experiences, Vygotsky provides us with a model of learning which emphasizes the role of talk and places social discourse at the centre. Most significant is the notion that children can learn effectively through interaction with a more knowledgeable other (which may be a peer or adult).
>
> (Corden 2000: 8)

The notion that children can learn through interaction underpinned Vygotsky's (1978) pivotal learning theory of the Zone of Proximal Development (ZPD). In essence he argued that as each new learning situation arises, we move from a state where we do not understand to a position where we can understand if supported through interaction with the more knowledgeable other, and from there to a situation where we are independent. The aim of the teacher is to support the pupil through this process either through class or group discussion. The theory of ZPD has often been connected in practice with the work of Bruner. He coined the term 'scaffolding' (Bruner 1985) to describe the process by which children needed initial support on engaging in a new activity and then have that support gradually withdrawn as they become more independent and are able to work unaided.

Some argue that 'the value of Vygotsky and Bruner's approach is to see the dichotomy [between transmission and progressive education] as false' (Mercer and Edwards, cited in Corden 2000: 12). But this claim is not entirely borne out in practice. For implementing Vygotsky and Bruner's theories effectively in the classroom demands 'high organisation based upon ideas' (Dewey 1966: 28–9). In other words, appropriate interventions require the 'more difficult task to work out the kinds of materials, of methods, and of social relationships that are appropriate to the new education than is the case with traditional education' (Dewey 1966: 29).

This is not to say that the work of Vygotsky and Bruner is not readily applicable to the teaching of literacy and the kind of literacy support demanded in all areas of both the primary and secondary curriculum (see Corden 2000 for an account of how this might be done). The NLS (DfEE 1998) for example requires whole class sessions along with group work. It suggests that different styles of writing are 'modelled' for pupils before they attempt them, thus providing a scaffold of a sort. In this way it is possible to apply a progressive approach to the literacy strategy although the very prescriptive lists outlined in the NLS suggest a more traditional stance. Yet crucially the delivery of the literacy hour will be determined by the existing philosophy of the teacher. The degree of interaction with the class will depend on whether the teacher views the content of the curriculum as something in effect to be 'transmitted' or 'constructed' through guided discussion and planned intervention.

Two positions have been starkly contrasted in this chapter in order to unravel some of the strands of the literacy debate. And part of the problem with the debate has been the shorthand use of the terms 'progressive' and 'traditionalist'. 'Progressive' teaching conjures up an image of children swinging from the light bulbs. A 'traditionalist' approach is one that will restore much needed order to the classroom. This chapter has, therefore run the risk of being equally stereotypical and, as we have seen there are those who wish to break down these barriers for that very reason, seeing the divide as unhelpfully sterile. Indeed in practice the delineations are less clear, the positions much more finely nuanced. Not everyone is neatly categorized into a camp. This is partly because 'progressive' and 'traditionalist' are in fact umbrella terms which represent a spectrum of views that often appear to meet somewhere in the middle. Yet they do constitute different approaches. A traditionalist or progressive teacher may be more at one end of the spectrum than the other – Richard Hoggart's views are not the same as Paolo Friere's; Chris Woodhead and David Blunkett may not always agree – but the range of views that these pairs represent place them on different sides in the literacy debate. That is not to say that on occasion the rhetoric will not be the same, but to understand why two people may, at one level, agree but draw very different conclusions we have to understand what is motivating their comments in the first place. What is their view of learning and to what end do they wish education to be put? Finally and perhaps most importantly we need to work out not only where others stand, but where we stand ourselves.

References

Ball, S.J. (1984) Conflict, panic and inertia: mother tongue teaching in England 1970–1983, in W. Herlitz (ed.) *Mother Tongue Education in Europe, Studies in Mother Tongue Education 1*. Enschede, NL: National Institute for Curriculum Development.

Ball, S.J., Kenny, A. and Gardiner, D. (1990) Literacy policy and the teaching of English, in I. Goodson and P. Medway (eds) *Bringing English to Order*. London: Falmer.

Barnes, D., Britten, J. and Rosen, H. (1972) *Language, the Learner and the School*. Middlesex: Penguin Books.

Blunkett, D. (1999) Commentary: moaners who are cheating your children, *Daily Mail*, 19 July.

Britton, J. (1974) *Language and Learning*. Middlesex: Penguin Books.

Brooks, G. (1997) Trends in standards of literacy in the United Kingdom 1948–1997. Conference paper. British Educational Research Association, University of York, 11–14 September.

Bruner, J. (1985) Vygotsky: a historical and conceptual perspective, in J. Wertsch (ed.) *Culture, Communication and Cognition: Vygotskian Perspectives*. Cambridge: Cambridge University Press.

Corden, R. (2000) *Literacy and Learning Through Talk*. Buckingham: Open University Press.

Department for Education and Employment (DfEE) (1998) *The National Literacy Strategy*. London: HMSO.

Department for Education and Employment (DfEE) (2000) *Transforming Key Stage 3: National Pilot English at Key Stage 3 Training 2000*. London: DfEE.

Departmental Committee of the Board of Education (1921) *The Teaching of English in England: Being the Report of the Departmental Committee Appointed by the President of the Board of Education to Inquire into the Position of English in the Educational System of England* (The Newbolt Report). London: HMSO.

Dewey, J. (1916) *Democracy and Education*. New York: Macmillan.

Dewey, J. (1966) *Experience and Education*. London: Collier Books.

Dombey, H. (1998) Changing literacy in the early years of school, in B. Cox (ed.) *Literacy is Not Enough: Essays on the Importance of Reading*. Manchester: Manchester University Press.

Freire, P. and Macedo, D. (1987) *Literacy: Reading the Word and the World*. London: Routledge.

Goswami, U. and Bryant, P. (1990) *Phonological Skills and Learning to Read*. Norwood, NJ: Lawrence Erlbaum Associates.

Graddol, D., Maybin J., Mercer, N. and Swann, J. (eds) (1991) *Talk and Learning 5–16: An Inservice Pack on the Oracy for Teachers*. Buckingham: Open University Press.

Guardian (1997) Leader article, 27 June.

Heath, S.B. (1983) *Ways With Words*. Cambridge: Cambridge University Press.

Hoggart, R. (1998) Critical literacy and creative reading, in B. Cox (ed.) *Literacy Is Not Enough: Essays on the Importance of Reading*. Manchester: Manchester University Press.

Kress, G. (1995) *Writing the Future: English and the Making of a Culture of Innovation*. Sheffield: NATE Papers in Education.

Kress, G. (1997) *Before Writing*. London: Routledge.

Marshall (2000) *English Teachers – The Unofficial Guide: Researching the Philosophies of English Teachers*. London: Falmer Routledge.

Meek, M. (1988) *How Texts Teach What Readers Learn*. Stroud: Thimble Press.

Meek, M. (1991) *On Being Literate*. London: Bodley Head.

Phillips, M. (1996) *All Must Have Prizes*. London: Little, Brown and Co.

Raban, B., Clark, U. and McIntyre, J. (1994) *Evaluation of the Implementation of English in the National Curriculum at Key Stages 1, 2 and 3*. London: School Curriculum and Assessment Authority.

Rowsell, J. (2000) Publishing practices in print education: British and Canadian perspectives on educational publishing. Unpublished PhD thesis, University of London.

Street, B. (1997) The implications of the new literacy studies for literacy education, *English and Education*, 31(3): 44–55.

Street, B. and Street, J. (1991) The schooling of literacy, in D. Barton and R. Ivanich (eds) *Writing in the Community*. London: Sage.

Tate, N. (1998) What is education for? The King's College London Fifth Annual Education Lecture. London: King's College London.

Vygotsky, L. (1978) *Thought and Language*. Cambridge, MA: MIT Press.

21	# Citizenship: what does it mean to be a good citizen?

Ann-Marie Brandom

Introduction

What does it mean to be a citizen in society, and what does it mean to educate for such citizenship? This is not a new question – Aristotle was driven to declare in *The Politics* that 'there is no unanimity, no agreement' over the nature of citizenship (1981: 168). In today's pluralistic, secular society, citizenship must promote a liberal democratic form of education (Hogan 1997: 51). Such a model itself is not neutral but it does underpin the latest version of the National Curriculum. Much of this underpinning is based on the work of T.H. Marshall who argued for a social citizenship (Marshall 1950, 1964), a citizenship that involved three interrelated elements, the civil, the political and the social.

The civil element stemmed from an understanding of 'individual freedom – liberty of person, freedom of speech and the right to justice'. The political element referred to 'the right to participate in the exercise of political power as a member of a body vested with political authority or as an elector of the members of such a body'. The social element referred to 'the whole range from the right to a modicum of economic welfare and security to the right to share to the full in the social heritage . . . prevailing in society' (all quotations from Marshall 1964: 78). These three strands form the basis of the current definition of what constitutes the effective education of citizenship: first, the social and moral responsibility given to, and expected of, pupils in school; second, their community involvement, learning about and becoming responsibly involved in the life and concerns of the community; third, the notion of themselves as politically literate, in other words aware of the scope of what it means to be an active citizen in society.

Underpinning Marshall's three stemmed approach then is the 'progressive' notion of the child as a future citizen. In other words his model anticipates the active engagement of the pupil in the decision-making process. This contrasts with a view that assumes a more passive model of learning in which the pupil needs to receive information to enable them to participate in adult life.

The government finally gave a formal place to citizenship in the National Curriculum in 2000. Evidence of the two models of learning, one progressive and one content laden, lies within it, but the government's solution to the potential tension between these two approaches may not be to everyone's liking because of the amount of prescribed content. Nor is there necessarily whole-hearted acceptance for the underlying rationale of this programme of citizenship. However, the emphasis given in the documentation on the skills of enquiry, communication, participation and intercultural discourse enables us to ask, what does it mean to be a citizen?

The statutory framework for Citizenship takes effect from August 2002. There is much work to be done for individual schools to formalize a programme of explicit citizenship in this time-frame but the importance of the subject has been reiterated:

> Citizenship gives pupils the knowledge, skills and understanding to play an effective role in society at local, national and international levels. It helps them to become informed, thoughtful and responsible citizens who are aware of their duties and rights. It promotes their spiritual, moral, social and cultural development, making them more self-confident and responsible both in and beyond the classroom. It encourages pupils to play a helpful part in the life of their schools, neighborhoods, communities and the wider world. It also teaches them about our economy and democratic institutions and values; encourages respect for different national, religious and ethnic identities; and develops pupils' ability to reflect on the issues and take part in discussions.
>
> (QCA/DfEE 1999: 12)

The government argued for the centrality of citizenship at a time when there were 'worrying signs of alienation and cynicism among young people about public life and participation, leading to their possible disconnection and disengagement from it' (Kerr 1999: 3). The context, in part, explains the government's approach. Their model of citizenship education emphasizes pupils' knowledge, skills and understanding of their role in society in order that they might better understand what participation in a variety of arenas might actually look like.

For pupils to know what citizenship is, the government argued, they must be given access to a curriculum that will give them confidence to begin the examination of what it is to be a respectful member of society. They then need to be encouraged to critique the status quo using a range of skills in order to understand better the diverse value systems of the local, national and international society to which they belong. Finally pupils, it suggests, need to be given the physical opportunity to participate in some form of community-based work to enable them to reflect on the role they will continue to play in their adult life.

The evolution of citizenship education in England

Until now, education for citizenship has not held a statutory place in the school curriculum. As such England is unique among its European, North American and Australian counterparts where civics or citizenship education has played an explicit role in education. This is not to say that individual schools in England have not been active on this front, it is simply acknowledging the insignificant role that citizenship has played until now in national legislation. What the Qualifications and Curriculum Authority (QCA) have endorsed, in providing a framework for the subject in the National Curriculum, is the opportunity for schools to wrestle with the issue of citizenship in their respective unique and individual situations. As a result of the QCA guidelines, the responsibility lies with the school to demonstrate how they can provide for citizenship education within curriculum time.

There have been periods of time when citizenship has been advocated in English schools (Batho 1990). One instance was in response to the rise of totalitarianism in Europe in the mid-1930s. In 1935 the Association for Education in World Citizenship (AEWC) was established to preserve the democratic fabric of society. The association was built upon the desire to emphasize the social responsibility of the individual citizen, an allegiance to the principle of freedom and an awareness of the political and economic factors that shape the modern world. These principles will begin to sound familiar when we compare them to the current National Curriculum guidelines for citizenship.

Attention was paid to the AEWCs definition of citizenship in the postwar years but no official programme was ever advocated at a national level. The subject was not taken forward and it was not until the rise of the comprehensive school system in the mid-1960s, and the introduction of social studies courses such as sociology, social studies or politics, that citizenship appeared, albeit at a low level, in the school curriculum. Although voluntary work in the community and participation in the broader life of a school were hallmarks of many educational institutions, it tended to be as a result of the enthusiasm of individual teachers (Fogelman 1997).

The National Curriculum

With the 1988 Education Reform Act, citizenship was given some form of legislative recognition. The National Curriculum contained not just an explanation of what was to be taught in each subject area, excluding the content for religious education, which was to be part of the 'basic curriculum', but a framework of guidance for 'cross-curricular themes'. The themes were provided as a means of augmenting the National Curriculum and were designed to give coherence to the educational experience of the pupil. The five themes were: health education; careers education and guidance; environmental education; education for economic and industrial understanding; and education for citizenship (NCC 1990a).

Non-statutory guidance was published for each theme (NCC 1990b). Schools were encouraged to develop their own policy document in response to the statement, 'Education for Citizenship develops the knowledge, skills and attitudes necessary for exploring, making informed decisions about and exercising responsibilities and rights in a democratic society' (NCC 1990b). Some schools did produce policy documents but it quickly became apparent that the pressure on curriculum time was so great that citizenship education had fallen by the wayside.

Even after the publications in 1990 of the report of the Speaker's Commission on Citizenship, *Encouraging Citizenship* and the National Commission on Education report (NCE 1993) there was little practical application of the blueprints on offer. Both reports endorsed the significance of citizenship and the former even attempted a definition of citizenship by referring to the work of the sociologist T.H. Marshall. The latter recommended that citizenship should be compulsory from the age of 7, but it was still up to schools to ensure provision and this was too problematic.

The review of the National Curriculum by Sir Ron Dearing in 1994 (Dearing 1994) could not find a formal place for citizenship. Representations were made to him but the slimming down of the subject content took priority (Fogelman 1997). The lack of any evidence of much good practice education in schools did not, however, hinder research into citizenship education. In 1991, for example, the Centre for Citizenship Studies in Education was established at the Leicester University. Surveys were carried out to ascertain schools' provision of citizenship and one such review, carried out in 1995, found that:

> 43 per cent of primary schools and 62 per cent of secondary said that it is an essential or very important part of the curriculum . . . on the other hand it was still the case for almost all schools that there was no mention, or only a very brief one, of citizenship education in the school development plan. About two thirds of schools (both phases) stated that pressures on the timetable had been a major constraint on their ability to provide citizenship education; lack of funding for resources and lack of staff expertise were also mentioned by significant numbers.
>
> (Fogelman 1997: 93)

The election of a Labour government in May 1997 provided an opportunity for change. The White Paper, *Excellence in Schools* (DfEE 1997) proposed that the teaching of democracy and education for citizenship be strengthened. To this end the Secretary of State for Education initiated the formation of an advisory group to establish the aims and function of citizenship in schools; to define in broad terms what effective citizenship should be; and make practical recommendations to the Qualifications and Assessment Authority (QCA) in the light of the Authority's review of the National Curriculum. The group was to be chaired by Professor Bernard Crick and the group's recommendations were to provide the framework for what citizenship education has become.

The *Final Report of the Advisory Group on Citizenship* now known as the Crick Report (Advisory Group on Citizenship 1998) was submitted in 1998. The report recommended that 5 per cent of curriculum time should be given over to the subject across the key stages. Subsequently reviewed by the QCA working party known as Preparation for Adult Life, the recommendations in the report formed the framework for citizenship in the revised National Curriculum 2000.

The Report called for citizenship education to be a statutory entitlement. Citizenship became statutory for all key stages and was incorporated into the Personal, Social and Health Education (PSHE) Programmes of Study at Key Stages 1 and 2. The date chosen for citizenship to be taught as a distinct subject at Key Stages 3 and 4 was August 2002.

As well as the recommendation of 5 per cent of curriculum time, the report also suggested that there should be a degree of interpretation permitted in the programmes of study in order to provide schools with a means of adapting the guidelines to the particular situation they were in. This too has been taken up, although in the future there may well be statutory schemes of work to follow, along with the publication of the assessment guidelines; at the moment, such flexibility exists.

National Curriculum 2000 requirements for citizenship

The Crick Report outlined the rubric of citizenship along three lines: understanding social and moral responsibility; becoming involved in the community and developing a political literacy. These have been adapted to provide the broad programmes of study outlined below. When delivering citizenship pupils are to:

- become informed citizens;
- develop skills of enquiry and communication;
- develop skills of participation and responsible action.

(QCA/DfEE 1999: 6)

To become an informed citizen, a pupil is required to have the opportunity to learn about a myriad of key political, social and cultural aspects. The requirements, which are very content laden, include learning about the law and the human rights and responsibilities that underpin society. Pupils are to be taught about the diversity of national, regional, ethnic and religious identities in society and they should understand the function of local and central government with the aim of appreciating the importance of their own participation now and when they are able to vote. They should understand how the voluntary sector operates and how significant the media is in affecting opinion. Finally they should learn about the global community and about resolving conflict (QCA/DfEE 1999: 14). Thus the model of citizenship is defined less through a conceptual process or framework but rather, as with the numeracy and literacy strategies, as a body of knowledge to be acquired. There is however obvious progression from Key Stage 3 to 4. The same topics are covered again at Key Stage 4, but in more depth and with more scope for analysis. This is designed to encourage further enquiry and the opportunity to form reasoned opinion.

In addition, although the programme seems to focus on the content, and there is no methodology laid down for addressing all the topics, it is the emphasis on skills that offers much scope for training pupils in intercultural dialogue. Pupils are to be taught to think, to justify, to contribute, to use their imagination, to negotiate and decide and to participate responsibly in school and in community-based activities. It is this last element that distinguishes the rubric on citizenship. Schools must provide opportunities for pupils to participate in voluntary work. The framework is not just theoretical, it is active and practical (QCA/DfEE 1999).

The importance of individual and corporate responsibility and participation within the framework is consistently emphasized. The learning outcomes are designed so that pupils have the opportunity to identify the many factors that influence society and begin to understand their own position within the political framework. As a result, they should be able to justify their personal opinion on these matters in the light of the issues they have studied – hence the focus on becoming politically literate. There is also an outline provided to indicate how citizenship can promote pupils' spiritual, moral, social, and cultural development as well as the key skills.

There is, as yet, no framework for the assessment of citizenship. Attainment targets have not been published in order to aid those responsible for the implementation of citizenship to devise appropriate schemes of work. There is no prescriptive explanation given of who is to be responsible for the delivery of the subject material; it is up to the school to organize. In the document itself, however, much of the content is provided with detailed cross-curricular links. Science (Sc), modern foreign languages (MFL), information and communication technology (ICT), music (Mu) as well as English (En), History (Hi), art and design (A&D) and geography (Gg) are all mentioned. For example requirement 1i 'pupils should be taught about: the world as a global community, and the political, economic, environmental and social implications of this' is linked with Sc2/5a, Hi/13, Gg/3b and MFL/4c (QCA/DfEE 1999: 14). Initial aid for individual subjects looking to include citizenship in their schemes of work would do well to read *Developing Citizenship in the Curriculum* (Edwards and Fogelman 1993) as it provides a summary for each subject in the National Curriculum linking this with key elements of citizenship.

Implications of the programmes of study

The revised National Curriculum lays out the framework and specifies that 5 per cent of curriculum time is allocated to citizenship. Schools are rightly concerned about where this time will come from. There is also a concern about who is to deliver the content of the programmes of study and how they will eventually be assessed. It is helpful that cross-curricular opportunities have been identified, but these have to be made explicit in curriculum planning. It is not clear whether there will be statutory schemes of work to adhere to which may well alter how schools deliver citizenship.

The most significant element of the statutory framework is the emphasis on participation. Schools must be able to offer some form of voluntary programme to students in order to allow them the opportunity to develop their commitment to their community. This could be in the form of a school council or voluntary community work. If citizenship is to be integrated into the present curriculum, schools must be prepared to examine the value system they uphold through the ethos of the school – because the school itself is a community and therefore acts as a model of citizenship. Pupils will automatically be acquiring knowledge, understanding and skills to cope in their school. They will glean very quickly the role they are to play in school, the extent of their rights and responsibilities and the nature of what is and is not valued. As Max Burkmisher says:

> If the school is a model . . . what is the school's vision? What is its purpose? Are the aims clear and understood and subscribed to by all? Is there clarity about values which underpin the aims? Do members of the school share in the discussion of these values? Do they measure their own practice against values? Are the values understood and shared by the wider community which the school serves? Given that we see our state as democratic, how democratic are our schools and in what ways can we make them more democratic?
>
> (Burkmisher 1993: 8)

Underlying the programmes of study is a commitment to respect both the individual and the diversity of communities in society.

Through their experience in and outside school, pupils will already be aware that there are structures in society that dictate authority. Citizenship can provide a means for pupils to reflect on their moral and personal development while learning how to acknowledge the value system that is in operation underpinning the democratic society in which they live. Since pupils will then be aware of their place in society, the Crick Report suggests it will become apparent that pupils have responsibilities to others in the community, hence the emphasis on the second aspect of effective citizenship, that of community involvement. This is not designed to be limited to the pupil's time in school either, this is education for life. The intention is to demonstrate to pupils the role the community plays and their life-long part in it. They need therefore to be made aware that personal decision-making and conflict resolution also have implications for all levels of society, from within families, to local community level through to the national, European and international level.

Conclusion

The implications of Marshall's three strands are not without their problems. The nature of the term 'active' citizenship demands response by the individual, yet any inherent inequality within society means that the response of some is curbed. Yes, lobbying Parliament in a democracy is your right, but it does not necessarily imply that things will change. In the same way, if pupils are to be offered a context for decision-making in a school, a context which, more often than not, takes the form of a student council, what powers if any does the council actually wield?

What kind of model of democratic rights are we promoting when we dictate in the first instance a certain moral code of acceptable behaviour? What right do we have as teachers to dictate to students what QCA have defined as good citizenship education? We are back to questions again. To find answers, we need to examine the underlying values operating in our educational system. Our educational system is caught up in the same dilemma; according to which value system has our national curriculum been developed? This question echoes the current debate over a 'liberal political theory . . . confronted by a diversity of beliefs and values' (Beck 2000: 136) (also see Chapter 4, this volume).

At no point in time is citizenship education advocating an anarchic model for pupils, yet our democratic society promotes, in fact demands, open debate concerning claims to possessing the 'right' understanding. Sources of truth are actively interrogated and scepticism reigns supreme. This in turn invites people to doubt authoritative institutions, preventing them perhaps to form allegiance, encourages them to ask the question why, and then provide their own alternatives to the assumptions of the day. If this is coupled with a diverse, multicultural society that has clusters of people who define their own authority structures separately, then there is confusion as to what makes a good citizen, let alone what makes for good citizenship education.

The example of the issue of homosexuality illustrates the complexity and potential contentiousness of the nature of critical discussion about how laws are passed. The ongoing debate concerning the recognition of homosexuality and the way it can or cannot be tackled in the classroom is surrounded by public controversy precisely because open debate is fostered in a democratic country. The legal framework may or may not be rewritten, but the issue itself is still controversial and thus has implications for the teaching of citizenship. What do you do when you are discussing the legal framework and a child in your classroom advocates homosexuality as a justifiable personal stance, but another child becomes very agitated because they believe that any expression of homosexuality is completely wrong? You are not promoting homosexuality in the class-room, but you are debating how law is made, how are you to deal with the controversy?

The question here is how teachers are to deal with controversial issues in the classroom. There is no rubric for the presentation of the topics on citizenship, but an endorsement to engage pupils with complex concepts and create an environment for healthy debate, discussion, respectful dis-agreement and critical thinking. The danger of this is that to engage pupils' thinking capacities is to allow them to question, and if you allow them to question they will begin to interrogate the autonomy they are permitted in school, they will challenge the status quo and they will perhaps lobby for change. The advocacy of education for citizenship is an exciting move forward in educational terms, if by education we mean the freeing of the child to question.

On the other hand if the nature of citizenship is to be slowly made prescriptive as assessment opportunities are written, then there may well be a dictation of the rubric and the current political literacy that is advoc-ated may not be permitted in the future. That may be too pessimistic a view; perhaps the only limitations placed on the nature of citizenship will be the approach of the teaching staff to the subject. It is important to note here that a school is not simply made up of teachers and pupils. There are also the administrators, school supervisors, cleaners, kitchen staff, technical support staff, librarians, volunteers, learning mentors from local businesses, the governing body, the local community and so on. All these people are members of the wider community and they too should be included in the links made with citizenship.

On a final note, it is the ethos of the school which will ultimately dictate the provision of effective citizenship education. The ethos of the school is upheld by members of its community. As a member of the school community you as a teacher must ask yourself what your understanding of citizenship is in order to make explicit your own value system. In doing this you will be able to feel confident in addressing the issues of citizenship because you will have answered the questions for yourself (Mead 1999).

Since pupil self-confidence is a vital ingredient to establish, it should also be the case that teachers are confident in the material they are handling and the critical thinking processes they are advocating. If you provide pupils with the skills with which to assess and analyse their role in society you may well be giving them the opportunity of a lifetime. If you simply ensure that they have learned how the United Nations Declaration of Human Rights came about, you may never hear them mention its significance again. Pupils need to own the process of democracy, not just be taught about it.

References

Advisory Group on Citizenship (1998) *Education for Citizenship and the Teaching of Democracy in Schools: Final Report of the Advisory Group on Citizenship*. London: Qualifications and Curriculum Authority.

Aristotle (1981) *The Politics*, rev. edn, T.J. Saunders (ed.). Harmondsworth: Penguin.

Batho, G. (1990) The history of the teaching of civics and citizenship in English Schools, *The Curriculum Journal*, 1(1): 91–107.

Beck, J. (2000) Citizenship and education for citizenship, in J. Beck and M. Earl (eds) *Key Issues in Secondary Education*. London: Cassell.

Burkmisher, M. (1993) Creating a climate for citizenship education in schools, in J. Edwards and K. Fogelman (eds) Developing Citizenship in the Curriculum. London: David Fulton.

Commission on Citizenship (1990) *Encouraging Citizenship*. Report of the House of Commons Commission on Citizenship. London: HMSO.

Dearing, R. (1994) *The National Curriculum Council and its Assessment: Interim Report*. London: NCC/SEAC.

Department for Education and Employment (DfEE) (1997) *Excellence in Schools*. London: DfEE.

Department for Education and Science (DES) (1988) *Education Reform Act*. London: HMSO.

Edwards, J. and Fogelman, K. (1993) *Developing Citizenship in the Curriculum*. London: David Fulton.

Fogelman, K. (1997) Citizenship education in England, in K. Kennedy (ed.) *Citizenship Education and the Modern State*. London: Falmer Press.

Hogan, D. (1997) The logic of protection: citizenship, justice and political community, in K. Kennedy (ed.) *Citizenship Education and the Modern State*. London: Falmer Press.

Kerr, D. (1999) Re-examining citizenship in England, in J. Torney-Purta, J. Schwille and J-A. Amadeo (eds) *Civic Education Across Countries: 22 Case Studies from the Civic Education Project*. Amsterdam: Eberon Publishers for the International Association for the Evaluation of Educational Achievement.

Marshall, T.H. (1950) *Citizenship and Social Class*. Cambridge: Cambridge University Press.

Marshall, T.H. (1964) *Class Citizenship and Social Development*. Chicago, IL: Chicago University Press.

Mead, N. (1999) The challenge of citizenship to religious education, *Resource*, 22(1): 12–15.

Mead, N. (2000) Identifying skills common to religious education and citizenship and the implications for initial teacher training. Unpublished lecture, delivered to the Conference of University Lecturers in Religious Education, 20 July.

National Commission on Education (NCE) (1993) *Learning to Succeed: Report of the National Commission on Education*. London: Heinemann.

National Curriculum Council (NCC) (1990a) *Curriculum Guidance 3: The Whole Curriculum*. York: NCC.

National Curriculum Council (NCC) (1990b) *Curriculum Guidance 8: Education for Citizenship*. York: NCC.

Qualifications and Assessment Authority (QCA) and the Department for Education and Employment (DfEE) (1999) *Citizenship*. London: QCA/DfEE.

Spiritual education

Ann-Marie Brandom, Mike Poole and Andrew Wright

Introduction

To achieve qualified teacher status (QTS) new teachers must demonstrate that they can 'plan opportunities to contribute to pupils' personal, Spiritual, Moral, Social and Cultural development' (DfEE 1998: 12). This chapter deals solely with the topic of spirituality. Why? Because in the first instance, although there are issues around definitions of what constitutes moral, social and cultural development, there are very specific difficulties in defining spirituality, not least being the fact that it is not necessarily a subject of comfortable public discourse. Second, although there are resources to support the delivery of spirituality across the curriculum, they do not address the issue of teacher confidence in handling spirituality in the classroom.

The requirement to be able to 'plan opportunities to contribute to pupils' personal, spiritual, moral, social and cultural development' (DfEE 1998: 12) reflects government concern that 'insufficient attention has been paid explicitly to the spiritual . . . aspects of pupils' development' (DfE 1994: 9). The 1988 Education Reform Act requires the promotion of 'the spiritual, moral, cultural, mental and physical development of pupils at school and of society' (DES 1988: 1). This requirement is reinforced by the Office for Standards in Education's (Ofsted) *Framework for the Inspection of Schools* (Ofsted 1993a) which expects inspectors to report on the provision made by schools for the spiritual development of children.

What exactly is 'spiritual development'? Is it merely a rhetorical reference to the conglomeration of experiences that constitute postmodern 'identity'? Or does it have a more substantial and critical role to play in the education of our pupils? We suggest that spiritual development is at the heart of the educational process since authentic education is inextricably bound up with ultimate questions of the meaning and purpose of life. This chapter develops a working definition of spirituality, explores the developing place of spirituality in education, considers spirituality as a whole-school issue, and finally, presents a case study designed to stimulate reflection on classroom practice.

What is spirituality?

Effective spiritual education in schools requires a clear understanding of what teachers are being asked to deal with. 'Spirituality' is a notoriously ephemeral concept; though it has something to do with the ultimate meaning and purpose of life, attempts at a tighter definition tend to prove elusive. The traditional equation of spirituality with Christian piety, in which the task of spiritual education was to nurture children into a confession of the Christian faith, seems disturbingly narrow in the context of our multifaith and multicultural classrooms. However there is a reai danger that, in resisting such Christian exclusivism, schools will inadvertently embrace a bland inclusive spirituality that, in trying to be all things to all people, ends up having nothing of value to say to anybody. Consequently, spiritual educators have embarked on a search for a flexible definition of spirituality, one acceptable to the broad sweep of public opinion yet at the same time open to the insights of specific spiritual traditions.

A frequent starting point in the search is the ambiguous relationship between spirituality and religion. For many, genuine spirituality is rooted in the sphere of the sacred, bound up with a desire to locate the ultimate meaning and purpose of life in some form of transcendent reality above and beyond the universe. The religious disciplines of prayer, worship and meditation enable the believer to enter into a spiritual relationship with God, Nirvana or some other conception of ultimate reality. Though the religious quest resonates with contemporary New Age sensibilities – in sharp contrast to the earlier rationalistic rejection of religious discourse as meaningless superstition – it is not without its problems. If we accept a necessary relationship between spirituality and religion, which specific religious tradition(s) ought we to teach in schools? In doing so do we not effectively disenfranchise the spiritual lives of atheists and agnostics?

A second starting point is the dualism between the physical material and spiritual/immaterial. Plato viewed the material world as transient and contingent, contrasting it unfavourably with the eternal and stable realm of spiritual forms (Hamilton and Cairns 1961). The ultimate meaning and purpose of our lives lies not in our physical bodies, which are destined to return to dust and ashes, but in the flourishing of our immortal souls. This Platonic dualism gave birth to an anthropology in which our spiritual selves are represented as 'ghosts in the machine' and 'spirits in the material world'. This dualism leads to forms of spirituality rooted in the ascetic renunciation of the physical world, such as a decision to resist the materialistic values of consumer capitalism or to follow the eight-fold path of Buddhism. A mirror image of this ascetic spirituality is to be found in the Epicurean celebration of the brute fact of human sensuality, sexuality and physicality.

A third starting point can be found in the idea of human freedom which places the introspective and self-conscious individual at the spiritual centre of the universe. This positioning can lead to the equation of spiritual health with psychological well-being and an ultimate concern for self-awareness, self-understanding and self-acceptance. Such introspective spirituality is cultivated by a variety of modern techniques such as therapy, meditation and counselling. Two important observations need to be made about this perspective: in the first place there is an increasing consensus that we are relational creatures, and that our self-understanding is as much dependent on our external relationships with society, culture and nature as it is on our internal self-understanding. Second, postmodern philosophers, such as Foucault, argue that our identities are in constant flux and consequently spiritual health depends not on our ability to 'find ourselves' but rather on our ability constantly to construct and celebrate multiple identities (Gutting 1994).

These three approaches to the complex question of spirituality are best seen as complementary and interconnected rather than as mutually exclusive: our ultimate spiritual concern needs to take account of our religious or secular worldviews, of the relationship of our inner selves to our bodies and to the material world, and of our developing identities as we seek to relate both to ourselves and those around us. This leads us to propose the following working definition of spirituality:

> Spirituality is the relationship of the individual, within community and tradition, to that which is – or is perceived to be – of ultimate concern, ultimate value and ultimate truth, as appropriated through an informed, sensitive and reflective striving for spiritual wisdom.
>
> (Wright 2000: 104)

Some comments will help clarify this definition:

- Spirituality here is intimately linked with personal identity as formed both by inner self-understanding and by our developing relationships with the world about us.
- The distinction between the way we see the world and the way the world actually is opens up the possibility of our spiritual values being either in harmony or dissonance with the actual order of things.
- It follows that our ultimate concerns may be pathologically misdirected, for example in a desire to dress in the latest fashion or in a more sinister need to victimize others on the basis of their race or sexual orientation.
- Spiritual truth is not neutral but value laden and demanding of our full engagement.
- Wisdom rooted in an ability to reflect in-depth on our experience of life, rather than abstract rationality or unrestrained emotivism, is the appropriate means of examining our spiritual commitments.
- The definition deliberately leaves the question of the material content of spirituality hanging in the air, not because the issue is unimportant but because the issue is too important prematurely to close down any options.

- The definition is offered not as a final statement but as a working model intended as a heuristic tool to enhance the possibility of cultivating spiritual literacy in schools.

Spirituality and education

There is no easy route from establishing a working understanding of spirituality to successful classroom practice. As a teacher you need to begin this journey by taking account of the legislation concerning spirituality, and of a range of approaches to spiritual education – traditionalist, progressive and critical (Wright 1998; Copley 2000).

When the 1944 Education Act referred to the spiritual dimension of education, it had in mind a specifically Christian spirituality. The context was that of a partnership between the state and the established Church of England that sought to utilize education as a means of bringing about the moral and spiritual rejuvenation of the nation in the aftermath of the horrors of the Second World War. The Act adopted a traditionalist model of education as cultural transmission that has its roots in the educational philosophy of John Locke ([1693] 2000). If the immediate task was to transmit knowledge through the traditional disciplines, the overriding aim was to cultivate those moral and spiritual virtues and habits of mind necessary for pupils to find their proper place in a civilized society. This fundamental task was to be achieved through compulsory religious education and daily acts of collective Christian worship. Pupils were to be nurtured into a Christian value system drawn from the Sermon on the Mount and the Ten Commandments. Spirituality was narrowly and exclusively Christian spirituality.

The 1960s saw a reaction against this traditionalist Christian pedagogy, driven by the recognition that – given the reality of an increasingly secular and pluralistic society – Christian values were being transmitted in an authoritarian manner which effectively silenced the voices of alternative spiritual traditions. The reaction against Christian traditionalism reconceptualized rather than rejected the task of spiritual education. In effect the source of spiritual values was relocated; no longer rooted in Christian revelation, they were instead to be found in the innate spiritual insight of children uncorrupted by society. Spiritual values were to be introspectively discovered rather than externally imposed. The task of the emergent progressive child-centred education that came to dominate the 1960s was to free children's spirituality from external constraint and enable them to discover their own inner spiritual selves. It was to Rousseau's romantic pedagogy rather than Locke's traditionalism that teachers turned for philosophical inspiration (Rousseau [1762] 1986).

The 1970s and 1980s saw a reaction against child-centred progressivism linked to sustained attempts to recover a traditional subject-centred education, a process exemplified in the introduction of the National Curriculum. The 1988 Education Reform Act (ERA) adopted a minimalist approach to spiritual education: schools must offer a balanced and broadly based curriculum in such a way that it 'promotes the spiritual, moral, cultural, mental and physical development of pupils at the school and of society' (DES 1988: 1). When the legislation was enacted, many observers assumed that this fleeting reference to spirituality would be treated as a mere rhetorical flourish that would have little direct impact on schools. The fact that, on the contrary, there has been a renaissance in spiritual education in schools since 1988 requires some explanation. Two key factors appear to have influenced this process. The first is the traditionalist concern of successive governments to utilize education as a tool for the moral rejuvenation of society (aided by the decision of Ofsted to report on the *provision* made by schools for the spiritual development of their pupils rather than the *outcomes* of this provision). The second factor was the response of teachers concerned with the rigid subject-centred nature of the National Curriculum who found in the reference to spirituality a Trojan horse that opened up the possibility of recovering a more flexible form of progressive child-centred pedagogy. As Tate observes, nobody 'wants their child to leave school clutching a handful of certificates, but no idea of how to be a human being' (Talbot and Tate 1997: 2).

The result has been a flourishing of spiritual education, coupled with a fundamental confusion concerning its nature, material content and pedagogical processes. There is an impasse between those traditionalists who wish to transmit clear spiritual values to children (either in the form of an inclusive liberal humanism or an exclusive Christianity pietism) and those progressives who see spiritual education as a means of undermining the incipient authoritarianism of the 1988 legislation (by freeing children to create their own spiritual identities against the backdrop of a child-centred education reconstituted within a postmodern framework). In recent years there has been an attempt to break the traditionalist–progressive deadlock through the development of a critical spiritual pedagogy based around five key principles.

1 *Spirituality is a controversial issue.* Since there is no public consensus regarding the ultimate meaning and purpose of life, teachers should acknowledge a range of competing and conflicting spiritual traditions. This strategy rejects a relativistic education that treats all spiritual perspectives as equally valid and invites pupils to create their own spiritual values on the basis of their untutored desires and inclinations. Such a move ignores the possibility that our ultimate concerns can be both morally unacceptable and intellectually inadequate.

2 *Spirituality enhances human freedom.* Critical spiritual pedagogy seeks to maximize the spiritual freedom of pupils by rejecting the paternalistic pedagogic strategies of both traditionalists and progressives. Traditionalists are paternalistic in imposing a single dominant spiritual tradition on pupils, while progressives are paternalistic in imposing on pupils the postmodern ideology that their immediate spiritual preferences are always valid. Authentic spiritual freedom, it is claimed, requires that pupils learn to engage critically with the ambiguous nature of spirituality.

3 *Spirituality is rooted in nurture.* Critical spiritual pedagogy accepts that spiritual nurture – understood as the induction of pupils into a specific value system – is an inevitable outcome of formal schooling. It rejects

the myth that schools can be spiritually neutral institutions: they will always work – if only implicitly – with a set of ultimate values that will help shape the spiritual lives of pupils. It follows that schools should openly embrace their role as transmitters of spiritual value and strive to bring spiritual integrity in all aspects of the life of the community.

4 *Spirituality must be appropriated critically.* The process of spiritual nurture must always be supplemented with a process of critical spiritual education. Nurture alone will produce only spiritually contented pigs while critical education will strive to form spiritually discontented philosophers. Pupils will need to be led towards a critical awareness of their own spiritual horizons, of the spiritual horizons of the school as an institution and of the spiritual horizons of a range of alternative spiritual traditions.

5 *Authentic spirituality demands spiritual literacy.* Critical spiritual pedagogy requires schools to equip pupils with appropriate levels of spiritual wisdom, thus enabling them to engage with spiritual questions in an informed, sensitive and intelligent manner. Pupils must be taught spiritual discernment, insight and understanding if they are to have the freedom to flourish as spiritual beings.

Spirituality in the whole school

It is time to ground the abstract discussion in the previous two sections in the concrete reality of schools and classrooms. Any discussion of the place of spirituality in the whole school needs to take account of the politics of education. The final two decades of the last century saw a polarization of authority and responsibility away from local educational authorities into both central government and individual schools. The current system gives central government the role of setting the broad educational agenda, and – via a complex system of surveillance and inspection – ensuring that individual schools successfully conform to this agenda. At the same time individual schools have significant levels of responsibility for their own development as they seek to organize and structure themselves to meet the demands of central government. This increase in local autonomy has led to a structural pluralism in which an increasingly diverse range of schools plough their own individual furrows. The minimalist nature of the legislation covering spirituality offers schools with a fair degree of autonomy in developing their provision for spiritual education.

Government advice on the implementation of spiritual education, presented in *Spiritual and Moral Development* (SCAA 1995), reinforces this picture of the autonomy of individual schools in their provision for spiritual development. The document offers no more than a generalized understanding of spirituality: spirituality is presented as being fundamental to the human condition, transcending ordinary everyday experience and concerned with the search for identity and meaning in response to death, suffering, beauty and evil; spirituality may be encountered in our beliefs, sense of awe, wonder and mystery, feelings of transcendence, search for meaning and purpose, self-knowledge, relationships, creativity and feelings and emotions; the promotion of spiritual development requires the nurturing of curiosity, imagination, insight and intuition (Wright 1998: 17). It is clear that this understanding leaves room for engagement with a broad range of specific spiritual traditions, both religious and humanistic, and does not preclude traditionalist, progressive or critical approaches. There is, though, a clear expectation that spiritual provision will be encountered in the school's ethos, its collective worship and in its explicit curriculum.

The spiritual ethos of the school will need to be a reality rather than an aspiration. The Department for Education and Employment (DfEE) expects schools to include a mission statement in their documentation that provides an opportunity for schools to make explicit their specific spiritual visions of the ultimate meaning and purpose of life in general and of education in particular. Mission statements vary from school to school, depending on each school's foundation. A state sponsored Muslim school, for example, is likely to have a very different spiritual vision than that of a multicultural school that grounds its values in the tradition of liberal humanism. The mission statement needs to be public property, articulated, owned and implemented by the whole school community. Gold and Evans claim that research demonstrates 'that a school where the purpose of education is clearly articulated and communicated is a far more effective school than one in which there is no obviously agreed purpose' (1998: 14).

The quality and integrity of a school's provision for spiritual education is likely to be reflected in its response to the vexed question of collective worship. A healthy mark of any community is its ability to celebrate its spiritual achievements and aspirations. All too often, collective worship reflects spiritual sickness rather than health. An apologetic attempt to appease Ofsted inspectors through a hesitant act of worship with which few can identify introduces a spiritual vacuum into the very heart of the school community. A school's core spiritual values need to be celebrated with dignity and integrity. This may take the form of either a religious act of worship or a secular assembly, since the legislation regarding collective worship is extremely flexible and makes available a range of religious and secular options.

The contribution of individual teachers to the spiritual life of the school will be reflected in their engagement with the institution's ultimate values. This need not – indeed frequently ought not – to be a process of blind acquiescence. A healthy spiritual community will be open to self-criticism if its spiritual values are either inappropriately formulated or implemented. More specifically, individual teachers will need to reflect on the place of spirituality in the classroom in their roles as form tutors and subject teachers.

Effective promotion of spiritual development in individual subject areas needs to respond to the ultimate questions about the meaning and purpose of life that are integral to each academic discipline. This applies to a geography teacher teaching about the weather system, to an English teacher addressing Keats' suggestion that 'Beauty is truth and truth beauty', and to a PE teacher inviting students to reflect on the importance of physical fitness. In each subject area there is opportunity to allow students to step back and see the larger picture of life, rather than simply knuckle down and improve their grades. Classroom teachers will need to ensure that the broader spiritual picture informs their lesson planning so that their classroom teaching effectively stimulates the critical, imaginative and creative dimension of their pupils' spiritual lives.

Science education – a case study

Ofsted (1993b: 17) emphasized that 'The promotion of pupils' spiritual, moral, social and cultural development is a "whole school" issue . . . other subjects [than religious education] can play no less significant a part in inviting pupils to reflect on the purpose and meaning of life'. There is not the space here to consider the spiritual dimension of every subject so our discussion is limited to a single case study, science. Some science teachers have found difficulty in 'promoting' the spiritual dimension of their subject and some have resented the requirement as an intrusion into 'teaching the facts'. However, far from adulterating science with metaphysics, the requirement is better seen as having a corrective role in showing science with a human face. It serves to redress some of the scientific imperialism of the early part of the twentieth century, which still lingers on as one strand of popular culture. As the foregoing discussion has indicated, the category 'spiritual' has many facets, several of which can help teachers show pupils the scientific enterprise in ways that neither exaggerate nor undermine its capabilities. They can be placed in four groups:

Awe, wonder and mystery
Young pupils find aspects of the natural world quite breathtaking, but increasing age is often accompanied by a blasé attitude. There is some justification for this change of attitude since something remarkable may seem like magic to a young child who has not yet understood the physical structures and processes involved. There is no good reason, however, why the sensations of awe, wonder and mystery generated by gazing into the night sky or studying how our bodies work should be diminished through increased learning, as though 'explaining' scientifically somehow 'explains away' non-scientific perspectives. Such sensations are most likely to be fostered and preserved if science teachers themselves experience and refer to them and are constantly aware of how little anyone knows of what there is to be known.

Curiosity, creativity and imagination
The role of curiosity in initiating scientific investigation needs no comment, but an understanding of the roles of creativity and imagination in scientific discovery has, over recent decades, grown considerably. The place of metaphor and conceptual models in promoting understanding of theoretical structures is now widely acknowledged in science as elsewhere.

Teachers might help pupils to see how this has worked by introducing them to such examples as the water circuit model of electricity flowing in a wire or the solar-system model of the hydrogen atom.

Meaning, purpose and identity

The question 'Why do I exist?' can have several meanings. It can be answered by reference to parental desires; it can be answered by a mechanistic description of the biology of human reproduction; it can be answered with reference to the purpose of a transcendent agent, God. The first two answers come from the behavioural and life sciences. The third answer lies outside the remit of science. Pupils sometimes ask for scientific proof that God exists. They have not spotted that it is no use going to science, the study of nature, for answers to religious questions about whether anything other than the natural world exists and to which the world owes its existence. It is beyond the competence of science to answer such questions and *Science in the National Curriculum* indicates that 'Pupils should be taught . . . to consider . . . the kinds of questions science can and cannot answer' (DfEE/QCA 1999: 37, 46). Nevertheless science studies may prompt such questions. 'Why is there something rather than nothing?' is a question of great antiquity which the noted scientist Stephen Hawking (1988: 174) has recently rephrased as, 'Why does the universe go to all the bother of existing?' A debate in class over this question could constitute an awareness of that which is of ultimate value.

More recently has come an awareness of the apparent 'fine-tuning' of the universe for life. If the physical constants of nature were even minutely different – some estimates give a minuscule difference of one part in one followed by 60 noughts as significant – we should not be here. Does this mean the universe is planned and purposeful? The mystery does not disappear by pointing out that this fine balance may result from an inflationary model of the universe. That simply pushes the question back a stage further to 'Why did the early universe have the properties which gave rise to an inflationary period, which in turn gave rise to the "fine tuning"?' It is important to remember when teaching science that there is more than one type of explanation. A scientific explanation of the existence of the universe in terms of a hot Big Bang is compatible with a religious explanation in terms of a purposeful creator. Failure to recognize a plurality of explanations is perhaps the most serious and probably the most common philosophical error encountered in science teaching. However such recognition provides an opportunity for a discussion on the variety of worldviews held by members of the class. Such acknowledgement of this diversity would again be addressing questions about ultimate value.

The first half of the twentieth century saw an elevation of the status of science to a level that could not be justified. Since science had been so successful in its rightful area of mapping the natural world, it was elevated by some philosophers to the position of the ultimate test of meaning, in a movement called logical positivism. Supposedly based on science, all statements had to be verified empirically if they were to be counted as meaningful and therefore possible candidates for truth. The system crumbled, however, because science itself contained assumptions, like the uniformity of nature, that could not be verified scientifically. Science as a subject does not have all the answers but because of the emphasis placed on 'proof', by definition this statement can negate notions of transcendence.

Feelings of transcendence

The term 'spiritual' has come into fashion in education over recent years, used in a way that encompasses those who do not hold specific religious beliefs as well as those that do. Although, as Ofsted (1993b: 21) has pointed out, 'Spiritual is not synonymous with religious, religious beliefs do form a major component of the broader concept of spirituality'. Religious beliefs have played a role in the development of modern science from the seventeenth century onwards, and studies of the interplay between these two disciplines have become big industry world-wide in academia over the last few decades. True, some sections of the media persist in an outdated confrontational approach and give to a few voices a disproportionate amount of air time to back up the notion of conflict. But academic historians of science have found the 'warfare model' inadequate to describe a set of relationships that is much more positive and interesting. Even the folklore accounts of the Galileo affair and the Darwinian controversies have been weighed in the balance and found wanting. Geoffrey Cantor, Professor of History of Science at Leeds has summed up a contemporary view of these episodes:

> Galileo can no longer be portrayed as the harbinger of truth and enlightenment who was pitted against reactionary priests . . . his censure resulted partly from his mishandling of a sensitive diplomatic situation. The other paradigmatic conflict concerns the Darwinian theory of evolution and centres on the Huxley–Wilberforce confrontation in 1860. These opponents are now viewed as trading minor insults in the heat of debate and not as exemplifying the necessary conflict between science and religion.
>
> (Cantor 1991: 290)

Teaching science in the National Curriculum provides many natural opportunities for introducing topics such as these from the history of science when the work of Galileo and Darwin are taught. In parallel with such historical episodes, it is valuable to include certain philosophical points about science, such as the nature of explanation, reductionism, scientific laws, language and models as well as the presuppositions of science. It has been largely due to misunderstandings about points like these that the idea of a mismatch between science and spirituality has arisen. A detailed discussion of such points and some practical classroom suggestions can be found in Poole (1995, 1998) and Charis Science (2000).

Conclusion

For many teachers, the current climate of education, with its stress on academic attainment at the expense of a commitment to the development of the whole child, is a cause of deep concern. There is a real danger of the soul of education being smothered by bureaucracy and a range of political agendas. Despite such concerns, the fact remains that teachers have a fundamental responsibility to develop the spiritual lives of their pupils by enabling them to engage in an informed, sensitive and intelligent manner with questions of the ultimate meaning and purpose of life.

References

Cantor, G. (1991) *Michael Faraday, Sandemanian and Scientist.* Basingstoke: Macmillan.

Charis Science (2000) *Resources for Spiritual and Moral Development across the Curriculum.* Nottingham: The Stapleford Centre.

Copley, T. (2000) *Spiritual Development in the State School. A Perspective on Worship and Spirituality in the Education System of England and Wales.* Exeter: University of Exeter Press.

Department for Education (DfE) (1994) Circular 1/94, *Religious Education and Collective Worship.* London: HMSO.

Department for Education and Employment (DfEE) (1998) Circular 4/98, *Requirements for Courses of Initial Teacher Training.* London: HMSO.

Department for Education and Employment/Qualifications and Curriculum Authority (DfEE/QCA) (1999) *Science in the National Curriculum.* London: HMSO.

Department for Education and Science (DES) (1988) *Education Reform Act.* London: HMSO.

Gold, A. and Evans, J. (1998) *Reflecting on School Management.* London: Falmer.

Gutting, G. (1994) *The Cambridge Companion to Foucault.* Cambridge: Cambridge University Press.

Hamilton, E. and Cairns, H. (eds) (1961) *Plato: The Collective Dialogues.* Princeton, NJ: Princeton University Press.

Hawking, S.W. (1988) *A Brief History of Time.* London: Bantam Press.

Locke, J. ([1693] 2000) *Some Thoughts Concerning Education.* Oxford: Clarendon Press.

Office for Standards in Education (Ofsted) (1993a) *Handbook for the Inspection of Schools: Part 2, Framework for the Inspection of Schools.* London: HMSO.

Office for Standards in Education (Ofsted) (1993b) *Handbook for the Inspection of Schools: Part 4, Guidance on the Inspection Schedule.* London: HMSO.

Poole, M.W. (1995) *Beliefs and Values in Science Education.* Buckingham: Open University Press.

Poole, M.W. (1998) *Teaching about Science and Religion: Opportunities within Science in the National Curriculum.* Abingdon: Culham College Institute.

Rousseau, J.-J. ([1792] 1986) *Emile.* London: Dent.

School Curriculum and Assessment Authority (SCAA) (1995) *Spiritual and Moral Development. SCAA Discussion Papers No. 3.* London: SCAA.

Talbot, M. and Tate, N. (1997) Shared values in a pluralist society, in R. Smith and P. Standish (eds) *Teaching Right and Wrong: Moral Education in the Balance.* Stoke-on-Trent: Trentham Books.

Wright, A. (1998) *Spiritual Pedagogy: A Survey, Critique and Reconstruction of Contemporary Spiritual Education in England and Wales.* Abingdon: Culham College Institute.

Wright, A. (2000) *Spirituality and Education.* London: Falmer.

Faith Hill and Margaret Sills

Introduction

Health education is generally thought to be a 'good thing'. In 1990, the National Curriculum Council (NCC) described it as 'an essential part of every pupil's curriculum' (QCA 1990: Foreword) and the revised National Curriculum for 2000 provides a framework for Personal, Social and Health Education (PSHE) as well as a statutory order for citizenship. The Department of Health (DoH) expects schools to play a major role in working towards the health promotion aims outlined in *Saving Lives: Our Healthier Nation* (DoH 1999). From 1999, the DoH worked in partnership with the Department for Education and Employment (DfEE) in promoting local healthy schools programmes and developing the National Healthy School Standard (NHSS).

From the very beginning of your career as a teacher, whatever your subject, you will probably be expected to teach health education or personal, social and health education (PSHE) through the informal curriculum and through your role as a tutor and to contribute to building a healthy school. You will also have responsibility for health related topics within your curriculum area. This chapter will help you to consider your role in teaching for health. It provides an opportunity to reflect on some of the more controversial issues involved and offers some general background and guidance to teaching health related subjects. First, it is necessary to clarify what we mean by 'health'.

Health is . . .

Health is a general term with many different meanings. If you ask a group of teachers, pupils, parents or governors what 'health' means to them, you will get a wide range of responses. For some, 'health' refers to the absence of disease and for others it is concerned with more positive attributes, such as personal fitness or total well-being. The most often quoted definition is from the Constitution of the World Health Organization (WHO 1946): 'Health is a state of complete physical, mental and social well-being, and not merely the absence of disease or infirmity'. The WHO Executive Board considered refining this to 'Health is a dynamic state of complete physical, mental, spiritual and social well-being, and not merely the absence of disease or infirmity' (1998). Either way (and you might like to reflect on the differences), the WHO definition is an important one for teachers because it places the emphasis on the quality rather than on the length of life. Young people are rarely interested in living to be 'old'! It is also an important definition because it highlights the multidimensional nature of health. Health educators and health promoters think of health not as a single commodity but as a rich and interrelated tapestry, involving mental, physical, spiritual and emotional aspects, and concerning groups, communities and the environment as well as individuals. What does 'health' mean to you?

Models of health education

Having looked at what we mean by health, we can move onto considering what constitutes health education. There are a number of different models or approaches to health education. The first is often described as a *bio-medical model* and is based very largely on medical approaches to health and illness. It is concerned with instructing individuals on how to live their lives in such a way as to avoid becoming ill. It is often criticized for being too authoritarian and top-down in its approach, and for ignoring all the complex issues involved in making real life choices about health issues. In schools, this model has been linked with 'Just Say No' campaigns and with the 'shock horror' approach, which seeks to prevent pupils behaving in certain ways by presenting gruesome and sometimes one-sided information. This approach is counter-productive in the long term.

The second model of health education is generally known as the *educational model*. Traditionally, it suggests that schools should provide young people with the facts about health and leave the decisions to them. This approach has its attractions: it fits with a philosophy of personal freedom and rational decision-making, teachers can ignore controversial moral and ethical issues, and it is easily accommodated within traditional teaching and assessment methods.

However, this educational approach has a number of problems. First, health is such a complex matter that the issues cannot be presented as straightforward 'facts'. Many important areas of health are highly controversial and young people need opportunities to consider a range of values and opinions as well as support in identifying and clarifying their own positions. They also need more than factual information to enable them to make and carry out healthy decisions. They need a range of skills, including decision-making and interpersonal skills, as well as those concerned with self-awareness, managing emotions and handling stress. For young people to adopt healthy lifestyles they also need a positive sense of self-esteem. Approaches to health education that address these concerns, emphasizing the importance and interdependence of work on knowledge, skills, and attitudes are within what is known as the *empowerment model*. This model is often reflected in practice and underpins many of the projects that were designed for schools by the Health Education Authority (HEA) in the 1990s.

The final model of health education is the *radical model*, which recognizes that poverty, poor housing and unemployment are major causes of ill-health. It is concerned with the many factors that affect health which are beyond the control of the individual. This includes the physical environment at both local and global levels. The radical model also addresses the effects on health of advertising, business interests and legislation. This model of health education stresses the importance of collective action to promote health. It is the most political of the models and, so far, plays only a small role in health education in schools.

As a teacher, each time you are asked to teach a health related topic you will have to choose between these different models. Which approach do you think you would be most comfortable with, and which would be most useful for your students? How could you combine different approaches?

Health promoting schools and the National Healthy School Standard

The European Network of Health Promoting Schools (ENHPS) was supported by the HEA with the aim of developing schools as centres promoting the health and well-being of pupils, staff, parents and the local community. The approach takes a holistic view of the nature of health, including mental, spiritual and physical well-being. It also recognizes the importance of the school environment, physical and social, in contributing to the health and well-being of pupils and staff.

The initiative built on the whole-school approach to health education and health promotion which recognizes that the messages young people receive about health are not confined to the formal health education curriculum. Much health education occurs in informal ways, for example, through extracurricular activities and chance discussions in the playground. It also occurs through the hidden curriculum. For example, the quality and nature of interpersonal relationships within a school will not only give young people messages about how to relate to others but will also influence their sense of personal worth and self-esteem. Unfortunately, many of the messages that young people are taught through the formal curriculum can be rapidly diluted by the ethos of the whole school. You may find young people being taught about personal hygiene in schools with very inadequate toilet facilities and nutrition education may not be reflected by the food choices provided in school canteens.

Samdal *et al.* (1998) found that students want to be treated fairly, to feel safe and to believe that teachers are supportive. Their findings endorse the notion that health promotion activities should also look beyond the classroom to the quality of students' school experience and the quality of the relationships with their teachers. Self-esteem, self-perception and a range of health behaviours affect present and future health and well-being; the development of these is underpinned by students' perceptions of, and experiences in, school (Coleman 1979; Schultz *et al.* 1987; Resnick *et al.* 1993; Hurrelmann *et al.* 1995; Samdal *et al.* 1998; Moon *et al.* 1999a, 1999b).

To be truly effective, the whole-school approach and the health promoting school initiative required radical changes in the way most schools in the United Kingdom were run and financed. However, some schools began moving in this direction and were further supported by the White Paper on *Excellence in Schools* (1997) which set out the government's intention to help all schools become healthy schools and the Independent Inquiry into Inequalities in Health (Acheson 1998) which recognized the crucial role of a sound education in promoting better health for all children and young people.

The National Healthy School Standard (NHSS) was launched in October 1999 as part of the Healthy Schools Programme led by the DfEE and the DoH and based at the Health Development Agency which, together with Health Promotion England, replaced the HEA in April 2000. The overall aim is to help schools become healthier schools, that is, successful in helping pupils to do their best and build on their achievements, through supporting the development and improvement of local programmes. The national accreditation process aims to ensure:

- programmes are based in sustainable education and health partnerships;
- the participation of schools and young people;
- quality management of local healthy school programmes;
- programmes are responsive to school and local needs, as well as national priorities;
- evidence is gathered to demonstrate effectiveness.

(DfEE 1999: 3)

All local education authorities (LEAs) are expected to be involved in an accredited education and health partnership by 2002 and all schools to be involved in healthy school activities through nationally accredited programmes by 2004.

The standards are organized in three sections: partnerships, programme management and working with schools. Equalities issues underpin all the standards, in particular the eight specific themes that are addressed, such as sex and relationships education, physical activity, PSHE and citizenship.

In practice, you will come across many schools that cannot yet be described as 'healthy' or 'health promoting'. As a new teacher, you will need to consider the type of school in which you wish to work and how far you personally want to adopt a health promoting role.

Curriculum issues

In 1990 the NCC defined health education as a cross-curricular theme and, although not a statutory subject in its own right, it was seen as playing an important part in contributing to the statutory duty on schools to:

provide a broad and balanced curriculum which:

(a) promotes the spiritual, moral, cultural, mental and physical development of pupils at the school and of society;

(b) prepares pupils for the opportunities, responsibilities and experiences of adult life.

(NCC 1990: Foreword)

Government guidelines were offered to schools in a key document entitled *Curriculum Guidance 5: Health Education* (NCC 1990). This booklet gave general guidance on health education in the curriculum and also spelt out nine key areas of study to be included at each of the four key stages:

- substance use and misuse;
- sex education;
- family life education;
- safety;
- health-related exercise;
- food and nutrition;
- personal hygiene;
- environmental aspects of health education;
- psychological aspects of health education;

(NCC 1990: 17)

For each area, more details were given for each of the key stages. For example, at Key Stage 3, in the area of the psychological aspects of health education, pupils should:

- know how labelling and stereotyping can have a negative effect on mental health;
- be able to receive praise and encouragement in order to promote the self-esteem and self-confidence essential to mental health;
- understand the emotional changes which take place during puberty; understand differences in maturation and have a positive self-image.

(NCC 1990: 17)

From this one example it can be seen that the 'empowerment' model is supported and that skills and attitudes are developed alongside the acquisition of knowledge.

The reason for revisiting each area at every key stage is to build upon and develop the work that pupils have already covered. It is very important to start with the needs and maturity of young people and to ensure that curriculum planning takes into account their developmental stage and previous learning. For example, sex education is included at each key stage because there are different aspects that need to be introduced as the young people grow towards adulthood. This process of programme planning to enable increasing complexity is referred to as a 'spiral curriculum' and is crucial to effective health education and PSHE.

Planning a spiral curriculum for health education as a cross-curricular theme is a daunting prospect and many schools faced with an already overloaded curriculum fell short of the ideals described in *Curriculum Guidance 5* (NCC 1990). As a subject teacher you need to be aware of the areas that come within your discipline and how these are linked developmentally. You also need to be familiar with the relevant work that is going on in other subjects and in other areas of the curriculum such as PSE (personal and social education), PSHE or other tutorial programmes. As a tutor you need to be aware of subject specific health education within the school and be able to identify the links with the pastoral curriculum (for more advice on this aspect of being a form tutor, see Chapter 26).

The revised National Curriculum for England, which came into force in September 2000, reinforced the links between the subject curriculum and the pastoral curriculum (QCA 1999). The two broad aims for the curriculum are reflected in Section 351 of the Education Act 1996, which requires that all maintained schools provide a balanced and broadly based curriculum that:

- promotes the spiritual, moral, cultural, mental and physical development of the pupils and society;
- prepares pupils at the school for the opportunities, responsibilities and experiences of adult life.

(QCA 1999)

This emphasizes the importance of PSHE and citizenship in helping:

to give pupils the knowledge, skills and understanding they need to lead confident, healthy independent lives and to become informed, active responsible citizens ... They learn to understand and respect our common humanity, diversity and differences so that they can go on to form the effective, fulfilling relationships that are an essential part of life and learning.

(QCA 1999)

The revised National Curriculum provides a non-statutory framework for teaching PSHE at Key Stages 3 and 4 from September 2000 and a statutory order for Citizenship which will be created as a new subject for all 11–16-year-olds from September 2002 (see Chapter 21). For Key Stages 1 and 2, there is a combined PSHE and citizenship framework. However, the following broad themes are common to the four key stages:

- developing confidence and responsibility and making the most of pupils' abilities;
- preparing to play an active role as citizens;
- developing a healthier, safer lifestyle;
- developing good relationships and respecting differences between people.

The PSHE framework includes aspects such as:

Pupils should be:
- taught to recognize how others see them, and be able to give and receive constructive feedback and praise;
- taught that good relationships and an appropriate balance between work, leisure and exercise can promote physical and mental health;
- given opportunities to feel positive about themselves.

Sex and relationship education

Although there is not space here to examine the curriculum in detail, it is important to say something about sex and relationship education because of its unique position in the curriculum. Sex education differs from other areas in its statutory position within the school curriculum. This position has been set out in legislation by the 1993 Education Act and is explained in the DfEE document *Sex and Relationship Education Guidance* (2000) that takes into account the revised National Curriculum published in September 1999 (QCA 1999) and the need for guidance arising out of the PSHE framework and the *Social Exclusion Unit Report on Teenage Pregnancy* (SEU 1999). This is the first time that schools have had a national framework to support work in this area.

Primary schools must have an up-to-date written policy on sex education and make it available to parents and pupils. Secondary schools must provide sex education including teaching about AIDS, HIV and other sexually-transmitted infections. This is to be done in a way that will encourage pupils to have due regard to moral considerations and the value of family life. The detailed content and nature of sex education is for schools to decide. Any parent can choose to withdraw their children from all or part of sex education where it is provided except for those parts included in the statutory Science National Curriculum (QCA 1999).

Many teachers are reluctant to teach about sex and sexuality. However, in many ways, teaching sex and relationship education is no different from teaching in any other sensitive area of the curriculum (see classroom strategies below).

The guidance document (DfEE 2000) states that sex and relationship education should be firmly rooted in the framework for PSHE rather than taught in isolation and should be equally relevant to both boys and girls.

> The objective is to 'help and support young people through their physical, emotional and moral development. A successful programme ... will help young people learn to respect themselves and others and move with confidence from childhood through adolescence into adulthood'.
>
> (DfEE 2000: 3)

Sex and relationship education has three main elements: attitudes and values; personal and social skills, and knowledge and understanding. It is defined as involving:

> lifelong learning about physical, moral and emotional development. It is about the understanding of the importance of marriage for family life, stable and loving relationships, respect, love and care. It is also about the teaching of sex, sexuality, and sexual health. It is not about the promotion of sexual orientation or sexual activity – this would be inappropriate teaching.
>
> (DfEE 2000: 5)

The issue of marriage has raised some controversial debate and needs to be dealt with sensitively. How do your values and beliefs relate to the question 'should we be promoting marriage above other ways of living?'.

How might this relate to the values, beliefs and experiences of your pupils within the context of their families and communities?

The guidance aims to:

- clarify what schools are required to do by law;
- give guidance on some of the issues involved in developing policy on sex and relationships education;
- show how it should be taught within the PSHE framework;
- guide schools and teachers on some of the sensitive issues schools may have to tackle when teaching sex and relationship education (as opposed to relationships education);
- outline some practical strategies for teaching;
- emphasise the importance of working in partnership with parents and the wider community;
- address some of the issues for schools concerning confidentiality.

(DfEE 2000: 6)

The role of the school's governing body and headteachers in the determination of the school's policy and programmes in consultation and partnership with the parents is crucial.

As noted previously, parents still have the right to withdraw their children from all or part of the sex and relationship education programme provided at school except for those parts included in the statutory Science National Curriculum (see Section 3 of the DfEE Guidance). Very few parents exercise this option but it does mean that schools must organize the curriculum in such a way as to allow for the possibility. Teachers need to be aware of the restrictions imposed by the Act and the detailed guidance and to ensure that they stay within the school policy. You should ask to see the policy document and any other guidelines used in your school. School policies should be set within the school's ethos and context. They should be written in a way that is clearly specific, achievable and set measurable time-related targets so that success or areas for development are identified easily. The policy document (usually no more than one page) should be accompanied by an implementation guide. You should ask for clarification on any points that are unclear. One point that new teachers often ask about relates to Section 28 of the Local Government Act 1988 which prohibits local authorities from promoting homosexuality. DfE Circular 5/94 made it clear that this does not apply to teachers or governing bodies acting on their own behalf (DfE 1994: 19; and DfEE 2000). This is usually taken to mean that, in practice, it does not apply to individual teachers and governors in schools.

Classroom strategies

the teaching methods used are as important as the content of the lessons . . . the participation of pupils is essential . . . Much of the teaching in health education will be based on the active involvement of pupils.

You may or may not agree with this quotation, but it is important to consider interactive teaching methods when planning health education.

It may surprise you that the quotation is not rhetoric from a 'trendy' educationalist, but from *Curriculum Guidance 5* (NCC 1990: 7). The importance of teaching methods is stressed over and over again in health education texts. This is partly because of the interdependence of knowledge, skills and attitudes discussed earlier, but it is also because of the sensitive nature of much health education. So, when planning health education strategies where should you start?

As with any other area of the curriculum, you should begin by clarifying your aims, objectives and learning outcomes. Then the most important issue to consider is sensitivity. Whatever health education topic you are covering, there will be aspects that may be particularly sensitive to one or more of your pupils. This may be obvious with topics such as sexuality, where pupils may have been abused or be facing difficult personal decisions. It is also true of less controversial topics. Nutrition, for example, can bring up concerns about body image, anorexia, mealtimes without family members because of bereavement or divorce, religious beliefs and a host of other potentially sensitive issues. However good a teacher you are, you can never hope to know all the personal concerns of all your pupils, so you should handle all health education topics with care. That means taking time to consider possible reactions to the work; being alert to signs of embarrassment or distress; being clear about your role and the extent to which you can offer support in and beyond the classroom; and knowing where to refer pupils for help when necessary.

In order to prepare your class for handling sensitive issues and to enable them to participate in group activities, it is important to establish a safe learning environment. This means actively building a climate of trust and empathy, where each individual feels involved and valued by the group. Most of the materials mentioned at the end of the chapter offer activities for establishing a positive classroom climate. These include icebreakers, relationship and group building tasks and problem-solving activities. Of all these activities, the most crucial to health education is the development of ground rules. You should encourage every class to negotiate and agree ground rules (that is to say, a set of statements about how the group proposes to work and learn together), and these should be monitored and reviewed regularly.

Having established a good working environment, you will be able to try out a wide range of teaching methods suitable to health education. These include formal information giving, audiovisual and other presentations, visits and the involvement of visitors. They also include interactive group methods, such as small-group discussions, games, simulations and role-plays. Schools are also experimenting with peer-group learning techniques and interactive drama presentations for some areas of health education. All of these methods can be useful and, by varying your approach, you can help to stimulate the pupils' interest, accommodate a variety of learning styles, and ensure they have some fun! It is then important to review and reflect on the activities in order to draw out and reinforce the learning that has occurred. Focus not only on the *what* but also on the *how* and *why* in relation to the learning associated with attitudes, skills and knowledge.

Support for health education

One really good piece of news for anyone starting to teach health educa-tion is that there is a wide range of support available. This partly comes in the form of teaching packs and other classroom materials that can save you a great deal of time in preparing lessons. Many of them were funded by the Health Education Authority (which no longer exists) and have been very carefully piloted in schools before publication. A list of selected resources is available from Health Promotion England (2000).

A word of warning, however – there is a vast amount of material on the market and not all of it is useful or appropriate for use in schools. This is particularly true of many videos that have been made for health education. You should always check the source of the materials and whether they are presenting a biased, stereotyped, discriminatory or inaccurate view. You should also consider whether materials would be appropriate for your groups in terms of age, sex, ethnicity, culture, school guidelines and so on. Always preview videos and familiarize yourself fully with other materials.

Support is also available in the form of individuals and agencies who will visit schools to help with health education programmes. This can range from the local general practitioner addressing an assembly through to drama groups running sessions on HIV and AIDS. Visitors can make a very positive contribution but are always far more effective when the pupils are actively involved in the visit. It is also important to be clear why you are involving outsiders, how they are contributing to the over-all programme and whether they have the skills to interact well with young people. Visitors have been traditionally involved in sex education and all school sex education policies should state the school's position on this.

The most valuable source of support that you are likely to come across will either be the local Healthy Schools Programme or your local Health Education or Health Promotion Unit, depending on your area. Both will have at least one person responsible for health education and promotion with young people who will be able to advise you on curriculum plan-ning, available materials and local concerns. They are unlikely to offer direct work with pupils but can often offer a variety of training for staff, parents and governors. They will also have materials available on loan and may well be able to organize free delivery of up-to-date resources to your school.

Conclusion

Health education and health promotion are important to the develop-ment of all pupils, and inevitably involve all teachers and most whole-school issues. Developing a healthy school and teaching particular health topics can be very challenging and demands carefully planning and sens-itive handling. Teachers have to choose from a number of different approaches and have to satisfy the demands of national legislation and school guidelines. However, there is a lot of support available and working in such a significant area of the curriculum can be very rewarding. Healthy schools can and do make a real difference to the lives of young people and the communities in which they live.

References

Acheson, D. (1998) *Independent Inquiry into Inequalities in Health*. London: Department of Health.

Coleman, S. and Syme, S.L. (1979) *Current Issues in the Socialization of Young People*. London: Methuen.

Department for Education (DfE) (1994) *Education Act 1993: Sex Education in Schools*, Circular 5/94. London: DfE.

Department for Education and Employment (DfEE) (1997) *Excellence in Schools*, White Paper. London: DfEE.

Department for Education and Employment (DfEE) (1999) *National Healthy School Standard Guidance*. London: HMSO.

Department for Education and Employment (DfEE) (2000) *Sex and Relationship Education Guidance*. London: HMSO.

Department of Health (DoH) (1999) *Saving Lives: Our Healthier Nation*. London: Department of Health/HMSO.

Health Promotion England (2000) *Resource List*. London: HPE (40 Eastbourne Terrace, London W2 3QR).

Hurrelmann, K., Leppin, A. and Nordlohne, E. (1995) Promoting health in schools: the German example, *Health Promotion International*, 10: 121–31.

Moon, A.M., Mullee, M.A., Thompson, R.L., Speller, V. and Roderick, P. (1999a) Health-related research and evaluation in schools, *Health Education*, (1): 27–34.

Moon, A.M., Mullee, M.A., Thompson, R.L. *et al.* (1999b) Helping schools to become health-promoting environments – an evaluation of the Wessex Healthy Schools Award, *Health Promotion International*, 14(2): 111–22.

National Curriculum Council (NCC) (1990) *Curriculum Guidance 5. Health Education*. York: NCC.

Qualifications and Curriculum Authority (QCA) (1999) *The National Curriculum for England*. London: DfEE.

Resnick, M.D., Harris, L.J. and Blum, R.W. (1993) The impact of caring and connectedness on adolescent health and well-being, *Journal of Paediatric and Child Health*, 29: 3–9.

Samdal, O., Nutbeam, D., Wold, B. and Kannas, L. (1998) Achieving health and educational goals through schools – a study of the importance of the school climate and the students' satisfaction with school, *Health Education Research*, 13(3): 383–97.

Schultz, E.W., Glass, R.M. and Kamholtz, J.D. (1987) School climate: psychological health and well-being in school, *Journal of School Health*, 57: 432–6.

Social Exclusion Unit (SEU) (1999) *Teenage Pregnancy*. London: SEU.

World Health Organization (WHO) (1946) *Constitution*. New York: World Health Organization.

World Health Organization (WHO) (1998) *Minutes of the 121st Executive Board Meeting*. Geneva: WHO.

Further reading

Anderson, J. (1994a) *Introducing Health Skills for Life. Health Education and PSE Materials for Key Stage 3*. London: Nelson.

Anderson, J. (1994b) *Health Education and PSE Materials for Key Stage 4*. London: Nelson.

Clarity Collective (1989) *Taught not Caught. Strategies for Sex Education*. Wisbech: Learning Development Aids.

Department for Education (DfE) (1995) *Drug Prevention and Schools*, Circular 4/95. London: Department for Education.

Emmett, V. (1994) The future of health education, *Health Education*, 3: 13–17.

Gray, G. and Hill, F. (1990–92) *What is Health*? (series of seven booklets on health topics). Oxford: Oxford University Press.

Gray, G. and Hill, F. (1994) *Health Education for 16–19s. Health Action Pack*. London: Health Education Authority.

Health Education Authority (HEA) (1991) *Health and Self*. London: Health Education Authority.

Heaven, P.C.L. (1996) *Adolescent Health. The Role of Individual Difference*. London: Routledge.

Henry, L., Shucksmith, J. and Philip, K. (1995) *Educating for Health. School and Community Approaches with Adolescents*. London: Cassell.

Lions and TACADE (1995) *Skills for Life – A Whole School Approach to Personal and Social Development for 11–16-Year-Olds*. Manchester: TACADE.

Ray, C. and Went, D. (eds) (1996) *Good Practice in Sex Education: A Source Book for Schools*. London: National Children's Bureau.

Standing Conference on Drug Abuse (SCODA) (1999) *The Right Approach: Quality Standards in Drug Education*. London: SCODA.

Stears, D. and Clift, S. (1995) Health, sex and drug education: rhetoric and realities, in J. Ahier and A. Ross (eds) *The Social Subjects Within the Curriculum*. London: Falmer Press.

Websites

http://www.cabinet-office.gov.uk/seu/1999/teenpreg.pdf – Social Exclusion Unit Teenage Pregnancy report.

http://www.DFEE.gov.uk – Department of Education and Employment. Curriculum Standards Guidance documents; Sex and Relationship Education Guidance; Non-statutory framework for PSHE and Statutory Order for Citizenship.

http://www.DFEE.gov.uk.circulars/DFEEpub – Drug Education: Getting the Message Across: summarizes 18 innovative projects.

http://www.drugscape.org.uk – Drugscape: A merger of the UKs two foremost drug information and policy organisations – the Institute for the Study of Drug Dependence (ISDD) and the Standing Conference on Drug Abuse (SCODA).

http://www.hda-online.org.uk – The Health Development Agency: finding ways to improve the public's health.

http://www.hpe.org.uk Health Promotion England. Resources and support – drugs and alcohol misuse, immunization, sexual health, children and families, and older people.

http://www.nc.uk.net – National Curriculum PSHE and Citizenship 2000.

http://www.ncb.org.uk – National Children's Bureau – Good Practice in Sex Education and other publicatiions.

http://qca.org.uk – Qualifications and Curriculum Authority.

http://www.who.int – The World Health Organization.

http://www.tacade.org – TACADE. Materials and resources for schools.

http://www.wiredforhealth.gov.uk – Government Policies and Guidance; Healthy Schools Programme; National Healthy School Standard.

Information and communications technology: policy and practice

Deryn Watson

Introduction

Never in education has there been so much interest, investment and sheer hype associated with any subject as that attached to information technology. From the late 1970s there has been substantial central and local government investment, supplemented by funds from parent/teacher associations (PTAs) and other sources, to put computers into every school. Following a series of initiatives, targeted on hardware acquisition, software development and in-service teacher training, information technology was identified as a component of the National Curriculum in 1989, a new subject area in its own right, with skills and competencies to be delivered and assessed (DES 1990). At the turn of the millennium, a further major initiative networking all schools for Internet access through the National Grid for Learning (NGfL) (DfEE 1997), combined with a new initial and in-service teacher training curriculum (TTA 1998), has maintained the rhetoric that IT is equated with the modern world, economic success and the future. So schools must embrace the technology; as the Prime Minister Blair stated when launching the NGfL:

> Technology has revolutionized the way we work and is now set to transform education. Children cannot be effective in tomorrow's world if they are trained in yesterday's skills. Nor should teachers be denied tools that other professionals are trained to take for granted. Standards, literacy, numeracy, subject knowledge – all will be enhanced by the Grid and the support it will give our programme for schools improvement.
>
> (DfEE 1997: 1)

To achieve this, schools have been exhorted to develop a whole-school policy for the use of IT. One perspective on the development of IT in education is that it has been an enormously successful and dynamic time.

A series of statistical bulletins shows that the number of computers in schools and the number of teachers who report using them has increased regularly since 1988 (DES 1989–1993; DfE 1995; DfEE 1997–2000). An alternative perspective, which I argue here, is that this period has been characterized by a confusion of purpose and lack of clarity of objectives.

In essence the use of computers in education has created some fundamental dilemmas. The overriding problem is a dichotomy of purpose. Is IT a subject in its own right, with a knowledge and skill base, or is IT a tool to be used mainly for the learning of other subjects? All the documents suggest both (HMI 1989; DES 1990; DfE 1995; DfEE 1999), yet few schools are able to achieve either to their own, or Ofsted's, satisfaction. Indeed research indicates that IT use in schools is not commonplace, and that barriers to the incorporation of IT into the syllabus identified throughout the 1990s persist (Gardner *et al.* 1992; Watson 1993; Watson and Tinsley 1995; Passey 1999).

Associated with a confusion over purpose are issues related to hardware availability and access, and teachers' perceptions of the relationship between using computers and their pedagogic intentionality. In essence many teachers may espouse the use of the computer to assist learning, and indeed use IT for their own personal work, but in reality few use it with classes on a regular basis. Using IT on a day-to-day basis, for pupils and for teachers, is still the exception, not the norm.

Dichotomy of purpose

Pedagogic vs vocational rationales

As early as the mid-1970s Richard Hooper, director of the first national government initiative, stated that there was a distinct difference between teaching people *with* computers, and teaching people *about* computers (Hooper and Toye 1975). During the 1980s, there was a proliferation of courses in computer science and computer studies for pupils at both 14 and 16-plus. Teaching about the computer, its architecture, systems design and programming, gained attention, and made increasing demands upon the availability of hardware. In contrast, the publication of a series of reports from subject associations, commissioned by the DES, highlighted the role of information technology for each subject area. The reports universally espoused the value of computer assisted learning (CAL) for their discipline.

This distinction has become increasingly blurred, however, until the role of the computer as a learning resource has become subsumed by a notion of 'information technology' skills and competencies. This notion has been bolstered by the NGfL, where the Internet is seen as a source of information for learners and teachers. Today, computers are used in schools mainly for two main groups – blocks of Year 7, 8 and 9 classes doing 'information skills' courses, learning to use a word processor or spreadsheet, and blocks of information and communication technology (ICT) GCSE examination classes. The relationship between these classes and the use of the computer to assist the learning of subjects, such as biology or geography, is tenuous. It is as if pupils are taught to drive a car theoretically, with six-week blocks of lessons, to use steering wheels, gears and brakes, but rarely actually take a vehicle onto the road for the purpose of travelling from A to B. How has this come about?

In part this is a reflection of an increasingly vocational agenda – IT is perceived as part of an equation that associates economic growth with modern technology (see Chapter 22 for a discussion of the vocational role of education). This places greater emphasis on the skills base than a more fundamental pedagogic purpose (Hawkridge 1990). The blurring of the distinction between learning *about* (vocational) and *with* (pedagogic) has been reflected in four documents that lie at the core of current national perspectives of IT that now influence schools.

Information technology from 5–16

The first policy articulation, in one of the national 'Curriculum Matters' series, presented the dual perception as it 'sets out to help schools devise a coherent strategy for making effective use of IT, both in the enrichment of existing subjects and in learning about the technology itself' (1989: iv). Under the aims, it stated clearly that: 'Although IT is only one of a host of important factors affecting society and schools today, it is unusual among current agencies of change in that it impinges directly on the learner at all ages; on the nature and content of study; and therefore on the curriculum and the teacher.' (HMI 1989: 2) In laying out a clear framework of purpose for the use of IT in schools, the pedagogic emphasis came first: 'Through the use of IT in the curriculum, schools will *also* be helping pupils become knowledgeable about the nature of information, comfortable with the new technology and able to exploit its potential' (HMI 1989: 2).

Although IT was to be delivered through subjects, both pedagogic and vocational purposes are reflected in the detailed aims; thus using IT is both 'to enrich and extend learning through the curriculum', and 'to help young people acquire confidence and pleasure using IT [and to] become familiar with some everyday applications' (HMI 1989: 2–3). 'IT concepts and objectives' are listed as communicating, data handling, modelling and so on; a subject such as geography is demoted to being merely a context for delivery. So IT concepts and skills are defined as separate from CAL for subject-based learning.

Information technology in the National Curriculum

The dichotomy noted above continues in the first National Curriculum Technology document (DES 1990); teachers are exhorted to use the computer in both roles, but one message, that of IT skills, appears to be more important than the other, that of curriculum use. Although in effect a condensed form of the IT concepts as outlined in the HMI document, not only are the vocational aspects dominant, they are also narrowly technocentric. For while pupils:

should be able to use Information Technology to communicate and handle information, design, develop, explore and evaluate models of real or imaginary situations; measure and control physical variables and movement;

they should also:

develop confidence and satisfaction in the use of information technology; develop the flexibility needed to take advantage of future developments in information technology.

(DES 1990: 51)

It is less easy to relate many of these capabilities to a subject-centred curriculum learning purpose.

The Dearing changes

By 1995 it had become apparent that the attempt to maintain the dual role of IT as a tool to deliver the curriculum and as a subject with a conceptual and skills basis in its own right was under substantial strain. In the Dearing National Curriculum review, IT became separated from technology (DfE 1995). IT capability was characterized by an ability to use effectively IT tools and information sources to analyse, process and present information, and to model, measure and control external events. It was necessary only to 'give pupils opportunities, where appropriate, to develop and apply their IT capability in their study of National Curriculum subjects' (DfE 1995: 1). So the role of a tool to support subject-based learning was reduced to a mere recommendation.

This shift away from supporting subject-based learning was sustained in other ways. The heavy investment during the 1970s and 1980s in the development of curriculum-focused software virtually ceased, with schools encouraged to use commercially based IT packages, a move that was criticized by the Parliamentary Office of Science and Technology (POST 1991) for both the reduction and inconsistency of a pedagogic agenda. This has been referred to as the 'commodification' of education. Thus it would appear that the pedagogic notion of CAL became more diffuse by the increasingly vocational notion of separate concepts and skills of information technology.

A new ICT curriculum for schools and initial teacher education

Finally in the revised National Curriculum (DfEE 1999), IT is confirmed as a separate subject in its own right, with assessments of attainment at four key stages as other subjects, but with an expanded name, information and communication technology, to reflect the growth of the Internet. In some respects, however, the pendulum would appear to have begun to swing back; the document clearly references other subjects where the ICT curriculum may be learnt. Thus while the tool is identified as a separate curriculum identity, it does have a pedagogic purpose. Schools are informed that 'It is for schools to choose how they organize their school curriculum to include the programmes of study for ICT' (DfEE 1999: 6).

This most recent curriculum articulation has been supported by the NGfL and by new teacher training initiatives, for both initial and in-service provision. The new national ICT curriculum for initial teacher training (TTA 1998):

> aims in particular to equip every newly qualified teacher with the knowledge, skills and understanding to make sound decisions about when, when not, and how to use ICT effectively in teaching particular subjects . . . It is the responsibility of the ITT [initial teacher training] provider to ensure that the ways trainees are taught to use ICT are firmly rooted within the relevant subject and phase, rather than teaching how to use ICT generically or as an end in itself.
>
> (TTA 1998: 1)

This should support the use of ICT within the pedagogic agenda. The curriculum itself is divided into two sections, one for effective teaching and assessment methods with a particular relevance to using ICT, and another which sets out the skills competence with ICT that trainees need. The recent QTS skills tests (TTA 2000) for assessing these competencies are the litmus test of this pedagogic intentionality; at the moment they are designed to ensure teachers have basic ICT skills such as putting data into a spreadsheet. The contexts are all related to general school functions, such as preparing for an open evening at school, and not their application in a subject context.

So after 20 years, schools and teachers still have to grapple with two rationales – one associated with learning the ICT tools and skills to reflect the use of ICT in the adult world, and the other to actually use the tools to further the rest of the curriculum. This dichotomy of purpose has inevitably been compounded by the practical and technical difficulties of implementing a flawed policy in schools. It is, I believe, this compounding of agendas that has made for problems of understanding of the role of IT within schools.

The reality in schools

Reconciling the conflict

Most secondary schools have appointed IT coordinators with the brief to define an IT policy and implement it. This involves tackling hardware and software, network maintenance and management, staff INSET, and reconciling the different perceptions of how, where and why IT should be used. Nor have the coordinators been able to start with a level playing field. Some schools have been active in CAL for many years, resulting in local patterns of use and resourcing highly dependent upon the interests and enthusiasms of particular staff. Because of the dictates of the National Curriculum, as outlined above, it is inevitable that the current overriding priority is ensuring that pupils are given opportunities to develop and apply IT skills progressively as they move through the school. Two central issues devolve from this, however: who is to provide the teaching for these IT skills and where will it happen?

A common strategy has been the development of IT skills courses, leading on to ICT or computers studies GCSE classes. The IT coordinator and other staff (who may now have taken specialist IT initial teacher training) are responsible for ensuring that all pupils attend these courses and so the statutory IT component is assured. Inspectors have reported, however, that pupils are often practising low level skills and there are often insufficient opportunities to apply the IT skills, learnt in these separate IT classes, to work in other subjects. As Ragsdale (1991) has noted, knowledge of IT skills does not mean these skills are always applied. Indeed, acquiring IT tool skills may be relatively easy, but gaining wisdom to use them effectively is not. Pupils are hampered from gaining such wisdom because they are learning these skills in isolation. It is sad to see pupils use a spreadsheet without a genuine need to explore and model a relationship in the data they are manipulating. They need to learn IT skills with a real task in mind and practice them regularly. This suggests, reinforced by the new initial teacher training curriculum, that they should use these skills regularly in the normal subject based classroom.

So the alternative is for different subject departments to deliver the IT curriculum. Some IT coordinators have analysed the component parts and then negotiated or persuaded departments to take on the responsibility for the teaching. A familiar pattern is for history or geography to take on responsibility for teaching databases, English for word-processing, and science or mathematics for modelling. This apparently logical approach has hit a number of snags. First, a number of subject departments may indicate a theoretical willingness to take part, but in reality they find their existing timetable is already squashed with competing curriculum demands. Second, a number of staff have been reluctant IT users themselves, and have baulked at taking on an IT teaching load. Even for confident IT users there have been problems. Where geography teachers may choose to use a data base to encourage pupils to pose and test hypotheses about a topic, for example population growth, at the same time they are now being asked to teach about data retrieval and ensure that a specific and measurable IT capability is delivered. Such teachers using IT have added complexity and potential conflict of purpose in what is otherwise a clearly geographically focused agenda.

A further problem with this approach is that there is a danger of formalizing IT delivery as being the responsibility of only some subjects. All the IT resources are focused on these, leaving isolated others who may want to use IT to assist learning in, for instance, art or foreign languages. There is little doubt that this approach is failing. The first survey of IT use in schools (DES 1989) showed that although half the teachers in secondary schools had been on initial awareness training, less than 25 per cent reported making significant use of computers, except for in computer and business studies, and on average less than 10 per cent reported that IT made a substantial contribution to their teaching and learning. The statistical bulletin (DfE 1997) still showed that less than 10 per cent of teachers (apart from those of computer and business studies) reported IT making a substantial contribution to teaching and learning – little change in the last 10 years of policy, training and investment. However the 2000 statistics show an increase to 30 per cent. The new training initiatives are designed to further overcome teachers' reluctance; we will not know until at least 2002 how successful they have been.

Neither policy is ideal, and their inadequacies explain the substantial criticisms of IT delivery by inspectors (Ofsted 1995). In the meantime however another whole agenda has emerged – using the Web as a source base of information, or rather Information with a capital I. It is here that many teachers and schools see themselves able to reconcile their problem. Using the Web to search for and download information needed for subject lessons, or even templates for the lessons themselves, will surely satisfy both requirements. There is a danger, however, that the fundamental purpose of education, to learn to know, is being swept aside by the need to acquire information. Where do pupils learn the wisdom of how to use information, to challenge its assumptions, its sources, indeed the very hegemony of 'Information'?

Underlying all approaches however are the related issues of resourcing and teachers' perceptions of the potential of IT for their subject. The reality of IT use in schools is more a reflection of these two concerns than the result of a coordinated implementation of whole-school policy.

Computers and rooms

Computers originally arrived in schools as stand-alone micro-computers, and were often located in the classroom of an enthusiastic teacher. Provision rapidly expanded until there was a bookable computer room, which may or may not have been networked. There is evidence to suggest that the advent of networked rooms contributed to a decline in the amount of CAL in a school (Wellington 1988). Today there are usually in schools a couple of computer rooms, with other clusters of machines in subject specialist areas.

For many years the type and configuration of the hardware has been a dominant issue in the field and talk of MS-DOS, processing speed, multimedia and now, Internet access has for a long time caused IT to be seen as synonymous with technical matters. This has been both overtly and covertly damaging. Decisions about purchase and computer room layout have too frequently been made on the basis of technical specification, rather than also considering the nature and use of the educational software and applications available. More importantly, this has helped to sustain a sense of technophobia, a sense of not being part of the inner circle of those who know about and can use 'the machines'. This phobia, which teachers do not display in other fields where machines are involved, has developed into a subtle myth. I believe that the myth is not actually about using the computer, but how to manage their use in the classroom situation. Many teachers own and use computers for their own work, but never use them in their classrooms.

The nub of the matter is of course that they are not using them in their classrooms – they are having to book a timetabled fixed resource and move the class there for a limited time (Watson 1990). It is ironic that limited time may be available for the very open-ended, exploratory work which demands flexibility. It is not the resource itself, but the restricted access to it, with all the related problems of pressure for everything to work correctly in the precious 50 minutes when teachers are in the room, that causes the problem. Furthermore, the amount of time available for CAL users to book the rooms has been severely limited by the increase in the blocks of IT skills classes. The new emphasis on the Web has led to a shift of location into school libraries or resource centres. This has facilitated increased access for individual pupils outside class, but does nothing to help the use of IT as part of direct classroom activities with a pedagogic intention in mind.

Schools do not have enough hardware to allow them to plan sensibly for coherent progression in IT skills used appropriately within curriculum settings. Learning with computers has severely declined in this climate. Schools are still relying on highly trained academic staff to act as both technicians for increasingly ageing hardware and coordinators of IT policy. This is clearly absurd. In the current resourcing and curriculum climate, schools are attempting to devise and implement IT policies that cannot be realistically delivered. Until there is a ratio of 1.5 machines to every pupil, and every teacher has a personal computer on their own desk, it is unrealistic for schools to be asked to deliver a balanced IT curriculum. It is certainly impossible to do justice to the very real and important conceptual issues about the nature of information and communication handling, and their role in society, in the light of technological capability.

In the meantime, targeted provision for specific groups, and encouraging and building on existing pockets of use and excellence can be the only way forward. Interestingly, in two research projects carried out during the early 1990s, the ImpacT study (Watson 1993) and PLAIT (Morrison *et al.* 1993), little discernible difference in effect was established between classes with widely different resourcing. It was the use to which the computers were put, and in particular the amount of process orientated material used, that appeared to have an impact on learning.

The subject teacher's perspective

Teachers wishing to explore the potential of IT for their subject have to invest much time exploring software and applications, often in isolation, and gain confidence in use within a classroom environment. They may need to move their class considerable distances to a timetabled computer laboratory. Success depends upon the considerable individual effort and enthusiasm that is required; success may be in the form of increased discussion and interest about the topic. Learning gains may not be as tangible and amenable to evaluation as the use of other resources. Evidence from research in classrooms in Spain, Canada, the Netherlands, and England (Olson 1990; Watson 1993; Albalat and Ruiz 1995; Veen 1995) suggests that teachers who succeed tend to be those who can clearly relate the use of IT to their pedagogic strategy for their own subject.

It is the keen IT users who manage, despite considerable organizational difficulties, to obtain access to resources and who are flexible in their approach to its use. In particular it is these teachers who recognize and enjoy the pedagogic potential of IT because it relates to their own philosophical underpinnings about teaching and the nature of their subject. (Watson 1993) They are at home with CAL; they 'teach geography (or history, biology, art and so on) with computers' rather than 'deliver IT'.

Unfortunately the DfEE statistics show that such users are the minority of the teaching population. This is supported by evidence that students on initial teacher training courses, whether BEd or PGCE, do not find much exemplar use of IT in their tutoring schools (Dunn and Ridgeway 1991; Mellar and Jackson 1992). Since those teachers who do regularly use IT in their classes are in the minority, it seems important to build IT policies around their success.

Implications

What can a new teacher do? It is clear that the problems with a national curriculum and IT school policies that are dominated by the delivery of vocationally-orientated IT skills courses may well be as alienating for new teachers as they appear to be for those already in post. Success in schools at the moment appears to hinge on those teachers who become convinced that using certain pieces of software can support their pedagogy and enhance the learning for their pupils. Once they are convinced, they familiarize themselves with the resource system to ensure access. Subject association journals provide software reviews and advice as they do for other teaching and learning resources. So the solution lies in your subject pedagogy, not in the IT world.

It is encouraging that students on initial teacher training have consistently prioritized two key questions about using IT in class – 'the ways IT could be used in teaching' and 'managing the use of the computer in the classroom' (Mellar and Jackson 1992; Lienard 1995). These are sound questions and relate to the issues discussed above. They were repeated in the McKinsey Report (1997). The potential role of IT in classrooms is enormous. The chances of realizing this are fraught because of a lack of clarity of purpose upon which to base policy and practice. Yet without a clear philosophical understanding driving forward and underpinning the role of IT for pedagogy, it will continue to be a much lauded but infrequently used innovation.

References

Albalat, J.Q. and Ruiz, F. (1995) Interpreting internal school influences on the educational integration of IT, in D. Watson and D. Tinsley (eds) *Integrating Information Technology into Education*. London: Chapman and Hall.

Department of Education and Science (DES) (1989–1993) *Survey of Information Technology in Schools: Statistical Bulletins*. London: DES.

Department of Education and Science (DES) (1990) *Technology in the National Curriculum*. London: HMSO.

Department for Education (DfE) (1995) *Survey of Information Technology in Schools: Statistical Bulletins*. London: DfE.

Department for Education (DfE) (1995) *Information Technology in the National Curriculum*. London: DfE.

Department for Education and Employment (DfEE) (1997) *Connecting the Learning Society, NGfL*. London: DfEE.

Department for Education and Employment (DfEE) (1997–2000) *Survey of Information Technology in Schools: Statistical Bulletins*. London: DfEE.

Department for Education and Employment (DfEE) (1999) *Information and Communication Technology in the National Curriculum*. London: DfEE.

Dunn, S. and Ridgeway, J. (1991) Computer use during primary school teaching practice: a survey, *Journal of Computer Assisted Learning*, 7(1): 66–70.

Gardner, J., Morrison, H., Jarman, R., Reilly, C. and McNally, H. (1992) *Pupils' Learning and Access to Information Technology*. Belfast: Queen's University of Belfast.

Hawkridge, D. (1990) Who needs computers in schools, and why? in M. Kibby (ed.) *Computer Assisted Learning; Selected Proceedings from the CAL '89 Symposium*. Oxford: Pergamon.

Her Majesty's Inspectorate (HMI) (1989) *Information Technology from 5 to 16*. London: HMSO.

Hooper, R. and Toye, I. (eds) (1975) *Computer Assisted Learning in the United Kingdom: Some Case Studies*. London: Council for Educational Technology.

Lienard, B. (1995) Pre-course IT skills of teacher trainees: a longitudinal study, *Journal of Computer Assisted Learning*, 11(2): 110–20.

McKinsey and Co. (1997) *The Future of Information Technology in UK Schools*. London: McKinsey and Company.

Mellar, H. and Jackson, A. (1992) IT in post-graduate teacher training, *Journal of Computer Assisted Learning*, 8(4): 231–43.

Morrison, H., Gardner, J., Reilly, C. and McNally, H. (1993) The impact of portable computers on pupils' attitudes to study, *Journal of Computer Assisted Learning*, 9: 130–41.

Office for Standards in Education (Ofsted) (1995) *Information Technology: A Review of Inspection Findings, 1993/94*. London: HMSO.

Olson, J. (1990) Trojan horse or teacher's pet? *International Journal of Educational Research*, 17(1): 77–84.

Parliamentary Office of Science and Technology (POST) (1991) *Technologies for Teaching: The Use of Technologies for Teaching and Learning in Primary and Secondary Schools*. London: Parliamentary Office of Science and Technology.

Passey, D. (1999) Strategic evaluation of the impacts on learning of educational technology, *Education and Information Technologies*, 4(3): 223–50.

Ragsdale, R. (1991) Effective computing in education: teachers, tools and training, *Education and Computing*, 7(1–2): 157–66.

Teacher Training Agency (TTA) (1998) *Initial Teacher Training National Curriculum for the Use of Information and Communications Technology in Subject Teaching*. London: HMSO.

Teacher Training Agency (TTA) (2000) *Qualified Teacher Status Skills Tests: Secondary – Information and Communication Technology*. London: HMSO.

Veen, W. (1995) Factors affecting the use of computers in the classroom: four case studies, in D. Watson and D. Tinsley (eds) *Integrating Information Technology into Education*. London: Chapman and Hall.

Watson, D.M. (1990) The classroom vs. the computer room, *Computers and Education*, 15(1–3): 33–7.

Watson, D.M. (ed.) (1993) *The ImpacT Report: An Evaluation of the Impact of Information Technology on Children's Achievements in Primary and Secondary Schools.* London: King's College London.

Watson, D. and Tinsley, D. (eds) (1995) *Integrating Information Technology into Education.* London: Chapman and Hall.

Wellington, J.J. (1988) Computer education in secondary schools: an electronic survey, *Journal of Computer Assisted Learning*, 4(1): 22–33.

14–19 education: broadening the curriculum

Peter Gill and Sally Johnson

Introduction

'I shall take it as self-evident that each generation must define afresh the nature, direction and aims of education' said the great educationalist Jerome Bruner in 1966. Yet in terms of the subjects covered, the National Curriculum for England and Wales is remarkably similar to the curriculum in place in grammar schools during the nineteenth century. This is not to say that there has been no criticism of the situation. In 1959 the Central Advisory Council for Education in England suggested that:

> The 'yield' of the whole educational system could be much increased if there were available a wider variety of forms of education and a wider choice of sequence in learning, so that every young person could find one that was designed to develop his [sic] potentialities in the most suitable way.
>
> (Ministry of Education 1959: 394)

This sentiment has been reiterated in many different forms over the intervening years but only towards the end of the twentieth century has a real attempt been made to satisfy the intention behind it. This chapter explores the history and evolution of academic and vocational education in England and Wales. It examines the philosophy and methods of Outcomes Based Education (OBE) and of new courses introduced such as General National Vocational Qualifications (GNVQ). The discussion considers whether postcompulsory educational provision available from September 2000 might be any more successful in broadening the choice of subjects taken and in encouraging a greater proportion of young people to achieve their potential.

Developing the secondary curriculum: an historical perspective

In the state sector, before 1944, only the children who passed an entry examination for grammar school received a secondary education. The rest, and by far the majority, remained in elementary schools until the age of 14. The 1944 Education Act extended secondary education to include all children up to the age of 15. The Act also instigated a tripartite system of schooling which largely mirrored the existing social class divisions. Grammar schools were retained and maintained high academic standards by selection through testing at age 11. They catered for the top 20 per cent of the ability range who sat General Certificate of Education (GCE) Ordinary and Advanced level examinations. As it happened, grammar schools tended to recruit mainly middle-class children and were generally located away from working-class areas. Technical schools were elevated to secondary status but aimed at a less academic and more practical approach for working-class children who would proceed to a craft or trade. Secondary modern schools were introduced for the rest of the newly enlarged school population offering a 'general education for life' and producing a workforce for the commercial side of industry (Maclure 1968: 209). The legislation put in place a modern, work-orientated education for the majority but the complete separation of the three different systems and their cohorts of children produced a general prejudice that technical and vocational education would never achieve the same prestige or esteem as the academic route (McCulloch *et al.* 1985).

Fifteen years later, in 1959, the Central Advisory Council for Education published a report entitled '15 to 18' – the Crowther Report (Ministry of Education 1959), which assessed the structure set up under the 1944 Act. This report specifically considered the balance between general and specialized studies and the interrelationship of the various stages of education, in order to provide an adequate supply of academic and vocationally qualified young people for all sectors of the workforce. The Council found several shortcomings and criticized the great waste of talent in a system which only enabled 12 per cent of pupils to stay in school to the age of 17. The Crowther Report made many significant recommendations, some of which are still being implemented today. The report suggested increasing the number of students who continue in education after the compulsory phase and recommended providing new and challenging courses for the middle ability range – 'an alternative road' – as a requirement for a coherent national system of practical education.

From the 1960s, comprehensive schools were phased in to locate children of all abilities and backgrounds in the same institution. The Certificate of Secondary Education (CSE) was introduced as a qualification for the 40 per cent of children below the GCE O-level standard. In fact the CSE was merely a watered down version of the O-level, locally administered, and it never gained the status it deserved. Perhaps its only lasting effect was to involve a generation of teachers in the examination and assessment process. This contributed to the compulsory inclusion of teacher assessment in the General Certificate of Secondary Education (GCSE) which amalgamated and replaced CSE and O-level. The GCSE was introduced in 1988 as a national school leaving certificate for the majority of the population in England and Wales (DES 1985).

One of the problems of the GCSE and the National Curriculum which followed shortly after was that the liberal academic tradition, as exemplified by the grammar school syllabus, was still too obviously apparent (Flude and Hammer 1990). The heavy hand of the old universities still loomed large. Many teachers realized that the system remained inappropriate for most pupils but attempts to introduce vocational qualifications usually failed because they were simply not designed for schools and the 14–16 age range. Few schoolteachers have the skills or qualifications to teach vocational topics and most schools simply do not have the facilities. An exception to this was the Royal Society of Arts (RSA) typing qualifications and many pupils (mostly girls) left school at 16 with RSA certificates in typing and office practice.

During the 1970s there was a growing realization in industry and commerce that schools were not producing enough leavers with useful skills. The perceived mismatch of educational content with industrial and economic need led to a number of initiatives by the government to try to alter the situation. Most of the initiatives came from the Manpower Services Commission, the arm of government responsible for employment and training rather than education. This intervention led to several years during which very different philosophies fought for control of the curriculum (McCulloch *et al.* 1985).

The most significant and successful of the schemes was the Technical and Vocational Education Initiative (TVEI). In its first manifestation the TVEI gave significant amounts of money to a number of schools to design and produce a heavily technologically oriented curriculum for 14–16-year-old pupils. Much of the money was earmarked for computers and other hardware and the level of spending gave rise to considerable envy in schools which had no access to such equipment. At this stage the TVEI curriculum was only for a small percentage of pupils even in the schools that did get the money and almost inevitably, given the liberal academic tradition referred to above, it was mostly the lower attainers that benefited. The academic–vocational divide remained intact. In the late 1980s the TVEI broadened its remit and offered money to schools that redesigned the curriculum such that *all* pupils received an education that was broadly technologically based (McCulloch *et al.* 1985). The sums of money were relatively modest but nonetheless welcome. It is interesting to note that aspects of the curriculum model that were being pushed by TVEI, such as core subjects and limited opportunity to specialize, were very similar to the rationale developed in the National Curriculum.

The fight for control of the compulsory school curriculum was won by the traditional liberal academics and the Department for Education, but for 16–19-year-olds the field was wide open. There was little alternative to A-levels for those staying on in the sixth form at school – but A-levels were designed as university entrance examinations and were taken by only a small percentage of the population. Even after the explosion in numbers of students entering higher education in the early 1990s, the proportion taking what could be called 'vocational' subjects (maths, science and computing) at A-level was still well under 10 per cent of the cohort.

There were a number of attempts to bring Business and Technician Education Council (BTEC) and City and Guilds courses into sixth forms, but most of the qualifications were very specifically vocational, related to only one trade or profession, and designed to be taught in further education (FE) colleges with their greater range of appropriate facilities. What was needed in schools was something more generalized and for a while a number of 'prevocational' courses were available. Probably the most successful of these were City and Guilds 365, the RSA Vocational Preparation and the Certificate of Prevocational Education (CPVE) sponsored by the Department of Education and Science (Youth Education Service 1985). These courses involved an extension of general education, the development of vocational interests and the acquisition of skills applicable to jobs and adult life.

Although to some extent Crowther's 'alternative road' was available to post-16-year-old middle ability students by the 1980s, the provision included many different courses that perhaps made choices complicated, even for those who were willing to take that route. It could be argued that the quality of much of this work was never fully recognized by students and their parents who still sought the academic path as a preference in postcompulsory education.

Society needed a flexible workforce with people able and willing to change trade or profession several times during their working lives. This flexibility implied a need for some sort of parity across qualifications. In order to ease the chaos of thousands of vocational and prevocational courses, the government created the National Council for Vocational Qualifications (NCVQ) in 1986 with a brief to bring together all the qualifications under one umbrella by the beginning of the new century. This was an ambitious project, partly due to the sheer difficulty of comparing very different skills, but also due to the independence of the different trades and professions who were proud of their own particular histories and status. To complicate matters further, the NCVQ tried to achieve parity not just within vocational qualifications but across the divide into academic qualifications. The resulting qualifications are named National Vocational Qualifications (NVQ) and are available at five levels.

In 1991 the government announced a new prevocational qualification available for full time students post-16 in schools and colleges, the General National Vocational Qualification (GNVQ). The GNVQ was to be linked to academic GCE A-level and National Vocational Qualifications accredited in the workplace through the National Qualifications Framework. An Advanced GNVQ was equivalent to two GCE A-levels and an Intermediate GNVQ to four GCSEs at grades A–C. Students with very low GCSE grades, or those who had not taken GCSEs, could enrol for Foundation level GNVQ courses.

Competence based qualifications

So far we have been referring mainly to vocational education as it developed in schools. However most vocational educational happens in the workplace and has developed a very different philosophy and practice. The key point about vocational education is that it is about skills, outcomes and competencies. Indeed apprenticeship training, from which it grew, has a much longer history than academic schooling and the vocational trainee was trained for exactly the skills in which he or she would be tested; the driving test is a good example. (If you have read Chapter 17 you will have identified this paragraph as referring to criterion referenced testing.) The model of initial teacher training introduced in 1998 with its requirements for Qualified Teacher Status (QTS) is also essentially a competence-led curriculum.

NVQs and GNVQs are examples of competence based qualifications. Before going into any detail about GNVQs it is important to make clear just what is implied by such a statement. Traditional school qualifications are based on the teaching of material defined in a syllabus the mastery of which is tested by a terminal examination. Pupils are expected to have covered the whole syllabus even though the examination can only sample part of the area covered. NVQs (and GNVQs up until 2000) are very clearly criterion-referenced qualifications. In any of their course specifications there are only outcomes to be achieved rather than content to be learned. The specification defines what the student should be able to do ('performance criteria'), in how many contexts these criteria should be met ('range statements') and how the competencies should be demonstrated ('evidence indicators'). There is no list of material to be covered, no reference to teaching or even if any should take place, and no time limit.

Bringing all existing vocational qualifications into line with this model has been enormously complex and has led to the generation of a whole culture with its own jargon, which is barely comprehensible to other practitioners in the field and quite incomprehensible to outsiders. As an example of these excesses consider the following which comes from the *Competence and Assessment Briefing Series*:

> A range statement defines the scope of an element of competence within a particular NVQ or SVQ. Range statements are made up of a series of dimensions (or categories for SVQ) under each of which there are range classes which are critical for the assessment of competent performance within the occupation. The range classes for each dimension identify critical differences in application and are mutually exclusive.

> (Mitchell and Bartram 1994: 5)

The school examination system had dabbled with criterion-referencing both in GCSE and the National Curriculum but mainly remained a traditional syllabus-led liberal education. The totally competence-led style of the GNVQ was at variance with the traditional school culture and teachers had severe problems in coping with both the change in philosophy and the large amount of paperwork involved in any scheme of assessment where the teachers themselves are the leading assessors (Murray and Gill 1995).

A further issue for teachers and students, in addition to the assessment load, was the overall structure of the GNVQ which differed greatly from the traditional GCE A-level. Although GNVQ Level 3 (Advanced) was meant to be equivalent to two A-levels it was organized as a modular course, with students taking 12 modules (eight compulsory and four chosen from a menu). Three modules of key skills: communication; application of number, and information technology (IT) were also incorporated and will be discussed later. All modules had to be passed but the final qualification was in a single area, for example 'Engineering' and was graded as 'Pass', 'Merit,' or 'Distinction'.

From its inception, GNVQ was successful in terms of the number of students opting to study for it, probably because of antipathy towards the GCSE A-level rather than the inherent attractiveness of the GNVQ (Solomon and Johnson 2000). On the other hand there were real problems with low student completion rates. Although there was no time limit for completing modules, the design had been to enable the Advanced level GNVQ to be completed in two years (as with the Advanced level GCE). In 1995 only 47 per cent of students registered two years before had completed their Advanced level GNVQ. The figures for the Intermediate and Foundation levels were 58 per cent and 20 per cent respectively. The success rate for A-level was about 70 per cent (for those taking and passing two GCE A-levels) within two years. In the light of the above mentioned difficulties the GNVQ was remodelled and relaunched in September 2000.

Provision from 2000

In his review of the National Curriculum, Sir Ron Dearing concluded that it would be desirable for schools to have more scope to include a range of options for 14–16-year-olds, which would complement a statutory core of subjects. Dearing saw this as offering many pupils a greater choice of GCSEs but he felt many others 'would be better served by courses of a more applied character' (Dearing 1993: 44). The report stressed that a mixture of academic and applied elements might prove motivating and helpful in the future when seeking employment.

Following the perceived success of the review, Dearing was asked to examine and reform the qualifications for 16–19-year-olds (Dearing 1996). However he was not given a free rein and his terms of reference made it clear that A-levels were sacrosanct, despite the fact that various groups (representing industry, commerce and higher education) consulted over many years had recommended fundamental changes to the traditional narrow diet of A-levels (National Commission on Education 1993).

As far as schools were concerned, vocational qualifications would continue to mean GNVQs. Dearing recommended a number of changes to them, mostly concerned with assessment. The original GNVQ style of assessment was based on the competence model adopted for NVQs. However GNVQs are not actually vocational qualifications – prevocational would be more accurate – and the assessment model had been found difficult to implement. The report recommended a greater proportion of the assessment by external examination and therefore less emphasis on teacher assessment of competence.

The main recommendations of the Dearing Report are itemized below together with the resulting changes which became effective from September 2000 (referred to as Curriculum 2000).

1 *Bring together the work of NCVQ and the Schools Curriculum and Assessment Authority (SCAA)*. This amalgamation took place in 1997 to form the Qualifications and Curriculum Authority (QCA) to oversee and regulate all academic and vocational qualifications. The aim of this merger was to bring greater coherence into the framework of qualifications and challenge pervasive attitudes inherited from the past towards the relative worth of achievement in the academic and vocational pathways.

2 *Rationalize the number of bodies involved in the awarding of qualifications*. The existing examination boards and vocational awarding bodies merged during the late 1990s to form three new centres for issuing course specifications, examinations and accreditation. EDEXCEL formed from the University of London Examination and Assessment Council (ULEAC) and BTEC. Oxford, Cambridge and the Royal Society of Arts (OCR) from the Oxford and Cambridge exam boards and the RSA. The Assessment and Qualifications Alliance (AQA) was created from City and Guilds along with the Associated Examining Board, Southern Examining Group and the Northern Examination and Assessment Board.

3 *Plain words and a common vocabulary should be adopted by the awarding bodies as soon as is practicable*. GNVQs were revised and launched in September 2000, along with other qualifications, such as revised GCE A-levels. The aim of the redesign of units was to reduce the overall burden of assessment while strengthening the external element and making clearer what students need to learn as opposed to what is assessed. The new specifications were written to be as comprehensible and jargon-free as possible. The entirely outcome-based model has been abandoned and the specifications contain details on what has to be learned as well as how they will be assessed. The assessment itself is a combination of internal portfolio and externally set and marked examinations, the latter typically counting for one-third of the available marks. Key skills remain an integral part of GNVQs, however, the award is no longer dependent on achievement of the key skills, which are now separately certificated as NVQ levels 1–3. For Foundation and Intermediate GNVQ the grades remain as Pass, Merit and Distinction.

4 *Students should have opportunities to take approved GNVQ units at Foundation and Intermediate levels from 14 onwards and to take those NVQ units approved for use in schools*. From September 2000, the new National Curriculum allows pupils an opportunity to study for GNVQs at Key Stage 4, alongside a core of GCSE subjects, as well as at post-16. This Part One GNVQ is available at two levels, in seven vocational areas: Foundation level will be equivalent to two GCSEs grade D–G; Intermediate level equivalent to two GCSEs grades A–C.

5 *The structure of A-levels and GNVQ should be brought into close alignment to enable students to build up a portfolio of qualifications across both pathways*. The A-level and the new Advanced Subsidiary (AS) syllabuses have become modular and are weighted against GNVQ Advanced (renamed Advanced Vocational Certificate of Education (VCE)) units, such that a full 12-unit Advanced VCE is equivalent to two GCE A-levels, a six-unit award is worth one A-level and a three-unit award (available initially in four vocational areas) valued as an AS level. The new AS qualification covers the first year of the A-level syllabus and is examined at the level

of achievement expected after one full year's advanced level study. Breaking down large awards into smaller fully examined credits is aimed at increasing a student's breadth of study and reducing the risk of non-completion. A/AS level and advanced VCE are to be graded on a common scale of A–E/U to improve equivalence for university entrance.

6 *A distinctive diploma at Advanced level should be created to recognize achievement in depth and breadth of studies.* This overarching certificate, designed as a mechanism to encourage a wider range of studies, is still under development and is not expected to be in place before 2003. The baseline of the model is placed at:

two A-levels;
one 12-unit GNVQ;
one A-level and a 6-unit GNVQ;
NVQ3.

Additional breadth is suggested through key skills plus a wider range of AS or 3-unit GNVQs in different subject domains.

This restructuring of the GNVQ is actually more fundamental than it might seem and is once again a sign of the liberal academic triumph. The strict outcome-led regime of the NVQ has been watered down and the new version of the GNVQ resembles the GCSE with the ratio of coursework to examination reversed. The title of *Vocational* A-level which has been adopted is misleading because true vocational education will inevitably take place mostly or entirely in the workplace. As stated earlier, GNVQs are *pre*vocational and there is a clear danger that they are becoming more and more like the old academic A-levels and the many students for whom that is an inappropriate model will find themselves clearly disadvantaged.

Key skills

A significant development introduced on the back of the original GNVQ and specifically encouraged in the Dearing Report (1996) was the idea of incorporating 'key skills'. This was not an entirely new idea because many schools and colleges had previously entered students for General Studies A-level to achieve the same thing. However, key skills were meant to be the transferable or generic skills that pupils would take from their education at school, into the workplace or higher education. The list adopted by the QCA is: communication; application of number; IT; working with others; improving own learning and performance; problem-solving (Solomon and Johnson 2000). The list is slightly arbitrary but exists in related forms in a number of other courses and countries at further and higher education level. Interestingly enough an almost identical list appeared as part of the original National Curriculum for England and Wales in 1989 under the title of 'cross curricular skills'.

Originally subsumed within the GNVQ, key skills now exist as stand-alone NVQs designed to be earned alongside the other sixth form qualifications and eventually further down the school and indeed in the workplace. Initially at school level there are only externally validated qualifications available in communication, application of number and information technology. As with other current GNVQs their assessment is by a combination of internally marked portfolio and externally set and marked examinations.

The separation of key skills was in response to the very real difficulties teachers experienced in incorporating and assessing them as part of the old GNVQ. However there is now a danger that they will be seen as just another subject (or subjects) to be passed and the very important principle of transferability will be lost. This is linked to the issue of the validity (see Chapter 17 for definition) of the externally set examinations. Exemplar tests issued before the commencement of the 2000 curriculum showed Level 2 Application of Number and Communication being assessed by *multiple choice examinations*. This may be partly defensible for application of number, but is plainly nonsense for communication, especially when the external tests are so heavily weighted. Multiple choice can be a good method of assessing recall but as a method of assessing transferable skills they are all but useless (Wood 1991).

There is a further issue in that the QCA list is not only arbitrary but also contains some very disparate elements. Is it really possible to impose the same structural and assessment models on such varied ideas as 'application of number' and 'improving own learning and performance'? The QCA model proposes just that. The former skill can probably be taught and, as a subset of mathematics, has been for centuries – but what about the latter? What are the relevant skills and competencies of 'improving own learning and performance' and how can they be taught and assessed reliably and validly? We simply do not know.

The range of 'topics' in the key skills curriculum is so wide and is underlain by such different philosophies (where they exist at all) that there is a real danger that they will fail completely to deliver what they claim. This is not a new criticism related only to the post-2000 curriculum. Whitson (1998), for example, has raised just these sorts of issues in relation to key skills in higher education but they have been ignored by the government and its agencies.

Conclusion

The range of philosophies and pressures fighting to control the school curriculum are much wider than the simple 'academic–vocational divide' that has been described in this chapter (see, for example, Williams 1961; Young 1971; Ball 1993). Nonetheless there is a polarity. We have tried to show how the education system in England and Wales has struggled to ameliorate several inherent difficulties generated by a curriculum inappropriate for many pupils that is perceived to have caused great wastage in the system over many years. The first way was to provide appropriate and motivating qualifications for the majority of young people in the middle ability range in order to retain them in education long enough to realize their potential. Second, an attempt was made to bring about parity of esteem between academic and more vocational courses through providing a single certificate of qualifications for entry to university or employment.

Third, the education system tried to broaden the range of subjects and types of qualifications that any one person can achieve in order to produce a workforce with greater transferability of skills.

From September 2000, the greater modularization of qualifications and overt equivalence of their worth through a new Universities Central Admissions System (UCAS) tariff, would appear to have put a more equitable structure in place. However it will be several years before it is clear whether or not a new broader curriculum is successful. Teachers can do a great deal to help but much is in the hands of outside agencies. Pupils and parents need to be persuaded that breadth is important, but the key players yet again are likely to be the universities or more particularly their admissions officers.

Will they use it? Will it work? Are the new courses available from 2000 more palatable and do they provide a better choice for broadening the range of subjects taken? Only time will tell, but we live in hope.

References

Ball, S.J. (1993) Education, Majorism and 'the curriculum of the dead', *Curriculum Studies*, 1(2): 195–214.

Bruner, J. (1966) *Towards a Theory of Instruction*. Cambridge, MA: Harvard University Press.

Dearing, R. (1993) *The National Curriculum and its Assessment*. London: School Curriculum and Assessment Authority.

Dearing, R. (1996) *Review of Qualifications for 16–19 Year Olds*, The Dearing Report. London: School Curriculum and Assessment Authority.

Department for Education and Science (DES) (1985) *GCSE, The National Criteria, General Criteria*. London: HMSO.

Flude, M. and Hammer, M. (eds) (1990) *The Education Reform Act 1988*. London: Falmer Press.

McCulloch, G., Jenkins, E. and Layton, D. (1985) *Technological Revolution? The Politics of School Science and Technology in England and Wales since 1945*. London: Falmer Press.

Maclure, S. (1968) *Educational Documents. England and Wales 1816–1967*. London: Methuen Educational.

Ministry of Education (1959) *15 to 18, A Report of the Central Advisory Council for Education*, The Crowther Report. London: HMSO.

Mitchell, L. and Bartram, D. (1994) The place of knowledge and understanding in the development of National Vocational Qualifications and Scottish Vocational Qualifications, in *Competence and Assessment Briefing Series*, 10: 15. London: Employment Department.

Murray, R. and Gill, P. (1995) GNVQ science – the road to success? *Education in Chemistry*, 32(1): 28.

National Commission on Education (NCE) (1993) *Learning to Succeed*. London: Heinemann.

Solomon, J. and Johnson, S. (2000) GNVQ Science at Advanced level: a new kind of course, in M. Monk and J. Osborne (eds) *Good Practice in Science Teaching, What Research Has to Say*. Buckingham: Open University Press.

Whitson, K. (1998) Key skills and curriculum reform, *Studies in Higher Education*, 23(3): 307–19.

Williams, R. (1961) *The Long Revolution*. Harmondsworth: Penguin.

Wood, R. (1991) *Assessment and Testing: A Survey of Research*. Cambridge: Cambridge University Press.

Young, M.F.D. (1971) *Knowledge and Control*. London: Collier-Macmillan.

Youth Education Service (1985) *The 14–18 Curriculum: Integrating CPVE, YTS, TVEI*. Bristol: Youth Education Service.

Further reading

Armitage, A., Bryant, R., Dunnill, R. *et al.* (1999) *Teaching and Training in Post-Compulsory Education*. Buckingham: Open University Press.

Bloomer, M. (1997) *Curriculum Making in Post-16 Education*. London: Routledge.

Edwards, T., Taylor Fitz-Gibbon, C., Hardman, F. *et al.* (1997) *Separate but Equal?* London: Routledge.

26 Beyond the subject curriculum: the form tutor's role

Jane Jones

Introduction

Your mental image of yourself teaching probably involves you explaining key elements of your subject. However, you will spend a significant amount of your time in school doing something for which you have had little preparation and which opens up innumerable opportunities to frustrate and fulfil. Almost certainly you will be involved as a form tutor within months of starting to teach. With the pressures on young people seemingly increasing with each generation, you will play a major part in the lives of large numbers of pupils in ways in which it is hard to imagine now. This chapter is an attempt to help you to prepare for the challenges that lie ahead beyond your role as subject teacher.

Chapter 12 on adolescence will provide an insight into the challenges facing young people in their everyday lives. In school, the role of the form tutor is crucially one of supporter, first port of call, guide – someone available on a daily basis who provides an anchor of stability. The work of the form tutor cuts across subject specialisms and emphasizes study and coping strategies as well as personal, vocational and life skills.

Tattum describes the character and ethos of a school as determined by 'decisions about the curriculum, the allocation of resources, the grouping of pupils and the arrangements made for guidance and welfare' (1998: 158). While government policy and funding largely determine factors such as school resources and the content of the curriculum, pupil grouping, student welfare and personal guidance, under the guise and auspices of the pastoral system, still remain within the decision-making processes of individual schools and teachers. It is these factors that may influence the success or failure of learners more than government legislation.

The pastoral system

There are over 4,500 secondary schools in England and within each of these the headteacher faces the demanding task of organizing the pupils, staff and other resources to produce an effective learning environment. During the setting up of the comprehensive system in the 1950s and 1960s, considerable thought and effort were given to developing an organizational system in which the individual pupil would feel valued, noticed and encouraged in their learning. Within many schools, a number of organizational subsets ('houses') were established. These varied in number from three up to 10 or even more, mainly depending on the size of the school. Within each house, tutors had a major responsibility for the welfare, discipline and pastoral care of their groups and became the link between the pupils in the school and the outside community, which included parents, careers services, social services and the courts.

Some schools set up vertical systems, in which three or four pupils from each year group were placed in the same tutor group. This system resulted in a mixed age group somewhat akin to a (very large) family, where younger pupils could rely on the help and support of older pupils as well as on their tutor. In return, older pupils took care of the younger ones in the tutor group, which assisted the development of their social and life skills.

However, while the vertical system provided a strong integrating system to support individual pupils, it also created problems, particularly administrative ones. For example, if a particular age group was required for medical examinations or had to select subject options, then messages had to reach the individual pupils concerned. In a school of 1200 pupils, there will be approximately 40 tutor groups each with around four pupils from each year. The logistics of messages reaching the right people at the right time sometimes proved difficult. Another problem involved the role of the form tutor who, at any one time, may have needed to concentrate on Year 11 pupils about to make choices for post-16 education, on Year 9 pupils preparing for the national examinations and on Year 7 pupils anxious about rubella injections. The difficulties imposed by having a representative sample of the whole school in each tutor group have increased as the administrative demands on teachers have grown since the mid-1980s.

An alternative to vertical systems are horizontal systems, in which tutor groups contain pupils from only one year group. This system mimics the arrangement pupils usually witnessed in their primary schools. The form tutor replaces their class teacher and the head of year is, in effect, the equivalent of their primary headteacher. Thus a secondary school organized into a horizontal system of year groups can be thought of as five or more primary schools working under one roof to the directives of the senior management team. Such a system, with heads and deputy heads of year (and/or a head of lower and head of upper school) working with a group of form tutors, creates a pastoral management structure which may, or may not, integrate well with the academic system of heads of department and subject teachers.

There are, of course, exceptions to the rule and some schools have combined horizontal and vertical systems with pupils belonging both to a house *and* a year group. In these schools the year group is the main organizational division with the house system bolted on for activities such as competitive sports. It is often the will to make a system work rather than the particular type of system that is the key to success.

The daily role of the form tutor

As form tutor, you are the one person who has daily contact with your group of pupils, monitoring their general well-being and possessing an exclusive overview of their progress across all subjects. Just 'being there' is an important factor, providing for the pupils an anchor of security in a large, sometimes impersonal institution, perhaps the only anchor of security for pupils with chaotic home lives (when a pupil mistakenly calls you 'Mum' or 'Dad' it can be a powerful reminder of how few adults actually talk *with* rather than *at* children).

Your own education, in terms of school studies and degree work will not have prepared you for the variety of routine and not-so-routine tasks that may face you as a form tutor. Reporting the death of a pet, checking a dental appointment card, collecting money for the day trip to Boulogne, listening to a complaint of bullying or tales of woe about an incorrect item of uniform might well constitute the daily 'pastoral agenda' of a form tutor – all within a fixed 10 minute slot of registration-cum-any other business time. The range of issues raised in those few minutes may be greater than in the rest of your day in school. Admitting to not knowing the right answer may be your philosophy during lessons and pupils may accept that as a virtue, but your responsibility as a tutor makes 'not knowing' unhelpful and possibly harmful for adolescents in your care.

Many of your pupils may come from very different backgrounds to yourself, may hold very different attitudes and may have faced a range of emotional experiences that you will never encounter except through them. The lives of some pupils may be so fraught with problems that you may wonder at how they manage to cope. Trying to empathize when you have no direct experience is challenging and not something that you can learn quickly. Learning to be a good form tutor may be more demanding than learning to be a teacher of your subject. The role is a highly skilled one requiring a range of personal qualities, skills and attitudes.

You can learn to be an effective form tutor by, for example, observing experienced tutors, talking to colleagues about your concerns, listening to pupils and hearing their views and by keeping up to date with official documentation with regard to pastoral concerns. To learn effectively, however, needs commitment on your part as well as access to the right information.

The role of the form tutor demands administrative competence coupled with the ability to think quickly about and around situations. With schools now obliged to report their attendance rates, filling in the register and 'chasing up' absences have become key tasks. A bona fide appointment is an 'authorized absence' and requires the appropriate notation in the register. It is easy to forget that the class register is a legal document, which can be used as evidence in a court of law. Do you record someone as 'present' if her or his friends say the pupil is 'talking to a teacher'?

As the attendance register fills up, truancy or other non-attendance related problems are quite easy to spot, especially if absence notes are not forthcoming. Absence notes themselves need monitoring, as they are susceptible to forgery. Some pupils intercept letters from school and forge convincing replies. However, some pupils quite legitimately write their own absence notes which are then signed by a parent who is perhaps not a speaker or writer of English. The tutor would need to know this so that appropriate channels of communication can be established. Indeed, the importance of establishing effective home–school communication cannot be overemphasized. Money is another issue: under what circumstances, if any, are you prepared to lend money to pupils? What do you do if you see a pupil carrying £50 in their pocket? The key thing to realize is that schools have policies and that, generally, knowledge of those policies reduces the dilemmas that you may face. You are not alone.

Bullying has become more of an issue in recent years. In the past, many schools would claim that they did not have a bullying problem. The evidence, collected over many years and in many countries, is that bullying is usually a much bigger problem than most teachers realize. A pupil who claims to have been bullied must always be taken seriously. A pupil asking for help needs time and reassurance, even if it is not immediately available. This gives a potent message first to those pupils who are bullied and, even more importantly, to would-be bullies who may be deterred by visible, decisive and speedy action by form tutors. Schools are required to have an anti-bullying policy and the form tutor needs to be familiar with this and with the associated procedures. So long as bullying is endemic to school life, many pupils will experience unhappiness as a result of incidents generated by the school culture. They need to know that the form tutor is the person to whom they can turn. With sensitive issues, counselling skills are needed and the form tutor, who is categorically not a counsellor, may well have to act as counsellor at times in situations where individual pupils need personal responses. As King (1999: 4) writes:

> The emphasis now is on equipping teachers with basic counselling skills: not training them as counsellors or to work as counsellors, but helping teachers perform their 'pastoral' work more effectively, and enabling them to recognize problems which need referring on to a specialist or a specialist agency.

Such basic skills, King (1999: 4) suggests, would involve 'listening skills, the skills of empathetic understanding, responding skills and a clear awareness of boundary limits'. Some schools have experimented successfully with peer counselling whereby older pupils are trained to listen to and to provide support for younger pupils. Keeping an eye on the education press can alert you to strategies that others have used successfully to deal with what for you might seem an intractable problem.

During the 1960s and 1970s, some schools were able to appoint counsellors, but their numbers have declined as budgets have been tightened and they have not on the whole been replaced in recent years. Counselling pupils will normally be part of the form tutor role but the lack of time and expertise will mean that many issues will, by necessity and perhaps to the benefit of a greater number of pupils, be explored within

the tutor group context. The task here is to create a supportive environment and to nurture support through activities such as role-play, drama,
debate and discussion. One-to-one counselling, with all the time implications involved, should still be the right of pupils, particularly those
for whom the form tutor is the only caring adult that they encounter on
a daily basis.

Tutor entitlement

In order to do the job effectively, the form tutor needs support and resources. Dolezal (1989: 12) states that every tutor has an entitlement to:

- information on, and time with, individuals;
- time with the group;
- time with the parents;
- time to prepare and access to resources;
- support for development via reflection, review and training.

Dolezal utilizes this paradigm to describe similar entitlements for pupils,
parents, year heads and subject teachers. In each case, she stresses the
importance of contact time, information accessing, appropriate resources
and support. Marland and Rogers (1997) stress the right of the tutor to be
fully briefed on their role and to be fully informed of the school's general
approach to personal, health and social education (PHSE) and to the
detailed content. In order to develop your knowledge and skills as a tutor,
you can consult the many publications and other resources available on
PHSE. There are many journals that you can consult on relevant topics,
for example, *The Journal of Beliefs and Values*, in which you will find
articles on issues such as sexuality and bereavement. *Pastoral Care in Education* is a particularly rich resource for tutors. In this journal you will find
discussions about topics as varied as work planners, careers education,
citizenship, bereavement courses, the development of study skills, personal development, behaviour management and the role of the form
tutor.

Responsibilities and problems take up a fair share of the tutoring time
available, but the picture is not one of unrelieved gloom. There are humor-
ous moments to be shared within the form group and many occasions
when you will be uplifted by their spontaneity, their acts of generosity
and by the care that they show for each other. Tutors should also celebrate the full range of achievements of their pupils, sometimes with due
pomp and circumstance if certificates are to be awarded, for example, or a
quiet word of praise to an individual pupil in another situation. Many
pupils tend to dislike being praised in front of their peers – possibly
because they are embarrassed or possibly because there is more status in
receiving a reprimand. However, good behaviour and good work benefit
from reinforcement through appropriate praise.

The negative self-image that results from inadequate feedback about a
pupil's ability can manifest itself when it is time to write self-assessments,
for example for a Record of Achievement. Pupils are notoriously lacking

in confidence when it comes to identifying their strengths and achievements although these can often be considerable. The form tutor needs to coax them out, thereby helping to increase the self-esteem of pupils and the construction of a more positive, more accurate self-image.

Assessment and communication

Another important function undertaken by the form tutor relates to assessment. The form tutor is the only teacher to have an overview of a pupil's progress across all subjects. Many schools have moved away from the end-of-year summative report and now build in progress reviews on a one-to-one basis in tutorial time. Some schools model this on the academic tracking of pupils as happens in schools in the USA. This system is more likely to be targeted at older pupils who may have GCSE support tutorials (Year 10 is a major transition time for pupils who may be launched into a different pace and style of learning and may quickly come to grief without support).

Coupled with this assessment role is that of communicator. The 'record book' or 'homework diary' serves both as a way of checking that homework is set and as a method of communicating with parents and guardians. As with any continuous monitoring, problems can be identified sooner rather than later, solutions negotiated, targets set and, of course, achievements recognized and rewarded. One issue here is the notion that although teachers are meant to be checking that pupils have recorded their homework, they are also de facto checking that their colleagues have been doing their job in setting homework in the first place. Sensitivity and the ability to be a supportive colleague are of the essence when you query a colleague's homework-setting.

Personal, health and social education

The concept of spiritual, moral, social and cultural (SMSC) education, which underpins the National Curriculum, emphasizes the need for a whole-school approach to the drawing up and delivery of a pastoral curriculum. All dimensions of a school and the curriculum as a whole contribute to the personal and social development of the pupils in some way. Nonetheless, pastoral programmes will be clearly identifiable in most schools and many topics, issues, activities and outcomes will be considered best handled by the form tutor as part of a tutorial programme. The tutor's role, which up to now may appear reactive and random, becomes coherent within the whole-school personal, health and social education (PHSE) structure. In the best systems observed by the inspectorate, teams of tutors work alongside a head of year on a range of issues related to personal development relevant to each age group. This often results in a pastoral curriculum constructed on the identification of 'critical incidents'. Thus a Year 7 group may undertake an induction programme, Year 9 may focus on 'options' and Year 11 may look at study skills or careers. While

Marland (1989) sees undeniable logic in this, he argues for a spiraling model whereby themes are constantly revisited but in different degrees and in different ways. It is important for form tutors not to be passive recipients of other people's materials and ideas but to show the initiative and creativity that they invariably demonstrate in their subject teaching. Tutors should seek to develop tutorial skills that can enhance the learning environment for the pupils and enable them to take advantage on a daily basis of all that the school offers. In the longer term, tutors help pupils to develop the skills and understanding needed to live confident, healthy and independent lives.

The form tutor's role in whole-school worship and moral education

Most schools have experienced some difficulty in responding to the legal requirement for a collective act of worship although as Gill (2000: 110) asserts: 'Most schools claim to make a regular provision for their pupils which, taken over a year, incorporate a broadly religious dimension'. The provision might include whole-school assemblies, tutor and year group assemblies and opportunities for individual silent reflection. In county primary, denominational and independent schools, she found that assemblies was considered an opportunity for the pupils 'to encounter the possibility of religious commitment' (Gill 2000: 109). In some schools, notably denominational, teachers were able to demonstrate and share their faith, while in others teachers experienced a personal dilemma, as Gill (2000: 110) explains,

> in the conflict they experience between their desire to be seen by pupils to uphold the law in respect of a religious activity in which they feel unable to participate, while retaining their standing with pupils as individuals of personal and professional integrity.

It will be important for you to assert your beliefs and to recognize your own personal dilemmas, but also to resolve and accommodate these within the culture and ethos of the school in which you have chosen to work. At the very least, you will be expected to accompany pupils to assemblies, support them in form assemblies and to undertake whatever tasks are required of you in that aspect of tutor time that comprises the collective act of worship.

Gill found a more fulsome acceptance by teachers of a responsibility to contribute generally to the moral development of the pupils. This, for example, took place in PHSE or form time and focused on social interactions and the application of moral principles such as justice and respect, and the discouragement of prejudice, bullying and racism. Gill found that the teachers sometimes organized structured debates while on other occasions spontaneous discussion arose as a result of 'critical incidents' in school.

Marland and Rogers suggest that the tutor's role is to identify issues and prompt group discussion enabling pupils not just to arrive at decisions but to focus on how to arrive at decisions. They argue that 'The process of tutoring is empowering the tutee, but with the giving of self-power must go the development of the ability to be sensitive and appropriately generous. Morality and ethics are at the heart of tutoring' (Marland and Rogers 1997: 26).

In my own research with adolescent girls, many said that they liked the opportunity to gather in a larger group, especially if pupils were presenting an assembly or if they had a special visitor or if the focus of an assembly was an issue of concern and interest to them. Likewise, they enjoyed debates on similar themes in PHSE, especially where they had an opportunity to air their views (and for these not to be scorned by tutors), and to be listened to with seriousness and respect. Gill, in her research, found that 'what young people value most is sincerity and relevance' (2000: 114). The pupils had strong feelings about apparent injustices and the problems of modern society and were greatly moved by natural catastrophes and other disasters, possessing an instinctive desire to want to help. As Gill suggests: 'Contemporary issues, current affairs and a wider discussion about the problems which confront the young in an imperfect world, they argue, should receive a much greater emphasis' (2000: 115). She echoes Marland and Rogers' suggestion for the need to create opportunities for pupil participation and involvement in the exploration of such issues. The form tutor has a role in helping to create such opportunities within the whole school SMSC framework and in helping the pupils to relate these concerns to their own lives.

Teacher–pupil interactions

Delamont (1983) investigated the interactions that exist between groups within schools, the most important of which were those between teachers and pupils. She eloquently describes how teachers spend considerable thinking and talking time 'sizing up' pupils. From the body of knowledge that teachers have gained through their professional training and their experience gained within school, a network of systems, strategies and beliefs underpin and direct the way teachers interact with pupils. Pupil behaviour in the lessons, snippets of information gained about pupils' home lives during the lesson and pupil attainment provide the main sources of information from which teachers build a picture of an individual pupil. Within two to three hours a week, in most secondary schools, a classroom teacher is expected to collect, reflect and act on the information gained from each of 30 or so pupils. It is not surprising that some pupils go unnoticed if their behaviour, lifestyle and progress do not immediately attract attention. On occasion, a particular action, piece of information or untypical standard of work can result in individual pupils being misunderstood by their teacher and, as a consequence, stereotyped in future interactions.

Systems and individuals

The pastoral system provides a framework for initiating and sustaining shared perspectives of individual pupils. In secondary school, pupils are frequently taught by 10 or more teachers and may be perceived differently by each one. This atomistic approach does little to help them to create a sense of identity as learners and as participants in the school system (see Chapter 12 for a discussion of identity). The form tutor's role within the system is to mediate between the teachers and the learners. By presenting a more complete picture of the pupils in a class to its teachers, you may ensure that future interactions take place in an informed and stable environment – neither marred nor exaggerated by uncharacteristic episodes or behaviours.

Handy and Aitken (1988) stress that one of the most important factors in organizational theory is how the organization is perceived by the individual, which, in the case of schools, must be the pupil. To provide an insight into this, I undertook a small-scale survey in a large, mixed London comprehensive in 1995. The main focus of the research was to investigate pupils' perceptions of the form tutor role. In all, 40 pupils across years 7–11 were asked:

- What do you think a form tutor is for?
- Who do you think is a good form tutor?

The pupils had very clear ideas and gave responses that were remarkable in their uniformity. The responses to the first question focused primarily on the pastoral support role, evidenced by comments such as 'to look after you', 'to see how you're doing' and 'to help you solve your problems'. Some aspects of organization and administration were identified such as 'to take the register', 'to watch punctuality' and 'to help the kids during fire drills'. Most surprising of all was the fact that almost every response given made reference to what the pupils saw as a central disciplinary function of the tutor role, expressed in a variety of ways: 'to teach you to behave', 'to stop us from talking and getting into trouble' and, more graphically, 'to stop us from getting up and ranging around and stop fights'.

Responses to the second question exemplified and validated these comments, the pupils suggesting the following qualities as essential for a 'good' form tutor:

- someone who listens;
- a sense of humour;
- being helpful and understanding;
- being strict and having the ability to keep order.

Typical responses were: 'She talks to people a lot and listens and she's good fun'; 'He's funny and he helps his tutor group and he's good at keeping order' and 'He's funny, but strict but he makes you laugh when he's strict'.

The usefulness of this small piece of research was a reminder of the expectations that the pupils have of the tutor. These reflect two very basic pupil needs: first individual care and support and second, the need for the teacher to maintain orderliness within the peer group. This concurs with Delamont's findings (1983: 90) where she states that the 'main strength of a teacher's position is that, in general, pupils want her to teach and keep them in order'. While the demands put on teachers by their pupils seem simple, the means of providing for their needs remains a difficult and diversified task for the form tutor. Sizing-up pupils is a continuous and evolving task for the form tutor who is in a unique position – perceiving pupils in a holistic manner, mapping their strengths and weaknesses and recognizing their successes and needs. As such, the form tutor fosters and supports the classroom interactions that can assist pupil learning.

Becoming a good form tutor

Far from being a marginal, time and status-squeezed role, the role of the form tutor is central to the fundamental aims of the school. Insofar as the tutor's role is to cohere all aspects of the pastoral and academic curricula, the tutor is accordingly 'the integrative centre for the school's whole curriculum' (Marland and Rogers 1997: 6). An important task is to consider how you can elaborate the developmental and creative potential of the form tutor role and the special contribution you have to make in each of your tutees' personal development. It is a role that is immensely rewarding. A good form tutor is never forgotten.

References

Delamont, S. (1983) *Interaction in the Classroom*. London: Methuen.

Dolezal, A. (1989) *Longman Tutorial Resources*. London: Longman.

Gill, J. (2000) The act of collective worship, in R. Best (ed.) *Education for Spiritual, Moral, Social and Cultural Development*. London: Continuum.

Handy, C.B. and Aitken, R. (1988) *Understanding Schools as Organizations*. London: Penguin.

King, G. (1999) *Counselling Skills for Teachers. Talking Matters*. Buckingham: Open University Press.

Marland, M. (1989) *The Tutor and the Tutor Group*. London: Longman.

Marland, M. and Rogers, R. (1997) *The Art of the Tutor. Developing Your Role in the Secondary School*. London: David Fulton.

Tattum, D. (1988) Control and welfare: towards a theory of constructive discipline in schools, in R. Dale, R. Fergusson and A. Robinson (eds) *Frameworks for Teaching*. London: Hodder and Stoughton.

Further reading

Burgess, R.G. (1988) House staff and departmental staff, in R. Dale, R. Fergusson and A. Robinson (eds) *Frameworks for Teaching*. London: Hodder and Stoughton.

Button, L. (1974) *Developmental Group Work with Adolescents*. London: University of London Press.

Davies, G. (1986) *A First Year Tutorial Handbook*. Oxford: Blackwell.

Hamblin, D. (1993) *Tutor as Counsellor*. Oxford: Basil Blackwell.

Qualifications and Curriculum Authority (QCA) (1997) *The Promotion of Pupils' Spiritual, Moral and Cultural Development: Draft Guidance for Pilot Work*. London: QCA.

Pring, R. (1984) *Personal and Social Education in the Curriculum*. London: Hodder and Stoughton.

Index

A-levels, 275
aims, of education, 34
  see also education, purpose of
assertive discipline, 151
assessment
  and classroom practice, 12
  and communication with parents,
    289
  GCSE and coursework debate, 30–1
  post-16, 277–8
attainment, and pupil organization,
    177–9

behaviour
  management strategies, 152–5,
    157–8
  sanctions, 125

child centred teaching, 222
children, pressures on, 29
class, 88–90, 103–4
classroom management, 5
Code of Practice, 194–5, 198–9
copyright, 127–8
corporal punishment, 126–7
curriculum
  and the classroom, 11–13
  development of, 274–6
  evaluation of, 89
  and the purpose of education, 28–9

defamation, 127
Dewey, J., 88, 221–2, 223

differentiation, 197
duty of care, 120, 122–3

education
  change, 32–3
  and political influence, 25–6
  purpose of, 37–9, 109–11, 235
  reform in England, 43–6
Education Act (1944), 89, 242
Education Action Zones (EAZs), 116
Education Reform Act (1988), 44–5,
    64–5, 91–3, 99, 121, 174, 231–3,
    239, 243
education policy, 10–11, 25–8, 102–3
education theory, 19–20
educational research, 27
effective schools, *see* school
  effectiveness
effective teachers, *see* teacher,
  effectiveness
eleven-plus examination, 90
English, and differentiation, 169–70
equality, *see* equity
equity, 87–8, 103–4, 176–7
ethics, and school management,
    38
ethnicity, 95, 104
examinations, history of, 91
Excellence in Cities, 102

Fish Report, 192–3
formative assessment, 165, 185–7
'Fresh Start' schools, 58

GCSE (General Certificate of Secondary Education), coursework debate, 30–1
gender
  differences during adolescence, 139–40
  differences in attainment, 91, 93–5, 140
  and social justice, 93–5
Gewirtz, S., 88
group work, 167

health and safety at work, 128–9
HMI (Her Majesty's Inspectorate), 75
home–school links, 99

ICT (Information and Communication Technology)
  and the national curriculum, 264–5
  and special educational needs, 199–200
inspection
  of information technology delivery, 268
  of spiritual development, 239–40

key skills, 280–1

Labour Government policy, 98, 224–5
  see also New Labour
league tables, effects of, 93
learning, 26–7
literacy, gender differences, 94
local financial management, 92–3

management, 14–15, 67
markets
  in education, 13–14, 27–8, 42–3, 52–4, 65–6
  and management, 14–15
marking, 186–7, 188–9
mathematics, and differentiation, 167–8

national curriculum
  and English as an additional/second language, 205
  as an entitlement, 67
  and information technology, 264–6
  and the pastoral curriculum, 255
  Personal, Social and Health Education (PSHE), 250, 255
  the place of Citizenship, 230, 231–3
  and purposes of education, 43–4
  and standards, 67

National Healthy School Standard, 252–3
negligence, 123, 129–31
neutrality, 40–1
New Labour, 45–6, 47–8, 53–4, 56–7, 111, 115–16

Ofsted (Office for Standards in Education)
  creation of, 76–7
  role of, 77
  and school evaluation, 55

parental choice, 52–4
Parent's Charter, 99–100
pastoral system, 285–6
pedagogical content knowledge (PCK), 144–5
performance-related pay (PRP), 70–1
Personal, Health and Social Education (PHSE), 289–91
  see also national curriculum
PGCE (Postgraduate Certificate in Education), 4, 69
physical force, use of by teachers, 125–6
Plowden Report, 99, 174
profiles, 185
progression, 146–7
punishment, see corporal punishment; sanctions
pupil
  cognitive growth in, 137–8
  development of identity, 138–9
  needs, 193–7
  organization, 163–4, 173–4
  physical development of, 136
  role of, 158–9
  self-image, 143–4
pupil recruitment, 46–7

qualifications, 276–7

race, and social justice, 95
reflection, 155–7
reliability, of assessment, 183–4

sanctions, 125
  punishment and the law, 129
scaffolding, pupil learning, 145–6, 226
scepticism, 39–40
school
  funding, 66
  organization, 285–6
  purpose of, 37–9
  self-evaluation, 78–7

school effectiveness, 15–16, 41–3,
    115–16, 151–2
science
    and differentiation, 168–9
    and spirituality, 246–7
sex and relationship education, 256–7
single-sex schooling, 95
standards, 25–6, 64, 65, 224
summative assessment, 184

teachers
    development, 8, 67–8
    effectiveness, 16
    evaluation of, 55–6
    interactions with pupils, 291
    as mentors, 8
    opinions about pupil organization,
        175
    'postmodern teacher', 18–19
    as a professional, 71
    as 'public intellectuals', 10, 19
    qualities, 4–5, 6–7
    role of, 6, 33–4, 120–1, 152–5,
        286–8
    status, 33
    workload, 187

teacher training
    and the inner city experience, 116–17
    quality of, 17
    regulation of, 68–9
teaching
    progressive methods, 12, 26
    strategies for health education, 257–8
Technical and Vocational Education
        Initiative (TVEI), 275
TGAT (Task Group on Assessment and
        Testing), 29–30
theory, see education theory
tripartite system of schools, 89–90
TTA (Teacher Training Agency), 68–9

urban education, 109–11
utilitarianism, 42

validity, of assessment, 183–4
Vygotsky, L., 166–7, 226

wait time, 190
Warnock Report, 192

Zone of Proximal Development (ZPD),
        226